Conflict
on the
Rio Grande

Conflict on the Rio Grande

Water and the Law, 1879–1939

DOUGLAS R. LITTLEFIELD

UNIVERSITY OF OKLAHOMA PRESS : NORMAN

Library of Congress Cataloging-in-Publication Data

Littlefield, Douglas R.
   Conflict on the Rio Grande : water and the law, 1879–1939 / Douglas
R. Littlefield.
        p. cm.
   Includes bibliographical references and index.
   ISBN 978-0-8061-3998-2 (hardcover : alk. paper) 1. Rio Grande—
Water rights—History. 2. United States—Boundaries—Mexico—
History. 3. Mexico—Boundaries—United States—History. I. Title.
   HD1694.A3L58 2008
   333.91'62097644—dc22
                                                          2008032893

The paper in this book meets the guidelines for permanence and
durability of the Committee on Production Guidelines for Book
Longevity of the Council on Library Resources, Inc. ∞

The manufacturer's representative in the EU for product safety is
Mare Nostrum Group B.V., Mauritskade 21D, 1091 GC
Amsterdam, The Netherlands, email: gpsr@mare-nostrum.co.uk

Contents

Illustrations

Figures

Maps

Acknowledgments

Writing a book on the history of water conflicts on the Rio Grande was a little like most water disputes in the American West—it seemed to go on forever. Nevertheless, I am indebted to many individuals who provided assistance over the years, some of who may have long since forgotten my original requests for help. One person who I know has not forgotten, however, is Professor Norris Hundley, Jr., because I have pestered him over the years with seemingly endless questions about various water issues in the West. I owe a great debt of gratitude to Norris. His comments and suggestions on this book undoubtedly have made it far better than it otherwise would have been. In addition, the example he set as a teacher, scholar, and editor constantly challenged me to enhance my own efforts in those areas. Moreover, as a colleague and friend, he provided highly appreciated advice and counsel.

Others with expertise in the history of water and the environment in the American West also deserve many thanks for reading early drafts of this book and in many cases answering a wide range of questions. These experts include Professors Harrison C. Dunning, Susan Neel, Richard Orsi, Donald J. Pisani, Alexander Saxton, Jim Sherow, Norman J. W. Thrower, and Daniel Tyler. All of them deserve my grateful thanks. Their help has saved me from many errors due to omission or lack of clarity.

The editorial staff at the University of Oklahoma Press also deserve my thanks for a careful review of the manuscript. Freelance copy editor Sally Bennett, in particular, warrants special recognition for her meticulous editing and her questions, which have made this book clearer and much more readable than it might have been otherwise.

In the research phase of this work, many individuals gave me assistance. In New Mexico, the archivists at the New Mexico State Records Center and Archives in Santa Fe provided me with vital help in locating and reviewing many files relating to Rio Grande history. There, my thanks go especially to Kay Dorman, Louellen Martinez, Arlene and Don Padilla, and Richard Salazar. In Las Cruces, Linda Blazer and Austin Hoover of the Rio Grande Historical Collections at New Mexico State University gave me a considerable amount of help and maintained an extremely pleasant archive in which to work. In Albuquerque, Jan Barnhart and Tim Wehrkamp of the Special Collections at the University of New Mexico contributed to my understanding of several aspects of the research in their holdings.

In Texas, the most useful materials were at the Eugene C. Barker Texas History Collection at the Center for American History at the University of Texas in Austin. At that archive, Ralph Elder deserves many thanks for his help in delving through the Richard Burges and Rio Grande Compact Commission files, particularly for recopying many of those files when the post office severely damaged a box in which they were being mailed. Bill Richter and Francis Rogers also contributed to my research efforts there.

Washington, D.C., was the location of the bulk of my research, especially the National Archives, which, at the time of my original archival work, housed the records of the Bureau of Reclamation. (These records have since been moved to the Denver branch of the National Archives.) My labors in Washington in Bureau of Reclamation files and in the records of numerous other federal agencies (many of which are now at the National Archives II in College Park, Maryland) would have been considerably more difficult without the valuable assistance of Chris Beam, Richard Crawford, Cynthia Fox, Ken Heger, Renee Jaussaud, Ed Schamel, and Charles South. In addition, Richard Baker of the U.S. Senate Historical Office and Ray Smock, historian of the U.S. House of Representatives, both provided helpful information on senators and congressmen involved in Rio Grande water struggles.

Once the National Archives moved all Bureau of Reclamation materials to its Rocky Mountain Branch in Denver, Joan Howard and Eric Bittner were extremely helpful there with requests to track down Rio Grande files I needed for clarification or to double-check for facts. In that regard, I also owe thanks to Brit Storey, historian for the U.S. Bureau of Reclamation, for his long-standing help, not only on the Rio Grande but also on research projects relating to many other Bureau of Reclamation projects.

Also shedding light on the Rio Grande apportionment problem were the Water Resource Centers at the Berkeley and Los Angeles campuses of the University of California. Beth Willard at UCLA provided encouragement and direction at the earliest stages of research, while Gerald Giefer at the Berkeley Water Resource Center helped direct me through the Frank Adams papers and other useful collections.

Although I did not have the chance to visit several archives whose collections proved to be useful, their staffs nonetheless deserve my thanks for lengthy telephone discussions and correspondence and for copying and mailing sections of relevant collections. Robin Bullock Tully and Paula McDougal at the Archives–American Heritage Center at the University of Wyoming provided access to several collections, including the Arthur P. Davis papers, and Dale Mayer at the Herbert Hoover Presidential Library was very helpful in sending sections of President Hoover's files.

My thanks also go to the staff of the Public Record Office in London, England, for copying multitudes of pages from the records of the Board of Trade and the Foreign Office. These documents helped me flesh out the details on the Rio Grande Irrigation and Land Company, the British parent corporation to the American Rio Grande Dam and Irrigation Company.

Several research assistants over the years have been extremely helpful. My thanks go especially to Christine M. Andersen, Sande DeSalles, Joseph G. Dobbins, and Alison Rapp, all of whom either waded through endless microfilm, endured many requests to find obscure published materials, or struggled to find illustrations for the text.

Also deserving credit in relation to illustrations is Cherie Northon of Anchorage, Alaska. Her help in designing a map that specifically identified places named in the text undoubtedly will save many readers much time in searching atlases (or, more recently, online maps). Cherie also has provided many other maps for consulting projects, which, as for this book, contributed immensely to their clarity and understanding. Bill Nelson also deserves thanks for his map of the irrigation systems in the Rio Grande Valley.

I also would like to thank the many fine lawyers I have worked with over the years on a wide variety of consulting projects relating to water rights and environmental matters in the American West. Without these attorneys' suggestions and comments on various reports and studies that I have done for their cases, my understanding of the significance of the history of the Rio Grande and its underlying legal questions would have suffered immensely.

Remembering everyone who lent a hand, provided support, or offered encouragement in preparing this work would be impossible. To those whom I undoubtedly have forgotten because of the many, many months that have elapsed since this book's inception, please accept my apology for the failure of my memory and also accept my appreciation for your contribution.

Finally, the two women in my life deserve special recognition. My wife, Christina B. Littlefield, answered multiple legal questions, provided suggestions in stylistic matters, and perhaps most important, endured endless hours of discussion on water rights and Rio Grande history. Her support goes well beyond what can be adequately acknowledged here. Special thanks also go to my daughter, Sara E. Littlefield, who has kindly tolerated far too many anecdotes about history in general but, despite this, still remains interested in that subject.

Conflict
on the
Rio Grande

Introduction

In November 1904, glowing accounts began to appear in newspapers in the western United States about an important turning point that had been reached in a long and bitter dispute over the apportionment of the waters of the Rio Grande. The decades-long controversy had pitted irrigators in southern New Mexico's Mesilla Valley against those farther downstream in the El Paso Valley, which encompassed farmlands around El Paso, Texas, and Juárez, Mexico (known in Mexico as El Paso del Norte). Each group had advanced a plan for a different major reservoir on the Rio Grande to solve its water needs, with one possibility being an international dam just above El Paso to be constructed jointly by the United States and Mexico and the other a commercial venture much farther upstream in New Mexico to be built by the Rio Grande Dam and Irrigation Company. The solution to the conflict, the press reported, had been reached at the 1904 National Irrigation Congress—a meeting of prominent politicians, businessmen, farmers, engineers, and water officials from around the West. The answer involved federal construction of a dam on the Rio Grande at Elephant Butte, New Mexico, about 125 miles upstream from the New Mexico–Texas border near the site favored by the corporate reservoir advocates. The Elephant Butte storage facility was to be built by the newly formed U.S. Reclamation Service (renamed the Bureau of Reclamation in 1923), and it would supply water to all of the formerly competing users in New Mexico,

The Rio Grande valley in Colorado, New Mexico, and western Texas, 1990. Map by Cherie Northon, Mapping Solutions, Anchorage, Alaska.

Texas, and Mexico. Together, Elephant Butte Dam and its related distribution system were to be known as the Rio Grande Project, and water supplies were to be allocated according to studies of irrigated and potentially irrigable lands to be conducted by the Reclamation Service. All of this was to be enacted into law and relevant parts incorporated into a treaty with Mexico shortly after the 1904 National Irrigation Congress adjourned.

Typifying the enthusiastic accounts of the conflict's resolution, the *Houston Post* announced that after "fighting for the past ten years, El Paso, New Mexico and Mexico came together today, buried the hatchet and will pull as one man for a great storage dam across the Rio Grande for the reclamation of arid lands in this section." The *Post* further added that this project meant "more for El Paso than can be told." Explaining that water users around El Paso and Juárez had abandoned the ambitious and long-debated proposal for an international dam a few miles above El Paso and Juárez in favor of the Elephant Butte reservoir much farther upstream as outlined by the Reclamation Service, the *Post* pointed out that the young agency already had federal funds to carry out its work, while money for the rival international facility was still lacking.[1]

Closer to the struggle along the Rio Grande in western Texas and southern New Mexico, the newspaper reports were even more laudatory. For example, New Mexico's *Rio Grande Republican* (published in Las Cruces) exulted that the National Irrigation Congress's effects would be long-lasting, especially in relation to the Rio Grande valley in New Mexico. "All seemed to be working for the reclamation of the arid lands," the *Republican* gushed, "that our citizens might have palacial [sic] homes surrounded with life's comforts, instead of poverty."[2] Downstream in Texas, the *El Paso Herald's* large headline boldly proclaimed "Unanimity," and the paper was filled with admiring commentary of how a consensus, "absolute, firm as a rock," had been reached "in sentiment and purpose, among representatives from the Rio Grande valley of New Mexico, Texas, and Mexico, with reference to plans for reclaiming the valley."[3] The *El Paso Daily Times* concurred. Under the banner "Elephant Butte Dam Approved—Joint Meeting of Texas, Mexico, and New Mexico Representatives Unanimously Favor Project," the *Times* recounted that the National Irrigation Congress had reached "a practical and amicable solution of the Elephant Butte Dam proposition—a question with which the people of this city have been wrestling for a number of years."[4]

The exhilarated press accounts were not merely examples of the local and regional boosterism that characterized the press throughout much of the American West in the late nineteenth and early twentieth centuries. Leading up to the promising reports had been many years of escalating dissension over limited Rio Grande irrigation water supplies. In the late 1880s, the dispute had mushroomed from a localized problem, affecting only a few farmers in the El Paso–Juárez area, into a major interstate and international altercation involving a multitude of officials and private parties on local, regional, and national levels on both sides of the Rio Grande (known in Mexico as Río Bravo del Norte). Thus, the announcement that this major river allocation issue had been resolved was remarkable reading for westerners. Indeed, the Rio Grande situation both before and after 1904 was covered heavily by the entire nation's press. Regardless of distance from the Rio Grande, many residents of the American West realized that they too eventually might face their own transboundary water battles, and therefore the news dispatches that the Rio Grande's apportionment difficulties had been settled by the Reclamation Service proposal were welcome tidings throughout the arid parts of the United States. Readers in the rest of the United States were enthralled by the controversy over the Rio Grande because it involved many different issues—foreign relations, the novelty of irrigation of desert lands, private enterprise and money versus government direction, questions of statehood status, and the powers of the different levels of government in the American federal system. The national fascination with the struggles on the Rio Grande was reflected in the fact that papers with readerships varying from major metropolises to small towns all carried news of events on the Rio Grande in the late nineteenth and early twentieth centuries.

Prior to 1904, few criteria established how water disputes that crossed borders might be resolved even within the United States, let alone internationally. Western water law was in its infancy when the Rio Grande strife began, and the manner of dividing scant irrigation supplies among claimants was ambiguous at best within individual states or territories. At the time, most western states and territories adhered to the legal doctrine of prior appropriation for governing water use and control, although the methods and details for establishing such claims varied enormously. In general, prior appropriation holds that whoever first puts the waters of a stream to beneficial use is entitled to continue to utilize that water ahead of the claims of all subsequent users. Such rights do not necessarily depend on real estate ownership, and water does not need to be used adjacent to source rivers or streams. The one consistent test for a continuing priority right is "beneficial use," although what that term precisely means is still a matter of considerable legal debate in the West. In times of shortage, the allotments of more-recent claimants (known in the jargon of water as "junior users" or "juniors") are curtailed in favor of older ("senior") rights. In other words, shortages are not shared proportionately among all claimants, and during droughts, juniors may receive no water at all while seniors receive their full allotments. Clearly, therefore, the oldest priorities are the best. Prior appropriative water rights in the West are considered property rights in much the same manner that landownership is a property right, and for that reason, water rights in the American West carry all the emotional and legal significance that real estate historically has throughout the entire country. Many westerners might argue that water rights are even more significant, because in the West, most land is worthless without water. Appropriative rights vary considerably from riparian water rights, which form the basis of eastern states' water laws. Riparian rights allow landowners adjacent to a stream to utilize its flow (such as to power a mill) but only so long as that use does not significantly diminish the supply to downstream users. Moreover, flows may not be diverted from watersheds, and landowners who are not next to streams have no claims to water at all. Fundamentally, appropriative water rights are based on the supposition of insufficient supplies, circumstances that exist in much of the American West; riparian rights assume adequate moisture nearly everywhere (such as through precipitation), a characteristic that typifies the East.[5]

Although considerable space had been devoted to prior appropriation in law journals and legal treatises by the early twentieth century, the details about how that doctrine applied in specific situations and how it differed from the East's riparian rights were still evolving.[6] The doctrine had emerged in the late 1840s and 1850s because of the necessities of water claims in the gold-mining areas of California, where many placer deposits lay away from streams and were located on public lands. Both of these circumstances meant that the doctrine of riparian rights was of little use to settle disputes over water, and prior appropriation had emerged as a practical result.[7] As water demands spread beyond the gold-mining regions, the legal ambiguities associated with prior appropriation intensified. In the region through which the Rio Grande flows above El Paso and Juárez, for example, there was a serious debate over the degree to which appropriation applied to various water uses under differing conditions throughout the late nineteenth and early twentieth centuries. Although Colorado's constitution specifically had endorsed priority as the basis for the state's water law in 1876,[8] the New Mexico Territorial Supreme Court did not sanction the doctrine until 1891, and the territorial legislature did not pass any statute accepting appropriation until 1905.[9] Texas's lawmakers had authorized priority of water use in 1889 (but only in the arid western half of the state). Nevertheless, that state's courts generally also protected riparian rights, and to cloud the issue more, Texas had no prescribed mechanism for recording the acquisition of appropriative rights until 1913.[10]

That was the situation within individual states and territories. How allocations should be accomplished on streams that crossed state lines (or territorial—New Mexico did not join the Union until 1912) was even more uncertain. At the time of the battle between the supporters of the Rio Grande Dam and Irrigation Company and backers of the international dam at El Paso, the U.S. Supreme Court was still several decades away from ruling in *Wyoming v. Colorado* (1922) that priorities could be considered as one factor in allocating supplies across state borders if neighboring states each accepted the appropriation principle.[11] That contention had been advanced in a few disputes in other parts of the West, notably in the events leading up to the Supreme Court's 1907 decision in *Kansas v. Colorado*— the first U.S. Supreme Court decision addressing interstate stream allocation. Nevertheless, the high court's justices in that case had begged the issue by merely suggesting that Kansas had not proven substantial injury by Colorado's uses of the Arkansas River. The justices added, however, that Kansas was entitled to an "equitable apportionment" of the Arkansas River and that Kansas could seek further redress if Colorado's uses of that stream's flows became more onerous. At that time, the Supreme Court did not address the validity of prior appropriation or riparian rights as those applied across state boundaries.[12] Moreover, the U.S. Supreme Court did not rule for over another half-century on whether Congress had the power to divide interstate streams. That question was not answered until 1963, when the justices declared in *Arizona v. California* that the 1928 Boulder Canyon Act had authorized a congressional allocation of the Colorado River among states of that watershed—a decision that said nothing about the history of interstate allocations as that had played out on the Rio Grande long before Congress passed the Boulder Canyon Act.[13]

Because of the uncertainties about how to address water rights across state and territorial borders, significant proposals to resolve that issue had emerged during the second half of the nineteenth century as alternatives to simply extending priorities across political boundaries. For instance, as early as 1878, the famed explorer of the Grand Canyon and director of the U.S. Geological Survey, John Wesley Powell, had proposed one theoretical means of interstate stream apportionment through the creation of irrigation districts throughout the western United States. Powell—who favored local control over water resources—posited that such districts could develop and disperse water within natural drainage basins regardless of state and territorial lines. Water users within these districts would regulate them.[14] Others took the opposite approach and argued for centralized control, suggesting that uniform water codes be drafted covering the entire arid portion of the country. In 1896, for instance, the head of the U.S. General Land Office called for a national commission to allocate and regulate interstate streams, and *Scientific American* supported a similar proposal in a March 1900 editorial.[15] Controversial propositions also emerged that included establishing water quotas for states sharing common rivers before the U.S. government could cede portions of the public domain to those states for reclamation.[16] Other proponents of unified authority maintained that the only viable approach to dividing rivers between two or more states was to let the federal government take charge. Well-known U.S. Army engineer Hiram M. Chittenden reached this conclusion in 1897, when he declared that a major reservoir system in the western United States was "absolutely essential." Chittenden added that "it is not possible to secure the best development of such a system except through the agency of the General Government."[17]

None of these interstate allocation solutions, however, was realistic for the American West of the late nineteenth and early twentieth centuries. After Powell made his proposal, it was widely condemned by westerners who were unwilling to yield control of "their" water to yet another layer of government that might act independently of other local, state, and national authorities. The autonomous basin-based districts contemplated by Powell, water users understood, could result in allocations contrary to some individuals' interests, and there might be no recourse through existing political channels because of the multiplicity of states or territories that might be affected. This was particularly true because many western state and territorial borders are straight lines based on meridians or parallels rather than being determined by topographic features of the land such as watersheds. Similarly, irrigators feared that any uniform water code spanning the entire West might undermine water rights acquired under the legal principle of prior appropriation. Even though water rights were not satisfactorily detailed under existing water law at the time, westerners were not about to give up whatever property in water that they had—certainly not in relation to water claimants across the border in an adjacent state or territory. Finally, turning the entire issue over to the U.S. government flew in the face of many westerners' common sense. With the public domain already comprising a substantial portion of the total acreage of the West (hence mostly subject to U.S. government control) and with the West having relatively few senators and congressional representatives compared to the more populated East, residents of the western United States strongly desired to retain whatever remaining home rule they had. Further federal regulation through U.S. government allocation of interstate rivers, westerners knew, would reinforce the region's status as a weak province dominated by the East.

On the Rio Grande in the late nineteenth and early twentieth centuries, therefore, however much El Paso water users might have strenuously asserted their claim to prior rights against upstream users in New Mexico, there was nothing in case law or statutory law to back up those declarations. Similarly, early general propositions for solving the question of water rights across state and territorial lines had not been eagerly embraced. The ambiguity of intrastate and transborder prior rights also was compounded by New Mexico's territorial status (until 1912), which raised the issue of whether a territory of the United States could or should be treated as an equal to a state in relation to interstate water law. Moreover, if there was little legal guidance on how water claims applied across state or territorial boundaries at the end of the nineteenth and in the early twentieth centuries, there was no rule for dealing with the international situation in relation to Mexico.

With the options for dividing waters across state, territorial, and national boundaries fraught with many perils and doubts, residents along the Rio Grande in southern New Mexico's Mesilla Valley and in the El Paso Valley in Texas and Mexico, therefore, had compromised at the 1904 National Irrigation Congress to retain as much local sovereignty as they could. In relation to the transboundary allocation question *within* the United States, this settlement portended—but preceded by years or even decades—similar negotiated agreements between states on other U.S. western streams, many of which took the form of interstate compacts. Like the situation on the Rio

Grande in 1904, many of these later accords were aimed at retaining local autonomy in water allocation matters in the face of growing federal intrusiveness. Rivers or lakes crossing the borders of two or more states that eventually came to have negotiated settlements in the West (defined to be areas including states lying partly or entirely west of the ninety-eighth meridian—others exist in the East) include the following, with the respective states involved: Animas–La Plata River (Colorado and New Mexico); Arkansas River (Colorado and Kansas); Bear River (Idaho, Utah, and Wyoming); Belle Fourche River (South Dakota and Wyoming); Big Blue River (Kansas and Nebraska); Canadian River (New Mexico, Oklahoma, and Texas); Colorado River (Arizona, California, Colorado, Nevada, New Mexico, Utah, and Wyoming); Costilla Creek (Colorado and New Mexico); Klamath River (California and Oregon); Lake Tahoe (California and Nevada); La Plata River (Colorado and New Mexico); Pecos River (New Mexico and Texas); Red River (Arkansas, Louisiana, Oklahoma, and Texas); Red River of the North (Minnesota, North Dakota, and South Dakota); Republican River (Colorado, Kansas, and Nebraska); Rio Grande (Colorado, New Mexico, and Texas); Sabine River (Louisiana and Texas); Snake River (Idaho and Wyoming); South Platte River (Colorado and Nebraska); Upper Colorado River (Arizona, Colorado, New Mexico, Utah, and Wyoming); Upper Niobrara River (Nebraska and Wyoming); and Yellowstone River (Montana, North Dakota, and Wyoming).[18]

The situation on the Rio Grande did not merely precede these other collaborative interstate river allocations; rather, events that transpired along the Rio Grande in 1904 exemplify the response to a "fragmented West," with multitudes of factions vying for control of the stream's waters.[19] This was a part of the broader contest for the economic subjugation of the arid regions of the West.[20] In the case of the Rio Grande, the factions compromised because the common good required cooperation. Contrary to Donald Worster's thesis in his landmark work *Rivers of Empire* (1985), that the evolution of water resource development and control in the West could best be characterized as a march toward a monolithic hydraulic empire, the situation on the Rio Grande suggested just the opposite.[21] The 1904 Rio Grande truce was locally achieved, even if it was brokered by a federal agency. In addition, the settlement's implementation quickly came to involve local and state authorities, quasi-governmental entities, and private organizations and businesses, as well as the U.S. and Mexican governments—a multitiered and interwoven fabric of negotiated settlement where no one strand of the agreement would hold without reinforcement from the others.

Isolated by miles of remote and arid terrain and with little convenient contact to other areas of the country, the communities in the Mesilla and El Paso valleys understandably wanted to remain on good terms with each other, especially because the regional economy was inextricably bound together regardless of state or international borders. As Arthur Maass and Raymond L. Anderson pointed out in their study of irrigation communities in several parts of the world, negotiated compromises are likely to take place when such accords are clearly in everyone's interests, where there is a sense of community and therefore mutual trust, and where all involved groups believe that a collaborative agreement will be mutually beneficial.[22] Under the circumstances that existed in the early twentieth century in southern New Mexico and western Texas (and adjacent areas in Mexico), compromise on the Rio Grande was especially vital because the interstate and international water conflict there was essentially a local problem.

Although similar in some respects to later negotiated interstate river settlements, the Rio Grande case was distinctive not only because it was the first such stream agreement affecting two or more states or territories but also because of the international features of the 1904 National Irrigation Congress compromise. The Rio Grande Project—as Elephant Butte Dam and the related distribution system were to be called—was to distribute water to irrigators in New Mexico, Texas, and Mexico according to studies conducted by the Reclamation Service that would fulfill the 1904 accord. As Secretary of the Interior Albert B. Fall later wrote in a 1923 letter to U.S. Senator Charles L. McNary, who chaired the Senate Committee on Irrigation and Reclamation of Arid Lands, "This project is unique among all reclamation projects of the United States in that it was conceived" partly to deliver Rio Grande Project waters to Mexico as determined by the 1904 agreement.[23]

The authorization for the Reclamation Service to build the Rio Grande Project and to determine the division of that venture's water supplies came from a 1905 federal statute that was based on the previous year's National Irrigation Congress compromise. This law provided the first answer as to how to divide the waters of any interstate river in the American West between two or more states. Whereas before 1905 there had been no legal remedy for allotting supplies across state and territorial borders, Congress's action created one formal means to accomplish that goal—federal legislation. Yet (as is discussed later in this book) this precedent for interstate river allocations remained largely unrecognized over the following decades. Indeed, not until the Supreme Court's 1963 ruling in *Arizona v. California* that the 1928 Boulder Canyon Act had created a congressional apportionment of the Colorado River was Congress's authority to make such divisions recognized.

Congressional action in 1905 did not merely divide the Rio Grande's waters within the United States—twenty-three years before the Boulder Canyon Act. The following year, Congress also accomplished the first international allocation of a stream shared by the United States and another country by ratifying a Rio Grande treaty with Mexico. The overall result of Congress's actions in 1905 and 1906 was that water stored at Elephant Butte Reservoir was to be delivered through the Rio Grande Project to an irrigation district in southern New Mexico and to those users downstream in western Texas and to Mexico in a ratio established by the Reclamation Service's studies.

Over the next three decades, growing Rio Grande water uses in northern New Mexico and Colorado caused the cooperative attitude seen at the 1904 gathering to spread to the entire Rio Grande basin above Fort Quitman, Texas (generally considered to be the point below which flows from the upper Rio Grande offer only minimal contributions to the basin below). This larger concurrence of how to allocate the entire upper basin's supplies was achieved through the negotiation first of the 1929 Rio Grande Compact (intended to be a temporary reprieve to allow various river investigations to be carried out), and then through the 1938 Rio Grande Compact. Both compacts covered the Rio Grande basin within the states of Colorado, New Mexico, and Texas above Fort Quitman, and the 1938 Rio Grande Compact specifically was intended to incorporate the provisions of the 1905 congressional apportionment in the larger, regional accord. Like the 1905 compromise and similar to the many other interstate agreements that were negotiated and implemented in the first half of the twentieth century, these later Rio Grande settlements were reached with considerable input from water users and their supporters who were most directly concerned as well as from a multiplicity of other entities.

This book not only examines the immediate factors that permitted the Rio Grande cooperative water settlements to take place but also describes the transformation of nineteenth- and early-twentieth-century law and changing attitudes about the role of government in coordinating the development of natural resources. In 1904, there was no precedent for dividing rivers among two or more states, and the Progressive-era faith in scientific management of natural resources was just beginning to replace the previous century's acceptance of rampant exploitation by private enterprise as the best method of extracting yet perpetuating nature's bounty.[24] The legal system was also changing. At the end of the nineteenth century, law as expressed in court decisions was no longer derived mostly from the moral values of the community, as it had been a hundred years earlier. Instead, litigation had become a means to further individuals' desires for economic and political power.[25] Changes in the goals of legislated law endorsed these shifting values. Legal historian J. Willard Hurst has characterized this evolution as the release of private individual creativity, and it could be seen in state (and territorial) general incorporation statutes permitting companies to be formed without specific laws sanctioning each individual corporation and in various economic incentives for certain types of land and water companies. Moreover, federal laws in the West were gradually accepting local customs in relation to water rights, and U.S. statutes were providing uniform procedures for rights-of-way across U.S. lands for reservoir and water companies and other access to the public domain.[26]

With all of these changes in the legal system just beginning to emerge around the turn of the twentieth century, the cooperative understanding that had been reached at the 1904 National Irrigation Congress had developed largely in a legal and philosophical vacuum. The result was a plan for federal government assistance with considerable local participation—a solution derived from a multiplicity of sources and many social, economic, and political levels of participation. The legal aspects of that remedy were similarly multiform and sprang from the American federal system of government, as well as the geographic and topographical differences of the country.[27]

Later, in the 1920s and 1930s (when the two Rio Grande compacts were completed), western water law was far more developed and the concept of government coordination of natural resources—with continued local involvement—was becoming a well-accepted tenet for Americans. Although Supreme Court litigation had established in 1907 (in *Kansas v. Colorado*) that each state was entitled to an "equitable apportionment" of interstate streams, the expense of such lawsuits and the apparently successful negotiation of the 1922 Colorado River Compact encouraged states to lean toward similar accords on other rivers such as the Rio Grande. President Franklin D. Roosevelt's New Deal policies augmented this motivation. As Richard Lowitt demonstrated in *The New Deal and the West* (1984), Roosevelt's ideas to overcome the Great Depression fostered an environment favoring coordinated natural resource management with input and participation by local, state, and regional interests.[28] As a result, federal agencies actively encouraged interstate compacts to allocate shared rivers, in many cases suggesting that federal funds for irrigation development might be withheld without such accords.

This book, therefore, deals with an emerging, diverse, and fragmented West—an area where local communities grappled over water issues as much among themselves as they did with the territorial, state, and federal governments and even a foreign power. The struggle was framed by transformations in legal theory and societal attitudes about the environment, and as these changes took place, the disparate elements of the West began to come to grips with their unique problems through negotiation and compromise. The Rio Grande thus reflects certain circumstances prevailing on other western rivers, but in addition, because of its unique setting geographically and its chronological primacy, the situation on the Rio Grande also stands apart from and heralds the evolution of water resource history in the American West.

CHAPTER I

A Dry River at El Paso and Juárez
An International Problem

Rioting in the late 1870s gave the first indication that serious trouble might be brewing along the Rio Grande in the area surrounding El Paso, Texas, and Juárez, Mexico. The unrest had been caused by conflicts over a vital natural resource for food preservation and other purposes—salt. The events that came to be known as the "salt wars" were particularly troubling because they ultimately led to murder and took place in an isolated international region with little governmental control along the border shared by the United States and Mexico. The resulting official investigations of the disturbances warned that future crises also might emerge over an even bigger problem in the area—water.

The inquiries had begun in the spring of 1878, when Colonel Edward Hatch, commanding officer of the Ninth Cavalry in the Territory of New Mexico, had been dispatched to San Elizario, Texas, a small town slightly downstream from El Paso and Juárez on the Rio Grande. Hatch was under orders to look into the uprisings, which had taken place on both sides of the Rio Grande, and to make recommendations for the prevention of similar disorders in the future. Hatch's report eventually reached the highest levels of the U.S. military, and the account solemnly explained that "a location of certain salt-ponds by one [Charles H.] Howard, and his attempts to

View of El Paso, Texas, in 1875. Courtesy Bureau of Reclamation, National Archives II, College Park, Maryland.

exclude the people from their free use, was the moving cause of the outbreak."[1]

Howard, a local politician, had moved to El Paso in 1872 from Austin, Texas. El Paso was then a stronghold of post–Civil War Radical Republicanism, and seeing an opportunity to challenge the ruling elite and to strengthen the local Democratic Party, Howard had allied himself with Luis Cardis, an Italian shopkeeper whose fluent command of the Spanish language made him well connected among the region's Mexican population. Howard's relationship with Cardis, however, had soured when Howard sought control over the area's salt ponds. Cardis had hoped to dominate the ponds in conjunction with other El Pasoans, including William Wallace Mills, brother of early El Paso resident and surveyor Anson Mills. As a result, Howard and Cardis became bitter enemies; Howard shot and killed Cardis on October 10, 1877.[2]

Colonel Hatch's report summarized what happened next. "The unprovoked murder of a Mr. Cardis, by Howard," Hatch wrote, "for daring to resist his claim to the salt-ponds, and for advising the people to resist it by proceeding in court, roused the population to a fury, and they collected in force in [San] Elizario, captured a small force of Texas Rangers, with whom was Howard, and put the latter and two or three other citizens to death."[3]

Hatch's report, and another drafted by a special military commission created to inquire into the fracas, estimated that before the rioting had ended, between five hundred and fifteen hundred people had taken part. Moreover, both accounts observed that only the arrival of U.S. troops under Hatch's command had prevented the bloodshed from expanding into a broader international conflict with Mexico, because many of that country's citizens crossed the Rio Grande regularly to obtain salt from the ponds.[4] The unwritten inference was that the attempt to restrict access to the salt ponds violated the common understanding that cooperative access to limited natural resources generally benefited everyone in isolated western communities.

Hatch's report and the review by the military commissioners offered the sobering assessment that similar future disturbances might erupt over control of water from the Rio Grande. The commissioners explained that they "regard[ed] as serious" the question of the "diversion and distribution" of water. Noting that the river frequently did not carry enough water to irrigate the farms in the arid valley encompassing El Paso and Juárez, the military tribunal warned that the issue of apportioning the scant water supplies between the two nations "must grow in importance, and may occasion trouble beyond the reach of diplomacy to settle."[5]

The military board's dire prediction soon materialized. Only two years after the salt riots, major conflicts erupted over the waters of the Rio Grande—the first such struggle between the United States and Mexico over a river the two nations shared. Much of the problem stemmed from the complex nature of the Rio Grande's basin in New Mexico, Colorado, and the valley around El Paso and Juárez. Known as the Río Bravo del Norte in Mexico, the Rio Grande is a major western stream draining roughly 175,000 square miles in the United States and Mexico.[6] After rising in the majestic peaks of Colorado, the river flows through that state's fertile San Luis Valley, then courses southward for more than 400 miles across New Mexico's arid deserts. Briefly forming a small part of the border between Texas and New Mexico, the Rio Grande subsequently becomes the international boundary between the United States and Mexico. From the point where the river begins to separate the two countries near El Paso to its mouth at the Gulf of Mexico, the stream flows about 1,200 additional miles—almost two-thirds of its total length.

By common understanding, the Rio Grande usually is divided into two distinct sub-basins at Fort Quitman, Texas (about 75 miles downstream from

El Paso), with the upper basin comprising about 34,000 square miles (about 20 percent) of the total drainage area. In this region, nearly all of the Rio Grande's flows are consumed by irrigation in Colorado, New Mexico, and the El Paso Valley in Texas and Mexico. In the basin below Fort Quitman, the Rio Grande receives most of its volume from tributaries on the Mexican side of the river.

The upper Rio Grande basin, with which this book is primarily concerned, can be subdivided into three natural areas. The uppermost region, the San Luis Valley in Colorado, is principally agricultural in nature with a relatively smooth topography surrounded by mountains except in the south near the Colorado–New Mexico state line, where the Rio Grande has cut an outlet for the southern portion of the valley. The northern part of the San Luis Valley does not drain into the Rio Grande and is variously known as the "dead" or "sump" area or more formally as the Closed Basin. The middle part of the upper Rio Grande basin covers the river's drainage area from the Colorado–New Mexico state line to San Marcial, New Mexico, almost three hundred miles to the south. In this reach, the river flows first for about seventy miles through a deep canyon surrounded by an arid mesa before the basin opens up near Embudo. From this point southward, the Rio Grande is dominated by a succession of narrow valleys separated by rocky canyons.

Immediately below San Marcial sits Elephant Butte. A huge geological formation, now partly submerged by the reservoir carrying its name, the butte bears a remarkable likeness to the head of a pachyderm. The land below Elephant Butte is barren except immediately along the river, where the stream flows through a succession of fertile valleys separated by canyons or narrows. Two of those immediately below Elephant Butte are the Palomas and Rincon valleys, while farther south lie the larger Mesilla Valley in New Mexico and the El Paso Valley in Texas and Mexico.

As the complex geography of the Rio Grande basin suggests, dissension over the river's waters was almost inevitable once settlement began to grow rapidly in the region. For example, barely two years after the salt riots and related murders, tensions over irrigation supplies along the border between Texas and Mexico had increased to the point that rumors abounded regarding the supposed plans of armed Mexicans to destroy an American diversion dam at Hart's Mill (near present-day downtown El Paso on the Rio Grande). As a March 19, 1880, letter to the editor in *Thirty-four*, a local newspaper, warned, "This dam is absolutely necessary to the irrigating of land cultivated in this vicinity; and if the Mexicans do come you may look out for war news."[7]

Two weeks later, forty-five residents of San Elizario petitioned the El Paso County Commissioners' Court for help in offsetting diminishing Rio Grande water supplies. Many Texans believed that these shortages had been caused by excessive Mexican diversions. Although in reality the smaller flows were more a result of a period of drought and increasing water uses far upstream in Colorado, the request was subsequently endorsed by other residents of San Elizario and by settlers in the nearby town of Ysleta, Texas. Claiming that over the previous few years the waters of the Rio Grande had become insufficient to irrigate crops and water cattle, the petitioners contended that the shortages had brought immense hardships to the area, and they sought a monetary grant to ease their burdens or, alternatively, relief from paying property taxes.[8]

The petition eventually reached Secretary of State William Evarts by way of Texas governor Oran M. Roberts. In his cover letter, Roberts conveniently ignored the fact that Mexican irrigators around Juárez had been using the Rio Grande's waters for many decades before Americans settled in the El Paso area—an omission that may have been prompted as much by his biases favoring large West Texas ranching and corporate interests as by the near total lack of international law on how a river shared by two or more countries ought to be apportioned among the nations involved. Nonetheless, Roberts cautioned Evarts that there was "a danger of trouble of a serious character in that section of our frontier if the Mexicans on the west side of the river are allowed to continue to take in their ditches all of the water that comes down the river during dry seasons, and thereby prevent our citizens from making crops." Although Secretary Evarts raised the matter with the American legation in Mexico and urged that the problem be resolved quickly, several years of heavy precipitation removed any sense of urgency.[9]

By the late 1880s, however, rain and snow had decreased once again throughout much of the West, and the new drought revived the question of how to allocate the Rio Grande's water supplies between Mexico and the United States. The issue resurfaced as the result of wing dams being built on the Mexican side of the river, allegedly to protect the bank from erosion. Unfortunately, the dams deflected the current toward the Texas shoreline, thus threatening to wear it away. From the American perspective, the dams not only called into question the interpretation of the 1848 Treaty of Guadalupe Hidalgo and the 1853 Gadsden Treaty, both of which had defined the middle of the Rio Grande's main channel as the international boundary, but also apparently violated an 1884 agreement between the

United States and Mexico providing that neither country could direct the river's current in such a manner as to cause the other side harm. Despite repeated American protests, in late 1888 the wing dams were still in place, and at least one was being extended completely across the Rio Grande with the obvious intention of not only controlling erosion but also diverting more water into Mexican irrigation canals. With a new international crisis looming, the U.S. Army was ordered to look into the matter, and the Army Corps of Engineers subsequently reported that the wing dams were a distinct violation of the 1884 accord. The corps further charged that the dams were "an invasion of the territorial sovereignty of the United States," and these findings resulted in additional official complaints to Mexico.[10]

As the U.S. government grappled with the wing-dam problem through the tedious formalities of international diplomacy, residents near El Paso and Juárez faced a new serious local situation. The drought of the late 1880s, which had contributed to the Mexican decision to extend the wing dam completely across the Rio Grande, also had taken its toll on the American side, where farms lay equally as parched and dusty as those south and west of the river. To find a solution to this immediate emergency, the El Paso City Council turned in the fall of 1888 to one of the community's prominent citizens, Anson Mills.

Born in Indiana in 1834, Mills had received an appointment to the United States Military Academy in 1855. He had left West Point before he graduated, however, later explaining in his self-published autobiography, *My Story*, that he had been judged "deficient in mathematics" in midyear exams. Claiming that he had resigned in humiliation over this failure, he had moved to the frontier in western Texas in May 1858, where he became a surveyor. In that capacity, he surveyed several forts for the U.S. Army and platted the sleepy hamlet of Franklin, Texas, which he later renamed El Paso after the narrow gorge through which the Rio Grande coursed just upstream from the town. With the outbreak of the Civil War, Mills accepted a commission in the Union Army; after that conflict, he served in the military during the Indian campaigns.[11]

Mills, who was home on leave from the Army Corps of Engineers when the El Paso City Council asked for his assistance, submitted to the community's leaders "a grand project for a dam and reservoir in the Rio Grande" to be built at the canyon four miles above the city. The concrete and stone dam, according to one newspaper account, would be sixty feet tall and create a lake fourteen miles long. Mills speculated that the new reservoir could

Brigadier General Anson Mills
in the early twentieth century.
From Anson Mills, *My Story,*
1918.

store the annual spring floodwaters and serve both the U.S. and Mexican
sides of the Rio Grande—an idea he had discussed informally with several
acquaintances on previous occasions.[12]

Apparently, Mills was not the first to consider damming the river above
El Paso; nevertheless, his proposal and fame as a city founder so impressed
El Paso's officials that, with their encouragement, Mills went to Washing-
ton, D.C., to meet with the U.S. Geological Survey's director, John Wesley
Powell. By the time Mills and Powell met, Powell had developed a consid-
erable reputation as an explorer, naturalist, and expert in the American
West. Born in New York in 1834, Powell had served in the Union Army dur-
ing the Civil War and lost an arm at the battle of Shiloh. Following the war,
Powell had taught at Illinois Wesleyan University and at Illinois Normal
University (today, Illinois State University), and he helped found the Illinois
Museum of Natural History. Beginning in 1867, he undertook a series of
expeditions to the West. In 1869—despite his lack of one arm—he led the
first of two exploratory parties down the Colorado River through the then-
unexplored Grand Canyon, during which he endured severe hardships and

the deaths of several companions. In 1881, Powell became the second director of the U.S. Geological Survey, a position he held until he died in 1894.[13]

A few months before Anson Mills went to Washington to meet with Director Powell and discuss the dam at El Paso, Congress had directed Powell to conduct a study of western water resources and possible reservoir sites, a review that later became known as the Powell Irrigation Survey. With much of the West being rapidly settled by the 1880s, the irrigation survey had been authorized in 1888—the same year that Anson Mills had proposed his dam at El Paso. The need for such an investigation had become readily apparent to federal lawmakers by the late 1880s. The drought of the second half of that decade, growing immigration to already crowded eastern cities, and the rapid filling of public domain lands that did not require irrigation to be productive (thus making them unavailable for further settlement) all had brought pressure to bear on Congress to do something to counter circumstances that many thought might lead to the decline of American individuality and an end to democratic values. The commissioner of the General Land Office, for example, had seen the need for such a reclamation study of the West when he had observed in 1885 that the disappearance of lands available for homesteading in areas with sufficient rainfall—the East and Midwest—was encouraging investors and companies to acquire considerable holdings in the arid West in anticipation of future settlement there.[14]

These and other factors had contributed to Congress's approval on March 10, 1888, of the Powell Irrigation Survey. The first large-scale hydrographic examination of the entire West, the Powell Irrigation Survey was not actually funded until late 1888.[15] Nevertheless, Mills's trip to Washington was in part founded on the hope that Powell would endorse the El Paso dam as part of his work for the irrigation survey, which, Mills hoped, might lead eventually to U.S. sponsorship for the project.

After hearing Mills's El Paso dam proposal, Powell was favorably impressed, and he requested that Mills meet with Secretary of State Thomas F. Bayard because of the international implications of the proposition. Bayard, in turn, asked Mills to draft a written plan for congressional consideration. Mills complied, and it was submitted to the federal lawmakers on December 10, 1888—only nine days after Congress had authorized funding for the Powell Irrigation Survey.[16]

In his proposal to Congress, Mills noted that for over two hundred years Mexicans annually had augmented a small natural dam of boulders with smaller rocks and willow branches at a site about three miles above El Paso.

The yearly effort was to improve the Rio Grande's flow into their main irrigation ditch, the Acequia Madre. Despite these exertions, however, floods usually washed the improvements away each spring and caused major changes in the river's channel. This sometimes left the Mexican ditch intake a considerable distance from any water. To Mills, the annual rebuilding was very inefficient. A much larger reservoir at the same location, he thought, not only would provide a satisfactory means of storing the floodwaters for later irrigation use but also could control water releases and confine the Rio Grande to a permanent channel, thus eliminating problems related to an unclear international boundary, such as smuggling and other crimes. With the river serving as a border between the two countries, Mills theorized that any plan to build a dam had to be truly international in character and the resulting reservoir had to be operated under the joint control of the United States and Mexico. Mills conjectured that this could be done through an international commission, both during construction and after completion. Demonstrating the poorly defined status of the emerging fields of western and international water law, Mills offered the suggestion in his proposal to Congress that the remedy "could be best brought about in this instance by treaty stipulations between the two countries."[17]

Mills believed that both the United States and Mexico should pay for the international reservoir, which he estimated would cost $100,000 for the dam itself, another $100,000 for the condemned land that was to be submerged, and a final $100,000 for the removal to higher ground of about fifteen miles of track belonging to the Atchison, Topeka and Santa Fe Railway. The resulting dam would be sixty feet high, creating a lake about fifteen miles long and seven miles wide. Mills calculated that about 1,653,000 acre-feet of water would flow each year into the reservoir, thus forming what would then be the largest artificial lake in the world. As far as dividing the stored water was concerned, Mills speculated that a quarter of it (413,250 acre-feet) would be lost to evaporation, a quarter could go to Mexican irrigators, a similar volume to Texas farmers, and the remaining 413,250 acre-feet could be used as a reserve to generate hydroelectric power (which was then becoming a viable source of energy) and to maintain a constant flow in the riverbed. Aside from the reserve water supply, Mills deduced—without much supporting evidence—that the 826,500 acre-feet used for irrigation on both sides of the river would water a huge area of a million acres and would make the desert bloom for a hundred miles below El Paso and Juárez. Furthermore, Mills's report to Congress enthusiastically asserted that the reservoir would allow sediment to settle, thus ending the frequent chore of cleaning downstream irrigation canals, and the study argued that when silt filled the reservoir, the dam could be raised by as much as an additional hundred feet to prolong its life. In other words, Mills's international dam proposal theoretically would solve a wide range of international and domestic problems in the El Paso–Juárez area.[18]

After Mills had presented his proposal to Congress, John Wesley Powell persuaded the Department of War to assign Mills to Fort Bliss, which had been established in 1849 in the vicinity of Juárez to protect American trade routes to southern California.[19] The War Department believed that with a formal assignment to Fort Bliss, Mills could assist the Powell Irrigation Survey's study of reservoir sites and reclamation possibilities on the Rio Grande. Nevertheless, the War Department's directive sending Mills to Fort Bliss specifically limited his examination of the river to sixty miles on either side of El Paso—orders that reinforced his bias in favor of the international dam site, since there were few other good reservoir locations within the sixty-mile range. Not only did Mills's military assignment help shape his favoritism for the El Paso dam site, so too did Powell's conviction that entire watersheds should be considered as units and water resources within these basins developed with little regard to interstate or international boundaries. Powell's theory in part stemmed from the reality that at the time there were no laws or accepted legal doctrines governing international or interstate allocation of stream flows. Because of these harmonious views, Powell ordered Mills to cooperate closely with Mexican interests in the Juárez area.[20]

From one perspective, Anson Mills's apparent motivation behind promoting the reservoir at El Paso can be interpreted as being a part of a contest among different groups for the economic conquest of the remote and arid regions of the West—circumstances that clearly had been an underlying cause of the salt wars a decade earlier.[21] Yet his predisposition to favor the dam site at that city did not rely entirely on his military orders; along with his brother, William, and various wealthy friends, Anson Mills had extensive landholdings on both sides of the river. Unquestionably, the value of these lands would increase dramatically with the completion of the international dam. Thus, Mills's incentive to see the plan succeed may have been driven as much by a desire for personal profit as by civic-mindedness, and these were sentiments that transcended the international border and affected major Mexican landowners in a similar manner.

On May 4, 1889, Mills arrived at Fort Bliss, where he met with Mexican government officials and local Juárez leaders. Explaining his project in detail to the Mexicans, Mills later observed that they received it "in a most encouraging manner." The Mexicans also gave Mills permission to establish one end of a cable for a gauging station on their country's soil, and in return, Mills invited the Mexicans to participate in all investigations for the proposed dam and reservoir—efforts that he believed would take only a few months—so that the Mexican government would fully understand the project from the beginning. Ultimately, Mills suggested that copies of all blueprints, maps, and working papers be given to Mexican officials "with a view to inducing the Mexican Congress (now in session) before their adjournment in January [1890], to pass a joint resolution authorizing their President to join the United States in the construction of the dam proper, and appropriating $150,000 for that purpose should our Government make a like appropriation; this for the purpose of gaining a year's time in commencement of the work." Mills also hoped to present similar documents to the U.S. Congress at its next session.[22]

As Mills pursued his studies of the international dam site, he was joined by prominent engineer William W. Follett. Born in Maine in 1856, Follett had received a degree in civil engineering from the University of Michigan in 1881, and following his graduation, he had found work with the U.S. Geological Survey.[23] With the El Paso dam proposal taking on considerable importance by 1889, the Geological Survey had assigned Follett to assist Mills in developing the technical details of the project. The United States also sent Colonel E. S. Nettleton, of the Powell Irrigation Survey, to review the Rio Grande situation. Mills coordinated work with Nettleton over the course of the next few months. In addition, Mills and Follett measured evaporation rates, studied sedimentation, surveyed the reservoir and dam sites above El Paso, and established a gauging station. Mills submitted the results of this research to the Geological Survey on October 10, 1889.[24]

Mills's report to the Geological Survey was considerably more detailed and realistic than either his casual suggestion to the El Paso City Council or his written proposal for Secretary Bayard and Congress, and it gave Mexico a sizeable interest in the entire project—a share that many Americans claimed was unnecessarily large and detrimental to American needs. Even more controversial, however, was Mills's opinion that Mexican citizens in the Juárez area had "prior rights" to the Rio Grande's waters. By the time Mills drafted his report, the water law doctrine of prior appropriation was becoming well established (if not equally well defined) in western states and territories. Essentially meaning first-in-time-first-in-right, priority contrasted sharply with the eastern doctrine of riparian water rights, which granted the authority to use water equally but only to those who owned land along waterways. Prior appropriation, in comparison, hinged on the chronological order of the claim to water, its rate of flow or quantity of the claim, and continued beneficial use. Appropriative claims did not depend on landownership next to a river, and supplies could be diverted away from lands adjacent to streams.[25]

Although the general outlines of prior appropriation were well under-stood in individual states and territories in the late nineteenth-century American West, the contention that priorities could cross state lines had been suggested, but not legally confirmed, in only a few local disputes—notably, along the Arkansas River in eastern Colorado and western Kansas.[26] Not until the 1922 Laramie River ruling in *Wyoming v. Colorado* did the U.S. Supreme Court hold that the doctrine of priority could be considered in allocating an interstate stream's waters where the neighboring states both adhered to the principle of appropriation. Even in this case, however, pri-orities were not implemented across the state line (as is sometimes mistak-enly assumed); rather, the apportionment to the two states was based on mass allocations derived from cumulative priorities.[27]

Thus, while the interstate aspect of water law was vague and remained so until well into the twentieth century, the relationship between upstream and downstream sovereign nations was even more ambiguous in 1889, when Mills argued that the long-standing prior rights of Juárez residents were being ignored by diversions in New Mexico and Colorado. Moreover, Mills declared that "the United States is under a moral obligation to indem-nify them [the Mexicans] for their loss or make some reparation, such as the construction of the projected dam and reservoir."[28] In a departure from the proposal he had given to Bayard and Congress, Mills contended that the "moral obligation" to Mexico required the U.S. government to pay for the entire El Paso reservoir project except for half of the dam itself, which would be Mexico's contribution. He also suggested that the U.S. government sus-pend restrictions on foreign labor so that Mexican workers could help build the dam on both sides of the Rio Grande and remove railroad tracks from the reservoir location. Finally, Mills advocated establishing an international commission to supervise construction and to administer the river's straight-ening as the boundary between the two countries. The constant shifting of the Rio Grande's main channel not only caused flooding and destroyed farmland but also complicated the determination of the position of the international boundary nearly impossible—a problem that made smuggling easy and the prosecution of criminals difficult because of uncertainties about jurisdictions. Mills hoped that the international dam would put an end to these problems.[29]

As to the dam, Mills's report to the Geological Survey called for building an international structure about three and a quarter miles above El Paso. According to Follett's calculations, the dam would create a reservoir fourteen and a half miles long and four miles wide at its most extreme points, holding 537,340 acre-feet of water. Scaling back his projections from those in the reports to Secretary Bayard and Congress, Mills estimated that the stored floodwaters—which would still create the biggest artificial lake in the world—would be sufficient to serve 100,000 acres on the U.S. side of the Rio Grande below the dam. This land, Mills suggested, "could be justly taxed for water rights should the Government see proper to reimburse itself for the investment." Aside from U.S. territory, Mills thought that an additional 125,000 acres on the Mexican side of the Rio Grande could be watered, but he made no provision for charging the Mexican lands for their water rights. Predicting that there would be a large amount of hydroelectric power generated at the dam, Mills proposed that income from energy sales could be used to repay construction costs. Mills recognized that silt accumulation was a major obstacle to the success of any dam on the Rio Grande, and he calculated that the filling of the reservoir with sediment would take a minimum of 150 years—a period of time that he hoped would be sufficient to allow engineers to develop a solution to this problem.[30]

Mills's Geological Survey report prompted widespread interest in the international dam proposition, and as a result, both he and John Wesley Powell appeared during 1889 before the Senate Select Committee on Irrigation and Reclamation of Arid Lands. Formed earlier that year and headed by Senator William Stewart of Nevada, this special congressional committee was charged with determining the best ways to reclaim the West and then to report its findings to the full Senate. The Select Committee on Irrigation and Reclamation gave considerable exposure to the need for western reclamation. As part of its work, for example, it held fifty-three hearings in various communities around the country. The committee also interviewed 382 witnesses and traveled 14,000 miles in addition to holding further hearings in Washington, D.C., in the winter of 1889–90. Thus, Mills's dam proposal and the committee's work were a logical combination, with each providing the other with increased exposure during a period when concern with irrigation-related matters was growing rapidly throughout the United States.[31]

In his testimony, Mills outlined his international dam ideas, and he explained that there were two sites near El Paso that could supply the valley below—one about a mile above the city and the other slightly upstream from that locale. Foreshadowing a later bitter conflict with irrigators in the Territory of New Mexico over the apportionment of the Rio Grande's water supplies, Mills added that there was another possible reservoir site located much farther upriver near Elephant Butte, New Mexico, but he dismissed that location on the grounds that, in his opinion, any facility there could hold only a tenth as much water as the international reservoir site. In discussing the advantages that a dam would bring to the El Paso area, Mills freely admitted that he would benefit personally from the reservoir because he owned acreage in the valley below the city. If the dam were built, Mills confirmed, his property would "become the best land in the whole country," but he contended that many others would similarly profit. Mills stressed, however, that without water everyone's lands were worthless.[32]

Although Mills had a direct interest in seeing the international dam constructed, Powell's enthusiasm for the proposal stemmed in part from his theories about equitably distributing waters of western streams based on the natural boundaries of river basins. Powell, who hoped that Congress would incorporate his ideas into legislation providing for an orderly development of the West's water supplies, thought that the Rio Grande, like all western rivers, ought to be divided into irrigation districts, which would be defined by watershed characteristics. These districts would exist independently of other political subdivisions and would be held in common by the people they served. The district's residents, in turn, would determine how best to administer allocations among themselves—an idea that was directly counter to the widely accepted (if not completely legally defined) understanding in the West that water rights were private property rights. Explaining his views to Congress, Powell suggested that a district could be formed in southern New Mexico's Mesilla Valley and in the El Paso Valley while other districts would assist areas farther upstream.[33]

Despite the apparent logic of Powell's idea, he recognized that even if this plan could be established across the interstate and international boundaries of the Mesilla and El Paso valleys, the apportionment of the waters within the district still might pose considerable difficulties. Noting that most Rio Grande precipitation occurred many miles above El Paso, while the lands to be irrigated were distributed among New Mexico, Texas, and Mexico, Powell reflected that the allocation of waters in a district covering the region confronted interstate and international problems. Nonetheless, Powell thought that no matter how the division was achieved, "the rights of all of the people now cultivating the soil should be maintained."[34] This could be accomplished best, Powell testified, by the construction of the proposed reservoir at El Paso. When combined with his plan of managing water in natural districts, the El Paso dam would maintain the rights of Mesilla Valley irrigators because they could divert the river's regular flow while El Paso Valley water users would benefit by the storage of return flows and floodwaters.[35] The "only hope for these valleys is through storage," Powell concluded, but he candidly admitted that "how the entire problem is to be solved by storage is not yet known."[36]

As the Senate Select Committee on Irrigation and Reclamation of Arid Lands concluded its hearings in Washington, two bills were introduced in Congress designed to make Mills's El Paso dam proposal the solution to the international problems involving the Rio Grande. These were the first legislative attempts to deal with dwindling Rio Grande water supplies in the El Paso–Juárez area, and the mere introduction of these bills suggested the growing belief on Capitol Hill that the apportionment of interstate and international rivers might be a federal as well as state and local concern. In the Senate, Texan John H. Reagan introduced a bill "concerning the irrigation of arid lands in the valley of the Rio Grande River [sic], the construction of a dam across said river at or near El Paso, Tex., for the storage of its waste waters, and for other purposes."[37] On the same day that Reagan introduced his bill, El Paso–area congressman (and future Texas governor) Samuel W. T. Lanham introduced a similar measure in the House of Representatives. Lanham, who believed that "the ultimate cost of the plan will not be more than the damage the Mexican people have sustained by our exhaustion of their water supply,"[38] called on the president to reach a negotiated settlement of Rio Grande border and water apportionment problems with Mexico that would involve building a dam at El Paso. Lanham's measure was referred to the House Committee on Irrigation of Arid Lands, a body that had only recently been created, which Lanham chaired.[39] For committee hearings on the bill, Lanham called for testimony from some of the same people who had appeared before the Senate Select Committee on Irrigation and Reclamation of Arid Lands, including Anson Mills and John Wesley Powell.[40]

In late February 1890, Lanham's committee returned his measure favorably to the full House of Representatives, although the committee clearly was concerned that the bill might be construed as sanctioning too broad of an undertaking—in effect, taking the place of a treaty with Mexico. To fend off such attacks, the Committee on Irrigation of Arid Lands spelled out how little authority the bill supposedly conveyed. Characterizing the measure as "inceptive and initiatory," the committee report stated that the bill contemplated "in its terms no present final or conclusive legislation." In addition, the committee suggested that the bill was "carrying no appropriation, but reserving any ultimate proposition on the subject to be controlled by the future judgment and discretion of Congress, after international consultations, and methods for concert of action shall have been considered and devised."[41] With these assurances, the Lanham measure was placed on the House calendar for later consideration.

Despite the guarded committee report on the Lanham bill, the specific nature of the opposition in the House of Representatives did not become visible until after the Senate had acted on the Reagan measure. Following a favorable report from the Senate irrigation committee,[42] when the measure moved to the Senate floor in March 1890, Senator Joseph N. Dolph of Oregon objected that Reagan's proposed legislation had not been reviewed by the Senate Committee on Foreign Relations. In Dolph's view, this was necessary because the Rio Grande apportionment and boundary issues were primarily international in character. Tennessee senator Isham G. Harris reflected the ongoing debate about the proper role of the federal government in sponsoring western reclamation projects by his disapproval of building a reservoir for irrigation, yet he did not oppose constructing a dam to settle the Rio Grande boundary problem. Reagan tried to overcome these complaints by pointing out that his bill still would have to be funded even if passed, but Dolph and Harris would not withdraw their objections. Further deliberations, therefore, were temporarily postponed.[43]

When debate on the Senate bill was revived on April 5, 1890, Reagan cited the hardships of the drought-stricken El Paso area as a reason for an immediate vote on the measure. Nonetheless, the prevailing sentiment among the senators was that the Rio Grande situation was really an international problem and that the Committee on Foreign Relations should therefore review the bill. The senators also objected that the measure conveyed too much power by consenting to federal reclamation and by taking the place of a treaty with Mexico. With unyielding opposition to Reagan's bill, the Senate eventually passed a substitute watered-down measure—a resolution asking the president to negotiate with Mexico to settle the Rio Grande problems. The resolution identified these difficulties as the lack of water during the irrigation season, flooding, and boundary changes that disturbed property titles, encouraged smuggling, and complicated other issues involving national jurisdictions. In an attempt to downplay any suggestion of federal involvement in domestic irrigation projects, no mention of a dam was made in the body of the resolution. The only reference to a reservoir at El Paso was in the title of Reagan's substitute bill: "International Dam in Rio Grande River near El Paso, Tex." Ironically, while the new resolution stemmed from the drive to have the international dam at El Paso built, the lack of mention of the reservoir in the text was later seized upon by opponents to demonstrate that Congress had never supported the international dam idea.[44]

When the Senate resolution was presented to the House of Representatives on April 29, 1890, Congressman Lanham urged its adoption in place of his bill since both measures embodied many of the same features. Even this did not prevent the same types of objections from arising in the House that had doomed Reagan's original stronger Senate bill. As in the Senate, some of Lanham's colleagues thought that the substitute resolution would provide an "entering wedge" for larger federal support for irrigation schemes—then a major issue to opponents of western reclamation. Others objected that the resolution had not been considered by the House Committee on Foreign Affairs. Regardless of these concerns, the effect of changing the Lanham bill to a resolution parallel to the Senate version softened the resolve of enough congressmen to win its approval the day it was brought to the full House of Representatives.[45]

The congressional joint resolution was the first step toward a compromise solution on the Rio Grande's apportionment between Mexico and the United States. Had the problem been simply an international one, however, the resolution might have paved the way for a relatively early settlement of the entire water dispute. Yet just as Anson Mills's El Paso dam began to appear to be the solution to the river's international water problems, questions concerning the river's apportionment within the United States added another factor to the already complex situation. Compounding the international controversy over the dam at El Paso, these new interstate issues made the question of the Rio Grande's division drag on for at least another ten years. Moreover, the conflict brought Congress more firmly into the picture as a participant in the solution of western water problems, although local needs and interests remained central to shaping congressional action.

CHAPTER 2

A Dry River in New Mexico and Texas

An Interstate Problem

The problem of dwindling Rio Grande water supplies in the El Paso–Juárez area was not merely a matter of international concern. The growing short-ages in the 1880s had attracted federal government attention because of the questions they had raised about an upstream country's obligation to meet a downstream sovereign nation's water needs. Yet as diversions proliferated all along the Rio Grande above El Paso, American farmers in the territory of New Mexico's Mesilla Valley were also adversely affected.

To New Mexicans, the water problem was primarily interstate in charac-ter. In this regard, New Mexico's problems were like several other interstate water issues that arose in the late nineteenth-century or early twentieth-century American West. As early as 1890 on the Arkansas River, for example, water users around Garden City, Kansas, had complained that upstream irri-gators in Colorado were depleting flows destined for western Kansas farm-lands. At about the same time, along the Laramie River, a proposal by Colorado's Larimer County Ditch Company to divert that stream's water supplies out of the basin angered downstream irrigators in Wyoming. And in the late 1870s, Arizona and California became involved in the earliest phases of a bitter struggle over the Colorado River—a controversy that has lingered to the present, along the way producing the first interstate river compact.[1] By 1920, other disputes had erupted between Nebraska and Colorado over the South Platte and Republican rivers. Some of these disputes were destined to become landmark U.S. Supreme Court water law cases.[2] So too was the Rio Grande, but for other reasons.

The New Mexico–Texas Rio Grande confrontation was distinct from the other contemporaneous interstate water conflicts for two major reasons. First, as noted in chapter 1, the early Rio Grande situation was compounded by international issues involving Mexico's claims to the river and the similarities between Mexican interests at Juárez to those of Texans at El Paso. (The Colorado River, too, eventually had international aspects to the struggle for its water supplies, but these were not as pronounced in the late nineteenth century as were the conflicts on the Rio Grande.) The dam at El Paso, New Mexicans realized, would bring no benefits to their region, especially since Texans—supported by international concerns—could be expected to fight any interference by New Mexico with the spring flood flows leaving the Rio Grande's headwaters in Colorado.

A second characteristic that made the New Mexico–Texas standoff atypical from the water controversies on the Arkansas, Laramie, and Colorado rivers related to New Mexico's political status and its geographic position of being sandwiched between the states of Colorado and Texas. Unlike the participants in the other early western interstate water rivalries, New Mexico was a territory and not yet a state. (New Mexico's role in the Colorado River interstate struggle took place after New Mexico joined the Union in 1912.) As a result, in the Rio Grande conflict, New Mexicans had considerably less power in Congress than did residents of Colorado or Texas—a political reality that did not exist along the Arkansas and Laramie rivers. Emphasizing the distinction, Colorado argued in the early stages of the conflict over the Arkansas River that Colorado's position was supported by the fact that it was a sovereign state and owed no obligation to the downstream state of Kansas any more than one independent nation was obligated to another country. Colorado later asserted a similar claim in the struggle with Wyoming over the Laramie River.[3]

On the Rio Grande, the situation was much different. There, New Mexico not only was not a downstream nation, it was not even a downstream state. As a result, although the Rio Grande yielded its own landmark Supreme Court decisions on water law, they were not centered on issues of one state versus another.[4]

Complicating the Rio Grande situation (as well as those on the Arkansas, Laramie, and Colorado rivers) was the uncertain status of state and territorial authority over water rights in the West and the ominous possibility that the U.S. government might eventually assert claims to all unused flows in western rivers for its own purposes. Many nineteenth-century westerners believed that when Congress had approved the Mining Act of 1866 (which had accepted local customs on public lands in relation to water use and control), 1870 legislation amending the Mining Act (which provided that land patents were to be granted subject to existing vested water rights), and the 1877 Desert Land Act (which directly extended prior appropriation to water used in the reclamation of arid public lands), federal lawmakers had transferred jurisdiction over water rights to state governments in the arid parts of the country.[5] As legal scholar Clesson S. Kinney explained in the 1912 edition to his authoritative tome on water law, "Each State has the power, either by legislative enactment, or by court decision, to adopt such a role governing the waters flowing or standing therein, as it sees fit."[6] Nevertheless, U.S. officials did not unanimously support this view. For example, while working for the Powell Irrigation Survey, Frederick Haynes Newell— later the second head of the U.S. Reclamation Service—had contended that the United States never had relinquished its control over water to the states, particularly on the public domain. Considering that much of New Mexico was still in federal hands, such an argument was antithetical to the position of nearly every irrigator in that territory. But even if states *had* gained control over water rights within their borders, the authority of territories such as New Mexico to regulate water allocation remained legally unknown.[7]

Geographically speaking, of greatest concern to New Mexico's water users were diversions in the San Luis Valley, an area in the south-central part of Colorado covering over 3,900 square miles and encompassing the uppermost portion of the Rio Grande basin. Although settlements had existed in the El Paso Valley as early as the sixteenth century and in New Mexico's Mesilla Valley since at least 1846, major American occupation in the San Luis Valley dated only from the 1860s. There had been little problem from San Luis Valley water use, however, until the completion of the Denver and Rio Grande Railroad and its spurs brought a heavy influx of farmers to the area in the late 1870s and early 1880s. Growing settlement in the San Luis Valley, in turn, stimulated ditch building and diversions from the Rio Grande for irrigation. When the Senate Select Committee on Irrigation and Reclamation of Arid Lands heard testimony in 1889 on the El Paso international dam proposal from Anson Mills and John Wesley Powell, canals in the San Luis Valley extended for almost 1,200 miles and were capable of supplying water to a million and a half acres—had there been enough water to do so.[8]

Most New Mexicans along the Rio Grande had seen the link between the growth of San Luis Valley agriculture and their water shortages. Although nearly all portions of New Mexico relying on Rio Grande water had been affected by the developments in the San Luis Valley, the region that had suffered the most was the Mesilla Valley. The area along the Rio Grande from El Paso northward into what is today the state of New Mexico had been well known to explorers for many years before Spaniards established the first settlements there, and in the seventeenth century, trading expeditions regularly traversed the Rio Grande valley on their journeys from Mexico City to Santa Fe and Taos. Conflicts with Indians, however, prevented any large-scale occupation of the region until the early 1800s, when a treaty between the Spanish and Indians paved the way for farms and villages to grow. In the late 1830s, the area around what is today El Paso and Juárez, which was governed by the recently independent Mexico, had a non-Indian population of about four thousand, and in the early 1840s, the Doña Ana colony was created slightly to the north of modern-day Las Cruces in the Mesilla Valley. Other communities and more farms followed, especially after the end of the U.S.-Mexican War in 1848, and within several decades, the Mesilla Valley had become a booming region with Las Cruces as its hub.[9]

The Mesilla Valley was one of the most productive farming areas in New Mexico by the middle of the nineteenth century—the local press referred to the region as the Egypt of the "American continent" and compared the Rio Grande to the Nile—but water scarcity had become critical there by the time the first international dam proposals had been introduced in Congress to solve the drought problem in the El Paso Valley.[10] Yet the international dam, as New Mexicans correctly understood, would do nothing for the Mesilla Valley, and the resulting reservoir would, in fact, flood some of the valley's best lands.[11] To correct the severe water situation in New Mexico, additional reservoirs on the Rio Grande appeared to be the answer, and calls for storing the Rio Grande's flood flows had begun to appear in 1879.[12] By the early 1890s, as Anson Mills developed his international dam plan for El Paso, some New Mexicans had begun to advocate a convention to address the water shortage problems in the Rio Grande valley.[13] Simultaneously,

Las Cruces, New Mexico, in the late nineteenth century, looking north on Main Street from the Loretto Academy, with Doña Ana Mountains in the distance. Courtesy Rio Grande Historical Collections, New Mexico State University, Las Cruces.

various enterprises organized to irrigate portions of the area adjacent to the river in New Mexico. Like the international dam proposal, the New Mexico schemes called for capturing floodwaters for later use.[14] Yet unlike the El Paso venture backed by Anson Mills, which assumed eventual federal sponsorship, the New Mexico projects were advanced by private water companies—a trait more common than government sponsorship for irrigation ventures in the late nineteenth century.

As was certainly true of the New Mexico proposals, most turn-of-the-century water firms' plans had been encouraged by changes in nineteenth-century American laws that were aimed at spurring economic growth, especially in the arid West. These were alterations in the legal system that historian J. Willard Hurst has characterized as the release of private individual creativity. Not only had the territory of New Mexico passed a general incorporation act in 1887 that allowed water companies to be formed without special legislative action for each new firm, but New Mexico's lawmakers also had declared that any works constructed by such companies were to be tax-free for the first six years. On the federal level, Congress had not only passed the Mining Act in 1866 and the Desert Land Act of 1877 but had also approved the General Revision Act of 1891, which authorized rights-of-way across U.S. public lands for reservoir and water companies.

This legislation became especially important to later events on the Rio Grande.[15]

Together, such laws and others like them had prompted a wide array of private reclamation enterprises throughout the West. Some ventures' plans focused on artesian wells and windmills; other proposals even involved rain making. Many of these undertakings' sponsors firmly believed that all that was needed was a little water to turn western deserts into an agricultural paradise. Water alone was thought to be sufficient to overcome poor soils because it carried nutrients in solution. Moreover, according to prevalent thinking, water would leach acids out of soils, kill detrimental insects and larvae, and discourage pests such as groundhogs and gophers. Indeed, many argued that "rain followed the plow" and that with irrigation, dry lands eventually, when cultivated, would increase precipitation and thus would convert themselves into more humid areas similar to the East. This now-discredited theory was that evaporation and plant transpiration on watered acreage would create clouds, which, in turn, would increase rainfall.[16]

All of these considerations went hand-in-hand with the era's conviction that nature could—and should—be harnessed to benefit humankind, and the stimuli brought about by nineteenth-century legal changes caused a deluge of water-supply businesses to be formed to take advantage of the new circumstances. Some of these were joint-stock (or "mutual") irrigation companies, in which the beneficiaries of the firm were also its owners. Others were private corporations. Regardless of form, however, each company vied with its competitors to secure control over the best irrigable lands and lock up related water rights.

In this regard, the Rio Grande was not unique. On the Colorado River, for example, Charles R. Rockwood had formed the Colorado Development Company in 1896 to provide water to what was then known as the Salton Sink in southern California. (He also changed the region's name to the more appealing "Imperial Valley" to attract settlers.) Rockwood secured the backing of irrigation engineer George Chaffey, who had developed reclamation projects in Australia and at the California communities of Etiwanda and Ontario. By the early 1900s, the California Development Company was delivering water supplies from the Colorado River to thousands of acres of former desert in southern California just north of the Mexican border.[17] Other reclamation ventures similar to Rockwood's sprang up throughout the West, including along the Rio Grande. Even the El Paso dam favored by Anson Mills had a private competitor for the same locale. That proposi-

Nathan E. Boyd with family and pets, ca. 1900. Courtesy Rio Grande Historical Collections, New Mexico State University, Las Cruces.

tion apparently never got beyond the incorporation stage, but the plan did receive widespread notice in the American press.[18]

In New Mexico, one of the largest private reservoir projects was planned by the Rio Grande Dam and Irrigation Company, which was organized by three El Paso merchants and chartered in New Mexico on January 12, 1893. Nathan E. Boyd, a medical doctor, later became the company's president, most outspoken champion, and largest investor. Boyd had been born into a rural Virginia family, and after moving west, he completed studies in 1882 at San Francisco's Cooper Medical College, the first medical school in the American West. Following his graduation, he spent several years in Sydney, Australia, and his growing prominence as a physician led to his appointment as editor of the *British Medical Journal* and a move to London.[19] Although Boyd eventually relocated to New Mexico, his time in England later gave him access to major British financiers for the Rio Grande Dam and Irrigation Company—investors who sought to cash in quickly on what appeared to be a lucrative opportunity.

For its technical plans, the Rio Grande Dam and Irrigation Company turned to one of its incorporators, John L. Campbell. Then El Paso's city engineer, Campbell had been El Paso County's deputy surveyor when Anson Mills first had proposed the international dam just above the city of El Paso. In 1889, Campbell had reviewed Mills's data on Rio Grande flows and specifications for the international dam, and Campbell later used this information in preparing the details for the Rio Grande Dam and Irrigation Company's works in New Mexico—much to Mills's dismay.[20] Under Campbell's direction, the firm produced plans "to construct irrigation works and consolidate under one corporate body certain irrigation rights and interests in the Rio Grande Valley, in southern New Mexico and El Paso County, Tex."[21]

The Rio Grande Dam and Irrigation Company intended to build a gigantic reservoir at Elephant Butte, New Mexico—about 125 miles upriver from El Paso—to provide water to the Mesilla and El Paso valleys, although most service would be in New Mexico. Also to benefit were the Palomas and Rincon valleys, two smaller areas along the Rio Grande upstream from the Mesilla Valley. The main dam at Elephant Butte was to be ninety-six feet high, creating a reservoir capable of holding more than 250,000 acre-feet of water—less than half the international El Paso reservoir's size but still bigger than any other artificial lake at the time. Eight miles downriver, a second, smaller, reservoir would be constructed, and between there and El Paso, two ten-foot-high diverting dams would be built to direct water released from the two storage reservoirs into irrigation canals. The diverting dams' foundations were to be deep enough to intercept the underflow of the river, which the company anticipated would increase from irrigation water seeping back to the river. In the same way as Anson Mills's initial proposal for the international dam had asserted that it would serve a ludicrously huge area of a million acres, the New Mexico plan had preposterous estimates of acreage to be watered by the Elephant Butte structure. Once the New Mexico canal network was completed, according to the Rio Grande Dam and Irrigation Company, 230,000 acres of Mesilla Valley lands would be under ditch, and by adding a "high-line" canal along nearby mesa lands, another 300,000 acres would be irrigated. The Rio Grande Dam and Irrigation Company also contemplated supplying water to lands beyond the Organ and Franklin mountains east of the Mesilla Valley, thus serving an additional 950,000 acres—bringing the total possible service area to nearly a million and a half acres.[22]

MAP
OF THE
RIO GRANDE VALLEY
FROM
ENGLE NEW MEXICO TO FORT QUITMAN TEXAS
SHOWING
DAMS, RESERVOIRS, CANALS
AND
IRRIGABLE LANDS
OF THE
RIO GRANDE DAM & IRRIGATION Cº

Proposed Reservoir

Elephant Butte Dam

N
W · E
S

Llano de Tularosa
450,000 acres irrigable

Organ Mts.

• Las Cruces

Mesilla Valley
110,000 acres irrigable

Level, cleared land ready for the plow

NEW MEXICO
TEXAS

Franklin Mts.

Mesa or uplands 500,000 acres irrigable

U.S.A.
MEXICO

• El Paso

Juarez •

El Paso Valley
80,000 acres irrigable
on the American
side of the river

Rio Grande

Area proposed for irrigation
Proposed irrigation canals

0   10   20   30 Miles

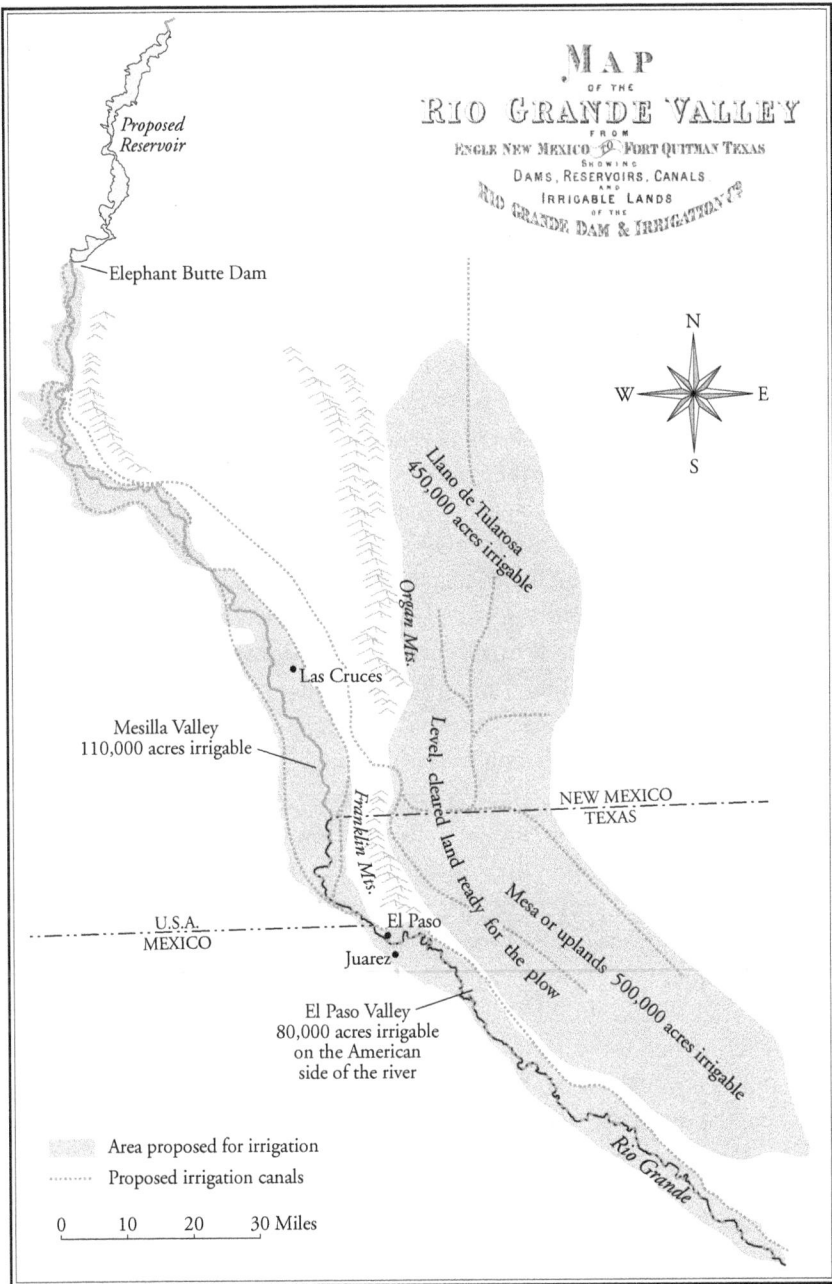

Irrigation systems of the Rio Grande valley proposed by the Rio Grande Dam and Irrigation Company, mid-1890s. Based on Map of the Rio Grande Valley from Engle, New Mexico, to Fort Quitman, Texas, in International Boundary Commission, *Proceedings*, 2: insert. Map by Bill Nelson.

The speculative nature of the Rio Grande Dam and Irrigation Company's plans reflected the late-nineteenth-century attitude that the natural environment was to be conquered in the pursuit of profit and "civilization." So too did the firm's almost total lack of attention to the "duty" of water—the quantity necessary per acre to raise crops. Although this omission in the company's strategy may have been attributable in part to the contemporary belief in some circles that newly farmed lands would increase humidity and precipitation and that water supplies would grow in direct proportion to lands irrigated, the Rio Grande Dam and Irrigation Company's lack of concern for the duty of water also was a reflection of how innovative irrigation farming was at the time. The firm's main reservoir was designed to hold 250,000 acre-feet of water, yet company officials optimistically boasted that their facility might eventually serve 1,480,000 acres (including the 950,000 acres beyond the Organ and Franklin mountains). Since the reservoir was to store mostly the spring floodwaters and not "normal" (year-round) flows, which were being seriously depleted by upstream irrigators, simple mathematics indicates that if all the projected acreage were to be served each year, the duty of water would be substantially less than 0.2 acre-feet per acre—this in a region where already-irrigated lands required anywhere from 2 to 6 acre-feet per acre (including transit losses due to seepage and evaporation). Such outlandish claims by irrigation promoters such as the Rio Grande Dam and Irrigation Company were not unusual in the late nineteenth century, and while they underscore the important and speculative role of private enterprise in developing western water resources, they also point toward how little actually was known at the time about irrigated farming techniques.[23]

Although the ambitious Rio Grande Dam and Irrigation Company undertaking had immense appeal in New Mexico, financing the project was not as easy as the firm's promoters would have liked. The company's original approach had called for landowners who wanted water to exchange half of their property and all their rights in existing community ditches for a perpetual and inalienable water right to their remaining acreage, which would be charged an annual "rental" (service) fee of $1.50 per acre. Typical of the language used at the time for water delivery contracts, the term "water right" did not mean a legal right to water the way it is understood today. Instead, the water right to be conveyed by the Rio Grande Dam and Irrigation Company was a contractual obligation by the firm to provide water to customers. For other income, stock sales and a bond issue would be used to finance construction of the dams and canals, and when water rentals paid off the bonds, the company would sell its land. Profits from real estate sales and continuing water rentals would pay dividends on the stock and make the holders of those securities very wealthy from the increase in stock value—at least, that was the theory.[24]

Although this financing method seemed feasible when the Rio Grande Dam and Irrigation Company was incorporated in 1893, that same year a severe economic depression began—the worst the United States had experienced to date and a crisis that would last until nearly the beginning of the twentieth century. Between 1893 and 1898, the unemployment rate in the United States averaged around 20 percent. In 1894, there were fourteen hundred strikes in the country, involving more than five hundred thousand workers, and outside the cities, a severe drought engulfed much of the West between 1893 and 1895.[25] These circumstances made it difficult to sell the Rio Grande Dam and Irrigation Company's securities to Americans and seriously crippled or bankrupted multitudes of other private irrigation ventures. To overcome this problem, the Rio Grande Dam and Irrigation Company gave Nathan Boyd a power of attorney, and Boyd went back to England, where he helped organize the Rio Grande Irrigation and Land Company, whose sole purpose was to own and finance the American firm.[26]

The British company, according to documents filed with England's Board of Trade, was chartered on October 10, 1895, and authorized to be funded at £500,000 at £1 per share.[27] This represented a potential capitalization of approximately £28,530,000 (2008 valuation), or in U.S. currency, about $56,110,000.[28] Following its formation, the British firm exchanged 300,000 shares and £26,500 in cash and debentures for control of the American company and that firm's official right to build the dam on the Rio Grande—an authorization the U.S. government had granted under the provisions of the 1891 General Revision Act before the El Paso international dam concept had gained widespread adherents. Of the 300,000 shares, 280,000 shares (worth $31,422,000 in 2008 U.S. dollars) went to Nathan Boyd and 20,000 ($2,244,000) to Reginald Chetham-Strode, who, with Boyd and several others had been an early sponsor of the American company. The cash and debentures also went to Boyd and Chetham-Strode. (The remaining 200,000 authorized shares were never issued.) The British firm's shares were to be credited to Boyd and Chetham-Strode as paid-in-full, although in the nineteenth century, payments for stock shares generally were not due until the issuing company called for them. Over the following four years, according to British government records, Boyd sold about a third and Chetham-Strode about half of their respective stock holdings to other investors.[29] Because its entire initial stock issue had gone to Boyd and Chetham-Strode (and credited to them as fully paid), the English company planned to borrow funds by bond sales. In effect, this highly speculative scheme gave Boyd an extremely large stake in the British firm with very little of his own money invested in it (although he subsequently bought a large portion of the company's bonds, probably with money raised by selling some of his stock).[30]

The British investment in the American Rio Grande Dam and Irrigation Company represented a unique aspect of English financial contributions to the development of the nineteenth-century American West. Many writers have acknowledged the role of British financial contributions to American railroads, but English investors sought many other economic opportunities as U.S. settlement took place beyond the ninety-eighth meridian. By the late 1800s, British backers of American railroads had grown wary of such investments because the English contributions had been largely in the form of bond purchases, which gave British sponsors no voting power in the American endeavors' administration. Struggles for dominance among the American railroad kings had left English investors merely as onlookers, and wealthy British citizens who desired to speculate in other American undertakings in the nineteenth century demanded a more direct role in management. The result was that English investors in nonrailroad enterprises in the American West frequently formed British firms such as the Rio Grande Irrigation and Land Company. These English companies, in turn, acquired or directly controlled American organizations, notably cattle, mining, and irrigation schemes. Many of these British enterprises demanded on-site supervision or at least occasional visits by English managers to America to oversee their investments.[31]

Such was the case with the English Rio Grande Irrigation and Land Company's acquisition of the American Rio Grande Dam and Irrigation Company, although that particular enterprise came to be almost entirely a Nathan Boyd venture. Not only did the British firm issue stock to obtain the American assets held by Boyd (which was then paid for by bond sales), but the English company also had an American manager: Nathan Boyd. Boyd's sale of the English firm's stock and his subsequent purchase of the company's bonds yielded the result that he held most of the British Rio Grande Irrigation and Land Company's securities, whether in the form of stocks or bonds. There were, nonetheless, other very prominent investors in the British firm; according to the records of England's Board of Trade and that country's Foreign Office, they included Colonel William J. Engledue, an English irrigation expert; the Earl of Winchelsea and Nottingham, who was also president of the National Agricultural Association of Great Britain; Samuel Hope Morley, a member of Parliament and a governor of the Bank of England; Arnold Morley, a former member of England's cabinet; and several other English lords and multimillionaires. Yet however prominent the British backers may have been, Boyd remained the key to the entire Rio Grande scheme.[32]

The Rio Grande venture was attractive to other bond investors not only because of Boyd's management and promotional efforts but also because of the Rio Grande Irrigation and Land Company's marketing publications. The purpose of the British enterprise was, according to its prospectus, "to acquire, by lease and assignment, the franchise rights, water rights, right of appropriating the waters of the Rio Grande (United States of America), contracts, properties, and undertakings of the Rio Grande Dam and Irrigation Company, and for the purposes of irrigating, colonizing, and improving the lands in the famous Rio Grande Valley, between Engle [near Elephant Butte], N. Mex., and Fort Quitman, Tex."[33] The English company's prospectus was bluntly candid in its assessment of profit potential and how investments in the New Mexico scheme would be protected. The British sponsors were well aware that the American firm's policy of having farmers exchange half their acreage for water rights had not yielded enough real estate–backed security to float bonds in the United States. Thus, to ensure that bonds would sell better in Great Britain, the English organization's prospectus hinted that recalcitrant landowners could be coerced to accept the land-for-water program—and under less favorable terms than the American firm had offered. Labeled "Private and Confidential," the English venture's prospectus explained that by acquiring the reservoir site at Elephant Butte, the company would dominate the entire flow of the Rio Grande in southern New Mexico. Thus, the prospectus concluded, "in controlling the water, the company will, to a great extent, control the irrigable lands."[34]

The conspicuous implication was that farmers who did not support the land-for-water exchange might get no water at all until they agreed to the program. Noting that while a few settlers had accepted the land-for-water trade on a fifty-fifty basis as initially proposed by the American firm, the English company's prospectus intimated that exchange terms would be less

generous in the future. "Obviously," the prospectus observed enthusiastically, "the remaining land owners must, in order to render their properties
of value, concede a large portion of their lands for water rights or purchase
the said water rights, at the ruling rate, from the company." Through such
tactics, the Rio Grande Irrigation and Land Company expected its American subsidiary to acquire forty thousand acres of irrigable valley lands.[35]

The English organization anticipated handsome profits. The sale of valley lands was planned to yield £400,000 (worth $44,888,000 in 2008). An
additional £3,000,000 ($336,662,000) would be earned from the sale of
water rights to cities and towns along the Rio Grande and to landowners
who could not be persuaded to trade real estate for water. Water rental fees
would bring in another £175,000 ($19,638,000) each year. Aside from this
income, the English holding company's prospectus pointed out that if the
high-line canal were built to serve mesa lands above the Rio Grande valley,
additional profits could be expected from the sale of acreage there, two-
thirds of which would be acquired through the same land-for-water
exchange program with cattle ranchers or bought directly from the U.S.
government. As if these profits were not enough, the prospectus noted that
under New Mexico territorial laws aimed at promoting irrigation, the American company's works would be tax-free for the first six years. Clearly, British
enthusiasm for watering the West was just as optimistic (and just as unrealistic) as its American counterpart.[36]

As the English Rio Grande Irrigation and Land Company was being
organized in Britain, the American-based Rio Grande Dam and Irrigation
Company's directors applied to the General Land Office under the terms
of the 1891 General Revision Act for a right-of-way to build Elephant Butte
Dam on federal public lands. On February 1, 1895, the U.S. government
approved the application, clearing the way for construction to begin immediately—or so the firm's officials believed.[37]

Yet the incorporation of the Rio Grande Dam and Irrigation Company
and its federal right-of-way approval soon precipitated vehement opposition
to the construction of Elephant Butte Reservoir by proponents of the international dam at El Paso. Justifiably fearing that the private dam at Elephant
Butte would interfere with the river's flows destined for the international El
Paso reservoir, Texans and Mexicans were infuriated that the New Mexico
project had been sanctioned by the U.S. government—an authorization
that seemingly ignored Texans' and Mexicans' claims to prior rights (even
if those had never been tested in court). For their part, the Rio Grande Dam

and Irrigation Company's sponsors argued that a reservoir at Elephant Butte could serve the Mesilla and El Paso areas adequately "without discriminating in favor of either the upper or lower valley," and they stoutly maintained that their dam would not interfere with any prior rights in Texas or Mexico, because it would only capture the Rio Grande's spring floodwaters. These annual flood flows had never been used in any significant manner by El Paso or Juárez irrigators.[38] International dam backers insisted, however, that because the river's regular flow was already fully appropriated, their facility had been designed to capture the same floodwaters that the Rio Grande Dam and Irrigation Company proposed to store at Elephant Butte. Thus, with international dam supporters becoming the leading foes of the Elephant Butte endeavor, the resulting stalemate escalated the water shortage into an interstate as well as an international struggle—an encounter in which the interstate facets soon came to dominate over the international issues.

The first evidence that Rio Grande water shortages had triggered interstate as well as international problems became apparent shortly after the Rio Grande Dam and Irrigation Company had obtained its right-of-way for Elephant Butte Dam. With no action by American authorities to correct the Juárez water shortages despite repeated pleas by Mexican officials, in October 1895 Mexico's foreign minister, Matias Romero, complained to Secretary of State Richard Olney about the near-total lack of water in the Rio Grande during the previous irrigation season. Romero declared that the 1848 Treaty of Guadalupe Hidalgo, the 1853 Gadsden Treaty, the 1884 agreement between Mexico and the United States, and international law all required the United States to respect the rights of Mexican citizens to have their share of Rio Grande waters. Relying on this legal reasoning, Romero insisted that steps "be taken to effect an arrangement with the Government of Mexico that will facilitate the fulfillment of international obligations and remedy existing evils as far as possible."[39]

Because Romero had raised the terms of treaties and international law—and because the State Department did not have its own legal office until 1931[40]—Secretary Olney sent Romero's letter to U.S. Attorney General Judson Harmon for his assessment of the two countries' rights and responsibilities in relation to Rio Grande waters. Olney asked specifically about provisions in the Treaty of Guadalupe Hidalgo relating to the Rio Grande as an international boundary, and he also wanted to know whether principles of international law substantiated Romero's contention that obstructions and diversions made by Americans on the Rio Grande were violations of Mexican legal rights.[41]

Harmon's answer became central to supporting Rio Grande water users' interests in New Mexico and Colorado against those at El Paso and Juárez, and by implication, the response gave ammunition to supporters of the Rio Grande Dam and Irrigation Company to use against backers of the international dam at El Paso. Harmon's analysis—which demonstrated how little actual law existed to address transboundary apportionment issues—found that the Treaty of Guadalupe Hidalgo and the 1884 agreement between the United States and Mexico had established that Mexico could object only to obstructions to navigation on the Rio Grande. Pointing out that, according to an 1850 exploration, the river's navigability ended about 150 miles below El Paso and Juárez, Harmon stated that American diversions obviously could not be interfering with navigability in the El Paso–Juárez area. Moreover, Harmon explained that the Treaty of Guadalupe Hidalgo, which had ceded Mexican land (including the Rio Grande's headwaters) to the United States at the end of the Mexican War, did not reserve any rights to Mexico for the use of the river's water for irrigation. Harmon concluded that the "fundamental principle of international law is the absolute sovereignty of every nation as against all others within its own territory."[42]

In short, according to Harmon, the United States had no obligation to provide any water to Mexico—a position that was so one-sided that it later was enthusiastically quoted by different upstream states against claims by lower parties on other streams. For example, Harmon's reply was subsequently used in 1903 by Colorado in the early phases of *Kansas v. Colorado* (decided by the U.S. Supreme Court in 1907) to justify Colorado's claim to sole and absolute control over the Arkansas River (a position not supported by the Supreme Court). Moreover, Harmon's opinion was even cited during later talks over how to apportion the waters of the Colorado River among that basin's states and in regard to Mexico.[43]

While Harmon's opinion sustained unlimited Rio Grande diversions in New Mexico and Colorado at the expense of those in the El Paso–Juárez area, Secretary Olney astutely recognized that Harmon's views would not settle the issue from the Mexican point of view. With the likelihood of an escalating international problem, Olney turned for help to the International Boundary Commission, established in 1889 to fix a permanent border between the United States and Mexico along the shifting channel of the Rio Grande. Anson Mills was the U.S. delegate to the commission.[44]

The International Boundary Commission's legal authority, however, only extended to matters relating to the location of the border between the two countries, and to deal with the Rio Grande's irrigation problems, a subsidiary international organization was created in 1896 to recommend how to apportion the river's waters between Mexico and the United States. Secretary Olney asked Anson Mills to work on the new International Commission on the Equitable Distribution of the Waters of the Rio Grande — known informally as the International (Water) Boundary Commission — in addition to his duties with the like-named International Boundary Commission. Romero appointed F. Javier Osorno as Mexico's representative to the new water commission.[45] Mills, Osorno, and their staffs then began to investigate the "best and most feasible mode, whether through a dam to be constructed across the Rio Grande near El Paso, Tex., or otherwise, of so regulating the use of the waters of said river to secure to each country concerned and to its inhabitants their legal and equitable rights and interests in said waters." Olney and Romero gave the commissioners eight months to produce a report.[46]

Although the commissioners could have investigated possible reservoir sites at locations along the entire Rio Grande, from the outset they assumed the solution to the El Paso–Juárez water shortages to be the international dam at El Paso. Anson Mills's dominant personality and his long-term support for that project likely contributed to this initial supposition, but the International (Water) Boundary Commission's prejudice in favor of the El Paso dam also was influenced by a timely protest lodged by residents of Juárez against the ambitions of the Rio Grande Dam and Irrigation Company — plans that were just then becoming widely known. Juárez farmers understandably worried that the Elephant Butte project would deplete all the remaining flows of the Rio Grande before the El Paso dam could be built.[47]

The International (Water) Boundary Commission's predisposition toward the El Paso dam and the Juárez protest — as well as the endorsement of the international dam by Mexico's president, Porfirio Diaz[48] — soon made that site the sole one being considered by the commission. To make the facility a reality, on August 17, 1896, the commission outlined a rough plan to obtain options on 27,000 acres to be flooded by the reservoir. In addition, the commissioners recommended seeking an agreement with the Southern Pacific and the Atchison, Topeka and Santa Fe railroad companies to move their tracks out of the reservoir area, and they determined that the State Department should negotiate with Texas to give up state-owned lands for the reservoir site. The International (Water) Boundary Commission also called on the State Department to arrange for the United States to cede to Mexico 100 acres of U.S. land in the territory of New Mexico just above El Paso so that one end of the dam would be in Mexico (the other end would be in Texas just across the river), thus creating a truly international structure. In a weakly disguised attempt to undercut the viability of the Rio Grande Dam and Irrigation Company's plans, the commissioners additionally suggested that the State Department urge Congress to become further involved in seeking a Rio Grande apportionment solution by passing laws prohibiting the private construction of any other dams and reservoirs anywhere along the Rio Grande and its tributaries. "This restraint," the commissioners observed, was "to be only so far as the appropriation of waters by these proposed dams and reservoirs might interfere with the present vested rights in Mexico and Texas below the [international] dam."[49]

While the commissioners sketched out the plans for the international reservoir, they also directed their engineers—one of whom was William W. Follett, who had helped Anson Mills develop the international dam plan in 1889—to locate the dam's exact site, to determine the depth to bedrock, to make working diagrams and cost estimates, to survey land to be ceded to Mexico, to investigate the flow of the river and its tributaries, to compile a list of all ditches and reservoirs on the Rio Grande and its tributaries, and to determine whether these facilities would interfere with the proposed dam.[50] The centerpiece to the engineering work became Follett's "Study of the Uses of Water for Irrigation in the Rio Grande del Norte," which was later printed in the *Proceedings of the International (Water) Boundary Commission* (1903).

According to Follett's survey, the region that had been hurt the most by Rio Grande water shortages was the El Paso Valley. Follett contended that many farms on both sides of the river in that area were being abandoned because of insufficient water, and he thought that Mexico's claims for damages caused by American upriver diversions were well founded. Although he blamed the downriver water shortages to some extent on drought and on the denuding of watershed forests in Colorado (which prevented the soil from retaining rainfall and allowed snow to melt more quickly), the relationship between forests and water supplies was controversial and only beginning to become clear to scientists of the day.[51] Regardless of the debate over the role of forests in water storage, Follett saw Colorado's increased irrigation uses of Rio Grande waters as the main culprit for the dwindling supplies. "The condition, therefore, to be considered at El Paso," Follett con-cluded, "is that of a dry river likely to recur every year"—a proposition that in the light of ever-increasing settlement was entirely realistic. Follett next turned his attention to possible reservoirs. Noting that there were two plans for major dams on the Rio Grande, one being that of the Rio Grande Dam and Irrigation Company at Elephant Butte and the other the international dam at El Paso, Follett stated that the facility at Elephant Butte "is not at all assured and may not even be a future probability." Follett acknowledged, however, that "its effect, if built, on the flow of the river would be very seri-ous, and so it should be carefully studied." Moreover, he warned that "if that dam is built at all, its use of water should be conditional on its stopping no flow when the supply of water at El Paso is short."[52]

Follett's engineering study of the Rio Grande basin was persuasive. In issuing its final report on November 25, 1896, the full International (Water) Boundary Commission relied heavily on Follett's findings in advocating the international dam plans. Whereas Follett had not directly endorsed either the Elephant Butte reservoir or the international dam at El Paso, the com-missioners already had committed themselves to a more partisan position by their decision several months earlier to secure options for the international dam site, and they continued to recommend that the reservoir be con-structed to solve the El Paso–Juárez shortages. Disingenuously accepting the idea that the Rio Grande Dam and Irrigation Company's project could also go forward, the commissioners nevertheless qualified that acceptance by taking the position that the El Paso Valley had prior rights to all Rio Grande water, both "normal" as well as flood flows. The commissioners declared that if both dams were to be built, the Elephant Butte structure "must in some way be restrained from using water already appropriated by citizens of the El Paso Valley, both Mexicans and Americans; and a method provided in case they violate these restraining rules for a prompt and efficient legal remedy for the parties injured." With this recommended restriction, the commissioners provided a detailed synopsis for the con-struction of the international dam—which they estimated would cost exactly $2,317,113.36—and for a treaty with Mexico to govern apportion-ing the stored waters.[53]

The report of the International (Water) Boundary Commission prompted Secretary of State Olney to ask Secretary of the Interior David R. Francis not to approve any more applications for rights-of-way anywhere on the Rio Grande above El Paso. To protect the international dam further,

Olney asked Francis whether there was any legal way to cancel the Rio Grande Dam and Irrigation Company's right-of-way for the dam at Elephant Butte and whether such a revocation could be "exercised without injustice to the parties directly and indirectly interested in that enterprise."[54]

Secretary Olney's queries raised important and complex issues concerning the federal government's authority to regulate international and interstate rivers as well as about the government's ability to withdraw a right already officially granted. These questions, in turn, were compounded by the ongoing debate over whether western arid lands should be ceded to the states for private reclamation or whether the federal government should undertake irrigation projects. Reflecting Populist antipathy toward large private enterprises as well as the anti–big government sentiments of the late nineteenth century, the issues underlying the withdrawal of Rio Grande public domain lands from entry by private enterprises and possible federal reclamation at El Paso also anticipated the Progressive era's infatuation with government-directed, scientifically managed natural resource development. The growing U.S. entanglement in the struggles over the apportionment of the Rio Grande, therefore, strongly presupposed greater federal control over all western natural resources, especially water, than had previously existed.[55]

Although there was no immediate answer to whether the United States could revoke its grant to the Rio Grande Dam and Irrigation Company, on December 5, 1896, Secretary Francis suspended review of all future applications for rights-of-way for canals and reservoirs on public lands anywhere in the Rio Grande basin in New Mexico and Colorado—an action that later became known contemptuously (mainly by Coloradans) as the Rio Grande "embargo." Significantly, however, Francis concluded that while he could prevent future rights-of-way from being sanctioned, he legally was unable to rescind those already granted, including the approval of the Rio Grande Dam and Irrigation Company's dam site at Elephant Butte.[56]

As the U.S. Interior and State departments were acting on the recommendations of the International (Water) Boundary Commission, Mexican officials also considered the commission's findings. Based on the commission's final report, Romero suggested to Olney that the United States and Mexico draft a treaty to provide for the construction of the international dam at El Paso and to apportion the waters of the Rio Grande between the two countries. The terms of the proposed treaty, which Romero forwarded several days later, were essentially those outlined by the International

(Water) Boundary Commission's November 25, 1896, report. Romero added an ominous note, however, when he charged that American diversions had caused damages to the Juárez area over the previous ten years in the amount of $35,685,000—insinuating that the United States owed Mexico this sum as compensation.[57]

Although Olney favored the idea of the international dam and a Rio Grande treaty, he was forced to deal with the fact that the issue had been severely complicated by the Rio Grande Dam and Irrigation Company's right-of-way grant. In his reply to Romero, Olney acknowledged that the U.S. government would be willing to negotiate, but he cautioned that in preparing to enter into deliberations, State Department officials had found themselves "embarrassed by greatly perplexing complications arising out of reservoirs, dams, etc., either already built or authorized through the concurrent action of the Federal and State authorities." Olney added that "just what legal validity is to be imputed to such grants of authority, or in what way structures completed or begun are to be dealt with, are questions under careful investigation and which must be disposed of before the United States will be in a condition to negotiate."[58]

With the recommendations of the International (Water) Boundary Commission clouded by the Rio Grande Dam and Irrigation Company's right-of-way and the inability of the Department of the Interior to revoke that grant, Olney searched for a way to stop the construction of the dam at Elephant Butte. Turning to Anson Mills, Olney inquired whether the Rio Grande could be considered navigable above El Paso. Olney defined a stream to be navigable if it could be used for commercial purposes—including even floating logs on a regular basis. His clear intent was to assert federal authority over the Rio Grande under the commerce clause of the U.S. Constitution and under the terms of laws enacted in 1890 and 1892 that required War Department approval for any structures that might interfere with a river's navigability.[59] If the Rio Grande Dam and Irrigation Company had not obtained the War Department's authorization under these laws, Olney reasoned, then the statutes could be cited to block the construction of the Elephant Butte structure. Olney also thought that the navigability argument could be used if the dam would affect existing U.S. treaty obligations to keep the lower Rio Grande open to commerce.[60] Mills, who approved of this strategy, replied in early 1897 that when the Treaty of Guadalupe Hidalgo had been concluded in 1848, the stream had been navigable below El Paso. He further reported that "this navigability of the river has been largely depleted, almost wholly destroyed, by the cutting off of the waters of the Rio Grande and its tributaries in Colorado and New Mexico."[61]

Mills may have declared the Rio Grande to be no longer navigable immediately below El Paso, but in his response to Secretary Olney, he did not rule out the possibility that the river previously might have been navigable even above that city. Therefore, with the navigability argument a possible means to eliminate the Rio Grande Dam and Irrigation Company's right-of-way, Olney then asked Secretary of War Daniel S. Lamont whether the firm had obtained the assent of the War Department to obstruct a navigable river. Olney also queried whether the Rio Grande could be considered navigable within the meaning of the 1890 and 1892 river obstruction laws. If Lamont found the Rio Grande to be navigable, Olney concluded, then litigation could be commenced to block the company's plans.[62]

Lamont referred Olney's questions to the U.S. Army Corps of Engineers. This was a particularly advantageous government agency to consult from the point of view of international dam supporters because of Anson Mills's affiliation with the corps—a fact probably not lost on Olney. The corps was also an appropriate choice because of its predisposition against private dams on American rivers, a prejudice stemming from the corps' fear that corporate-owned structures might fall under the regulatory powers of other federal agencies, thereby diminishing the corps' authority and autonomy.[63] On the basis of an investigation, the army engineers reported that the Rio Grande was indeed navigable during periods of high water. At such times, according to the corps, the river was unquestionably navigable at, and even above, El Paso. The engineers also determined that the stream could certainly be used in commerce[64]—a key to the landmark legal definition of navigability according to the U.S. Supreme Court's 1870 decision in *Steamer Daniel Ball v. United States*—even if that commerce was only floating logs or flatboats.[65] In conclusion, the engineers added that a dam at Elephant Butte would interfere with navigation not only at El Paso but also well below the city.[66]

After a delay for nearly two months caused by a change in presidential administrations, the new secretary of war, Russell A. Alger, asked the Department of Justice on May 4, 1897, to take legal action against the Rio Grande Dam and Irrigation Company. Three days later, Acting Attorney General Holmes Conrad notified the U.S. district attorney in New Mexico to file suit against the firm, alleging that its officials had not cleared the company's plans with the secretary of war.[67]

With this action, the U.S. government had committed itself to blocking a previously granted right by attempting to prove that a nearly bone-dry river was commercially navigable. This effort was of dubious ethical and legal merit, since it ignored the fact that the international dam at El Paso likewise would interfere with the Rio Grande's alleged navigability. But on a broader level, the federal suit against the Rio Grande Dam and Irrigation Company also challenged the widely held western belief that arid states and territories controlled the allocation of waters within their borders. This issue virtually begged Congress to become more involved in interstate and international river apportionment, particularly on the Rio Grande.

CHAPTER 3

The United States versus the Rio Grande Dam and Irrigation Company

Legal historian Morton J. Horwitz wrote that by the end of the nineteenth century, law, as expressed in court-related activities, no longer reflected the paternalistic moral sense of the community that it had been in the eighteenth century. Rather, litigation had evolved into proceedings that reflected individuals' desires for economic and political power.[1] Such was certainly the situation underlying the U.S. government's lawsuit against the Rio Grande Dam and Irrigation Company. The official motive behind the suit was to expedite a solution to the international problem with Mexico. New Mexicans, however, perceived the real goal to be the limitation of water resource development within their territory to enhance the value of lands around El Paso and Juárez held by prominent Texans such as Anson Mills and his colleagues. In filing the suit against the Rio Grande Dam and Irrigation Company, federal officials argued that they were only protecting existing water rights in Texas and Mexico, but New Mexicans thought otherwise and rallied to support the company against the overwhelming powers and almost limitless funds of the U.S. government. Clearly, the Rio Grande Dam and Irrigation Company faced a formidable opponent, yet despite the seemingly mismatched might of the litigants, no easy settlement was forthcoming.

Because of the international and interstate aspects of the case, the Rio Grande Dam and Irrigation Company's battle to use its right-of-way at Elephant Butte took on major significance to all involved. To foreigners with an interest in Rio Grande matters—especially British investors in the Rio Grande Irrigation and Land Company and Mexican water users near Juárez—the lawsuit raised questions about the U.S. government's integrity and reliability. English backers of the Rio Grande Irrigation and Land Company wanted the litigation ended, but they were uncertain about the extent to which they should ask their government to intervene with U.S. authorities. To Mexicans, in contrast, the lawsuit represented the fulfillment of U.S. obligations to protect their rights to sufficient water from the Rio Grande.

Foreign interests aside, to the U.S. government, the Rio Grande litigation became one of the earliest tests of U.S. authority over western rivers—federal challenges to claims of state supremacy in water-related matters that escalated through such later U.S. Supreme Court cases as *Kansas v. Colorado* (1907), *Winters v. United States* (1908), *Wyoming v. Colorado* (1922), *United States v. Appalachian Electric Power Company* (the so-called *New River* case, 1940), *Nebraska v. Wyoming* (1945), and *Arizona v. California* (1963).[2] Also, federal officials saw the Rio Grande suit as a determination of the United States' ability to manage scarce natural resources and foreign affairs without interference by private, state, or territorial interests.

To residents of New Mexico, the case reinforced their belief that New Mexico's territorial status relegated them to being second-class citizens whose needs were subjugated to those of an economic and political elite around El Paso—a ruling class that included Anson Mills and was well connected to society and federal authority in Washington, D.C.[3] Of course, the Rio Grande Dam and Irrigation Company (as its plans and sponsorship by British financial powers had made clear) was hardly an ordinary small irrigator like most Mesilla Valley farmers, but New Mexicans overlooked this discrepancy. To them, the firm represented New Mexico's water, and for that reason, the lawsuit provided a major impetus behind a statehood drive to fortify New Mexico's political strength.

Finally, to El Pasoans, the suit against the Rio Grande Dam and Irrigation Company demonstrated the need for upstream irrigators to acknowledge the prior rights of downstream appropriators, even if those rights were in another state (or in this case, territory) or country. Such recognition was necessary to El Pasoans to protect the sanctity of water rights as property even if the law did not yet formally accept the validity of such claims crossing political boundaries.

With so many points of view involved, it is not surprising that the courts took twelve years to decide the case—including three appeals to the U.S. Supreme Court, one of which established the lawsuit as a landmark in American water law. Even after the legal fight had ended in the United States with a final Supreme Court decision against the Rio Grande Dam and Irrigation Company, international arbitration over the loss of the firm's assets continued for another decade.[4] Clearly, *United States v. Rio Grande Dam and Irrigation Company* was a prime example of, as Horwitz would have concluded, "the inevitable political and redistributive functions of law."[5]

Secretary of War Russell A. Alger's request that the Department of Justice take action against the Rio Grande Dam and Irrigation Company triggered the first salvo in the long battle. Late in May 1897, U. S. Attorney William B. Childers filed a complaint in New Mexico's Third Judicial District Court to restrain the firm from building its dam at Elephant Butte, and the court immediately issued a temporary injunction preventing any more work on the river until the case could be heard fully. Because of the American company's relationship with the English Rio Grande Irrigation and Land Company, Childers subsequently filed an amended bill of complaint naming the British parent firm as an additional defendant.[6]

The complaint was the one of the first attempts by the U.S. government to wrest control of a major western river from private developers by arguing that irrigation works would interfere with a particular stream's potential navigability. But it was not the only such action. This tactic also was used a few years later to block Charles R. Rockwood's ambitious plans for a private reclamation system along the lower Colorado River—a venture that interfered with the United States' proposals for developing that western stream. In Rockwood's case, the United States opposed Rockwood's diversions from the Colorado River in 1904 even though he previously had filed for those water claims with California officials at about the same time as the earliest phases of the Rio Grande litigation were taking place. With the Rio Grande case still in court as late as 1904 with no final decision on the merits of the navigability argument, the United States could hardly allow Rockwood's work to go forward on the Colorado—a river that no one disputed was navigable in its lower reaches—while simultaneously maintaining that the Rio Grande was navigable.[7]

In the Rio Grande case's 1897 complaint, the U.S. government charged that that river was navigable from the Gulf of Mexico to about 350 miles below El Paso—where rapids blocked the way—and then farther upriver from El Paso to La Joya, New Mexico (slightly downstream from Elephant Butte). The United States also contended that the upper reach of the Rio Grande had been used for floating logs, rafts, and poles, while steamboats had plied the lower portion of the river. These activities, the U.S. argued, made the Rio Grande an artery for commerce and thus subject to federal regulation under the U.S. Constitution. The government also alleged that the proposed dam at Elephant Butte and related diversion works would "so deplete and prevent the flow of water through the channel of said river below said dam, when so constructed," that the Rio Grande Dam and Irrigation Company's plans would "seriously obstruct the navigable capacity of the said river throughout its entire course from said point at Elephant Butte to its mouth." The complaint further denied that federal officials had granted any authority to the company to build the reservoir at Elephant Butte—despite the Department of the Interior's grant of a right-of-way to the firm for the dam. Moreover, the government's lawyers argued that treaty obligations prohibited any interference with navigation on the river.[8]

Among those handling the defense for both the British and American companies was Albert B. Fall. Destined to play a lengthy role in the history of Rio Grande water allocation, Fall had been born in Frankfort, Kentucky, in 1861. He moved west in 1881 seeking relief from respiratory ailments, and after living in Texas for several years, he relocated to New Mexico in 1887. There, after reading law in his spare time, Fall began a legal practice (although he maintained an office in El Paso). As a lawyer, Fall represented many irrigation and mining companies, and his prominence and backing for New Mexico's statehood propelled him into a series of ever-higher political and judicial offices. These positions eventually culminated in his becoming one of New Mexico's first U.S. senators after that state's admission to the Union in 1912. Later, Fall served as a secretary of the interior—in which capacity he played a significant role in Rio Grande affairs—until he resigned that position in 1923, shortly before the Teapot Dome oil field scandal clouded his reputation.[9]

In response to the U.S. government's complaint, Fall and two other attorneys for the Rio Grande Dam and Irrigation Company stated that the site of the proposed reservoir at Elephant Butte was wholly within the territory of New Mexico and therefore did not come under the terms of U.S. treaties with Mexico. In addition, the lawyers affirmed that the Rio Grande Dam and Irrigation Company had complied with acts of Congress when its officers had filed for the right-of-way for the reservoir at Elephant Butte under the 1891 General Revision Act.[10] This was a point that the *Rio Grande Republican* (published in Las Cruces) reiterated as demonstrating the futility of the complaint, and a position that the *El Paso Tribune* apparently supported when it editorialized that there was sufficient water for both the Elephant Butte structure and the international dam.[11] The lawyers for the Rio Grande Dam and Irrigation Company also contended that the firm had met the requirements of all laws of the Territory of New Mexico regarding the construction of irrigation works. Adding that the Rio Grande Dam and Irrigation Company fully intended to respect the prior rights of water users below Elephant Butte, the attorneys denied that the Rio Grande had ever been navigable above Roma, Texas (hundreds of miles downstream, near the Gulf of Mexico), and they asserted that the firm's plans would not affect navigability at any point below the proposed dam.[12]

Westerners ridiculed the absurdity of the government's claim that the Rio Grande was navigable upstream from El Paso. As the *Los Angeles Times* explained on July 12, 1897, the navigability argument "is regarded by New Mexicans knowing that stream as farcical in the extreme." The newspaper then quoted one New Mexico resident, John M. Ginn, who had been asked to provide affidavit testimony in the case. The Rio Grande, Ginn had stated, "is a dangerous, treacherous sandbar, quicksand stream" that never had been capable of navigation. The paper added that according to Ginn's statement, steamboats could only ascend the river above El Paso "by the aid of wings."[13]

The district court did not take long to reach its decision. On July 31, 1897, the court declared that based on a review of "affidavits, extracts from geological reports, agricultural reports, reports of engineers and of the Secretary of War, histories, and other sources of information," the Rio Grande was not navigable in New Mexico. The court then dismissed the suit, and U.S. Attorney Childers immediately appealed to the New Mexico Territorial Supreme Court—an action no doubt partly prompted by the fact that the Mexican members of the International (Water) Boundary Commission were then in Mexico City reporting favorably on efforts by the United States to secure the construction of the international dam at El Paso.[14]

Despite the appeal to the territorial supreme court, some New Mexicans were heartened by the lower court's decision and hoped for a quick resolution to the case. The *Rio Grande Republican*, for example, enthused, "We feel that it is safe to say the case will soon be disposed of and the question once [and] for all will finally be settled by the supreme court of the United States, whether the Rio Grande is or is not navigable. Prompt action is all that we ask. We learn further, from good authority, that as soon as this question is settled that the English stockholders are ready to put the money up to complete the work. It is said that eleven millionaires who have not heretofore taken stock, are now ready to subscribe, among them being the manager of the bank of England."[15] Other western papers reported favorably that U.S. Attorney Childers was going to abandon the argument that the Rio Grande was navigable at or above El Paso and instead merely assert that the river's flows contributed to navigability much farther downstream, near Laredo, Texas.[16]

Yet while some westerners remained optimistic that the case would end soon, the suit and its appeal to the higher court triggered outrage in New Mexico's Mesilla Valley because of the benefits the Rio Grande Dam and Irrigation Company's project promised to bring to the area. Nathan Boyd, the firm's president (who rarely understated his point of view), later observed that "landowners of the valley, to a man, favored the company's undertaking, as lands now practically valueless, or, where irrigated from community ditches, worth but little more than a few dollars per acre, rapidly appreciated in selling value so soon as the company began work upon its canal system, large blocks being contracted for by subsidiary companies and sold to settlers at $100 an acre."[17] In addition, the hypocrisy of the government's position in the suit was not lost on New Mexico's water users. As one infuriated Mesilla Valley farmer pointed out in his angry letter of protest to President William McKinley, if the main argument against the Rio Grande Dam and Irrigation Company was that its proposed reservoir at Elephant Butte would impede navigation, so too would the international dam at El Paso, as would existing diversion dams all along the river.[18]

European investors in the English Rio Grande Irrigation and Land Company were equally dismayed with the litigation. With thousands of applications to purchase New Mexico lands flooding the firm's London office (according to Nathan Boyd), William J. Engledue, president of the British corporation, desperately sought some means to accommodate Mexico's Rio Grande water claims so that the Elephant Butte project could go forward. Proposing to the U.S. State Department that the federal government subsidize part of the Elephant Butte venture's costs, Engledue suggested that in exchange, the Rio Grande Dam and Irrigation Company would deliver water to Mexico at six shillings per acre as an annual water service charge—the same rate to be levied on American irrigators.[19] Nothing came of Engledue's idea. Prompted by the increasing federal desire to regulate all western natural resources that typified emerging Progressive-era ideology and by the undefined state of western water law, the U.S. government had little to gain and much to lose if a territorial government and a private corporation could prevail in this important battle over a major western river.

Like the district court, the New Mexico Territorial Supreme Court rapidly arrived at a decision, rendering its opinion in favor of the American and English companies on January 5, 1898. In reaching its conclusion, the territory of New Mexico's highest court first considered the question of U.S. treaty obligations to Mexico and found that both countries had merely agreed not to construct any works below El Paso that would interfere with the common use of the Rio Grande. The United States had no other responsibility to Mexico, the court ruled, and it observed that "no obligation devolved upon the United States to conserve the waters of the river above that point [El Paso] for the purpose of facilitating navigation below it."[20]

Having dismissed treaty duties, the New Mexico Territorial Supreme Court next addressed the question of navigability. In the court's opinion, this issue turned on the applicability of the congressional acts of 1890 and 1892 regarding navigable waterways. Taking note of the lower court's finding that the Rio Grande had been used just twice to convey merchandise in New Mexico, and that on those occasions entrepreneurs had only floated a raft and telegraph poles, the Territorial Supreme Court stressed its dissatisfaction with the navigability argument. "It is perfectly clear," the court opined, "that the Rio Grande above El Paso has never been used as a navigable stream for commercial intercourse in any manner whatever, and that it is not now capable of being so used. . . . Dams have been created and maintained at El Paso for nearly 200 years, by which the river has been obstructed, and its waters diverted for irrigation to both sides of the Rio Grande. But never until the present time, so far as we can ascertain, has any question been raised by anyone as to interference with any use of the river for purposes of navigation."[21]

Not only was the Territorial Supreme Court unconvinced that the Rio Grande was navigable in New Mexico, but the justices also saw through the legal jargon to the real reason for the lawsuit. "It seems clearly apparent that the [international dam] work at El Paso to which the United States has committed itself, tentatively at least," the court wrote, "is not designed to preserve or improve the navigable capacity of the river, but to facilitate the distribution of the waters which may be gathered by obstructing the stream for the benefit of riparian occupants, and that the object of this proceeding is not to serve a public benefit from the navigation of the Rio Grande, but rather, under the guise of a question of navigability of the stream, to obtain an adjudication of the interests of rival irrigation schemes, in aid of one locality against another." The court then lashed out at the government's contention that federal authorities should be the arbiters of western water disputes on non-navigable rivers. "Manifestly, neither the acts of Congress cited nor the provisions of the treaty [of Guadalupe Hidalgo] have any application to questions of this kind, and they cannot be invoked to settle conflicting local interests, whose determination must necessarily depend upon entirely different considerations."[22]

Having disposed of the issue of the Rio Grande's navigability within New Mexico, the Territorial Supreme Court then focused its attention on the stream below El Paso, yet the justices did not directly answer whether the lower river was navigable. Instead, they determined that Congress had intended that in a conflict between water uses for navigation or reclamation on a western river such as the Rio Grande, irrigation should prevail. Based on all of these considerations, the New Mexico Territorial Supreme Court thus upheld the lower court's ruling.[23]

Understandably, the New Mexico press was elated by the decision, and the El Paso newspapers were equally disappointed. Commenting on January 14, 1898, the *Rio Grande Republican* agreed with the New Mexico Territorial Supreme Court's assessment that the litigation was a pretext, as the court had written, "to obtain an adjudication of the interests of rival irrigation schemes, in aid of one locality against another." Observing that the *El Paso Times* was still backing "General Mills and Max Weber [the German consul at Juárez and a prominent businessman in the area] in their efforts to stop the building of the Elephant Butte dam and reservoir," the *Republican* declared, "These gentlemen are fighting this enterprise because they believe that if this dam should be built, that it would supply that valley below El Paso on both sides of the river and that the International dam would be delayed for at least some years, and that, then, they would not be able to have a 'finger in the pie' in the distribution of Uncle Sam's dollars and the early sale of their large tracts of land below El Paso."[24]

Demonstrating that the Rio Grande case also was prompting strong opinions elsewhere in the West, the *Denver Republican* printed a lengthy editorial supporting the New Mexico Territorial Supreme Court's decision. Yet the paper also expressed concern about what the navigability line of reasoning implied for non-navigable streams that supplied flows to downstream navigable waterways. Repeating the key points of the Territorial Supreme Court's ruling, the Denver newspaper noted that because New Mexico was not yet a state, the territory thus was subject to greater federal control over its rivers and waterways. Nevertheless, the *Republican* worried that the navigability claim, insofar as it applied to the Texas reach of the Rio Grande, someday might be used to support federal authority over the New Mexico part of the river no matter what its navigability status or New Mexico's statehood circumstances. Anticipating the U.S. Supreme Court's 1940 ruling in what became known as the New River case—a decision that greatly distressed western water interests because it extended federal authority to even non-navigable streams in certain circumstances—the *Republican* pointed out that "if congress has a right to interfere with irrigation enterprises because many miles farther down a river is navigable, then there is hardly any limit to its authority over irrigation. In that case it could put a stop to irrigation in Colorado, because certain streams which cross the state boundary are navigable farther down. . . . This consideration of itself should suffice to make the supreme court of the United States question the existence of such authority."[25] Nearly all westerners agreed with the Denver newspaper's perspective, and they continued to follow the Rio Grande case closely for that reason.

Ignoring the Territorial Supreme Court's chastising, the U.S. government appealed the New Mexico decision to the U.S. Supreme Court. Counsel for both sides argued *United States v. Rio Grande Dam and Irrigation Company* in the Supreme Court in early November 1898, and the high court issued its opinion six months later.[26] The Supreme Court pointed out that the original trial court—supported by the subsequent opinion of the New Mexico Territorial Supreme Court—had determined only that the Rio Grande was not navigable within New Mexico, but the U.S. Supreme Court noted that neither New Mexico court had addressed the issue of navigability below El Paso in any substantive detail. Central to this issue was the U.S. Supreme Court's observation that the trial court had taken "judicial notice that the Rio Grande was not navigable within the limits of New Mexico." The high court's ruling hinged on this phrase, especially on the use of "judicial notice"—a legal term that essentially meant that the lower court had ruled on the basis of common knowledge without the need for supporting evidence or testimony. It was reasonable, the U.S. Supreme Court commented, for courts to take judicial notice that some streams were navi-gable and others not, but the justices opined that it might not be a matter of common knowledge at what place between a stream's mouth and its source navigability ceased. Because the Supreme Court believed that a basis other than judicial notice was needed to determine where navigability ended on the Rio Grande, the justices remanded the case to the New Mexico Third Judicial District Court for additional testimony and evidence.[27]

The U.S. Supreme Court's ruling may have been a victory for the gov-ernment, but the Rio Grande Dam and Irrigation Company viewed it as only a temporary setback. The firm's secretary, W. T. Johns, was certain that the company would ultimately win the case. Assuring treasurer Henry D. Bowman in late May 1899 that the final outcome would support the Rio Grande Dam and Irrigation Company's position, Johns shrugged off the lower court's forthcoming second review, and he explained that "all our lawyers agree that the decision is very favorable to us and there is nothing to prevent our going on with the big dam at once."[28]

Unlike the professed lack of concern on the part of Rio Grande Dam and Irrigation Company officials, other westerners had stronger views of the Supreme Court's opinion. Residents of El Paso and Juárez hailed the ruling. Max Weber, the German consul in El Paso, declared that the Supreme Court's decision was an affirmation that "no private corporation or individual can obstruct the flow of the water" and that the decision would "now pave the way for the signing of a treaty between Mexico and the United States and that congress and the senate will now be able to legislate on this vital point for the relief of the arid west."[29] In contrast, Coloradans were deeply worried. One Denver editorial writer lamented, "The principle involved in this case is one of vital interest to Colorado. If the federal government, on the sham plea that navigation is being interfered with by the construction of a dam and the use of water for irrigation three or four hundred miles away, can put a stop to said use of water, it can shut down every ditch in the San Luis valley. It is danger-ous to allow such a principle to receive the affirmation of the supreme court of the United States."[30] The *Fort Collins Weekly Courier* concurred, pointing to another Colorado stream that might be adversely impacted by the outcome of the Rio Grande case. The litigation might "have a serious effect on the value of water rights in both the Rio Grande and Arkansas valleys of this state," the *Courier* warned, "for if diversion of water at Elephant Butte is illegal it must also be illegal at other points higher up on the river. The same rule will also apply to the Arkansas River."[31]

Regardless of the conflicting views (or perhaps partly because of them), the Rio Grande Dam and Irrigation Company did not begin work on the dam at Elephant Butte following the Supreme Court's ruling, since there was still some risk of a final adverse decision in the litigation. As it turned out, the decision not to proceed with construction was a critical mistake— one that came back to haunt the firm several years later.

In the meantime, the district court set a hearing for November 1, 1899, to determine the impact of the Rio Grande Dam and Irrigation Company's proposed Elephant Butte structure on the navigable portion of the river. As that date approached, however, government attorneys asked for a continuance until February 5, 1900. The official explanation was the need to gather more evidence, but additional reasons included buying time to attempt a negotiated settlement and to send an emissary to Mexico City to discuss tactics in the lawsuit.[32] The district court was unwilling to wait until February, however, and it granted a delay only until December 12, 1899—another factor that proved crucial later in the case.[33]

When the trial resumed, extensive evidence was presented,[34] and based on this documentation, Judge W. F. Parker of the Third Judicial District Court ultimately found that the Rio Grande was navigable between its mouth at the Gulf of Mexico and Rio Grande City, Texas (downstream from El Paso). Yet noting that there was "no direct testimony in this case showing that any given quantity of water in the Rio Grande passing El Paso reaches Rio Grande City, the head of navigation, and there accomplishes any certain effect upon the navigability of the stream," Judge Parker concluded that "the intended acts of the defendants in the construction of a dam or dams, or reservoir, and in appropriating the waters of the Rio Grande, will not substantially diminish the navigability of that stream within the limits of present navigability."[35] Judge Parker's decision generally pleased upstream Rio Grande interests and their supporters, but they nonetheless were wary of a foe that seemed willing to fight on at all costs. "The unjust prejudice of the government at Washington against the west," Colorado's *Aspen Tribune* declared (in an editorial reprinted from *Field and Farm*), "was never so openly avowed as when it . . . sent a man here to fight the question of Colorado's rights to the use of the waters created in the state as was developed in the recent Elephant Butte case." The *Tribune* urged its readers to remain vigilant and warned, "It is well for us to be on our guard as there is a strong movement on foot in the east to rob us of our birthright and take from us that which God has given as one of his greatest blessings. The enemy has a black eye just now, but this does not end the contest."[36]

Notwithstanding the "black eye," the day after the district court had issued its second ruling, U.S. Attorney Childers asked the court to set aside the findings of fact and grant a rehearing. Childers maintained that "new evidence" had been excluded from consideration by the court's refusal to grant his previous request to continue the trial to February 5, 1900, and the court's insistence on starting the second hearing on December 12, 1899. Rejecting the motion, the district court dismissed the bill of complaint against the Rio Grande Dam and Irrigation Company, and the U.S. government then filed an appeal to the New Mexico Territorial Supreme Court, alleging that not all the facts had been considered by the lower court, because of its denial of Childers's earlier continuance motion.[37]

Strongly suggesting that Childers's request to reopen the case in the lower court had been a legal maneuver to substantiate the appeal, Attorney General John W. Griggs told Secretary of State John Hay that it was unfortunate—despite U.S. Attorney Childers's claims to the court about the existence of additional facts—that the United States had no formal measurements of the contributions made by the upper Rio Grande to the lower river to dispute the Rio Grande Dam and Irrigation Company's claims. To remedy this situation, Griggs noted that William Follett of the International (Water) Boundary Commission had been a very persuasive witness at the second hearing in the lower court, and he suggested that Hay direct the commission under Follett's supervision to study seepage and evaporation from the Rio Grande below El Paso. These examinations, Griggs believed, would provide the "new evidence" that the government professed it had not been able to introduce in the lower court. Moreover, Follett's position as Anson Mills's subordinate would probably guarantee a favorable interpretation of any ambiguous information. Griggs expected a second adverse ruling from the New Mexico Territorial Supreme Court, which would be appealed to the U.S. Supreme Court, and he told Hay that Follett's study should be done "in the belief that the [U.S.] Supreme Court will send the case back for another trial." Six days later, Hay wrote to none other than Anson Mills to have him place Follett in charge of the task.[38]

Mills, whose opposition to the Rio Grande Dam and Irrigation Company's plans was well known by this time, thought that because the suit against the firm was partly to satisfy Juárez's water needs, Mexican officials should also play a role in measuring the river. Accordingly, he asked the Mexican representative to the International (Water) Boundary Commission, Jacobo Blanco, to join the survey. After consulting with his government, Blanco agreed—in effect bringing the resources of the combined

U.S. and Mexican governments to bear against the Rio Grande Dam and Irrigation Company in the pending litigation. In addition, Mexico's involvement made it abundantly apparent that one of the central goals of the lawsuit was for the U.S. government to take control of western rivers—in this case, through the federal authority to conduct international diplomacy. On February 13, 1900, the joint commission directed William Follett, as the U.S. consulting engineer, and his Mexican counterpart, E. Corrella, to proceed with the work of measuring the river.[39]

As the engineers' investigation of the Rio Grande went forward, the New Mexico Territorial Supreme Court heard the second appeal in *United States v. Rio Grande Dam and Irrigation Company,* which was based almost entirely on the claim that the U.S. government had not been given ample time to prepare its supposed "new evidence" and present related testimony.[40] The Territorial Supreme Court took a dim view of the second appeal. Affirming the lower court as to the findings of fact regarding the navigability of the Rio Grande, the New Mexico justices ruled "that the whole matter was thoroughly gone into, and we conclude that the facts as set forth in the findings of the learned judge below, are sustained by the evidence, and we adopt the same as the findings of the court."[41] As to the contention that the government had not been granted enough time to prepare its case properly, the court was less than charitable. In a stinging rebuke, the court lambasted the U.S. attorneys. "We think no sufficient diligence has been shown by the government in this case in regard to this evidence," the court charged. "From the time of the issuing of the mandate by the Supreme Court of the United States remanding this cause for this investigation, the government took no steps whatever to furnish this evidence."[42] As if to scold the government more, the Territorial Supreme Court observed that aside from the initial request to change the hearing date from November 1, 1899, to February 5, 1900, U.S. Attorney Childers had not subsequently asked for additional time to secure evidence. On these grounds, the Territorial Supreme Court once again upheld the district court and the position of the Rio Grande Dam and Irrigation Company.[43]

With the Territorial Supreme Court's castigation, Childers began to worry that the federal government eventually might not prevail, and he decided not to appeal to the U.S. Supreme Court again unless higher officials in the Department of Justice specifically instructed him to do so. Childers was not alone in his desire to let the litigation die. Officials at the Rio Grande Dam and Irrigation Company also wanted to avoid a new appeal by the government to the U.S. Supreme Court not only because they were ahead in the legal battle but also because of soaring attorneys' fees. In August 1900, Nathan Boyd tried to forestall an appeal by citing national politics to Attorney General Griggs. Boyd told Griggs that the Rio Grande Dam and Irrigation Company's problems stemmed not from water-related issues but instead from political concerns relating to the forthcoming U.S. presidential election, and Boyd suggested that the lawsuit was being manipulated by the federal government to gain support in Texas (at the time, a strongly Democratic state) for Republican President William McKinley's reelection campaign. Because Boyd thought that the presidential race might be close, he threatened to campaign for Democratic (and Populist) candidate William Jennings Bryan unless the government let the case rest with the decision of the New Mexico Territorial Supreme Court.[44]

Politics aside, Boyd may have had another motive—a direct personal monetary reason—for wanting to see the litigation end. Earlier that year, Boyd had been named receiver for the English Rio Grande Irrigation and Land Company.[45] Feeling the financial burden of the lengthy lawsuit, the firm's bondholders had decided to liquidate the company's holdings rather than wait for the outcome of further legal appeals by the American subsidiary. The British company's notice explained to its bondholders, "Owing to the prolonged and costly litigation in which the above company has been involved with the United States Government, the Capital of the Company has become exhausted. The litigation is still pending, the United States Government having appealed against the last Decision of the Courts. . . . For nearly a year the Company has been kept going by advances made by the principal Debenture Holders but in view of the further expense that will be entailed before the final decision of the United States Courts can be obtained, and the impossibility of raising Capital by placing either the Shares or the Debentures of the Company whilst the question of the Company's Titles remains in any degree the subject of litigation, the Directors found it necessary" to call for the appointment of a receiver of the company.[46]

The notice had been sent to all of the Rio Grande Irrigation and Land Company's bondholders. According to British government records, Boyd was by far the largest owner of the firm's securities, possessing or having a direct interest in outstanding bonds valued in 1900 at £37,450 (£2,136,897, or about $4 million as of the year 2008) of the total of £47,000 (£2,681,820, or a little more than $5 million in 2008).[47] Thus, Boyd may have cited the 1900 election to U.S. officials as a reason for dropping the case, but clearly an end to the lawsuit also would have brought him immense financial benefits.

Regardless of Boyd's reasons for wanting to preclude any appeal, Attorney General Griggs offered to compromise, in part because of the political considerations that the Rio Grande case raised.[48] With the importance of the Rio Grande litigation well understood by western voters and politicians alike, the government's new stance apparently was designed to prevent the humiliation of a second loss by federal officials in the U.S. Supreme Court prior to the national election. Yet even after McKinley had been safely returned to the White House following the 1900 election, the government still wanted to avoid the embarrassment of another adverse ruling by the high court and a possible new hearing in the lower court. This time, however, the Justice Department's reluctance to press the case stemmed from the findings of Follett and Corrella, none of which were of much use to the government's case. Follett and Corrella, who had issued their report on the lower Rio Grande barely two months after the election, had determined that only 16 percent of the total flow of the Rio Grande passing San Marcial, New Mexico (about forty miles above Elephant Butte), arrived at Roma, Texas—in their opinion, the head of navigation. This quantity, the engineers believed, was sufficient to raise the level of the lower river an average of a mere six inches. Thus, with considerable doubt as to whether a half foot of water would convince the courts that the upper river played a critical role in making the lower portion navigable, government officials continued to seek a compromise with the Rio Grande Dam and Irrigation Company rather than press on in court.[49]

To negotiate a settlement, Special Assistant Attorney General Marsden C. Burch held a series of meetings in El Paso with Rio Grande Dam and Irrigation Company officials, and he offered the firm a "proportionate share of the waters of the Rio Grande" if the company guaranteed not to "seriously interfere with navigation."[50] Ignoring the fact that the international dam at El Paso—which was to be constructed even with the dam at Elephant Butte in place—also would disrupt navigation and hold back flows to the lower river, Burch asked the Rio Grande Dam and Irrigation Company to recognize senior water rights on both sides of the El Paso Valley to guarantee that enough water would flow down the river each year to fill the international reservoir. Nathan Boyd—whose unwillingness to compromise on the recognition of the El Paso Valley's alleged senior water rights had grown in direct proportion to his bitterness over the unending litigation—refused the offer.[51] The U.S. government then modified its position, offering to accept the decision of the New Mexico courts as final if the Rio Grande Dam and Irrigation Company would recognize senior water rights for 40,000 acres on just the Mexican side of the El Paso Valley. Boyd still balked, viewing his stand as a matter of personal integrity.[52]

Boyd's adherence to principle was justifiable in his view because he believed that New Mexico should not be compelled to accept a status inferior to that of any state and because at that time there was no clear legal doctrine requiring the recognition of priorities across state or national boundaries. Yet his attitude seriously jeopardized the Rio Grande Dam and Irrigation Company's already difficult financial situation. With the litigation having been in the courts for four years, lawyers' fees were mounting at an alarming rate. As one of the American firm's officials had observed well before the compromise discussions began, the American and British companies might eventually win the court battle, but "it makes one sweat drops of blood to watch for the fiscal results."[53]

With Boyd's consistent rejection of all settlement proposals, government officials felt that there was no alternative but to go forward with the appeal to the U.S. Supreme Court. Claiming that they had not had enough time to obtain evidence, the government's lawyers contended in the U.S. Supreme Court hearing in November 1901 that a new trial should be ordered. The high court rendered its decision in early March 1902. Writing for the majority, Justice John Marshall Harlan observed that the Rio Grande Dam and Irrigation Company's proposed reservoir at Elephant Butte raised a question of "great importance" concerning navigation, "one that could not properly be made and concluded within the time ordinarily required for the preparation of an equity cause for final hearing."[54] The Supreme Court thought that the lower court should have postponed the final hearing from December 12, 1899, to February 5, 1900, as had been requested by U.S. Attorney Childers, to allow the government time to finish obtaining its evidence. Moreover, the Supreme Court held that the motion for a rehearing should have been granted for the same reason. Rejecting the New Mexico Territorial Supreme Court's opinion that "no sufficient diligence has been shown by the government in this case in regard to . . . [obtaining its] evidence," the U.S. Supreme Court concluded that since "the record does not show that the representatives of the Government were chargeable with a want of diligence in their preparation of the cause, we think that the decree should be reversed and the cause remanded, with liberty to both parties to take further evidence."[55]

The U.S. Supreme Court's decision was a major blow to the Rio Grande Dam and Irrigation Company's supporters, who realized that even if the government could not win the case on its merits, the firm could be ruined financially through endless litigation. This understanding prompted E. V. Berrien, who had replaced W. T. Johns as secretary for the company, to ask New Mexico Territory's governor, Miguel A. Otero, to intercede and help negotiate a settlement. Berrien suggested a plan. The Rio Grande Dam and Irrigation Company would step aside and allow the U.S. government to build the dam at Elephant Butte—not at El Paso—if the government would repay investments made by the British and American Rio Grande companies' sponsors. This idea seemed reasonable to Berrien, since Congress was then debating an expansion of the federal government's role in irrigation development in the West—discussions that three months later led to the passage of the Reclamation Act of 1902. Berrien thought that his offer would appeal to the U.S. government because a federal dam at Elephant Butte would cost considerably less than the proposed international dam at El Paso, and the plan would benefit the Rio Grande Dam and Irrigation Company because the government's savings could be used to reimburse the firm's investors. Furthermore, Berrien contended that Mexico could be persuaded to accept his solution if the United States would guarantee delivery of at least 30,000 acre-feet of water per year to the Juárez area.[56]

Despite the logic of Berrien's proposal, nothing came of it, because of Nathan Boyd's adamant opposition to any settlement requiring the acknowledgment of prior rights in the El Paso–Juárez area. To Boyd, the guaranteed supplies to Mexico appeared to be just such a recognition. Thus, for the time being, the Rio Grande Dam and Irrigation Company did not actively press the case in court, and negotiations came to a standstill. Over the next year, the American firm, facing an opponent whose resources would permit a victory through attrition if not through a court judgment, concerned itself with reorganizing its remaining assets as the International Mining, Land, and Cattle Company—a corporate name that strongly intimated that the old organization was out of the irrigation business for good.[57]

The government likewise did nothing about the case because the enactment of the Reclamation Act on June 17, 1902—three months after the Supreme Court's second decision—allowed the newly created U.S. Reclamation Service to start a review of the relative merits of the Elephant Butte and international dam sites. Eventually, however, almost a year after *United States v. Rio Grande Dam and Irrigation Company* had been remanded to the Third Judicial District Court, the government reopened the case by bringing a supplemental complaint against the company.

The new charge was filed on April 7, 1903. Seizing on a technicality, the revised complaint pointed out that the 1891 General Revision Act, which allowed rights-of-way for canals and reservoirs on public lands and under which the Rio Grande Dam and Irrigation Company originally had secured its dam location, provided that grants would be forfeited if they were not used within five years. Because the initial injunction against the Rio Grande Dam and Irrigation Company had been lifted by New Mexico's Third Judicial District Court on July 31, 1897, and was never reinstated, the government's new complaint contended that the firm had lost its right to build Elephant Butte Dam because well over five years had elapsed since that date.[58] Reluctantly ruling in favor of the government, the Third Judicial District Court held that the company had indeed forfeited its authority to build the dam at Elephant Butte. The court then issued an injunction against any work at the site.[59]

Two more years passed before the Rio Grande Dam and Irrigation Company appealed, and during this interim, there was considerable uncertainty among the firm's American supporters about how best to proceed. Part of the delay undoubtedly centered on the pending interstate lawsuit over the Arkansas River in *Kansas v. Colorado*—a case that two midwestern newspapers characterized in nearly identical stories as "regarded by some as the most important suit of the kind ever instituted in this court."[60] Because of the significance of the Arkansas River case, many observers believed that it could have an impact on matters on the Rio Grande, particularly when, in March 1904, the U.S. government filed a petition to intervene in the Arkansas River case to assert control over all western rivers. Federal lawyers claimed that while the Arkansas River was not navigable in Colorado or Kansas, it was navigable in Indian Territory (which became Oklahoma in 1907) and in the state of Arkansas. The United States further observed in the Arkansas River case that the U.S. Constitution gave the federal government authority over all navigable rivers. Moreover, the U.S. government contended that it had a vital interest in *Kansas v. Colorado*, especially because of the government's position in the Rio Grande Dam and Irrigation Company litigation and the claim of navigability in that lawsuit. Federal lawyers went still further in the *Kansas* filing and stated that the United States had a vital role in that case because the United States owned over a million acres of public lands west of the ninety-eighth meridian that were uninhabitable without irrigation. Many of these lands were in Kansas and Colorado (much like the U.S.-owned large areas along the Rio Grande in Colorado and New Mexico). Public domain lands, the U.S. government suggested, could be settled under the terms of the 1902 Reclamation Act, which gave the United States a vital interest in the outcome of the *Kansas v. Colorado* litigation (facts that also applied to the Rio Grande). In the Arkansas River lawsuit, the federal lawyers believed that neither Kansas nor Colorado should prevail in its claims to the interstate stream because "either contention, if sustained, would defeat the object, intent, and purpose of the reclamation act, prevent the settlement and sale of arid lands belonging to the United States, and especially those within the watershed of the Arkansas River west of the ninety-eighth degree west longitude, and would otherwise work great damage to the interests of the United States."[61]

With the Arkansas River litigation still before the U.S. Supreme Court following the adverse ruling in the Rio Grande case by New Mexico's Third Judicial District Court, the ultimate outcome of the *Kansas v. Colorado* case clearly would have major implications for the Rio Grande lawsuit. This was probably a factor in the decision by Rio Grande Dam and Irrigation Company officials not to appeal the district court's decision immediately to the New Mexico Territorial Supreme Court.

Also prompting a delay in the Rio Grande case, however, was the fact that backers of the English Rio Grande Irrigation and Land Company had turned to their government's authorities for help. With substantial investments by many prominent British citizens in the parent Rio Grande Irrigation and Land Company, British officials understandably were concerned by the Rio Grande case, but they too appeared uncertain about how to proceed. In late 1904, for example, bondholders in the British firm asked England's Foreign Office to seek a settlement to the Rio Grande dispute in international arbitration. As a result, the British ambassador to the United States, Sir H. M. Durand, had asked the U.S. government to agree to such proceedings.[62] Nevertheless, four months later, Durand wrote to the British Foreign Office in response to a query as to what additional aid he might provide in America, saying that "any action by him [Durand] would rather harm the co. than otherwise." Durand suggested "vigorous legal action by the co."[63] During the balance of 1905, according to Foreign Office records, further communications among Durand, English foreign secretary Lord Lansdowne, and U.S. secretary of state Elihu Root attempted to find some resolution to the Rio Grande situation, yet little came of this correspondence.[64]

The cause for the holdup in the Rio Grande case was not merely due to the British and American Rio Grande companies' depleted finances and the parallel litigation on the Arkansas River; the delay also centered on Boyd's fervent opposition to new government attempts to arrive at a compromise. While publicly Boyd had softened and expressed a willingness to be a part of settlement so long as an accord did not include subordinating New Mexico's water rights to those of downstream users—a position he argued was in the best interest of the territory (and, of course, his company)—in private, he was strongly opposed to any agreement with the El Paso area.[65]

Boyd's conflicting positions stemmed from what had become a near-pathological desire to link Anson Mills—to whom Boyd traced most of his company's troubles—to criminal misconduct. Believing that if Mills's supposed misdeeds could be exposed, Boyd was certain that they would discredit the entire El Paso international dam proposal and vindicate his own Rio Grande Dam and Irrigation Company plans for Elephant Butte. Between 1903, when the lower court reinstated its injunction against any further work at Elephant Butte, and 1906, when the New Mexico Territorial Supreme Court upheld that decision—a ruling that several Colorado newspapers declared was "of much importance" to more than one state because it meant "that no more irrigation works can be built" on an interstate stream "by private enterprise unless it can be shown that they will have no influence upon the capacity of the stream below"[66]—Boyd carried on a bitter personal campaign against Mills through an endless stream of published diatribes and constant letters to federal officials. (In fact, Anson Mills later recalled, some of this correspondence was so alarming that the Secret Service declared Boyd to be a "dangerous man" and barred him from further personal conferences with State Department officials.) Even after the New Mexico Territorial Supreme Court's decision, Boyd continued to write to a large array of top government administrators demanding "justice" and the prosecution of Anson Mills and his alleged cohorts. In addition to declaring that Mills had abused the power of his position on the International (Water) Boundary Commission by promoting the international dam at El Paso (which was probably true), Boyd insisted that Mills also had perjured himself by affirming under oath that the Rio Grande was navigable above and below El Paso (which, according to the U.S. Supreme Court, was open to question). Boyd's obsession with punishing Mills for the Rio Grande Dam and Irrigation Company's problems eventually grew to encompass other federal officials, and Boyd charged that those who had refused to prosecute Mills over the years were obviously part of Mills's plot. To Boyd, therefore, people such as Attorneys General John W. Griggs, Philander C. Knox, and William H. Moody (all of whom had played roles in the case against Boyd's company) were either criminally liable or, at the very least, morally reprehensible.[67]

Because the U.S. Reclamation Service had continued to examine the merits of the Elephant Butte and international dam sites as the years had passed, some Reclamation Service officials also shared Mills's culpability in Boyd's eyes. This further stalled a final appeal by the Rio Grande Dam and Irrigation Company to the U.S. Supreme Court. As the government studies had gone forward, that Reclamation Service's assistant chief engineer, Arthur P. Davis (who had suggested that the government might step in and build the dam at Elephant Butte), quickly came to achieve the same despicable status in Boyd's mind as the vilified Anson Mills. In one particularly vitriolic letter written in response to Davis's negative analysis of the company's plans—typical of many that Boyd wrote concerning Davis and Mills—Boyd claimed that Davis was "mentally and morally depraved" and that he showed "a cynical contempt for the canons of public and official decency." Moreover, Boyd charged that in reviewing Davis's critique "one is almost driven to account for its extraordinary irrelevancy by concluding that it was written by a congenital idiot, borrowed for such purpose from the nearest asylum for the insane."[68]

Boyd's desire to send Mills and his supposed co-conspirators to prison overshadowed taking the Rio Grande Dam and Irrigation Company's case to the U.S. Supreme Court for a third time. While Boyd took no immediate action to appeal the 1906 New Mexico Territorial Supreme Court decision, the government also did not press the case and went forward with its own plans for a federal dam on the Rio Grande. Ironically, this structure was to be built at Elephant Butte, not at El Paso—the very plan suggested by the Rio Grande Dam and Irrigation Company's secretary, E. V. Berrien, several years earlier. In fact, U.S. officials became so certain of ultimately prevailing that they declined a 1907 offer by the British embassy to arbitrate a settlement.[69] The government's lack of concern about an appeal also reflected federal officials' Progressive-era convictions that their plans for the Rio Grande were in the best interests of the basin because the plans were based on objective engineering expertise, whereas the ambitions of Boyd's firm— according to U.S. authorities—were founded on a greedy desire to monopolize land and water. This paternalistic attitude encouraged government officials to ignore the patent injustice of blocking the Rio Grande Dam and Irrigation Company's efforts on the technicality that the firm had not exercised its right-of-way grant within the required five years. If "Dr. Boyd's company had been bona fide capitalists, instead of wildcat promoters," declared Reclamation Service engineer Benjamin Hall self-righteously, "they could have legally done six years actual work without molestation [after the temporary injunction had been lifted]."[70] Hall conveniently ignored the fact that during that period the litigation was still before the courts, and the "wildcat promoters" would have been foolish to have invested large sums of money building a dam that they might ultimately have had to tear down or abandon.

Eventually, Nathan Boyd grasped the futility of his campaign to see Anson Mills in jail, and he took the Rio Grande Dam and Irrigation Company's case to the U.S. Supreme Court for the last time. The justices heard arguments on December 3, 1909, and handed down their ruling ten days later, upholding the decisions of the Third Judicial District Court and the New Mexico Territorial Supreme Court revoking the company's right-of-way at Elephant Butte. The U.S. Supreme Court said nothing about whether a just resolution had been reached by the lower courts, preferring to rely on the purely legal point that the firm had forfeited its rights by not acting within the five years allowed by law.[71]

Despite the Supreme Court decision, Boyd continued to battle for compensation for his own and his companies' losses, although he preferred not to recognize the legal reality of the five-year work-allowance time frame on which the final decision by the high court had rested. For example, in a 1911 filing with English government authorities seeking reimbursement for funds that he had expended in defending the two firms in court, Boyd wrote,

> The [Rio Grande Irrigation and Land] Company has been ruined by the suit to enjoin the completing of its works on the Rio Grande. Failing, after seven years of such litigation, to prove that the said works would obstruct the navigation of a non-navigable stream, the United States government, as a last resort, supplemented its bill of complaint and prayed the courts to declare the company's charter rights and right of way forfeited because the company's Elephant Butte dam, so-called, had not been completed within the five years prescribed by the Act under which the company's right to impound the flood waters of the Rio Grande had

been acquired. The courts have so declared forfeited the company's said rights, thereby penalizing the company for not doing the very thing it was enjoined, pending the said litigation, not to do.[72]

Even as late as the 1920s, Boyd was still seeking reimbursement through international arbitration, a claim that he ultimately lost on November 28, 1923. Time had not mellowed Boyd's quest to impugn Anson Mills's reputation, however. The international tribunal that heard Boyd's petition for compensation for the British Rio Grande Irrigation and Land Company's investors observed that the case was "unusual" because of the "attacks made on high officials of the Government of the United States in papers accompanying the British Memorial." These included assertions that parties such as Mills had "with impunity commit[ted] perjury and prostitute[d] their official positions in the interests of graft," and as a result "of the aforesaid dishonest practices of the high officials[,] the people of New Mexico . . . have directly and indirectly been robbed of many millions of dollars."[73]

An embittered Nathan Boyd died in March 1926—ten years after the U.S. government completed construction of Elephant Butte Dam very near the location where his company would have built its dam. With Boyd's death went all hope that the backers of the Rio Grande Irrigation and Land Company might recover any of their investment. As the firm's liquidator wrote in his annual filing with British authorities several months after Boyd had passed away, "In March last, the receiver [Boyd] died without having received any concession from the U.S. Gov't. The prospects of anything now being realized for the Stock Holders are very remote." Although the Rio Grande Irrigation and Land Company did not cease to exist formally until February 11, 1949,[74] the path had been cleared years earlier for an apportionment of the waters of the Rio Grande based on the federal government's intervention in the interstate feud over the allocation of the river's waters.

CHAPTER 4

Congress Seeks a Solution

The Culberson-Stephens Bills

Although the formal interstate struggle over Rio Grande waters initially had started in the courts with the U.S. government lawsuit against the Rio Grande Dam and Irrigation Company—litigation that in part reflected an economic contest between competing water users in the Mesilla and El Paso valleys—Congress soon became involved. Federal lawmakers had taken up irrigation-related issues in the West as early as 1873, when they had commissioned a hydrographic survey of California. Although that study had been limited to just one state and did not involve the actual construction of any irrigation works, Congress's authorization of the Powell Irrigation Survey in 1888 broadened the government's commitment to reclamation studies to embrace the entire arid West. The failure of many private irrigation ventures, the major economic depression after 1893, and the lack of success of the 1894 Carey Act—in which Congress had sidestepped the water development issue by granting public domain lands to western states for state-sponsored irrigation projects—ultimately led to the passage of the 1902 Reclamation Act. This law sanctioned the federal government's construction of irrigation works on the condition that settlers who benefited would repay the costs.[1]

While the Reclamation Act is widely acknowledged by modern historians as a major turning point in western irrigation because of Congress's direct involvement in a national reclamation program and that plan's relationship to intrastate water rights,[2] few writers have recognized that even before the Reclamation Act was passed, Congress had been grappling with another important water-related issue — how to apportion interstate and international streams. This is probably partly because no modern writer has suggested that Congress possessed the authority to allocate interstate and international rivers prior to the U.S. Supreme Court's 1963 decision in *Arizona v. California* interpreting the 1928 Boulder Canyon Act as a congressional allocation of the Colorado River among that basin's states. Indeed, at least one scholar has contended that the Supreme Court's reading of the Boulder Canyon Act was flawed and that Congress intended no such interstate apportionment of the Colorado by passing that law.[3]

Regardless of the meaning of the Boulder Canyon Act, the historical record is clear that in the late nineteenth and early twentieth centuries, Congress devoted considerable time to the question of how to divide interstate and international rivers, notably the Rio Grande. Much as events leading to the passage of the Reclamation Act illustrated a growing desire by federal authorities to have a significant voice in shaping emerging irrigation-related water law in the West, the issue of how to divide the Rio Grande also was occupying Congress's attention, particularly on an interstate basis. This question ultimately led to a legislated apportionment of the Rio Grande's flows in 1905 — the first division of an interstate river's waters by federal lawmakers. Although this was a congressional allocation, the division was initially sanctified by local water users, and the federal lawmakers simply carried out the wishes of those on the scene.

Prior to the debate over whether a dam should be built at El Paso or at Elephant Butte, Congress never before had dealt with the allocation of a stream between two states. Nonetheless, beginning in the late 1890s, Texas's congressional delegation eagerly took up the issue after supporters of the international dam at El Paso reasoned that they might obtain their objective more quickly through legislation than through court action against the Rio Grande Dam and Irrigation Company. This rationale appeared all the more reasonable after the initial court rulings in favor of the firm. With Congress being more easily swayed by public pressure than the courts were, the skirmish in the legislative arena between backers of the Rio Grande Dam and Irrigation Company in New Mexico and proponents of the El Paso international dam in Texas grew considerably more heated than in the litigation. Arthur P. Davis — future chief engineer and eventually director of the U.S. Reclamation Service—later remarked in retrospect, "[F]or many years the fight between these two projects and their interested valleys raged and produced a deep seated antagonism between their people such that each valley became more anxious to kill the competing project than to promote and establish its own."[4]

Part of the hostility that Davis described stemmed from the fervent conviction in the El Paso Valley that upriver water users intended to deplete the Rio Grande's flows so severely that El Paso and Juárez farmlands would return to desert. The historical record to some extent substantiated this belief, especially by the increase in upstream diversions after the late 1880s, although these were largely in Colorado's San Luis Valley. Also contributing to the antipathy between the El Paso and Mesilla valleys were backers of the Rio Grande Dam and Irrigation Company, such as the firm's president, Nathan Boyd, who charged that the proposal for an international dam at El Paso was a scheme designed solely to deprive a politically weak territory of water to benefit a handful of wealthy El Paso speculators such as Anson Mills.[5]

The rival local sentiments fueled the U.S. government's litigation against the Rio Grande Dam and Irrigation Company as well as simultaneous congressional battles over authorizing the international dam at El Paso and dividing the impounded waters between Mexico and the United States. The legislative struggles centered on a series of measures that collectively came to be called the Culberson-Stephens bills, named after Senator (and former Texas governor) Charles A. Culberson and El Paso–area congressman John H. Stephens, the Texas federal legislators who introduced most of the proposed laws. The timing of events in the Rio Grande Dam and Irrigation Company court case substantially determined the bills' movements through Congress, and the measures brought the Rio Grande water issues to a Congress in which Texas was considerably more influential than the territory of New Mexico. In the Fifty-fifth and Fifty-sixth Congresses (1897–99 and 1899–1901), for example, Texas held thirteen seats in the House of Representatives in addition to the state's two U.S. senators. By comparison, the territory of New Mexico had only one nonvoting delegate to the House and no senators. After the congressional reapportionment following the 1900 census, Texas gained three more House seats, while New Mexico continued to have only its lone nonvoting delegate.

Because of Texas's powerful congressional presence and New Mexico's impotence, the Culberson-Stephens bills greatly strengthened the interstate facets to the Rio Grande apportionment battle, and the struggle became intimately linked with the question of New Mexico statehood. While El Pasoans pressed Congress to approve the international dam, New Mexicans urged Capitol Hill to allow their territory to become a state to protect the Rio Grande Dam and Irrigation Company's Elephant Butte project and to give them a better footing to fight Texas's attempted raid on the river's water. New Mexicans had sought statehood for many years in the last decades of the nineteenth century, but the territory had failed in this goal, in part due to xenophobia and prejudice against the region's large Hispanic and Catholic population. The interstate allocation issue added renewed urgency to New Mexico's statehood quest to protect its Rio Grande water supplies.[6]

The Culberson-Stephens bills grew out of a variety of factors, including the work of the International (Water) Boundary Commission, correspondence between Anson Mills and the State Department, the decision of the Justice Department to file suit against the Rio Grande Dam and Irrigation Company, and the initial government defeats in the litigation. Recognizing that Congress might be able to do what the courts had not accomplished, shortly after the company had been vindicated by the New Mexico Territorial Supreme Court for the first time, Congressman Stephens and Texas senator Roger Q. Mills (Charles Culberson's predecessor on Capitol Hill) introduced resolutions asking the executive branch for all documents pertaining to the Rio Grande for review. In April 1898, President William McKinley responded by submitting the proceedings of the International (Water) Boundary Commission, a draft of an incomplete treaty negotiated in 1896 between the United States and Mexico based on the commission's recommendations, and all related correspondence from the departments of Interior, State, and War. Although Congress had requested these materials to study the Rio Grande water problem, legislation directly addressing the matter was postponed on May 22, 1898, when the U.S. Supreme Court remanded the Rio Grande Dam and Irrigation Company case to the New Mexico Third Judicial District Court for the first time, asking for a fuller hearing on the issue of navigability.[7]

Congressional backers of the El Paso international dam tried to hinder the Elephant Butte effort in whatever manner they could while waiting for the second lower court decision. For example, in a ploy that officials of the Rio Grande Dam and Irrigation Company charged was aimed at scuttling their venture, international dam proponents succeeded in having Congress tack onto a bill permitting tram roads and canals on public lands a proviso preventing any canal right-of-way from interfering with prior water rights— meaning, of course, El Paso's. When Rio Grande Dam and Irrigation Company president Nathan Boyd successfully lobbied to defeat this amendment, international dam sponsors offered a substitute that prohibited construction of reservoirs anywhere on the Rio Grande in the territory of New Mexico without congressional authorization. Boyd also managed to prevent this restriction from passing, but other—and, as Boyd saw them, more insidious—provisions were added to what Boyd characterized as "innocent, noncontentious measures" that would have limited farming in New Mexico to the area then irrigated (about 200,000 acres), a constraint that plainly would have made the construction of Elephant Butte Dam nearly pointless. While such proposed legislation might be seen in one perspective as the emergence of the Progressive era's drive toward scientifically managed and coordinated control over western rivers, these bills also accurately reflected competing local factions in the El Paso and the Mesilla valleys seeking to secure for themselves the economic benefits that either the international or Elephant Butte dam would bring. Whatever the underlying motivation for this legislative action, Boyd's vigilance and protests by his supporters were all that overcame these threats to the Rio Grande Dam and Irrigation Company's project.[8]

More-direct assaults on the Rio Grande Dam and Irrigation Company's plans emerged in Congress shortly after the Third Judicial District Court upheld the ruling in favor of the Rio Grande Dam and Irrigation Company for the second time. The connection between the court's ruling and the introduction of the first Culberson-Stephens bill was obvious. With the government having lost again in the litigation, in early 1900 Anson Mills encouraged the State Department—with which Mills had close ties because of his position on the International (Water) Boundary Commission—to ask federal lawmakers to press the international dam cause. The Texas congressional delegation was more than willing to oblige. Mills then helped Congressman Stephens draft a bill to sanction the international dam, and with this help, Stephens introduced in the House of Representatives a measure "to provide for the equitable distribution of the waters of the Rio Grande River between the United States and the United States of Mexico, and for the purpose of building an international dam and reservoir on said river at El Paso, Tex." Stephens bluntly explained that the bill's purpose was to restrain the Rio Grande Dam and Irrigation Company in the event that the U.S. Supreme Court held on an appeal from the lower courts that the firm had a right to build the proposed reservoir at Elephant Butte. Within a few days, Senator Culberson introduced a similar measure on the other side of Capitol Hill.[9]

The Stephens and Culberson bills were nearly identical. To protect the international dam, both measures provided that no one could appropriate water in the territory of New Mexico to which others had prior rights (meaning, from Culberson and Stephens's point of view, residents of the El Paso Valley). Demonstrating Anson Mills's influence in shaping the bills, the twin measures allocated exactly $2,317,113.36 from the U.S. Treasury to build the international dam. This was the precise amount that had been specified in the International (Water) Boundary Commission's November 25, 1896, report to Secretary of State Richard Olney and Mexican foreign minister Matias Romero—a study that had strongly endorsed the El Paso dam and that Mills had helped draft. The Stephens and Culberson bills also directed the secretary of state to secure an agreement with Mexico to help build the international dam at El Paso and to divide Rio Grande water as also had been recommended by the International (Water) Boundary Commission.[10]

The Culberson-Stephens bills angered New Mexicans, and the publicity accorded to the measures was amplified by the New Mexico Territorial Supreme Court's hearings in April 1900 on the government's appeal of the lower court's second decision upholding the Rio Grande Dam and Irrigation Company. Residents throughout New Mexico realized that although the bills and litigation directly affected only the Rio Grande watershed, the implications for the entire territory were foreboding. Believing that if either bill passed or if the government won in court, Texas's assault on the Rio Grande would be just the first of many attacks on the territory's water supplies, New Mexicans protested in a variety of ways. For example, the *Rio Grande Republican* called on New Mexico's delegates to the Trans-Mississippi Commercial Congress, then meeting in Houston, to secure a resolution condemning the Culberson-Stephens bills. The measures, the newspaper declared, violated "every principle of right and justice."[11] Simultaneously, New Mexicans also deluged Territorial Governor Miguel A. Otero's office with complaints. Otero reacted to the crisis by calling for a convention to be held in Albuquerque on May 15, 1900. When the delegates assembled, they quickly passed motions directing Otero to send representatives to Washington, D.C., to protest in person against the Culberson-Stephens bills.[12]

Senator Charles A. Culberson
of Texas, date unknown.
Courtesy Eugene C. Barker
Texas History Center,
University of Texas, Austin.

Congressman John H.
Stephens of El Paso, ca. 1912.
Courtesy Library of Congress.

Of the two measures, the Stephens version received the most scrutiny, since the House Committee on Foreign Affairs—to which the bill had been assigned—held public hearings, partly in deference to the New Mexico delegation's presence in the nation's capital. Among the first to testify at the committee hearings was Harvey B. Fergusson, New Mexico's former delegate to Congress. Fergusson was incensed. If the Stephens bill were truly equitable, Fergusson demanded, why then was the state of Colorado not subject to the same prohibition as New Mexico against appropriations on the Rio Grande above El Paso? Pointing out what he viewed as an obvious attempt by Texas to take advantage of New Mexico's territorial status, Fergusson made it clear that should the Stephens bill or anything like it ever be passed, continued growth in Colorado would ultimately mean that New Mexico would receive little, if any, Rio Grande water.[13]

Also testifying before the House Committee on Foreign Affairs was D. N. Marron, another New Mexico protester. Charging that a "syndicate" had been formed in El Paso to promote the international dam at that city and to speculate in lands the reservoir would serve, Marron provoked an outburst from Congressman Stephens, who angrily denounced Marron's allegations. Stephens insisted on proof to support Marron's accusation, and Stephens staunchly maintained that the impetus for the dam came from Mexican complaints, not Texas speculators. Yet Marron's allegations were not just rhetoric, as Harvey Fergusson then demonstrated. Substantiating the charges, Fergusson pointed out that evidence introduced in the Rio Grande Dam and Irrigation Company litigation had identified Anson Mills's brother, William W. Mills, as the head of a group that had "bought up lands for a hundred miles south of El Paso, on both the Mexican and Texan sides [of the river]." Stephens, who claimed to know William Mills well, countered that he was "not worth $500," yet when pressed, Stephens could not deny that the court record proved that a syndicate did exist and that it had connections with William Mills.[14]

Aside from Fergusson and Marron, other representatives from the Albuquerque convention who had traveled to Washington objected to the Stephens bill because it required that the reservoir behind the international dam be completely full to satisfy Mexico's irrigation requirements regardless of New Mexico's needs. Condemning a provision giving half of the reservoir's waters to Mexico, the New Mexican protesters contended that this would effectively block subsequent appropriations in their home territory, thus carrying out an interstate and international apportionment in which

New Mexico would get nothing.[15] Such complaints about the Stephens bill, while not succeeding in killing it, achieved a partial victory. Securing the intercession of members of the House Committee on Territories—who looked more favorably on New Mexico's concerns—to block action by the Committee on Foreign Affairs, New Mexicans were able to prevent further hearings on the Stephens bill until after the November 1900 election.[16]

Even with this temporary triumph in the House of Representatives, backers of the Rio Grande Dam and Irrigation Company were still faced with the Culberson bill in the Senate. Shortly after the adjournment of the hearings on the Stephens bill in the House, the Senate Committee on Foreign Relations, which had received the Culberson bill for review, issued a favorable report. Observing that the international dam at El Paso would create a regular and uniform flow of the Rio Grande, the Senate committee believed that the moderated current would prevent changes in the river's channel and stabilize the international boundary.[17] The report also suggested that the international dam would improve the navigability of the Rio Grande, settle Mexico's damage claims attributed to dwindling water supplies, and provide a reliable flow of irrigation water to both sides of the stream. Underscoring the uncertain state of existing international water law, the Senate committee's report found that "a feasible mode will be provided for regulating in the future the use of the waters of the river so as to secure to each country concerned and to its inhabitants the legal and equitable rights in said river." The report, however, did not specify what constituted those "legal and equitable rights," and somewhat disingenuously, it concluded that "these rights will be accomplished without injury or injustice to any State or Territory through which the river flows."[18]

New Mexico's Governor Otero immediately took a strong stand against the Culberson bill, observing sarcastically, "As I understand it, this bill is similar to what is known as the 'Stevens [sic] bill' which was introduced in the House at its last session. If that bill becomes a law, they might just as well build a wall around the territory, and if it becomes a law in the shape that the Stevens [sic] bill was introduced, it will require a standing army in New Mexico to see that its provisions are enforced. They should tack an amendment on to a law of that kind providing that 'the men who vote for the passage of such a bill should be the ones sent out here to see that it is enforced,' as I am rather of the opinion that such a law will mean untold trouble in the territory, and could never be enforced in the world without the sacrifice of lives of many men."[19]

While Otero, Fergusson, and others were assailing the Culberson bill, New Mexico's territorial delegate to Congress, Bernard S. Rodey (widely known as "Statehood Rodey" because of his many activities aimed at gaining New Mexico's admission to the Union), was taking another approach. Rodey urged Mississippi senator Hernando D. Money, who sat on the Senate Committee on Foreign Relations, to ask the full Senate to postpone considering the Culberson bill until the complete record of the court proceedings in the Rio Grande Dam and Irrigation Company litigation was available for review. Rodey thought a deferral would be appropriate because if the U.S. Supreme Court upheld the Territorial Supreme Court's second decision in the case, then the outcome of voting on the Culberson measure would probably be affected. Responding to the request, Money promised that he "would not permit the passage of any section of this bill that would in any way empair [sic] the rights of the citizens of New Mexico to all the water to which they had ever been entitled."[20]

Several petitions sent to the Senate reinforced Money's determination to delay a vote on the Culberson bill.[21] The most prominent and detailed of these was Nathan Boyd's testimonial of January 10, 1901. In this protest, Boyd emphatically declared that the Culberson bill hardly could be considered an "equitable proposition"—a phrase that foretold the difficulties that later would arise in defining "equitable apportionment" after the U.S. Supreme Court had established that standard in its 1907 *Kansas v. Colorado* ruling as the basis for dividing interstate streams.[22] The Culberson measure's injustice, Boyd argued, was the result of a deliberate effort by the executive branch of the U.S. government to mislead Congress by withholding vital background information on the Rio Grande situation. According to Boyd, executive branch officials who had assembled the collection of documents in response to Congress's 1898 request for Rio Grande–related materials had omitted selected records that supported the Rio Grande Dam and Irrigation Company's position. This deception, according to Boyd, was intended to deprive "the people of New Mexico and Colorado of their legitimate right to the use of the waters of the Rio Grande, and in particular to destroy the legally acquired and vested rights of the Rio Grande Dam and Irrigation Company." Moreover, Boyd charged that "practically every paper that militates against the 'international dam' proposition was suppressed either in part or in whole, while every paper favorable to the international dam project and to Mexico's claim was included." Worse still, Boyd added that "even Attorney-General Harmon's [1895] opinion [that Mexico had no claim to Rio Grande waters], an authoritative and definite official state-ment, directly bearing on the subject, was entirely omitted."[23]

Boyd's petition then addressed the merits of his company's project, and he suggested that Mexico's claims for damages could be satisfied at a consider-ably smaller cost than building the international dam by providing Juárez farmers with waters stored in a reservoir at Elephant Butte. In addition, the proposed Elephant Butte structure, Boyd asserted, even had the support of El Pasoans except for those who would directly profit from the international dam—meaning, of course, Anson Mills, his brother, and their colleagues. Warning the Senate that most El Pasoans were concerned about "the serious danger that a large storage dam just above the city would entail" owing to its possible failure, Boyd offered as proof of Texas's approval of his company's project a resolution passed by the El Paso Chamber of Commerce. (Perhaps not coincidentally, the proclamation had been approved in September 1900, shortly after the New Mexico Territorial Supreme Court had upheld the Rio Grande Dam and Irrigation Company for the second time.) With the weight of this logic compelling to Boyd, his petition stated that the Senate's "sense of justice" should defeat any bill for the international dam.[24]

As the campaign against the Culberson-Stephens bills continued, it became increasingly tied to the drive for New Mexico statehood. New Mex-icans fully understood that part of the strategy of the international dam back-ers was to have Congress authorize the project at El Paso before statehood was granted to New Mexico. This would eliminate possible opposition from a voting New Mexico congressional delegation (however small it might be) and might permit Congress to control the appropriation of Rio Grande waters in New Mexico because the territory was subject to greater federal authority than it would be as a state. Although many contemporaneous observers believed that Congress had left water rights issues to the individ-ual states with the passage of the 1866 Mining Act and later federal legisla-tion,[25] there was still some question about whether such laws applied to western regions that remain territories. Pro-statehood New Mexicans such as Nathan Boyd saw this aspect of the Rio Grande struggle as a reason why New Mexico's entrance into the Union as a full-fledged state was impera-tive. Believing that the territory's inferior political status deprived it of suffi-cient power to combat the international dam scheme, Boyd urged Governor Otero to take matters into his own hands and call a state constitutional con-vention even before Congress authorized such a move. Although Califor-nia had done precisely this in 1849 before that state was admitted to the

Union in 1850, Boyd's proposal, in Otero's view, was too aggressive. Otero could not support such a plan at that time (although within a few months, he called for a meeting to press Congress for an enabling act), because he believed it would undermine existing support for New Mexico statehood — backing that was already thinner than statehood for California had been five decades earlier.[26]

The frantic New Mexico activities against the Culberson-Stephens bills paid off for the time being, and neither measure came to a final vote before the Fifty-sixth Congress adjourned on March 3, 1901. Nonetheless, when the new Congress convened shortly thereafter, Representative Stephens and Senator Culberson again introduced bills to build the international dam at El Paso. Both measures, which were essentially the same as those of the previous legislative session, were referred to the respective House and Senate committees on foreign affairs for consideration, and on the House side of Capitol Hill, New Mexico's nonvoting delegate to Congress, Bernard Rodey, lobbied to secure Colorado's opposition to these new measures on the grounds that the Culberson-Stephens measures would be as detrimental to that state as to the territory of New Mexico.[27] Additional, but slightly different, versions of these bills were introduced by Stephens, fellow Texas congressman Albert S. Burleson of Austin, and Senator Culberson in April 1902. According to Boyd, the reason for the differing forms was that the earlier bills would have restricted further appropriation of Rio Grande floodwaters in both New Mexico and Colorado, whereas the later measures applied only to New Mexico. Boyd charged that supporters of the Culberson-Stephens measures had become wary of alienating all western states' congressional delegations because of the limitation imposed on Colorado in the initial bills. Therefore, according to Boyd, the Culberson-Stephens measures had been modified in the later versions to apply only to New Mexico, which had no voting power in Congress and had little clout on important congressional committees.[28]

Such direct attacks on New Mexico strengthened Governor Otero's conviction that statehood was as imperative as the defeat of the Culberson-Stephens bills. Otero's resolve that New Mexico had to join the Union was fortified by the U.S. Supreme Court's second ruling against the Rio Grande Dam and Irrigation Company, sending the case back to the lower court for more evidence and testimony. Seeking to protect the territory's interests, Otero urged congressional delegate Bernard Rodey to bring to the attention of the secretary of the interior and the attorney general the assaults on New

Mexico by Congress and the courts, and Otero asked the New Mexico leg-islature for funds to defend the "territory's rights" in the Rio Grande Dam and Irrigation Company case.[29]

Boyd also took up the campaign against the new Culberson-Stephens (and Burleson) bills by printing and distributing a lengthy "analysis" of the Rio Grande water problems, much of which was an emotional invective against Anson Mills and his supporters. Whereas Boyd had sent a lengthy written report and protest to the Senate when the previous Congress had been considering the Culberson-Stephens bills, this time Boyd mailed his criticism directly to Secretary of State John Hay. Asserting that if any of the bills passed, Texas and Mexico would claim such extensive senior rights to Rio Grande waters that New Mexico would "be limited to the present area under cultivation," Boyd insisted that "competent authorities have declared that a scientific and comprehensive system of storage reservoirs on the Rio Grande and its tributaries in New Mexico would provide sufficient water for approximately 3,000,000 acres, if not more, of highly productive alluvial land."[30] Aside from this questionable contention, Boyd asked why the United States should fund the international dam at El Paso when his Ele-phant Butte facility would supply all the water required for irrigable lands both above and below El Paso and at far less federal expense. Moreover, Boyd maintained, the government's projected cost of the international dam had been considerably underestimated, and the proposed treaty with Mexico contained unjustifiable admissions of U.S. liability for damages attributable to water shortages in the Juárez area. These arguments notwith-standing, Boyd ultimately returned to haranguing his favorite culprit, con-cluding that "Gen. Anson Mills and his associate promoters know that it would be useless to ask Congress to build a great dam, at enormous cost, to impound water for the El Paso Irrigation Canal Company [which supplied the American side of the river in Texas], so therefore they lay much stress upon the alleged wrongs . . . [done to] Mexico."[31]

The New Mexico protests against the new Culberson-Stephens bills and Boyd's campaign—despite his charges against Mills—were successful in securing yet another delay on the international dam legislation. Instead of a vote on the Culberson-Stephens measures, on June 6, 1902, powerful Colorado senator Henry M. Teller asked the full Senate to request that President Theodore Roosevelt (who recently had been elevated to the pres-idency following William McKinley's assassination) deliver to Congress all reports, correspondence, and relevant information on the Rio Grande water problems. This resolution had the effect of postponing any formal action on the Culberson-Stephens bills until the materials had been received and reviewed.[32]

Regardless of the Rio Grande Dam and Irrigation Company's 1902 victory over the Culberson-Stephens bills, early the next year Congressman Stephens introduced yet another bill to build the international dam at El Paso. Within a few weeks, Senator Culberson had followed suit on the other side of Capitol Hill, but these new bills were largely symbolic.[33] Several factors made it unlikely that they would have received the amount of attention given to the previous Culberson-Stephens bills, although one Albuquerque newspaper urged New Mexicans to remain vigilant.[34] First, with the U.S. Supreme Court having remanded the Rio Grande Dam and Irrigation Company case to the New Mexico courts for the second time in March 1902, the firm's supporters had begun to realize that the government could crush the company through endless appeals. Second, Boyd's backers had fallen by the wayside, embarrassed by his relentless accusations against Mills, which, whether true or not, had become increasingly frequent and alarmingly irrational. Third, Kansas had recently filed suit against Colorado over the apportionment of Arkansas River flows between those two states, and westerners were watching that case for any precedent it might establish in relation to other interstate streams— including the Rio Grande.[35] Fourth, in a ploy to drive a wedge between Elephant Butte Dam backers and those who urged New Mexico's admission to the Union, Senator Culberson intended to propose an amendment to a congressional measure authorizing statehood for Arizona, New Mexico, and Oklahoma. Linked to the bill, however, was the proviso that the U.S. government would gain complete control over the Rio Grande—a move that obviously would eliminate the Rio Grande Dam and Irrigation Company.[36] Finally, the U.S. Reclamation Service, created by the Reclamation Act in June 1902, already had started its own studies of the Rio Grande to see whether the long-standing controversy on the river could be settled under the terms of the new law. This made congressional approval of a final Culberson-Stephens bill unlikely until the Reclamation Service had completed its review. Furthermore, the passage of the Reclamation Act and the growing popularity of the Progressive-era tenet that scientific, centralized regulation of natural resources was preferable in many cases to development by private enterprise also had persuaded most supporters of the Rio Grande Dam and Irrigation Company—including Governor Otero—to abandon the firm's cause in favor of intervention by the U.S. Reclamation Service.

Thus, in the end, the Culberson-Stephens bills contributed to the apportionment controversy by making the attacks on the Rio Grande Dam and Irrigation Company and New Mexico's water supply double-pronged, coming from Congress as well as the courts. Such a two-headed offensive demonstrated an activist role of both case and statutory law in shaping the history of the arid West in the late nineteenth century. Legislative action in the form of the Culberson-Stephens bills had been directed at the economic development of the El Paso and Juárez area—much as a similar legislative stimulus underlay the chartering of the Rio Grande Dam and Irrigation Company and that firm's acquisition of a right-of-way to build Elephant Butte Dam under the terms of the 1891 General Revision Act. With the legislative arena creating conflict between different economic interests, settling the problem was left to the courts. In this context, the federal lawsuit against the Rio Grande Dam and Irrigation Company, as legal historian Morton Horwitz would have argued, suggests that litigation in contract and property law in the late nineteenth century performed a politically and economically redistributive function.[37] Clearly, the lawsuit against the Rio Grande Dam and Irrigation Company was directed at garnering political support in Texas for the El Paso dam and at economically benefiting the El Paso–Juárez area at the expense of New Mexico.

Both case and statutory law, therefore, played key roles in laying the groundwork for an interstate and international apportionment of the Rio Grande. Yet in the conflict between the international dam and the Elephant Butte venture, how case and statutory law were used largely was determined by competing local interests. Profoundly shaping the evolution of water use and control in the southern New Mexico and western Texas region, the litigation and the final disposition of the 1903 Culberson-Stephens bills together set the stage for a compromise—an agreement that would derive from a different congressionally directed apportionment of Rio Grande waters among New Mexico, Texas, and Mexico. Although this was to be a legislative answer, it was to stem from a new set of principles guiding federal involvement in western resource development—a set of precepts that emphasized scientific and comprehensive planning for the management of natural resources, not the exploitation of those resources to benefit private enterprise. Nevertheless, the legislated solution was defined on the local stage and illustrated westerners' continuing reluctance to allow the federal government to have a free hand in regulating scarce water resources.

CHAPTER 5

The Compromise of 1904

After decades of struggle over the Rio Grande, a workable solution to the bitter apportionment problem appeared with the passage of the Reclamation Act on June 17, 1902. The law—sometimes called the Newlands Act after Nevada congressman (and later, senator) Francis G. Newlands, who had sponsored the legislation—represented the culmination of years of pressure by western states and territories for a feasible means of financing and building large-scale irrigation works.

The Reclamation Act grew out of a multitude of circumstances in the 1890s. Filled with turmoil, the decade witnessed a series of unsettling events—both natural and manmade. One of the most significant was a depression that hit the United States in 1893. In 1894, 30 percent of all workers in the country were unemployed, and the financial crisis did not begin to turn around until nearly the beginning of the twentieth century. The economic emergency was compounded by the arrival of thousands of new immigrants to the United States—many coming from southern and eastern European countries whose cultures and religions differed from those of more-long-term Americans. These two factors, in turn, set the stage for numerous strikes and other unrest. Moreover, the growth of large corporations with few governmental restraints, combined with the emergence of powerful urban political bosses, created a sense of helplessness among many.[1]

Outside the cities, many American farms had been crippled, especially in the West. Cattle grazing had been especially hard-hit by the winter blizzards and summer heat of the late 1880s. Simultaneously, much of the easily accessible public land available for homesteading had already been claimed, leaving only arid regions open to further settlement. In response, westerners had sought means to bring more water to barren lands to accommodate additional homesteaders. This was a goal shared by many easterners, who believed opening new lands to farmers would relieve the social and economic stresses facing the cities. All of these factors enhanced the West's clout in Congress, a power shift created by the admission to the Union of more western states after the Civil War. This added regional political muscle did not significantly change the House of Representatives—whose membership was dependent on population—but western strength in the Senate grew with each added state. The new western senators helped lay the groundwork for federal support for reclamation. At first, this backing took the form of the Carey Act of 1894, which authorized each western state to obtain up to a million acres in support of reclamation projects. This legislation was followed eight years later by the Reclamation Act, which gave direct federal support to irrigation in the West.[2]

Under the Reclamation Act's provisions, proceeds from public land sales in western states and territories were to go into a revolving fund for constructing reservoirs and other irrigation facilities. Farmers who benefited from the works would pay for them over a period of time (originally ten years but later extended on many projects), and the recovered money would help underwrite subsequent works. All of this would be administered by a new agency, the U.S. Reclamation Service (after 1923, the Bureau of Reclamation), under the direction of the secretary of the interior.[3]

The Reclamation Act, which marked the beginning of direct federal support for irrigation projects in the West, set the stage for a congressional apportionment of the Rio Grande. Moreover, the creation of the Reclamation Service established an agency whose precise goal was to overcome the problems associated with western aridity through social manipulation, scientific study, and efficient management of natural resources. Mostly engineers, the leaders of the Reclamation Service were drawn from a line of work that accepted the Progressive era's idealistic view that they and other professionals could be agents of social change through the careful use of technology. The engineers of the Reclamation Service believed, as one scholar of the period has noted, "that human society followed laws as predictable as those which govern the universe or natural world, and that engineers, as 'logical thinkers' trained to weigh evidence carefully and without bias, could solve a wide range of social and economic problems."[4]

Under those circumstances, it is not surprising that the fledgling Reclamation Service saw finding a solution to the Rio Grande's complex interstate and international water difficulties as an opportunity to help establish the agency as the premier federal influence in western resource development. In this regard, Reclamation Service officials were more than willing to build on earlier U.S. government interest in the Rio Grande and eventually to propose a new solution to dividing the river—one that involved an interstate apportionment between New Mexico and Texas sanctified by Congress as well as a treaty allotting supplies to Mexico. The Reclamation Service's plan, however, was made possible only through a locally achieved compromise among a large body of water users in the Mesilla Valley and those in the El Paso Valley on both sides of the international boundary. In this regard, irrigators attempted to retain some degree of autonomy from federal dominance in water allocation matters.

Even before the Reclamation Act had been passed, the hydrographic branch of the U.S. Geological Survey, which later became the Reclamation Service, had been active in compiling data on western rivers through activities such as the 1888 Powell Irrigation Survey. Building on this background, in early 1902—just months before the Reclamation Act had become law— the hydrographic branch had sent Arthur Powell Davis to New Mexico and El Paso to report on the best method of resolving the Rio Grande stalemate. Davis was an appropriate choice for the assignment, given the strong sentiments among backers of the international dam at El Paso and those supporting the Elephant Butte proposal. Having served with the Geological Survey since his uncle, John Wesley Powell, had hired him in 1882, Davis favored decentralized local control of reclamation projects while supporting Progressive-era principles of centralized planning and federal supervision.[5] These seemingly contradictory ideals ultimately found expression in both the 1902 Reclamation Act and the solution that emerged to solve the Rio Grande's apportionment problems.

Once he had arrived in New Mexico, Davis examined the Rio Grande Dam and Irrigation Company's Elephant Butte reservoir site and concluded that it would not permit the construction of a storage facility large enough to serve the Mesilla and El Paso valleys adequately. The ideal site, Davis believed, existed a short distance downstream (still more than a hundred miles above the international dam location at El Paso). Davis reported his findings to the Geological Survey and urged that a more comprehensive investigation of the area be made. In mid-1902, the newly formed Reclamation Service followed up on Davis's recommendations. After several preliminary studies, the Reclamation Service's chief engineer, Frederick Haynes Newell—a long-time proponent of federal sponsorship for western irrigation development and the unofficial author of the 1902 Reclamation Act—sent consulting engineer Benjamin M. Hall to coordinate further work and to write a full-fledged proposal for a dam near the Elephant Butte site favored by Davis.[6]

Hall was destined to become one of the most important figures in achieving an interstate and international apportionment of the Rio Grande—an allocation that he fully intended for Congress to carry out through appropriate federal legislation and a treaty with Mexico. Born in South Carolina in 1853 and raised in Georgia, Hall had graduated from the University of Georgia with a degree in engineering in 1876. He subsequently taught mathematics for several years at North Georgia Agricultural College (today, North Georgia College and State University) before finding other employment as an engineer in water supply and mining investigations in Georgia's goldfields. This training led Hall to provide his expertise as a consultant to the U.S. Geological Survey in 1896. Eight years later, he joined the Reclamation Service as a supervising engineer and played a central and vital role in achieving a settlement dividing the Rio Grande's waters among Mexico, Texas, and New Mexico. He also helped develop other Reclamation Service projects in New Mexico. Subsequently, after leaving the Reclamation Service, Hall became the head engineer in charge of developing a major irrigation plan for Puerto Rico.[7]

As the Reclamation Service's Rio Grande investigations progressed in 1903 and early 1904, interstate and international events simultaneously combined to lay the groundwork for a compromise proposal to end the dispute over the river's water. On the interstate level, the ongoing proceedings in the U.S. Supreme Court in *Kansas v. Colorado*, originally filed in 1901 over the apportionment of the Arkansas River, had driven the point home to New Mexicans that interstate water struggles were not limited to their territory's conflict with Texas. In the Arkansas River litigation—which water users throughout the West were following closely—Kansas had contended in its bill of complaint that "[t]he volume of water in the bed of the [Arkansas] river flowing from Colorado into Kansas was and should be, and would be, very large, but for the wrongful [Colorado] diversion of the same."[8] Kansas also argued that each summer the Arkansas River above Wichita went dry, and Kansas asserted that Colorado's diversions caused diminishing crop returns in the Arkansas River basin in Kansas. Kansas concluded its complaint by asking the Supreme Court to prohibit any new Colorado appropriations from the Arkansas River.[9]

Kansas's arguments before the Supreme Court regarding reduced Arkansas River flows were substantiated in large measure by the claim that that state held riparian rights to the stream.[10] This was not a popular position in New Mexico, where the public had long accepted prior appropriation as the basis for allocating streams. Nevertheless, while the underlying water law theories may have differed in the conflicts over the Arkansas River and the Rio Grande, both were similar in that water uses along the Arkansas River in Kansas and Colorado dated back well into the nineteenth century—circumstances that were also true for irrigation in Texas and New Mexico on the Rio Grande. Another aspect that mirrored the situation on the Rio Grande was that many ditches in the downstream Kansas reaches of the Arkansas River predated those upstream across the state line in Colorado.[11] New Mexicans therefore realized that the outcome of the *Kansas v. Colorado* case could have significant implications for their battle with Texas over appropriations on the Rio Grande.

One crucial difference, however, distinguished the Arkansas River and Rio Grande interstate water disputes—a distinction that was well understood by New Mexicans and worried them. Unlike the situation on the Rio Grande, both Kansas and Colorado were states and ostensibly equals in the federal Union, with Kansas having become a state in 1861 and Colorado in 1876. Along the Rio Grande, both Colorado and Texas (which joined the Union in 1845) had long been full-fledged states. Yet at the time of the *Kansas v. Colorado* litigation, New Mexico remained a territory of the United States—a political status that made the Rio Grande case significantly different from the water dispute on the Arkansas River because New Mexico's officials fully understood that they could not argue that their territory was an equal in sovereignty to Texas or Colorado.

Despite the differences between the circumstances on the Rio Grande and on the Arkansas River, the *Kansas v. Colorado* case was clearly of such major import to the outcome of the conflict on the Rio Grande that New Mexico's leaders believed they had to become involved in the Arkansas River case one way or another. Therefore, as a strategic move in the Rio

Grande matter, New Mexico's officials considered supporting a state in the Arkansas River conflict whose interests most closely aligned with those of their territory on the Rio Grande. Although many years later, during interstate compact negotiations, New Mexico would strenuously protest Colorado's bid to keep whatever Rio Grande water Colorado wanted, in 1904 New Mexico's territorial delegate to Congress, Bernard Rodey, and the territory's solicitor general, Edward Bartlett, considered intervening in *Kansas v. Colorado* to support Colorado's claim to total control over the waters of the Arkansas River as one of the state's sovereign rights. Rodey and Bartlett thought that backing Colorado's position in *Kansas v. Colorado* would strengthen New Mexico's stance against Texas's claim to the flow of the Rio Grande. With New Mexico's officials considering intervening in *Kansas v. Colorado* and with that lawsuit receiving considerable coverage in the western press, New Mexico's irrigators realized that the outcome of that case might have a profound influence on their own trouble with Texas.[12]

On the international level, events also had been leading toward a compromise proposal on the Rio Grande. Much as the interstate aspects of the Rio Grande struggle had similarities with other river disputes between states, so too did the international situation along the Rio Grande have parallels involving conflicts with foreign nations on other streams. Along the lower Colorado River, Charles Rockwood's California Development Company had been carrying out studies and engineering work aimed at diverting the Colorado's waters to southern California's Imperial Valley (then known as the Salton Sink). Rockwood's efforts were interfering with Colorado River flows destined for Mexico, and as along the Rio Grande near Juárez, the Colorado River situation was exacerbated by speculation and large landholders on both sides of the international border. Much as they had done on the Rio Grande, Mexican authorities had grown uneasy over Rockwood's plans for the Colorado River, and they had lodged protests with the United States over the Colorado's diversions.[13]

Regarding the Rio Grande, the Mexican ambassador to the United States, M. de Aspiroz, sent his objections to Secretary of State John Hay over the continuing water shortages in the Juárez area on June 3, 1904. Aspiroz told Hay that until 1882 there had been a plentiful supply of water in the Rio Grande to irrigate large parts of the valley below El Paso on both sides of the river. Since then, however, American diversions had caused the Mexican population in the Juárez area to decrease to less than half its previous size. Echoing the 1896 conclusions of Matias Romero, the Mexican foreign minister,

Aspiroz asserted that the decline in the number of farmers had cost Mexico $35,685,000, and he cited records of the International (Water) Boundary Commission to prove these claims. Aspiroz pressed for a quick solution — either by the U.S. government's support for the international dam at El Paso or by payment of damages.[14] With the Colorado River situation also demanding attention, Secretary Hay then urged the Department of the Interior to find a solution. Hay suggested for the Rio Grande that the new Reclamation Act of 1902 might provide an answer.[15] This was a solution that was also beginning to emerge with respect to the Colorado River and California's Imperial Valley water needs, although a resolution to that problem took longer to find, owing to a multitude of factors.[16]

Within the Interior Department, the Aspiroz and Hay Rio Grande communications were referred to Frederick Newell of the Reclamation Service for an appropriate answer, and he promptly drafted a proposed reply to Secretary Hay. In a separate cover letter to the director of the Geological Survey, Charles D. Walcott (who officially oversaw the Reclamation Service until it became a separate agency in 1907),[17] enclosing the suggested response, Newell explained that the U.S. government had been put "in a particularly unfortunate position by the fact that its principal representative [to the International (Water) Boundary Commission], General [Anson] Mills, has certain financial interests at El Paso which may have warped his judgment." Newell thought that Mills's "admission of the damage to Mexico" showed poor judgment because the Mexican claims were, in Newell's opinion, "exorbitant and absurd," and he added that Benjamin Hall, whom Newell deemed "thoroughly loyal without preconceived notions for or against Mexico," had been appointed to work on the situation and suggest a solution.[18]

Despite these conclusions, Newell's draft communication to Secretary Hay was considerably less candid than the cover letter to Walcott, no doubt in part because Mills, in his role with the International (Water) Boundary Commission, was under State Department jurisdiction. Declaring that U.S. citizens in Texas suffered from Rio Grande water shortages as much as Mexican farmers, Newell blandly advised Hay to tell the Mexican ambassador that "every reasonable effort will be made by the executive departments to remedy the unfortunate conditions."[19]

By October 1904, Benjamin Hall had completed his examination of the Rio Grande apportionment problem, and the result was his landmark report, "A Discussion of Past and Present Plans for Irrigation of the Rio Grande Valley."[20] This study marked a major turning point in the struggle over water allocation in the Rio Grande valley. Not only did it strongly endorse Newell's view that federal administration was the most efficient means of water resource development in the West, but Hall's report also supported the Progressive-era concept that solutions to serious natural resource problems, such as those that existed on the Rio Grande, were best left to experts and professionals to devise solutions. Hall's study also had further significance because, while it laid the foundation for a locally achieved compromise apportioning Rio Grande flows among water users in New Mexico, Texas, and Mexico, it also tacitly invited Congress to consecrate that accord through legislative action — the first such effort by federal lawmakers to divide an interstate river's water supplies.

Hall's analysis projected that a Reclamation Service reservoir at Elephant Butte could store 2,000,000 acre-feet of water — enough to furnish 600,000 acre-feet annually to farmers for several years if drought prevented replenishing the reservoir with spring flood flows. Hall believed that this water could irrigate a total of 180,000 acres annually in the Rio Grande valley, with 110,000 acres being served in New Mexico, 20,000 acres in Texas above El Paso, and 50,000 acres below that city on both sides of the river. Comparing his proposal to the plan for the international dam at El Paso, Hall found that a Reclamation Service reservoir at Elephant Butte would hold three to four times the international reservoir's capacity. In addition, although a storage facility at Elephant Butte would have a slightly higher evaporation rate than one at El Paso, it would have no losses by overflow such as those contemplated for the international dam to maintain the river's channel. Finally, Hall noted that a reservoir at Elephant Butte would flood less valuable land than the El Paso structure, which, Hall's report observed, would drown thousands of acres of fertile Mesilla Valley farms.[21]

Having shown the Elephant Butte location to be superior, Hall's study then addressed the division of water to be stored by the reservoir. Texas had not been covered by the terms of the original Reclamation Act, because the state's earlier existence as an independent republic meant that it had no federal public lands to help underwrite the reclamation fund. Acknowledging this point and the fact that no Rio Grande apportionment treaty then existed with Mexico, Hall asserted that a congressionally directed interstate allocation and an international agreement could allow the river's waters to supply New Mexico, Texas, and Mexico in predetermined amounts. As Hall viewed the situation, the Elephant Butte site had the advantage of being in New Mexico and therefore subject to the operations of the U.S. Reclamation

Elephant Butte before the dam's construction, ca. 1909, with a new wagon road down Ash Canyon to the construction site. Courtesy Bureau of Reclamation, National Archives II, College Park, Maryland.

Service. Hall then made it clear that he saw a congressional division of the river—with appropriate State Department input concerning Mexican interests—as the solution to the Rio Grande's problems. "The project can be so planned that legislation by Congress can allow Mexico and Texas to participate," Hall explained. He cautioned, however, that "the extent and manner of this participation is a matter that must be arranged and decided on by Congress and the Department of State. All that the Reclamation Service can do at present is to make plans and estimates for work in the territory of New Mexico that will not conflict with any action that may be taken by Congress and by the Secretary of State for restoring water to which the El Paso Valley in Texas and Mexico has laid claim by virtue of ancient prior appropriation and continuous use."[22] The phrase "ancient prior appropriation and continuous use" had ominous implications that would carry over into the proposed legislation to include the El Paso Valley under the provisions of the Reclamation Act.

Even without a new law allowing Texas to participate in the benefits to be achieved under the Reclamation Act and without a treaty with Mexico, Hall still believed that irrigators below El Paso on both sides of the Rio Grande could benefit from water stored behind Elephant Butte Dam, although these supplies would have to be released into the river as they left New Mexico. In true Progressive-era fashion, however, Hall's report contemplated that federal legislation and a treaty would bring better management of the river.[23]

Although Hall anticipated that Mexico's allotment of Rio Grande waters under a new treaty would be delivered in the river's bed, he planned to serve New Mexico and Texas irrigators in a new federal reclamation system to be called the Rio Grande Project. This would include Elephant Butte Dam (which Hall initially preferred naming Engle Dam after a small nearby town, to avoid the likelihood that his proposed structure would be confused with the dam planned by the Rio Grande Dam and Irrigation Company).[24] In addition to the major reservoir, the Rio Grande Project would encompass a diversion dam and headworks near Leasburg, New Mexico (about forty miles above El Paso), a large canal that would run down the east side of the Mesilla Valley, and other distribution works. The west side could be supplied, Hall surmised, by a separate canal, by pumping, or by pipes across the river. Hall suggested that the Leasburg diversion dam be built first, to furnish irrigation water to the canals while the major storage reservoir at Elephant Butte was under construction.[25]

With his report in hand, Hall issued a press announcement to begin a public relations drive for the federal dam at Elephant Butte. Hall and his fellow Reclamation Service engineers Arthur Davis and W. H. Sanders also visited the New Mexico towns of Las Vegas, Engle, and Las Cruces to obtain support for construction of Elephant Butte Dam and the Rio Grande Project. Hall realized that Texas's backing for his conception was vital, but with the Reclamation Act not then covering the El Paso Valley, the federal government could plan officially only for New Mexico. Therefore, the public relations efforts were initially limited to that territory.[26]

Of the towns visited by the Reclamation Service engineers, Las Cruces, the economic heart of the Mesilla Valley, was the most important. With area residents well aware that the U.S. government might provide an answer to the Rio Grande apportionment difficulties, Reclamation Service engineers met with about two hundred New Mexicans at the local courthouse on October 20, 1904. Outlining their plans, the engineers told the assembly that their

Mexican diversion dam on the Rio Grande near Juárez, 1904. Courtesy Bureau of Reclamation, National Archives II, College Park, Maryland.

presentation would form the basis for a formal recommendation to the secretary of the interior, who, at the time, held the sole authority to approve or reject Reclamation Service projects. The proposal received the meeting's strong support, and the assembled throng unanimously adopted resolutions in favor of the federal venture. Even those El Pasoans who attended the Las Cruces gathering were favorably impressed, so much so that the day after the event, the *El Paso Herald* prematurely trumpeted "El Paso Approves the Reclamation Plan."[27]

Enjoying this solid public backing, Hall then set out to win broader support for his plan. While Hall recognized the important role that official lawmaking institutions such as the U.S. Congress would play in implementing his scheme, he also realized that the power structure of the United States involved more than just legislatures, courts, and executive agencies. In fact, as Hall well knew, the American legal process was sometimes profoundly shaped by informal and nongovernmental institutions such as interest groups, trade associations, and private organizations.[28] This understanding

Las Cruces diversion dam, 1904, to be replaced by the more modern and permanent facilities of the Rio Grande Project. Courtesy Bureau of Reclamation,
National Archives II, College Park, Maryland.

led Hall to turn his attention to the Twelfth National Irrigation Congress,
which was scheduled to meet in El Paso on November 15–18, 1904.

The national irrigation congresses, which had been held yearly since the
first gathering in Salt Lake City in 1891, had evolved into one of the most
important forces behind federal involvement in reclamation in the western
states.[29] The delegates to these conferences included prominent state and
national politicians, irrigation engineers, educators in the field of agriculture,
members of commercial organizations, officials of private water companies,
and other leaders of public opinion.[30] Their numbers and influence allowed
them to bring immense pressure to bear on federal and state legislative bodies, and past achievements had included the 1894 Carey Act and the 1902
Reclamation Act. Hall believed that support by the 1904 National Irrigation
Congress for a dam at Elephant Butte and the Rio Grande Project would
result in its formal authorization by the secretary of the interior, the passage
of related federal legislation extending the Reclamation Act to the El Paso

Valley in Texas, and the ratification of a treaty with Mexico. These actions, Hall hoped, would end the fight over the river's apportionment forever.

Hall's opportunity for a favorable reception at the 1904 National Irrigation Congress was encouraged by the important role the young Reclamation Service was set to play at that conference. Frederick Newell had been named the chairman of the engineering and mechanics section, a position that allowed him to designate speakers for that part of the program. In his capacity as chairman, Newell had invited many of the most prominent irrigation engineers of the day, including men such as Joseph B. Lippincott and Elwood Mead. Lippincott—then a supervising engineer for the Reclamation Service—was a former topographer for the U.S. Geological Survey who later played instrumental (if controversial) roles in developing San Francisco's water sources from the Hetch Hetchy Valley in Yosemite National Park and Los Angeles's supplies from California's Owens Valley. Lippincott also later served as an engineering consultant for many irrigation districts and cities in the western United States.[31] Mead, a former territorial and state engineer for Wyoming, was chief of investigation and drainage irrigation for the U.S. Department of Agriculture in 1904. Mead later supervised irrigation investigations in Australia and eventually became commissioner of the U.S. Bureau of Reclamation.[32]

In addition to inviting Lippincott and Mead to the 1904 National Irrigation Congress, Newell had directed all Reclamation Service officials in the western part of the United States to attend. Furthermore, aiming to highlight Hall's proposal as much as possible, Newell had scheduled the second annual conference of Reclamation Service engineers to be held in conjunction with the irrigation congress. In short, Newell did everything possible to give Hall's plan a complete and highly visible review at the El Paso meeting.[33]

The Reclamation Service's public relations drive in New Mexico paid off by convincing a disproportionately large number of delegates with Rio Grande connections to attend the gathering. Of the fifty-eight delegates from New Mexico, twenty-three were from the lower Rio Grande area of the territory. Prominent New Mexicans who expected to be present included the territorial delegate to the U.S. Congress, Bernard Rodey; former territorial governor L. Bradford Prince; and the banker and treasurer for the Rio Grande Dam and Irrigation Company, Henry D. Bowman.[34] A large group of Texans with Rio Grande ties also expected to be present. Of the forty-one Texas representatives going to the 1904 National Irrigation Congress, twenty-two represented the El Paso Valley near the New Mexico border. These included El Paso–area congressmen William R. Smith and John H. Stephens (whose district had included the El Paso area until 1903, when it had been redrawn in accordance with the results of the 1900 census), as well as Felix Martinez, a leader of the business community in the region. Martinez was then chairman of the irrigation committee for the El Paso Chamber of Commerce, but his renown went well beyond that organization. Also expecting to appear at the irrigation congress was distinguished El Paso attorney Richard F. Burges, who was widely respected for his knowledge of the emerging field of western water law. Burges was to act as the legal representative for water users on the Texas side of the El Paso Valley for decades after the 1904 gathering.[35]

Although the public relations effort convinced many delegates with Rio Grande interests to attend the Twelfth National Irrigation Congress, the most formidable obstacle that Hall faced in securing the adoption of his plan was persuading the El Paso–area representatives to drop the international dam proposal in favor of a federal reservoir at Elephant Butte. Furthermore, Hall had to convince the El Pasoans that the Reclamation Service project was different from the venture proposed by the Rio Grande Dam and Irrigation Company, which El Pasoans such as Anson Mills had strenuously opposed for over ten years. With these problems in mind and with a strong desire to avoid a public controversy between Elephant Butte and international dam advocates at the irrigation congress, Hall invited Texas congressmen Smith and Stephens to the Reclamation Service engineers' meeting—held the day prior to the official opening of the 1904 National Irrigation Congress—to review the new Elephant Butte Dam proposal at length. Hall knew that Stephens's endorsement was critical because of the congressman's role in sponsoring the House of Representatives' versions of the Culberson-Stephens bills, and Smith's approval was deemed equally important because at the time, he represented much of the El Paso area. In addition, the support of both congressmen was crucial to obtaining later federal legislation extending the Reclamation Act to the El Paso Valley, thus permitting a full interstate apportionment to take place within the Rio Grande Project.[36] After considerable discussion, the Reclamation Service engineers convinced Smith and Stephens that Hall's plan would satisfy the needs of the Texas part of the El Paso Valley, and the engineers and congressmen then adjourned to the first session of the Twelfth National Irrigation Congress, where Hall was to present his proposal.

Introducing Hall to the assembled crowd, Frederick Newell boldly announced that the Reclamation Service intended the proposed federally built Elephant Butte Dam to solve both the interstate and international problems on the Rio Grande. Newell explained that "the Secretary of the Interior and the Secretary of State hope to see, through the expenditure of the reclamation fund, some solution possibly, about the question confronting us on the Rio Grande." Newell then turned the program over to Hall.[37]

Hall's presentation embodied essentially the same points he had covered in his written report to Newell the previous month, and he emphasized to the delegates that his plan involved an apportionment of water to be stored at Elephant Butte Reservoir, which would provide irrigation supplies for about 110,000 acres in New Mexico, 20,000 acres in Texas above El Paso, and 50,000 acres below the city on both sides of the river. These figures, however, were to be adjusted based on later Reclamation Service surveys as construction of the distribution system took place. Significantly, Hall's division left Texas's share of Rio Grande waters below El Paso subject to whatever allotment Mexico might receive. Hall later wrote that "in making plans for this Rio Grande Project, the engineers of the Reclamation Service have recognized the existence of these interstate and international questions, and have provided as much water for the El Paso Valley in Texas and Mexico as would have been supplied by the proposed international dam at El Paso, but they have not stated how this El Paso Valley water should be divided between Texas and Mexico; neither have they expressed any opinion as to the sovereign rights of the Territory of New Mexico, the State of Texas, or the Republic of Mexico."[38]

Hall's explanation to the 1904 National Irrigation Congress was followed immediately by a presentation on the underflow of the Rio Grande by Charles S. Slichter. A professor and later graduate school dean at the University of Wisconsin, Slichter was a consulting engineer for the U.S. Geological Survey. Hall had asked Slichter in July 1904 to study the groundwater situation because those familiar with the Rio Grande had long suspected that there was a connection between groundwater and surface river flows. To Hall, removing this potential source of controversy was especially important regarding the division of waters between users above and below El Paso because if there was significant groundwater movement past the city, any apportionment of the Rio Grande's surface flows would be meaningless without including underflows. With Slichter's research aimed at addressing this problem, the professor had determined that "the origins of the ground waters, or the supply of ground waters . . . is the water contributed by the river itself or lost by the river."[39] Slichter also found that there was little groundwater flow below "the Pass," the narrow gorge just above El Paso that was to have been the site of the international dam.[40] Thus, Slichter's presentation confirmed that an apportionment of the Rio Grande as proposed by the Reclamation Service was indeed feasible.

Hall's report and Slichter's conclusions caused an instant sensation among the irrigation congress delegates — so much so that a mass meeting for all interested parties was scheduled later that day to air Hall's proposal more fully. Within hours, according to the *El Paso Herald*, "the immediate and personal interest of the meeting to the people of El Paso and the surrounding country attracted one of the largest crowds of the convention to the main hall." Over three hundred people jammed into the special afternoon session, where Hall again outlined his plan. As in his morning presentation, he specifically avoided discussing diplomatic and legislative problems that would have to be overcome, such as passing a law to extend the Reclamation Act to the El Paso Valley in Texas and negotiating a treaty with Mexico. Focusing instead on the engineering aspects of his idea for Elephant Butte Dam and the Rio Grande Project, Hall hoped to garner the broadest possible support for a localized compromise without creating debate on issues he believed best left to the U.S. and Mexican governments.[41]

When Hall had completed outlining his proposal, delegates from Texas and New Mexico were quick to embrace it, and this endorsement demonstrated how thoroughly the interstate aspects of the Rio Grande's division had come to dominate the international concerns. J. A. Smith, president of the El Paso Chamber of Commerce, spoke for many Texans when, according to the *El Paso Herald*, he "made a ringing speech in which he declared that the international [water] boundary commission had been superseded, so far as the [El Paso] dam was concerned, by the reclamation service."[42] New Mexicans also backed Hall's plan, and Bernard Rodey, although asserting that New Mexicans above Elephant Butte were not relinquishing any claims to Rio Grande waters, introduced a resolution approving "the proposal of building the Elephant Butte Dam as a happy solution of a vexed question that has embarrassed the parties interested, providing . . . [for] an equitable distribution of the waters of the Rio Grande with due regard to the rights of New Mexico, Texas, and Mexico." With El Paso and Mesilla Valley interests satisfied, all of the American delegates present passed the motion, although Mexican representatives refrained from voting until they could consult with their government.[43]

While the Mexicans caucused, the New Mexico and Texas delegates created a committee to agree on further steps to be taken. Meeting to iron out any differences they might have, the Americans sought to present a united front to Mexico regarding how much water that country should receive in any accord dividing supplies below El Paso.[44] The need for American harmony stemmed from several vital considerations. First, Hall's proposal had suggested that there would be enough water from Elephant Butte Reservoir to irrigate 50,000 acres in the El Paso Valley on both sides of the river, but he had not spelled out how that water would be apportioned between Texas and Mexico. Thus, the Mexican allotment would significantly affect Texas's proportionate share of Rio Grande waters. Second, the still-outstanding Mexican demand for water or damages because of American diversions was an international issue—theoretically a thornier problem than merely dividing irrigation water within the United States. American unity in any treaty negotiations, therefore, was essential. Third, acknowledging that if Mexican prior rights were recognized in any treaty discussions, El Paso's almost certainly also would be, the Americans understood that because many New Mexicans had long fought such recognition, the problem required discussions among themselves before Mexico's delegates were included.

As the American faction worked to eliminate the interstate differences, the Mexican delegates to the irrigation congress chose their five emissaries to the committee, and early on November 18, 1904—the final day of the conference—the full fifteen-member council met to consider Hall's proposal. After reviewing the plan in depth, the Mexicans offered a limited endorsement of the federal Elephant Butte Dam proposal, agreeing to leave the determination of the extent of Mexican irrigable acreage below El Paso to Reclamation Service studies. These surveys later would be verified by the Mexican government. In effect, this process would allow the Reclamation Service to create the Texas allocation at the same time. In response to the Mexican committee members' approval, the New Mexico and Texas panel members passed a resolution accepting the Mexican position, and the fifteen committee members next turned to former New Mexico territorial governor L. Bradford Prince to bring their resolutions before the full irrigation congress. Prince subsequently announced to the complete assembly later that day that a compromise on dividing the Rio Grande's waters had been reached by the committee of fifteen, and he read the resolutions passed by the Mexican and American committee members into the record. Prince then asked the Twelfth National Irrigation Congress to add the weight of its entire membership to the accord, and that body—including the Mexican participants—overwhelmingly approved a resolution endorsing the Reclamation Service plan to apportion the Rio Grande.[45]

The achievement of a mediated compromise apportioning Rio Grande waters was a major coup for the young Reclamation Service, and Benjamin Hall was justifiably gratified with the support for his proposal. Exulting in his success the day after the irrigation congress adjourned, Hall told Arthur Davis that the delegates' "full agreement and endorsement of the Reclamation Service plan was the crowning glory of the Irrigation Congress." Hall explained the manner in which the resolution of support had been achieved, and turning to how the backers of the international dam at El Paso had been overcome, he gloated, "The results were more than satisfactory. They were nothing short of miraculous. It would have done your heart good to see those old sinners flocking to the mourners' bench. I had been doing missionary work among them for some time, but I had not expected such a land slide [sic]. Even old [Bernard] Rodey got religion, and said he was willing to let Mexico have some water. Old Max Weber [the German consul at Juárez and a prominent irrigator on the Mexican side of the river] died hard, but he came in all right in the round up. I fear that General [Anson] Mills will not survive the issue. So far as I know, he has not a single adherent left. The city and the whole valley are enthusiastically in favor of our plan."[46] Hall added that backers of the Reclamation Service's proposal had "nailed the Congressmen [Smith and Stephens] also, and [they] will keep the ball rolling"—a reference to the need for the U.S. Congress to extend the Reclamation Act to the Texas side of the El Paso Valley and to approve a treaty with Mexico.[47]

While Hall was understandably pleased with the outcome of the 1904 National Irrigation Congress, satisfaction with the compromise extended well beyond Reclamation Service employees. The *Atlanta Constitution* was quick to boast that Hall was a former resident of Georgia and that it was his plan that had solved the Rio Grande stalemate.[48] In addition, Senator Francis Newlands of Nevada—the official sponsor of the 1902 Reclamation Act and an attendee at the irrigation congress—told the *Washington Post* that the El Paso gathering had been "one of the most important held yet," and he added that "it practically settled the controversy between New Mexico and Texas and the international contest between the United States and

Mexico."[49] The agreement reached at the 1904 National Irrigation Congress also was widely hailed for other reasons, not the least of which was that the accord suggested that interstate and international disputes on other western rivers might be resolved through similar scientific analysis, efficient planning, and negotiation.[50] This was a point of particular importance to Colorado because of the large number of streams that state shared with its neighbors, and multiple Colorado newspapers carried accounts of the compromise on the Rio Grande.[51] Indeed, the concept of negotiated settlements for shared rivers based on professional and systematic study was so widely hailed that within a year, President Theodore Roosevelt had appointed a special commission—which included Frederick Newell of the Reclamation Service—to negotiate with Mexico over the waters of the Rio Grande and Colorado River and with England over the Milk River, which crossed the international boundary from Montana into Canada.[52]

Moreover, the settlement on the Rio Grande appeared to those in the southern New Mexico and El Paso area to be a preferable solution to the interstate and international issues instead of continuing the still-pending Rio Grande Dam and Irrigation Company litigation. This was especially true because the other major interstate river conflict at the time, *Kansas v. Colorado*, was still in front of the U.S. Supreme Court, and in that case, the United States was arguing that the federal government ought to have complete control over all navigable western rivers. Rio Grande water users thought eliminating the litigation over their river removed that case as a possible means of a similar claim to federal authority.

Of far greater importance to Rio Grande water users, however, was the fact that the 1904 National Irrigation Congress accord was discerned by all involved as a permanent solution to apportioning Rio Grande waters—one that was locally achieved but would subsequently be implemented by appropriate federal legislation and a treaty with Mexico. The *El Paso Herald*, which had covered the irrigation congress closely for its readers, spelled out how delegates viewed the final decision to back Benjamin Hall's plan. "The conference [held by the fifteen committee members] patently was not looked upon as in any respect as a temporary compromise," the *Herald* rejoiced. "The purpose expressed by all the committeemen was to arrive at a permanent working agreement in favor of the Elephant Butte Dam."[53] The "permanent working agreement," as everyone understood—particularly after Hall's presentation was printed nearly verbatim in the local press—was that Elephant Butte Dam would serve approximately 110,000 acres in New Mexico, 20,000 acres in Texas above El Paso, and 50,000 acres below that city on both sides of the river and that the final exact allocations would be left to future Reclamation Service surveys.[54] All that remained was for the U.S. Congress to enact a law extending the Reclamation Act to the Texas part of the El Paso Valley and to approve a treaty with Mexico. This would formalize the local compromise reached at the 1904 National Irrigation Congress.

CHAPTER 6

The 1905 Congressional Apportionment of the Rio Grande

With the 1904 National Irrigation Congress endorsement of Benjamin Hall's Elephant Butte Dam proposal, implementing the local compromise became vital to obtaining a permanent end to Rio Grande water conflicts. On the interstate level, two major steps had to be taken. One of these was to create organizations in the Mesilla and El Paso valleys to work with the Reclamation Service in the construction of Elephant Butte Dam and the Rio Grande Project's distribution system. The Reclamation Service preferred contracting with water users' associations instead of individuals because these groups could collect charges for maintenance and repayment obligations from farmers on behalf of the government. Dealing with such organizations was also consistent with the Progressive-era and Reclamation Service philosophy of centralized planning and federal supervision of locally controlled irrigation systems—an ideology that squared with westerners' desires to manage their own water-resources destinies.

An equally important step toward fulfilling the interstate aspects of the 1904 compromise was the extension of the 1902 Reclamation Act to the U.S. side of the El Paso Valley. Texas was not covered by the original terms of the Reclamation Act because it had no federal public lands to help underwrite the reclamation fund; without legislation allowing part of the Rio

Grande Project to be built in the El Paso Valley, Reclamation Service officials realized that they would have to release waters for lands below El Paso
into the riverbed at the southern boundary of New Mexico. This was a
potentially wasteful procedure that conflicted with the prevailing sentiments that favored efficient natural resource management. Such a process
also would cause a great deal of water to be lost to American farmers in
Texas by what were essentially unregulated Mexican diversions along the
Rio Grande. For these reasons, shortly after the 1904 National Irrigation
Congress had ended, the Reclamation Service began a drive to have the
U.S. Congress extend the Reclamation Act's provisions to Texas's lands
below El Paso.

By eventually bringing the U.S. side of the El Paso Valley under the terms
of the Reclamation Act, Congress formally sanctioned the irrigation congress's compromise of 1904. More noteworthy, however, was that this legislated approval of the 1904 accord—passed by the U.S. Congress in
1905—authorized the Reclamation Service to carry out the first true apportionment of any interstate stream. Occurring twenty-three years before Congress passed the 1928 Boulder Canyon Act, which the U.S. Supreme Court
ruled in *Arizona v. California* (1963) was the earliest legislatively sanctioned
division of a river (the Colorado) between two or more states, the 1905 Rio
Grande law was, in fact, the first such congressionally directed interstate
stream allocation. In addition, the extension of the Reclamation Act to the
El Paso Valley also preceded by seventeen years the earliest Supreme Court
decree apportioning an interstate river (*Wyoming v. Colorado* in 1922) and
the first interstate compact dividing a stream's waters (the 1922 Colorado
River Compact).[1] Thus, the 1905 law broadening the Reclamation Act to
cover the U.S. side of the El Paso Valley was the earliest interstate apportionment of a western river in any form, whether legislated by Congress,
ordered by the Supreme Court, or negotiated in compact form.

Perhaps equally important, however, was the fact that the 1905 congressional division of the Rio Grande was demonstrative of an ever-widening
federal interest in western water affairs, an entanglement that was to
become increasingly complex not only on the Rio Grande but also on many
other western rivers. This U.S. involvement in water issues in the West par-
alleled growing federal concern with scientifically managing a variety of the
region's resources, including forests, ranges, and mineral lands. Progressives
in President Theodore Roosevelt's administration such as Reclamation
Service Chief Engineer Frederick Newell and Gifford Pinchot, head of the

Franklin Canal in El Paso before reconstruction by the U.S. Reclamation Service, date unknown. The Franklin Canal was the main distribution system for the U.S. side of the Rio Grande below El Paso and Juárez. Courtesy Bureau of Reclamation, National Archives II, College Park, Maryland.

Bureau of Forestry in the Department of Agriculture, believed that only a coordinated and comprehensive approach to western resource management would allow these national assets to be utilized productively for years to come. The drive to have Texas included under the terms of the Reclamation Act, therefore, was consistent with that view. Only with Texas covered by that law, Reclamation Service officials realized, would the U.S. part of the Rio Grande Project operate at maximum efficiency.[2]

Following the 1904 National Irrigation Congress, however, Rio Grande irrigators were more immediately concerned on the local level with forming organizations to work with the Reclamation Service than with promoting new federal laws. Demonstrating the continuing involvement of grassroots participation in shaping the final outcome of the Rio Grande's apportionment, within weeks of the National Irrigation Congress, about thirty-five businessmen and landowners assembled at the El Paso Chamber

Franklin Canal in El Paso after reconstruction by the U.S. Reclamation Service, date unknown. Courtesy Bureau of Reclamation, National Archives II, College Park, Maryland.

of Commerce to establish the El Paso Valley Water Users' Association. To underscore the continuing desire to work with Mesilla Valley farmers toward implementing the Reclamation Service's plan, those present at the El Paso gathering decided to send a delegation to New Mexico's organizational conference. Shortly thereafter, New Mexicans scheduled a meeting for December 22, 1904, in Las Cruces to create the Elephant Butte Water Users' Association.[3]

When the New Mexico water users convened (with many delegates wearing badges bearing the motto Dam the Rio Grande), El Paso interest in their proceedings had blossomed, and about fifty Texans traveled north to join approximately two hundred Mesilla Valley residents at Las Cruces. With this being the first chance for farmers who had not attended the irrigation congress to air their views on the Reclamation Service proposal, they came to hear Benjamin Hall explain his ideas in person. As had been the case at the irrigation congress, Hall's presentation was persuasive, and the meeting ended with the decision to continue the process of establishing the Elephant Butte Water Users' Association for New Mexicans who would benefit from Elephant Butte Dam and the Rio Grande Project.[4]

Although Rio Grande farmers focused primarily on forming water users' groups, the Reclamation Service simultaneously prodded Congress to take steps to implement the 1904 compromise. In this endeavor, the agency worked closely with Texas's congressional delegation. While in theory the 1902 Reclamation Act initially had given complete authority to the secretary of the interior to approve irrigation projects as well as the power to regulate nearly all other aspects of new reclamation undertakings, in practice, much of the real power lay with the Reclamation Service. The Reclamation Service's near-autonomy lasted until 1914; Congress then, in responding to complaints regarding poorly conceived projects and overextended financing, changed the Reclamation Act to require congressional approval for all new irrigation projects.[5] Nevertheless, before 1914 on the Rio Grande, cooperation between Congress and the Reclamation Service was necessary to create the Rio Grande Project because—unlike many other early reclamation efforts—the Rio Grande Project was interstate as well as international in character. Both aspects necessitated congressional attention. For the interstate part of the 1904 compromise to be realized, Congress would have to extend the 1902 Reclamation Act to the El Paso Valley in Texas, and for the international portion of the 1904 accord to fall into place, Congress would have to ratify a treaty with Mexico.

Addressing the interstate aspects of the 1904 agreement, at about the same time that the irrigators in Texas and New Mexico were creating their respective water users' associations, Congressman John Stephens submitted to the House of Representatives a bill "extending the operation of the irrigation reclamation act of Congress to the State of Texas in certain cases."[6] The measure was premature, however, and soon was replaced by another bill with the same goal authored by Reclamation Service head Frederick H. Newell.[7]

By the time Newell wrote his proposed law to extend the Reclamation Act to the El Paso Valley, he had developed a considerable degree of expertise in western water matters. Following an engineering education in the 1880s, Newell had gone to work for the U.S. Geological Survey and eventually became a hydraulic engineer within that agency. As a Geological Survey employee, Newell had worked on a variety of rivers, including

Temple of Agriculture, housing the offices of the Elephant Butte Irrigation District (originally the Elephant Butte Water Users' Association), 1922. Courtesy Bureau of Reclamation, National Archives II, College Park, Maryland.

overseeing sixteen men along the Rio Grande making stream measurements. After the Hydrographic Division of the Geological Survey had been formed in the late 1890s, Newell directed that division's projects. Eventually, he became one of President Theodore Roosevelt's principal environmental advisors (along with Chief Forester Gifford Pinchot). Indeed, Newell had drafted the 1902 Reclamation Act—a measure that President Roosevelt had signed into law.[8]

Introduced in the House of Representatives on January 18, 1905, by Congressman William R. Smith, the lengthy title of Newell's measure to implement the 1904 National Irrigation Congress compromise clearly described its purpose: "A bill (H.R. 17939) relating to the construction of a dam and reservoir on the Rio Grande, in New Mexico, for the impounding of the floodwaters of said river for the purposes of irrigation, and providing for the distribution of said stored waters among the irrigable lands in New Mexico, Texas, and the Republic of Mexico, and to provide for a treaty for the settlement of certain alleged claims of the citizens of the Republic of Mexico against the United States of America." The phrase "and providing for the distribution of said stored waters among the irrigable lands in New Mexico,

Texas, and . . . Mexico" spelled out the bill's intent to legislate an apportionment of Rio Grande waters, and subsequent congressional debates firmly established that the division being contemplated was to be carried out by the Reclamation Service based on Benjamin Hall's estimates and the local compromise reached at the 1904 National Irrigation Congress.[9]

The Newell-Smith measure, which was referred to the House Committee on Foreign Affairs to be considered in conjunction with one of the final Culberson-Stephens international dam bills, expanded the Reclamation Act to the El Paso Valley in Texas and authorized the secretary of the interior to build Elephant Butte Dam and the Rio Grande Project. This part of the Newell-Smith bill was consistent with nearly everyone's understanding of the 1904 local accord. Yet in what became the measure's most controversial provision, the bill also called for a study of any senior Mexican Rio Grande water rights, the official recognition of those rights, and the negotiation of a treaty to liquidate Mexican damage claims.[10] Such terms reflected Newell's concern for careful and detailed planning, but they outraged New Mexicans, who believed that their water rights—which were held under New Mexico's territorial laws—were not subject to Mexican (or Texan) claims of seniority. With no case or statutory law then recognizing appropriative water rights across state lines, New Mexicans believed that their claims existed independently of any similar claims in the El Paso and Juárez areas. Moreover, the years of struggles by the Rio Grande Dam and Irrigation Company to fend off the proposal for an international dam at El Paso, as well as New Mexico's lengthy battle for statehood, further underscored New Mexicans' determination that no federal law should sanction prior rights in the El Paso and Juárez areas.

The issue of Mexico's alleged prior rights led to the first overt demonstration that the U.S. Congress planned to authorize the Reclamation Service to apportion the Rio Grande between New Mexico and Texas through the Newell-Smith bill. When the measure reached the floor of the House of Representatives on January 26, 1905, Massachusetts congressman William S. McNary emphasized the importance of the legislation by observing that there had been "a controversy between New Mexico and Texas for some time about the right to use this water." McNary added that because of this strife, New Mexicans had "been unable to build a dam and unable to use the river water because of the claim that Mexico down below El Paso is entitled to a large share of this water." Wyoming congressman Frank W. Mondell understood the situation clearly and explained that the aim of the Newell-Smith measure was to resolve the lengthy dispute. Mondell pointed out that an agreement had been reached "by the representatives of Mexico at the recent irrigation congress at El Paso, and by the people of New Mexico, Colorado, and Texas represented at that meeting." (Mondell mistakenly included Colorado, which was not a direct participant in the 1904 accord.)[11] Further clarifying the Newell-Smith bill's objective in response to a query from Congressman Charles L. Bartlett of Georgia, Mondell stressed that the proposed law was to provide "a happy solution of a long standing controversy, not only between the people of the United States and the Republic of Mexico, but also between the people of New Mexico and Texas."[12]

Mondell's allusion to Mexico's role in the apportionment conflict underscored that the legislators fully recognized the connection between the interstate and international aspects of the Rio Grande's problem and that the lawmakers saw the Newell-Smith bill as the best alternative to address the interstate part of the issue. For example, Representative Albert S. Burleson of Texas suggested that measures such as the Culberson-Stephens bills actually had proven counterproductive by only dealing with the international problem and not considering the dispute between New Mexico and Texas. Burleson then described his conviction that the 1904 National Irrigation Congress had approved a complete solution and that in passing the Newell-Smith bill the legislators would be implementing the interstate portion of that compromise by federal law. Burleson explained, "[L]ast year an international irrigation congress was convened in the city of El Paso, and as a result of the action taken by that congress the people of the territory of New Mexico and the people of the State of Texas living at and below the city of El Paso, and many Mexican citizens who are interested, all united upon the proposition embodied in this bill as the most feasible and practical means of settling this long-drawn-out controversy."[13]

Even Congressman Stephens—an author of the Culberson-Stephens bills discussed in chapter 4—completely agreed with the purpose of the Newell-Smith measure. Speaking on the House floor, Stephens's explanation of the bill's intent reflected his intimate knowledge of the entire Rio Grande conflict. Not only had Stephens fiercely opposed the reservoir at Elephant Butte proposed by the Rio Grande Dam and Irrigation Company, but even after his district had been redrawn as a result of the 1900 federal census, Stephens had continued to work closely with the area's new representative, William Smith, to resolve the Rio Grande quandary. Given

Stephens's thorough familiarity with the apportionment difficulty, there can be little doubt that his interpretation of the Newell-Smith bill accurately portrayed the measure's intention. "I will state," Stephens declared, "that at the irrigation congress held last year at El Paso, the delegates from New Mexico, composed of Mr. [Bernard S.] Rodey, the governor, and other prominent citizens of New Mexico, and a committee from El Paso and old Mexico met in that congress and agreed upon and adopted a series of resolutions. . . . *The main features have been embodied in this bill.*"[14]

Regardless of Congress's belief that the Newell-Smith bill would carry out the 1904 compromise apportionment on an interstate level, New Mexicans reacted with hostility when copies of the proposed legislation reached the Mesilla Valley. Believing that the measure gave away New Mexico's irrigation supplies by accepting El Paso's and Mexico's claims to senior water rights, New Mexicans saw the bill's recognition of downstream priorities as a surreptitious attempt to circumvent the irrigation congress accord under a false guise of harmony. Because New Mexicans did not believe that the 1904 compromise had included any legitimization of prior rights in the El Paso Valley (either in Texas or in Mexico), they concluded that the Newell-Smith bill was an even more insidious means to guarantee water to Texas and Mexico at the expense of upstream users than had been the despised Culberson-Stephens bills.

Demonstrating the deep distrust of the Newell-Smith measure on the part of New Mexicans, N. C. Frenger, a prominent southern New Mexico attorney and secretary of the Elephant Butte Water Users' Association, fired off a panic-stricken telegram to Benjamin Hall charging that the proposed law was an "absolute surrender of New Mexico rights." Assuming that Hall would agree, Frenger insisted that the Reclamation Service take action to block the bill's passage. Nathan Boyd, publicly still vigilant for New Mexico's rights, also wired Hall, warning that if the Newell-Smith measure was approved, he would not drop the Rio Grande Dam and Irrigation Company's third (and, as it turned out, final) appeal to the U.S. Supreme Court. Boyd reasoned that if the appeal went forward, the federal government's plans could not proceed since the Rio Grande Dam and Irrigation Company might ultimately prevail in its struggle to build its own dam at Elephant Butte. Under these circumstances, Boyd believed, New Mexico landowners would not pledge their support for the Reclamation Service project. Concluding that the Newell-Smith measure was "fatal to the sovereign rights of New Mexico," Boyd asserted that the bill also was "opposed to the principles agreed upon with [the] Texas delegates [at the 1904 National Irrigation Congress]."[15]

With Newell, Benjamin Hall's boss, as the author of the bill, it is not surprising that Hall did not share Frenger's and Boyd's concerns. In an attitude that typified the Reclamation Service's dealings with water users on many early irrigation projects, Hall patronizingly dismissed the New Mexicans' fears with a sarcastic note to Arthur Davis, then the Reclamation Service's assistant chief engineer. Reviewing the New Mexico correspondence, Hall quipped, "I wired you this morning the substance of these two statesman-like messages and hope my telegram may reach you in time to save the country. Personally I have not been uneasy about the matter, as I felt that you and Mr. Newell were fully competent to take care of the 'sovereign rights of New Mexico.' I have not seen an authentic copy of the Smith bill, as I am somewhat out of the world [meaning not in Washington, D.C.], but I hope it is not as bad as my 'constituents' seem to consider it. Hoping that you will be able to keep things from getting too badly balled up, I am, Very truly yours, B.M. Hall, Supervising Engineer."[16]

Hall's response to Frenger was considerably more diplomatic than had been his letter to Davis. Seeking to calm Frenger's anxiety, Hall assured him that if the Newell-Smith bill passed in "a form that does not give due consideration to the interests of New Mexico, there will be ample opportunity to amend it." This statement, of course, conveniently ignored the fact that the Reclamation Service directly had shaped the terms of the bill in the first place. Adding that the agency's officials could not "undertake to control the actions of Congress," Hall blandly remarked that if asked for advice, the Reclamation Service would "have the interest of New Mexico at heart." Hall offered little further encouragement, but, demonstrating his belief that the Newell-Smith bill's intent was to apportion the waters of the Rio Grande, he stated that "if Congress sees fit to adopt the engineering project, but change the basis of water distribution, we have no power to interfere." Hall concluded bluntly that "it rests with your representatives and your friends in Congress to see that you get a reasonable, if not fully equitable, share of water."[17]

New Mexicans were alarmed by Hall's cavalier attitude, and their worries mounted when the Newell-Smith bill passed the House of Representatives and was referred to the Senate.[18] With the approval in the House, New Mexicans in the Mesilla Valley turned their attention to defeating the measure on the other side of Capitol Hill—ironically, along with an identical bill introduced in the Senate by Charles Culberson — or to having the legislation amended to drop the recognition of prior rights in Texas and Mexico. Significantly, while New Mexicans lobbied to block both bills in the Senate, the congressional debate continued to underscore the legislators' desire to pass a law apportioning Rio Grande waters among users above and below El Paso based on the 1904 National Irrigation Congress accord.

Leading the attack against the twin bills, the Elephant Butte Water Users' Association and the Las Cruces Chamber of Commerce turned to the El Paso Valley Water Users' Association for assistance and proposed that the measures be altered to delete references to prior rights at and below El Paso. Such a modification would have been consistent with the agreement reached at the 1904 National Irrigation Congress, but the Texans refused, fearing that this concession might lose Mexico's support for the entire compromise. With the failure of this tactic, Mesilla Valley interests immediately wired various U.S. senators asking to delay the bills until a New Mexico delegation could reach Washington, D.C.[19]

In the meantime, Herbert B. Holt, president of the Elephant Butte Water Users' Association, asked Charles E. Miller, a member of New Mexico's legislature, to persuade the territory's other lawmakers to oppose the Newell-Smith and Culberson bills. Including a draft of a proposed resolution protesting against the measures with his letter to Miller, Holt explained that the Newell-Smith and Culberson bills conflicted with the terms of the 1904 National Irrigation Congress agreement by recognizing El Paso's prior rights. Holt's opinion was particularly noteworthy because not only was he a lawyer, but he also had been one of the fifteen committee members from New Mexico, Texas, and Mexico who had reached the original accord at the irrigation congress. Filling in the details, Holt spelled out exactly what his perception of the compromise was. The provision of the law acknowledging the El Paso Valley's prior water rights, Holt argued, was in direct contravention of the understanding reached at the irrigation congress. In addition, he confirmed that those present at the 1904 gathering had accepted the Reclamation Service's estimates that with a federal dam at Elephant Butte, 110,000 acres could be watered in New Mexico, 20,000 acres supplied in Texas above El Paso, and an additional 50,000 acres irrigated at and immediately below El Paso on both sides of the river. In addition, according to Holt, all of these lands would be treated equally regardless of priorities.[20]

The New Mexico opposition to the Newell-Smith and Culberson bills surprised many El Pasoans. Believing that both measures embodied the complete terms of the 1904 compromise, the Texans responded indignantly to the New Mexico complaints. The El Paso Valley Water Users' Association, for example, sent an urgent wire to Newell expressing bewilderment over the New Mexico uproar. Contrary to the position taken by the New Mexicans, the Texas water users requested Newell's support for the Newell-Smith and Culberson measures: "Cannot conceive motive [behind the] opposition [of] parties [in] New Mexico to Smith [and] Culberson bill[s]. Your positive declaration to them of its fairness and value to all concerned and the dangers of losing project if it fails we feel will cause them [to] withdraw opposition and endorse it. Your patriotic services [on] our behalf have our deepest sense of gratitude and in the name of all those interested we plead [with] you to assist us [in the] present emergency."[21]

Yet despite the Texans' request for intervention, Reclamation Service officials declined to involve the agency in what they perceived to be largely a political battle in Congress.[22] Adding to the Reclamation Service's reluctance to take sides openly, Newell's role in drafting the House of Representatives' measure made the agency especially leery about interceding, and with the large international and interstate stakes involved, Reclamation Service officials thought they could ill afford to alienate either Texas or New Mexico and still maintain the agency's credibility for expertise in western reclamation matters.

Even if the Reclamation Service *had* decided to intervene on Texas's behalf, however, New Mexico had a powerful Senate ally in its opposition to the Newell-Smith and Culberson measures. Shortly after the Newell-Smith bill was reported back from the Senate Committee on Foreign Affairs, Senator Henry M. Teller of Colorado entered the fray. Teller had long supported New Mexico's opposition to Texan and Mexican claims to priority because of the much younger irrigation systems in Colorado's part of the Rio Grande watershed, the San Luis Valley. Teller's backing for New Mexico also stemmed from his state's position in *Kansas v. Colorado*, which was then working its way toward a resolution by the U.S. Supreme Court. In that litigation, Colorado's lawyers were contending that upriver states had no obligation to deliver any water whatsoever to their downstream neighbors, a position that they argued was supported by Attorney General Judson Harmon's 1895 opinion that the United States had no duty to provide any Rio Grande water to Mexico. Teller thought that Colorado's stance in the *Kansas v. Colorado* case applied equally well to New Mexico in relation to Texas and Mexico. Joining the battle over the Newell-Smith and

Culberson bills, Teller offered an amendment to delete the offensive recognition of El Paso and Juárez prior rights, and by the time the House measure had reached the Senate floor, Teller had convinced its supporters to back his modification. Teller's persuasiveness was partly aided by Herbert Holt's resolution opposing the Newell-Smith and Culberson bills, which, at Charles Miller's request, had been passed by the New Mexico legislature and delivered to Congress.[23]

While officially presented as an amendment to the Newell-Smith bill, Teller's motion deleted everything after the measure's initial enacting phrase, inserting instead what was to become the final language extending the 1902 Reclamation Act to the El Paso Valley in Texas. This revised version of the bill passed the Senate without debate, and on February 21, 1905, it was accepted by the House of Representatives. Using a pen subsequently given to the City of El Paso because of the importance it represented, President Theodore Roosevelt then signed the bill into law.[24] (The Reclamation Act was extended to the entire state of Texas the following year.)[25]

The new act appeared simple, but it contained several important provisions. First, giving the federal government considerable authority to end the Rio Grande dispute, the law provided that if the secretary of the interior determined that there were enough lands in New Mexico and Texas that would benefit from the Elephant Butte Reservoir and that the cost of building the dam and irrigation works would be returned to the reclamation fund, the Reclamation Service could construct the system "should all other conditions as regards feasibility be found satisfactory." This proviso was subsequently interpreted by the Reclamation Service as being a congressional directive to build Elephant Butte Dam and the Rio Grande Project in line with Benjamin Hall's proposal to the 1904 National Irrigation Congress. The feasibility requirement also meant that the Reclamation Service would determine the extent of irrigable lands in New Mexico and Texas—as Hall's plan had called for—and the specific acreage would be identified by the secretary of the interior based on those studies. The widely held understanding by local interests, however, was that the formal irrigable land surveys would come close to Hall's original 1904 estimates, and water stored at Elephant Butte Reservoir would be apportioned among New Mexico and Texas accordingly. Thus, when ultimately carried out by the Reclamation Service, the irrigable land surveys would fully implement the congressionally sanctioned interstate apportionment between the two states through the construction of the Rio Grande Project.[26]

Despite the historical significance of the 1905 legislative division of the Rio Grande, legal scholars of the day failed to recognize its importance—or, for that matter, that it had occurred at all. Such prominent legal writers as Albert E. Chandler, Henry P. Farnham, Clesson S. Kinney, Joseph R. Long, John Norton Pomeroy, and Samuel C. Wiel either totally ignored interstate allocation issues in their water law treatises or discussed litigation as the only possible solution to river disputes among states.[27] This was in part because the earliest interstate apportionment decision by a federal court did not take place until 1898, and that ruling—*Howell v. Johnson*—was not a U.S. Supreme Court decision.[28] Even the 1907 landmark U.S. Supreme Court ruling in *Kansas v. Colorado* did not actually divide an interstate river but only established that the court could do so at a later date if it so desired. As Kinney concluded in the 1912 edition of his *Treatise on the Law of Irrigation*, "[W]hen the first edition of this work was published in 1893, there was no law upon the subject of the application of the Arid Region Doctrine of appropriation, either statutory or case, as specially applied to interstate rivers. In fact, nearly all the law upon the subject has been developed within the last ten years."[29]

The legal writers of the day missed the vital importance of the 1905 congressional division of the Rio Grande for two significant reasons. First, the apportionment had been accomplished through a law extending the 1902 Reclamation Act to the El Paso Valley, thus allowing the Rio Grande Project to be built and water to be divided within the federal irrigation system according to Reclamation Service surveys, as Benjamin Hall had proposed. Nothing in the text of the law spelled out the river's allocation even though Congress's desire to apportion the waters within the Rio Grande Project in accordance with the agreement mediated by the 1904 National Irrigation Congress mediated was unmistakably evident in the legislators' deliberations. Without hearing or reading the debates, therefore, legal writers would have been unaware of the law's river-division aspect.

A second reason why early legal writers failed to notice the significance of the 1905 apportionment of the Rio Grande is that Congress did not see its legislation as establishing a bold example for resolving future water conflicts among states. With little law—either case or statutory—bearing on interstate water disputes, the legislators took the position in their discussions that the 1905 law was merely an imprimatur of the widely hailed 1904 National Irrigation Congress accord. To the congressmen and senators, the truly important event had happened on the local level the year before they acted to extend the Reclamation Act to the El Paso Valley. Because much of the West was still extremely isolated and unsettled, federal lawmakers had little reason to suspect that similar compromises would ever be needed or achieved on other interstate and international rivers.

With Congress unaware of its act as a possible precedent for future interstate water problems and legal writers of the time also failing to perceive the importance of the law, it is not surprising that more-recent legal scholars, such as Robert E. Clark, Wells A. Hutchins, and George William Sherk, as well as experts on interstate compacts such as Supreme Court Justice Felix Frankfurter, Jerome C. Muys, Vincent V. Thursby, and Frederick Zimmermann, also reached the conclusion that until the 1963 Supreme Court ruling in *Arizona v. California*, dividing an interstate river could only be accomplished by litigation or compact.[30]

The 1905 allocation of the Rio Grande was not merely a recognition that interstate river priorities could be enforced where both states accepted the doctrine of appropriation and that those rights could be compromised.[31] In fact, the congressional debates over the bill implementing the 1904 Rio Grande agreement made it abundantly clear that acceptance of all priorities had been rejected in favor of a division of the river's water supplies to be carried out by the Reclamation Service. As Arthur Davis explained after the measure had become law, the new legislation did not acknowledge prior rights anywhere on the Rio Grande. "The bill provides for the extension of the provisions of the Reclamation Act to that portion of the State of Texas that can be irrigated from the Rio Grande," Davis told Hall. "Nothing is said about prior rights, and it is the understanding with both the Texas and New Mexico delegations that all lands receiving water from the Engle [Elephant Butte] reservoir will stand on the same basis." In other words, waters within the Rio Grande Project were not being apportioned by priorities but instead would be divided within that project according to Reclamation Service surveys. Davis believed that such an approach was "a broad-minded, generous view for these landowners that hold water rights." "It seems to me," he concluded, that it "augurs well for the future of the project."[32]

With the battle over prior rights resolved, the Reclamation Service and the two water users' associations turned their attention to moving forward with other aspects of Hall's proposal. Farmers in both New Mexico and Texas were eager to participate in the project, and thus neither the Elephant Butte Water Users' Association nor the El Paso Valley Water Users' Association had any difficulty in obtaining pledges to repay the cost of building the

Rio Grande Project. In November 1905, Herbert Holt reported to Newell that New Mexico landowners had committed 124,304 acres to the Elephant Butte Water Users' Association—well over the organization's quota of 110,000 acres. Simultaneously, Texans had pledged 59,000 acres. The Texas commitment, according to Hall, made the Rio Grande Project "feasible" as required by the 1905 law bringing the El Paso Valley under the provisions of the Reclamation Act, although the precise number of acres of Texas lands to be served still depended on how irrigable acreage in the El Paso Valley on both sides of the Rio Grande would be divided between the United States and Mexico under a future treaty.[33]

The successful membership campaign by the two water users' associations meant that further organizational steps for the Rio Grande Project could take place. One of these was to secure the project's water supply under New Mexico law. To do this, Benjamin Hall notified New Mexico's territorial irrigation engineer, David L. White, on January 23, 1906, that the Reclamation Service planned to appropriate 730,000 acre-feet of Rio Grande water per year to be stored at Elephant Butte Reservoir. Hall's 1906 appropriation was supplemented two years later by an application for all the remaining unappropriated waters of the Rio Grande.[34]

All that remained to formalize the relationship between the Reclamation Service and the water users was the contractual arrangement under which the Rio Grande Project would be built and its cost repaid to the reclamation fund. Although the water users had taken preliminary steps to create their associations in late 1904, the time necessary to incorporate both groups, to secure pledges, and to negotiate details on the working plans with the Reclamation Service delayed the signing of a contract between the two water users' associations and the U.S. government for over a year. Ultimately, on June 27, 1906, an agreement was executed by representatives of the Elephant Butte Water Users' Association and the El Paso Valley Water Users' Association. The joint accord provided that only members of the two organizations would be eligible to receive Rio Grande Project waters and that liens on farmland would secure repayment of project costs. Reimbursements to the government were to be made under the terms of the 1902 Reclamation Act in ten installments, the first becoming due when water was delivered to the project's farms. The water users' associations were to guarantee and collect payments from individuals on the behalf of the U.S. government.[35]

The signing of the contract established a working partnership between the federal government and those who would benefit from the Rio Grande

Project. This was an alliance in which power flowed two ways—with the federal government's future actions in relation to the Rio Grande Project decidedly shaped by local concerns. In no sense was this a top-down monolithic venture directed solely from Washington, D.C. Rather, the contracts between the two water users' associations and the U.S. government allowed the Reclamation Service to begin work on the Rio Grande Project, and the arrangement began to fulfill the interstate part of the local 1904 compromise. Yet while the Elephant Butte Water Users' Association had membership pledges far exceeding its estimated allotment of 110,000 acres within the Rio Grande Project, the determination of the final number of irrigable acres in Texas was still subject to the negotiation of a treaty with Mexico, an international accord that the Reclamation Service had simultaneously been working toward securing.

An International Apportionment

The 1906 Treaty with Mexico

The formalization of the New Mexico and Texas water users' relations with the U.S. government and the extension of the Reclamation Act to the El Paso Valley had implemented part of the 1904 National Irrigation Congress compromise. These actions had established that the Reclamation Service would apportion the river among American irrigators in the Mesilla and El Paso valleys based on Benjamin Hall's estimates of irrigable acreage and that the water users would pay for the construction of the distribution system within the Rio Grande Project. Moreover, the establishment of contractual relations between the water users' groups and the Reclamation Service guaranteed that authority over the Rio Grande Project would be decentralized, with power spread among the government, the water associations' leaderships, and the many individuals who would benefit from the construction of the Rio Grande Project. In short, while the project would be centrally planned and supervised by the U.S. government's engineers, the contracts ensured that a decision-making process comparable to federalism would exist to handle the day-to-day details in allocating Rio Grande water—a procedure that partly satisfied western desires for autonomy in water matters and partly corresponded with U.S. government aspirations for federal authority over rivers in the arid part of the country.

While the contracts moved the U.S. part of the 1904 compromise closer to implementation, the international issue of providing dependable water supplies to Mexico—which had raised the apportionment question in the first place—was still unsettled. Without a resolution of this problem, water deliveries to American farmers in the El Paso Valley would remain insecure and subject to Mexico's diversions. This, in turn, would affect the extent and success of that part of the Rio Grande Project to be built below El Paso on the Texas side of the river. To carry out the international aspects of the 1904 compromise, Reclamation Service officials began to encourage other parts of the executive branch of the government to negotiate a treaty guaranteeing a fixed amount of water to Mexico. Such planning for the international aspect of the 1904 compromise echoed contemporaneous efforts to coordinate western resource planning in other branches of the federal government.[1]

The Reclamation Service also urged Congress to appropriate money to cover Mexico's proportionate cost of Elephant Butte Dam. Because Hall's estimate of serving 50,000 irrigable acres below El Paso had not been assigned specifically to either Mexico or Texas but covered both sides of the El Paso Valley, the satisfaction of Mexico's water claims would simultaneously define the U.S. allotment for the Rio Grande Project in Texas. With much at stake for American water users in the El Paso Valley, it is not surprising, therefore, that Texas's congressional delegation played a prominent a role in securing the federal funds and in ratifying a treaty with Mexico.

The question of Mexican claims to Rio Grande waters had not been ignored when the congressional debate over broadening the 1902 Reclamation Act to cover the El Paso Valley had taken place. On several occasions, there had been attempts to incorporate methods in that legislation to establish Mexico's quota of the river's supplies—in effect, legislating a treaty with a foreign power. This objective, however, met considerable resistance in Congress because including even a part of Texas under the terms of the Reclamation Act was extremely controversial owing to the state's lack of public federal lands to support the reclamation fund. Congressional backers of the 1904 compromise quickly realized, as a result, that complicating the matter by providing "American" water to another country would have spelled defeat for any bill extending the geographic range of the Reclamation Act within the United States. For these practical and political reasons, the measure bringing the Texas part of the El Paso Valley under the provisions of the Reclamation Act did not mention Mexico.[2]

Without specific congressional direction on what to do about Mexican demands for Rio Grande waters, the head of the Reclamation Service, Frederick Newell, faced a dilemma. To clarify the situation, Newell asked Secretary of the Interior Ethan A. Hitchcock, shortly after the Reclamation Act had been extended to the Texas part of the El Paso Valley, whether the Reclamation Service should plan to use all of the Rio Grande Project's water in the United States or whether some supplies should be reserved for possible assignment to Mexico. Newell pointed out that he needed this information to estimate the project's total costs, and he suggested that to find an answer, a conference with the State Department ought to be called. Such a meeting also was necessary, Newell believed, because the U.S. government was involved in a similar international apportionment dispute over the Milk River between the state of Montana and Alberta, Canada.[3] As with the Rio Grande, the Reclamation Service was making plans for a major irrigation project on the Milk River, and actions with regard to either river might influence policies affecting the other.

The Milk River situation stemmed from railroad baron James J. Hill's interest in irrigating northern Montana. Hill, who controlled the Great Northern and Northern Pacific railroads, understood that with adequate irrigation, lands near his rail lines would become extremely valuable. The Northern Pacific by itself held more than 13 million acres in Montana, a large block of which lay in the Milk River watershed. Hill believed that by damming the outlet of St. Mary Lake and diverting that water into the north fork of the Milk River, that stream would carry water at least 150 miles (over two-thirds of which was in Canada) and would serve about 250,000 acres near Chinook and Malta, Montana. The Geological Survey had investigated the Milk River's irrigation potential in 1900, and the stream had become one of the first projects contemplated by the Reclamation Service. Nevertheless, land speculation and the task of negotiating a treaty with Canada and Great Britain (the latter of which represented most Canadian interests in foreign affairs at that time) over the Milk River's waters and those of its tributaries had delayed the project for some time.[4]

The Milk River was particularly bothersome to federal authorities not only because of the difficulties between the United States and Mexico on the Rio Grande but also because the Reclamation Service had plans for the Colorado River, where transboundary issues affected both Mexico and southern California. That the three international rivers were linked was crystal clear to U.S. government officials as well as to observers in the press.

The *Washington Post*, for example, reported on April 15, 1905, that President Theodore Roosevelt had named a three-member commission "to deal with contentions relative to irrigation schemes on [the] Canadian and Mexican boundaries" involving the Milk River, the Rio Grande, and the Colorado. Those controversies, the *Post* acknowledged, stemmed in part from the near-total lack of legal information on how to address such conflicts, and as a result, the paper stated that the commission would have to "deal with some entirely new questions of international law relative to riparian rights." Because the Reclamation Service was intimately involved in all three situations, Roosevelt had chosen Newell as one of the three commissioners. (The other two commissioners were William L. Penfield, a solicitor for the U.S. State Department, and Marsden C. Burch, a special assistant attorney general who several years earlier had attempted unsuccessfully to broker a settlement with the Rio Grande Dam and Irrigation Company.)[5]

Throughout the spring of 1905, the Milk River problem increasingly concerned U.S. officials, particularly when the Canadian government insisted that international river negotiations cover other waterways shared by the United States and Canada. With that list including the Niagara River, streams in northern Minnesota, the Great Lakes, and the St. John River (which flowed from Maine into New Brunswick), talks between Canadian and U.S. authorities became exceedingly difficult.[6] The Milk River, however, remained the largest point of contention between the two countries, especially as the Reclamation Service moved forward with its plans for the Milk River Project on the U.S. side of the border. The *Manitoba Free Press* charged that American water planners wanted "the whole stream," and the Canadian paper warned that the Reclamation Service's proposal would "have the effect of diverting this stream from Dominion territory."[7] The result, the *Free Press* suggested ominously, might be that Canadians would have to retaliate and redirect all the Milk River's tributaries to stay on the Alberta side of the international boundary.[8]

In response, the *Great Falls (MT) Tribune*—hardly a disinterested observer—attempted to cool the heated tempers. Claiming that everyone on both sides of the border might benefit by adhering to known legal principles, the *Tribune* suggested that by applying the tenet of riparian rights, all water users in both countries would be treated fairly.[9] Nevertheless, riparianism required that water could only be used by landowners adjacent to a river, and even then, the flow had to be returned to that stream largely undisturbed for use by downstream riparian claimants. Although not many west-

erners knew the details of water law (particularly as undefined as that subject remained at the time), ranchers and farmers fully understood that irrigation was a consumptive use of water, one that would diminish useable
flows. Even among those who were up to date on water law theory, events
on the Rio Grande had amply illustrated over the previous decade that no
one knew whether any existing water law doctrine applied across international boundaries.

By the end of May 1905, the Milk River dispute had become so con-
tentious that negotiations had ground to a halt as the Americans and Canadians argued the fine points of international law and whether other streams
would be included in the talks.[10] Nevertheless, water matters on the southern boundary of the United States continued to move forward. Unlike the
Milk River and potential transboundary irrigation uses of that stream, the
Rio Grande had the advantage of having had the 1904 National Irrigation
Congress consider how best to allocate that river's flows between irrigators
in southern New Mexico and around El Paso and Juárez. With the exact
allocations between water users in Texas and Mexico remaining uncertain,
Newell cautioned that the United States should be wary of creating precedents on how such diplomatic problems were handled. In light of the parallel Milk River problem, Newell therefore believed that the State
Department ought to be consulted regarding the Rio Grande Project and
whether Mexico should be included in the Reclamation Service's planning.
Ignoring the firm commitment made to Mexico by the American delegates
to the 1904 National Irrigation Congress, Newell added that if Mexican
demands were to be considered at all, they ought to be acted upon as quickly
as possible so as not to delay construction of Elephant Butte Dam and the
Rio Grande Project.[11]

Newell's query led to several high-level conferences among officials of
the Departments of Interior, Justice, and State, and these meetings resulted
in the conclusion that the decades-old Rio Grande conflict with Mexico
had to be resolved. Yet how much Rio Grande water Mexico should receive
remained uncertain, and Newell was directed to provide a preliminary version of a treaty covering this issue. Newell then turned to Reclamation Service legal counsel Morris Bien to outline the features of a possible agreement
with Mexico.[12]

Born in New York in 1859, Bien had graduated from the University of
California in 1879 with a degree in civil engineering. Further education
had earned him a law degree in 1895 from Columbian University (today

known as George Washington University) and a master's degree in law the following year from National University Law School (now also a part of George Washington University). Prior to studying law, Bien had worked as a topographer for the U.S. Geological Survey, and during his law school years, he had been employed by the General Land Office. There, his duties included analyzing rights-of-way requests for irrigation ventures in the American West. Following the creation of the Reclamation Service in 1902, he moved to that agency to take charge of land and water legal matters. In addition, he reported on rights-of-way and irrigation legislation for the Department of the Interior until his retirement in 1924.[13]

Bien was a logical choice to carry out Newell's request for a possible treaty allocating some Rio Grande flows to Mexico. Not only did Bien have legal training and a background in land and water issues, but at about the same time that the 1904 National Irrigation Congress had reached its compromise on allocating Rio Grande flows, Bien had started drafting a model water code for use within the United States. Most western states and territories at the time had no record of existing diversions, no consistent methods of recording new water rights claims, no adequate means of supervising the distribution of water, and no simple ways to adjudicate water disputes. With the Reclamation Service embarking on the construction of many irrigation systems in different states and territories, to facilitate such endeavors, Bien had been directed to provide a template or standardized form for western water laws.[14] Bien therefore seemed especially well qualified to draft a treaty with Mexico over an international allocation of the Rio Grande's flows.

In response to Newell's request, Bien addressed what he thought would be the most controversial aspects of any treaty providing water to Mexico. Noting that according to the 1895 opinion offered by Attorney General Judson Harmon, the United States had no legal obligation to satisfy Mexico's claims to Rio Grande waters, Bien nonetheless recommended that future international harmony might make granting water to Mexico worthwhile. Bien added that if the water were delivered to Mexico without charge, this might even promote good public relations. Bien explained in a draft of a letter to the secretary of the interior that "the United States might, therefore, be willing to permit a supply of water to become available for the irrigation of lands within the limits of Mexico upon the same basis as such water is furnished to its own citizens." "Such a course," Bien suggested, "would doubtless meet all considerations of business equity, as conditions have gradually arisen where [the United States'] own citizens [below El Paso] have been deprived of water as well as those of a foreign country, and it hardly would be expected that the Government would be more generous to foreigners than to its own people. In order, however, to exemplify its good will towards a neighbor, the Government might be justified in going still further and appropriating a sufficient sum of money to pay the proportional cost of the water delivered to the lands in Mexico." Bien concluded that such an approach was consistent with the compromise reached at the 1904 National Irrigation Congress, which had endorsed the delivery of free water to Mexico.[15]

While government officials considered how to handle Mexican water claims, residents throughout the Rio Grande valley demonstrated that they still intended to play an important role in Rio Grande water issues. For example, taking matters into his own hands to see that the full 1904 compromise was implemented quickly, Hughes D. Slater—the editor of the *El Paso Herald*—campaigned tirelessly for a treaty with Mexico. Even before Newell had been directed to draft an international accord, Slater, whose views carried considerable weight in the El Paso area,[16] mailed to Newell ideas for negotiations with Mexico. Slater also offered to help with the international talks. Newell, however, replied that for the time being the Reclamation Service assumed that the Rio Grande Project would be built without any water going to Mexico.[17]

Newell's reply did not dampen Slater's enthusiasm for a treaty with Mexico, both to satisfy Mexican claims and to protect American interests in Texas (and, presumably, American interests on the Mexican side of the international border in the Juárez area). Continuing to advocate the treaty idea among Reclamation Service officials involved with the Rio Grande Project, Slater sent Bien a specific proposal for a negotiated settlement together with a draft of an explanatory cover letter to the secretary of the interior, both of which reaffirmed Rio Grande valley residents' commitment to the 1904 National Irrigation Congress compromise. Slater's cover letter to the secretary of the interior traced the history of the Rio Grande conflict between the United States and Mexico and noted Attorney General Harmon's opinion that the United States had no obligation to provide any water to its southern neighbor. Nonetheless, like many Texans who had supported the international dam at El Paso, Slater thought that "in the interest of 'comity' or neighborly good will" the United States should concede something to Mexico. Slater proposed that the United States provide Mexico with water at about two and a half acre-feet per year for 22,000 acres—his own estimate of formerly irrigated Mexican lands denied water by upstream American diversions— and he stated that he believed the people of New Mexico and Texas supported such an international apportionment. The total resulting annual obligation of 55,000 acre-feet, Slater explained to Bien, should be delivered free of charge to compensate for Mexican damages, a concept endorsed by the irrigation congress committee of fifteen that had agreed to the 1904 compromise.[18] (The principle of the United States supplying water to Mexico for existing acreage and doing so without cost was subsequently used as the foundation for talks with Mexico leading to a 1944 treaty that addressed allocating supplies along the entire Rio Grande all the way to the Gulf of Mexico, as well as on the Colorado and Tijuana rivers. American negotiators of this later international accord pointedly referred to the earlier Rio Grande treaty as a precedent for how to deal with Mexico.)[19]

Slater recognized that it might be politically unacceptable to provide water without cost to Mexico while American farmers would have to pay for their supplies. Nevertheless, he recommended that if Mexicans were required to contribute to the expense of delivering their water, they should pay no more than their proportionate share of building Elephant Butte Dam and the Rio Grande Project. To determine this amount, Slater suggested multiplying $40—Hall's estimate of the Rio Grande Project's per-acre expense—times the estimated 22,000 irrigable acres in Mexico, thus creating a total bill to Mexico of $880,000. This amount, Slater believed, should be paid in gold by Mexico in one lump sum to avoid the need to collect foreign payments once the Rio Grande Project was opened.[20]

As to other terms of the treaty, Slater proposed that Mexico's water be delivered in the bed of the Rio Grande at the head of the Mexican Acequia Madre and that the diversion point for that canal be established permanently downstream from the intake of El Paso's main irrigating ditch, the Franklin Canal, to avoid any American disputes with Mexican ditch tenders. Aside from the diversion dams for the Acequia Madre and the Franklin Canal, no other dams would be allowed on the river between El Paso and Fort Quitman, Texas—generally considered the point where the upper Rio Grande's flow was fully depleted. With these terms, Slater was certain that all the United States' obligations to Mexico would be fulfilled, and Mexico, therefore, would waive all claims to damages or more water.[21]

Bien shared Slater's proposal with the architect of the 1904 accord, Benjamin Hall, who heartily approved the plan. With Hall's endorsement,

Slater became an unofficial ambassador to Mexico. Meeting with a "Mr. B."—in all likelihood, Jacobo Blanco, Mexico's member of the International (Water) Boundary Commission and one of the fifteen committee members at the 1904 National Irrigation Congress who had accepted Hall's compromise proposal—Slater explained that he personally preferred to provide water to Mexico without charge, as the irrigation congress had endorsed, but Reclamation Service officials thought it would be more appropriate for Mexico to pay for its share of building Elephant Butte Dam. Blanco's response was that while the draft treaty was "in substantial accord with the agreement reached at the irrigation congress," the proposition that Mexico pay for its allotment of Rio Grande waters was entirely new. Blanco warned that the Mexican government would never agree to such terms.[22]

Blanco's other principal objection to the proposed treaty was that he believed that the amount of water suggested as Mexico's share was too small (a claim later echoed by Mexican authorities in the negotiations leading to the 1944 treaty). Citing the resolutions passed by the irrigation congress the previous fall, Blanco argued that the meeting's delegates had agreed that a formal survey of previously irrigated Mexican lands should be undertaken to determine Mexico's apportionment of Rio Grande waters. Slater countered, however, that such a study would be both time-consuming and costly, and he suggested that Mexico accept instead the conclusions on irrigable acreage reached in 1896 by the International (Water) Boundary Commission—on which Jacobo Blanco had sat. The commission's report, Slater pointed out, had determined that Mexican canals in the Juárez area had had a combined capacity of three hundred cubic feet per second and that the irrigation season had lasted about a hundred days each year before American diversions had become a problem. Slater noted that by converting the cubic feet per second to a daily acre-foot basis and then multiplying by the hundred days, the International (Water) Boundary Commission's estimate yielded about 59,400 acre-feet annually, a figure Slater thought Blanco could hardly reject, given his role in reaching the 1896 conclusions.[23]

Discussions continued, and based on Slater's diplomatic efforts, on June 3, 1905, Hall sent Newell a revised draft of the treaty for consideration and approval by the Washington Reclamation Service office.[24] The new version rounded off the International (Water) Boundary Commission's estimate of 59,400 acre-feet for Mexico's annual Rio Grande water uses, calling for the United States to build Elephant Butte Dam and to provide to Mexico in the bed of the river 60,000 acre-feet of water per year. (Delivery in the river's bed left maintenance of the Rio Grande's channel to the Acequia Madre a responsibility of Mexican authorities.) Mexico's daily allotment was to be in proportion to supplies for the U.S. side of the El Paso Valley, except in case of drought, when both countries would share equally in reductions (a concept later used in negotiating the Colorado River part of the 1944 treaty). Mexico's water would be free of charge, with the United States paying the full cost of storage and delivery. The treaty draft also stipulated that the agreement was not a recognition of the legitimacy of Mexico's damage claims against the United States, and in exchange for the guaranteed water supplies, Mexico would waive all rights to other Rio Grande waters above Fort Quitman, Texas (again, also a feature of the 1944 treaty in relation to the Colorado River).[25]

Newell submitted the treaty proposal to Secretary of the Interior Ethan Hitchcock in October 1905. Hitchcock then forwarded it with his approval to Secretary of State Elihu Root, who sent it on to the Mexican ambassador to the United States, Joaquin D. Casasus. In late March 1906, Casasus responded with Mexico's requests for changes in the treaty. Demanding that Mexico's annual allotment of Rio Grande waters be increased from 60,000 to 75,000 acre-feet, Casasus also wanted the water delivered to the mouth of the Acequia Madre and not simply provided in the river's bed, thereby making the United States responsible for channel maintenance. Furthermore, Casasus asked that Mexico be guaranteed half of any water flowing in the river from dam overflows, excess releases, or storm runoff between Juárez and Fort Quitman.[26]

The Reclamation Service was unwilling to accept any of Mexico's alterations to the treaty. Government officials thought the 60,000 acre-foot figure was adequate because that amount had been reached by the International (Water) Boundary Commission in 1896 as a fair estimate of Mexico's needs. Also, based on Slater's knowledge of local opinions, the figure was acceptable to American water users in southern New Mexico and around El Paso. In addition, Reclamation Service leaders believed that for the United States to ensure delivery of Mexico's water to the mouth of the Acequia Madre would impose maintenance responsibilities on the United States for the Mexican canal's headgate, which, because of river channel changes, frequently had to be adjusted. Finally, the Reclamation Service contended that granting Mexico a right to the small and irregular flow of Rio Grande water between Juárez and Fort Quitman would seriously complicate future relations between the U.S. and Mexican sides of the El Paso

Valley. Thus, the Reclamation Service steadfastly maintained that no alterations in the treaty should be allowed.[27]

In light of the fact that the United States was upstream and therefore could negotiate from a position of strength in the vacuum that existed in international law on such matters, there was little reason to expect that the Mexican government would try to force changes in the proposed treaty. Nonetheless, well before Mexico had made its formal reply to the draft in March 1906, Texans had started to press Mexico to accept the U.S. version of the treaty. As early as January of that year, while Mexico was still considering the wording submitted to Ambassador Casasus, Congressman William Smith wrote to El Paso water lawyer Richard Burges urging him to encourage "those at Jaurez [sic] who are interested [to] bring some influence to bear upon the authorities at the City of Mexico to expedite action by them."[28]

Even after Mexico had replied to the U.S. treaty proposal, Texans continued to be active in opposing any changes. Once Casasus had responded with Mexico's demands, Congressman Albert Burleson, who had been laboring behind the scenes in Washington to garner congressional support for the treaty, expressed his distress to both the State Department and the Department of the Interior over Mexico's insistence on receiving 75,000 acre-feet each year. Burleson also advised Burges that he would oppose any such modifications to the treaty in Congress, because he was well aware that any additional water that went to Mexico would be at Texas's expense.[29]

With the treaty still not accepted by Mexico by mid-May 1906, Burleson became exasperated. Like many other Texans, he resented the fact that the determination of Texas's share of Rio Grande waters hinged on the completion of the treaty with Mexico. Burleson's displeasure with the Mexican demands was all the more understandable because to achieve the 1904 National Irrigation Congress compromise, Texas's water users had already agreed not to insist on recognition of their Rio Grande rights as being senior to those in New Mexico. Realizing that without the treaty, Texas's share of the Rio Grande's flows would remain entangled in endless disputes with Mexico while New Mexico would benefit to the fullest extent possible by the construction of Elephant Butte Dam, Burleson was galled by the Mexican position. He complained to Burges, "I have grown weary in my efforts to get this treaty into shape for submission to the Senate." Testily, Burleson added, "I have been working upon this general scheme for seven years, and I did think when the treaty was proposed by this government to Mexico, offering to give the people of Juarez, who own the land on that side of the river, 60,000 acre-feet per annum, that they would jump at the opportunity to accept the offer; and this obstacle, which has been thrown in the way by the Mexican government asking for more [water], is very provoking to me, and if it is insisted upon it means that the treaty will not be further pressed and that the Senate of the United States will not even be given the opportunity to pass upon it."[30]

The Texas stance was soon conveyed to Mexican officials, who fully understood that their downstream status made further discussions futile. In late May 1906, the Mexican government backed down, and Ambassador Casasus signed a treaty embodying essentially the same features as the Reclamation Service's original proposal.[31]

Texans, after having played a pronounced role in drafting the treaty and in securing its acceptance by Mexico, then turned their attention to having it ratified by the U.S. Senate. Texas's efforts in this regard were important to stop a fledgling effort by Colorado's Rio Grande water users to have the treaty defeated on Capitol Hill. Ever since 1896, Colorado water users had chafed under the so-called Rio Grande embargo—the restriction that had been imposed by Secretary of the Interior David R. Francis to block the Rio Grande Dam and Irrigation Company's reclamation plans. The embargo had prevented new dams or diversions anywhere on the river above El Paso, and Coloradans recognized that the approval of the treaty with Mexico would forever remove the possibility of putting Mexico's 60,000 acre-feet to use in their state. As a result, Colorado's congressional leaders had started a drive to defeat ratification of any Rio Grande treaty with Mexico. To thwart the Colorado insurrection, Burges advised Congressman Burleson that the treaty's supporters in El Paso were "ready to take any steps in our power to further the early ratification of the treaty." Such efforts by El Pasoans and Burleson's tireless endeavors in Washington were successful. The U.S. Senate ratified the treaty on June 26, 1906, and President Theodore Roosevelt officially approved it on January 16, 1907.[32]

The treaty between the United States and Mexico, like the 1905 law extending the Reclamation Act to the El Paso Valley, was another formal step in implementing the 1904 National Irrigation Congress compromise. The actual construction of Elephant Butte Dam, however, remained to be accomplished. The biggest single impediment to beginning work was obtaining an appropriation from Congress. While in theory the reclamation fund was to be utilized to pay for Elephant Butte Dam and the Rio Grande

Project, in reality the Reclamation Service had vastly overcommitted itself to projects throughout the West, substantially draining the agency's resources. For example, money earmarked for the Hondo Project—an effort to revitalize a failing private irrigation system on a tributary of the Pecos River—had taken most of the Reclamation Service's budget for New Mexico.[33] Moreover, public land sales, which were supposed to provide the initial operating revenue for the reclamation fund, were not yielding enough money to fulfill all the Reclamation Service's obligations. Under these circumstances, only a week after the Rio Grande accord had been reached at the 1904 National Irrigation Congress, the Reclamation Service had recognized that financing Elephant Butte Dam from the reclamation fund would be close to impossible.[34] Arthur Davis explained the situation to Benjamin Hall on February 28, 1905—only three days after the Reclamation Act had been extended to the U.S. side of the El Paso Valley. "There is not sufficient money now and cannot be for several years to carry out this [Rio Grande] project," Davis lamented. "The funds on hand," he continued, "and in prospect for reclamation purposes are all allotted for about three years to come for projects which the service is now committed." Worse still, Davis added that after that date, the return of money that might become available from irrigated parcels as well as from the sale of other lands would be insufficient for a project as large as Elephant Butte Dam. Thus, Davis believed that it was unlikely that contracts for the main dam could be signed within the following five to six years.[35]

These were circumstances that Rio Grande water users in New Mexico and Texas found difficult to accept after the arduous work in reaching the compromise at the 1904 National Irrigation Congress and after securing passage of the 1905 law extending the Reclamation Act to the El Paso Valley. With the completion of the 1906 treaty with Mexico, desperate Rio Grande valley residents turned to Congress for a special appropriation to build Elephant Butte Dam. The rationale for this funding, from the point of view of water users in New Mexico and Texas, was that Americans should not have to pay for the cost of providing Mexico with the treaty-guaranteed 60,000 acre-feet of water per year. Once again taking a leading role, the Texas congressional delegation worked diligently to acquire the appropriation, and their efforts focused mostly on satisfying Mexico—a strategy encouraged by the Reclamation Service.

The initial request to Congress was for $1,000,000, a figure that was not wholly arbitrary, although it certainly gave that appearance. The amount derived from Reclamation Service estimates of the ratio that Mexico's 60,000 acre-feet per year bore to Elephant Butte Reservoir's total annual water supply. With somewhat convoluted reasoning, Hall explained to Newell how the $1,000,000 figure had been reached. "We expect to use 600,000 acre-feet per annum for irrigation," Hall observed. "It will require one-seventh of that amount turned loose from the reservoir to make 60,000 acre-feet after losing 30% in transit from the Engle [Elephant Butte] Dam to the head of the Mexican Ditch. One seventh of 600,000 is 85,714, 30% loss from which is 25,714. After making the subtraction we have only 60,000 acre-feet, the amount that we expect to deliver to Mexico. As the entire project will cost $7,000,000 and the Mexican treaty will require one-seventh of the water turned loose from the reservoir, at least $1,000,000 should be appropriated for that purpose."[36]

While this rationalization ignored the fact that the $1,000,000 amount had been determined from just one year's water use and that Elephant Butte Dam would certainly supply Mexico with water until the reservoir filled with silt decades in the future, Hall nevertheless noted that the Mexican ambassador wanted to meet with Reclamation Service officials to discuss having the agency support the appropriation in Congress. For his part, Newell believed that having the Reclamation Service do anything to back the funding effort would be impractical. Instead, he told Hall that the matter should be pressed by the people of Texas through their senators and representatives. "Unless they take the initiative," Newell stated categorically, "it is impossible to do anything."[37]

Newell may have found it impractical to support the congressional appropriation in public, but he was more than willing to work behind the scenes to obtain the money. In a strongly worded letter to Congressman Burleson, Newell affirmed that building the Rio Grande Project was out of the question until Congress approved the $1,000,000 grant. Newell did not merely express his certainty that construction could not go forward without the funds, however; he added a draft of legislation necessary to secure the money—wording that ultimately turned out to be almost identical to the final form of the appropriation act providing the $1,000,000 to build Elephant Butte Dam.[38] While Newell lobbied on Capitol Hill, Davis pressed the cause on the State Department, explaining that the $1,000,000 was for the cost of carrying out the provisions of the 1906 treaty. In addition to the money to build the dam, Davis proposed that Congress also should provide an allotment each year to cover Mexico's share of maintenance costs, and he testified in support of the funding before the House Committee on Appropriations.[39]

Even Nathan Boyd beseeched Congress to make the financial allotment, albeit for rather unusual reasons. Boyd, whose Rio Grande Dam and Irrigation Company had just lost its third appeal to the New Mexico Territorial Supreme Court, believed that the 1906 treaty giving Mexico 60,000 acre-feet of water annually was a new scheme promoted by the backers of the old proposal for an international dam at El Paso, including Anson Mills and his associates. The way Boyd saw it, since the Mexican 60,000 acre-feet could be applied to lands with no maximum acreage restrictions comparable to the 160-acre limit imposed on Americans in Reclamation Service projects, the supporters of the international dam—who had large landholdings in Mexico near Juárez—would have a benefit not enjoyed by American farmers in Texas or New Mexico. This advantage, Boyd thought, stemmed from the facts that the Mexican water would be provided without charge (and paid for by Americans served by the Rio Grande Project) and that the size of the Mexican landholdings was unlimited, making the Mexican acreage held by the international dam sponsors more cost-efficient and much more valuable. Therefore, to thwart the enrichment of what he perceived to be his long-time adversaries, Boyd told Attorney General Henry Moody that the Rio Grande Dam and Irrigation Company would dismiss its pending third appeal to the U.S. Supreme Court if the secretary of the interior would recommend that Congress appropriate the $1,000,000 for Elephant Butte Dam and if the government would repay losses suffered by investors in his company.[40]

Not surprisingly, Boyd's offer was ignored in Washington, but after the intense lobbying by Reclamation Service officials, the State Department, the Mexican government, and American water users, Congress responded in early 1907 by adding to a general appropriations bill a paragraph authorizing $1,000,000 for Elephant Butte Dam.[41] Relieved that the money was finally available to begin construction of the facility, Congressman William Smith assured Richard Burges that El Paso's interests stood on solid ground.[42] The project could finally go forward to complete the fulfillment of the 1904 compromise.

CHAPTER 8

The Reclamation Service Begins Work

By early 1907, the groundwork for implementing the 1904 National Irrigation Congress compromise had been fully laid. Simultaneously, the evolution of the American legal system during the preceding decades had had a major impact in shaping the way in which the accord would be carried out. Originally chartered under nineteenth-century laws aimed at encouraging private economic growth in the American West, Nathan Boyd's Rio Grande Dam and Irrigation Company was facing the final denouement of the U.S. government's lawsuit to halt the firm's endeavors, and within two years, the U.S. Supreme Court would ultimately rule against the company's efforts to build a dam at Elephant Butte. Unlike early nineteenth-century court actions, which tended to reflect a paternalistic sense of the community's collective values, this suit was more typical of an emerging legal formalism that strove to perform a redistributive function in relation to wealth and power.[1] In the Mesilla and El Paso valleys, this meant removing private enterprise in water allocation along the river and replacing it with a partnership between the U.S. government and local interests. (Simultaneously, similar events were under way on the lower Colorado River.)[2]

Complementing the role of litigation in leading to a Rio Grande agreement, informal democratic legal action also had played a part in achieving a solution to the region's water problems. As one recent scholar has observed, democratic activities by organizations with no official legislative capacity frequently can have enormous impacts on constitutional deliberative bodies because of the influence the informal groups carry through their memberships.[3] This was certainly true in relation to the irrigation congress's approval of the 1904 Rio Grande compromise. Without that body's endorsement of the Reclamation Service's plan for Elephant Butte Dam and the Rio Grande Project, any early solution to the river's difficulties would have been unlikely. The weight of the irrigation congress's proceedings was further enhanced by the relatively undefined status of western water law, especially in relation to interstate and international streams. Without well-understood legal tenets on how to divide the waters of rivers that crossed state or national boundaries, the recommendations of the 1904 National Irrigation Congress carried greater import to national legislators and virtually invited them to become directly involved.

While informal democratic action by the irrigation congress had played a key role in bringing about the various elements in the 1904 Rio Grande apportionment, changes in the goals of formal legislation also had helped implement the accord through the 1905 law extending the Reclamation Act to the El Paso Valley, the 1906 treaty with Mexico, and the 1907 $1,000,000 appropriation to build Elephant Butte Dam. Once favoring private enterprise over government involvement, congressional bias had swung, by the early twentieth century, toward an adherence to the Progressive-era creed of scientific management and comprehensive planning through a partnership between government experts and local concerns.[4] This alliance formed the basis for the Reclamation Service's plan for Elephant Butte Dam and the interstate and international division of waters to be stored at the reservoir.

Although the legal system in relation to western water issues had evolved by early 1907 to a point at which it could contribute to a resolution of the problems concerning the division of the Rio Grande's waters, actual construction on Elephant Butte Dam and the Rio Grande Project presented a host of new questions. As building got under way, American water users immediately learned of the many factors that might influence the Rio Grande Project's ultimate dimensions. Although Mexico's quota of Rio Grande waters had been established by the 1906 treaty, the final distribution between Texas and New Mexico of the river's remaining flow was not yet determined. Because the ultimate allocation of the project's water to irrigators in New Mexico and Texas would have an impact on land values and on the proportionate construction costs to be repaid to the federal government, water users in both states played key roles in pressing the Reclamation Service to expand their respective parts of the project and to decrease acreage across the state line. Such competition for the economic conquest of the land was typical of growth in many parts of the American West,[5] and it had been one of the fundamental difficulties in preventing a Rio Grande water distribution agreement prior to 1904. The struggle for material gain by competing regions threatened to undermine the fragile irrigation congress compromise. Ultimately, only through an uneasy cooperation between water users and the Reclamation Service was a total collapse of the 1904 agreement avoided.

The interstate competition between New Mexico and El Paso water users encouraged widespread land speculation, a problem vastly compounded by the Reclamation Act's requirement that landholdings be 160 acres or smaller to receive federal water. This farm size restriction had been part of the political price to obtain support in Congress for the Reclamation Act. Many politicians feared that any federal subsidy for reclamation in the West would contribute to the growth of large farms, which would have an unfair competitive edge over small family farms in the East. Thus, limiting the acreage that could receive water supplies under the Reclamation Act's provisions would help block the formation of huge farms underwritten by government-provided water.[6]

Understandably, on many Reclamation Service projects throughout the West where existing farms were to receive water—including the Rio Grande—owners of large parcels did not want to sell their acreage in small units until water became available. This, of course, would make the land more valuable. Underscoring this belief, land prices skyrocketed on Reclamation Service projects during the first ten years after the Reclamation Act had been signed into law. For example, the average price for improved farmland on the first twenty-five Reclamation Service projects shot up nearly 800 percent between 1902 and 1913. This was precisely what sponsors of federal reclamation originally had opposed, not only because they were against profiteering but also because such dramatic surges in land values discouraged the settlement of small farm units. As early as 1901 and 1902, Frederick Newell had wanted the legislation that eventually became the Reclamation Act to require landowners who held large blocks of acreage to sell most of that land to obtain water supplies for the remainder. Shortly after the Reclamation Act had passed, federal officials still clung to the goal of seeing large private holdings broken up to receive reclamation project irrigation waters. As the secretary of the interior explained in 1905, "It is obviously not the intent of the reclamation act to irrigate at public expense large private holdings and increase the wealth of a small number of men unless the public receives an equivalent gain. The strongest argument for the law is, not that it adds to the wealth of the State, but that it builds the greatest number of homes and creates a community of owners of the soil who live on the land and derive their sustenance from it."[7] This idealistic vision was not shared by large landholders in the western states and territories, and the results in many places were stalemates and angry confrontations between U.S. officials and reclamation project landowners. The Rio Grande was no exception, and the competition between southern New Mexico and western Texas over the final dimensions of the Rio Grande Project encouraged the conflict over speculation between landowners and the Reclamation Service.

Land speculation was intimately tied to another issue that proved divisive as construction on the Rio Grande Project moved forward. That problem was whether hydroelectric power should be developed at Elephant Butte Dam and along major delivery canals. Irrigators generally favored generating power to help offset repayment obligations and to pay for more lands to be included within the respective parts of the final Rio Grande Project than Benjamin Hall had originally forecast. In addition, electricity was a relatively new energy source in the early twentieth century, with many urban areas beginning to switch from gas to electric lighting, both indoors and out. The first large hydroelectric power plant had gone into operation at Niagara Falls in New York in 1895, and in 1904, that facility was producing 20 percent of all the electricity used in the United States.[8] Nearly simultaneously, various electric appliances were becoming widely available through assembly-line production techniques pioneered by Henry Ford. Thus, the development of hydroelectric energy appeared to be the wave of the future; this was true along the Rio Grande and elsewhere in the American West, where multitudes of mountain streams created ample opportunities for power generation.

Irrigation promoters and others had enthused about the West's hydroelectric power possibilities as early as the 1880s, believing that this new energy source would benefit mining, transportation, and farming in addition to supplying urban areas. Eventually, hydroelectric power was generated on many Reclamation Service projects, with the largest facilities being constructed on the Salt River Project in Arizona and on the Minidoka Project in Idaho.[9] Yet many other projects also came to include the generation of electricity, leading ultimately to the Boulder Canyon Project on the Colorado River in the late 1920s. On the Rio Grande (as elsewhere), the debate over whether electricity should be generated complicated the land-speculation problem. Both issues were crucial in the Reclamation Service's final decision in how to apportion lands within the project (and hence, water) between farmers in New Mexico and Texas.

Speculation in Rio Grande valley land erupted shortly after the 1904 compromise had been reached, and the greed for increased real estate values demonstrated that the Reclamation Act's idealistic limitation of providing federal water only to farms of no more than 160 acres was almost meaningless in the face of rampant economic opportunism. At first, the speculation problem was worst in New Mexico's Mesilla Valley—in part because before the Reclamation Act was extended to the El Paso Valley in 1905, the Reclamation Service was not certain about the extent to which canals could be built in Texas. After the El Paso Valley was covered by the Reclamation Act, land speculation spiraled out of control in both New Mexico and Texas.

Business letterhead used by the Elephant Butte Realty Company vividly illustrated the focus on land sales and the role that the Rio Grande Project played in those transactions. A large elephant labeled "Uncle Sam" spouting water through its trunk onto a bounteous farm was at the top of this stationery, while in the background was a body of water identified as the Rio Grande held back by a huge structure labeled "Government Irrigation Dam." The entire scene was illuminated by a massive sun with beams of light radiating out in all directions. The stationery heading so clearly emphasized the speculative nature of land sales at the time that one Reclamation Service employee had forwarded the letterhead to Chief Engineer Frederick Newell with the caustic observation written on the back, "Mr. Newell: That you may see the New Mexico idea of the Rio Grande Project."[10]

The desire to gamble on increasing real estate values along the Rio Grande was widespread among all landowners, and large and small property holders alike sought to get rich from the government's largesse. That multitudes of farmers were seeking to cash in on their acreage can be seen from the Reclamation Service's noting in 1910 that the value of cultivated lands within the first unit of the Rio Grande Project (acreage served by the

Letterhead, Elephant Butte Realty Company, ca. 1908. Courtesy Bureau of Reclamation, National Archives Branch, Rocky Mountain Region, Denver.

Leasburg Diversion Dam) had skyrocketed from between $20 to $40 per acre to $100 to $300 per acre. Even raw land had climbed wildly in value during the same time, soaring from between $3 to $10 per acre to $20 to $40 per acre. According to a contemporaneous news account, such a dramatic increase in real estate values was a "great impetus to agricultural development," but the newspaper also reported that it had had a decidedly unfavorable impact on cultural diversity within the Rio Grande Project. The paper observed that because of the escalation of property values, "the majority of the land is now in the hands of [Anglo-]Americans . . . while previous to the advent of the reclamation service it was controlled by farmers of Mexican extraction."[11] With such sizeable increases in land values, speculation had become so uncontrollable within a few years of the start of construction on the Rio Grande Project that Reclamation Service head Frederick Newell unhappily observed that "the water users instead of working with us to solve present difficulties are devoting their energies to selling land."[12]

Driving part of the land-speculation problem was a debate over precisely where the Rio Grande Project's distributing canals would be located. Not merely involving real estate values, this controversy also centered on the possibility of developing hydroelectric energy from the venture—a goal highly compatible with the Progressive-era belief in comprehensive natural resource management. How waters from Elephant Butte Dam would be physically carried down the Rio Grande valley became an increasingly important concern as construction on the Rio Grande Project moved forward, and two competing proposals emerged—both touted by supporters as the most efficient and cost-effective methods to run the system. One called for a high-line canal to be built along mesa lands well above the river, with offshoots feeding major ditches below. Proposals for so-called high-line canals appeared on many reclamation projects throughout the West, essentially for the same reasons as on the Rio Grande. To proponents of the Rio Grande high-line canal, this distribution system would increase the irrigable area (and related land values) of the entire Rio Grande Project and would allow the generation of hydroelectric power from drops in elevation along the canal in addition to the electricity that could be created at Elephant Butte Dam. The electricity would provide opportunities for new economic enterprises, and income from energy sales could be used to offset Rio Grande Project construction charges. Moreover, advocates argued that the high-line canal would decrease the need for drainage ditches by eliminating seepage from the riverbed, which in some places was actually above surrounding valley lands because of past flooding and levee buildup. Because the high-line canal primarily would enlarge the irrigated acreage in New Mexico's part of the Rio Grande Project, to broaden the high-line canal's appeal, its backers asserted that it could easily deliver water to the city of El Paso—then a rapidly growing metropolis.

If a high-line canal were not built, the other option to convey Elephant Butte Reservoir waters to farmlands below, sometimes called the "low-line" canal proposal, was simply to use the Rio Grande's bed or a combination of the river and lower valley canals. Supporters of the lower system claimed that the high-line canal would be too costly to construct and that even hydroelectric power revenues would not offset the additional building expense. The most cost-efficient approach, they believed, was simply to use the riverbed. Low-line backers contended that there was no significant market for hydroelectric power that could be generated only when water was released from Elephant Butte Dam during the summer irrigation months. This was a sizeable problem in an era when there was no national or regional power grid to transfer energy to satisfy shifting seasonal demands. Low-line supporters also questioned whether the reservoir could store enough water to serve more Rio Grande Project lands than the Reclamation Service had projected in 1904 and still offer municipal supplies to El Paso.

One of the earliest advocates of the high-line canal was El Paso water lawyer Richard Burges. Together with a large group of other prominent individuals, Burges developed a plan in 1910 to use hydroelectric power generated at Elephant Butte Dam and at various locations along a high-line canal to operate an electric interurban railroad. The line would be built in the El Paso and Mesilla valleys. Undoubtedly motivated in part by the huge success Henry E. Huntington had achieved in establishing the Pacific Electric Railway as the largest interurban system in the nation—a streetcar network that served the entire Los Angeles basin and ran on power from hydroelectric generating plants in California's Sierra Nevada—Burges and his colleagues hoped to accomplish the same feat in the El Paso and Mesilla valleys. With regional boosters of the day frequently comparing the agricultural yields of the Rio Grande region to those of southern California, Burges and his collaborators sought to create another parallel in relation to transportation systems. Regardless of high hopes and considerable scheming, however, the joint interurban and hydroelectric energy plans failed to materialize, partly because Elephant Butte Dam was not completed until 1916, and then without power-generating facilities, owing to their cost. The publicity fostered by the interurban railroad idea, however, kept the high-line canal proposition—and the question of how Rio Grande waters would be divided between New Mexico and Texas—alive well after the interurban proposal had been shelved.[13] (Funding for hydroelectric generation at Elephant Butte Dam was not authorized until the mid-1930s, and the dam's power plant went into operation in 1940.)[14]

Even after the demise of the electric railroad venture, however, the high-line canal proposition remained appealing. Quickly coming to represent more than just an alternative water delivery system, the canal and its energy-creating components were seen by many of the area's residents as methods to bring the best aspects of a civilized society to the arid Mesilla and El Paso valleys. With uses for electrical energy proliferating and with increasing settlement in southern New Mexico and western Texas, champions of the high-line canal claimed that the hydroelectric energy the canal could produce was essential to the future prosperity of the region. Furthermore, proponents argued that the high-line canal could convey high-quality, inexpensive water to El Paso. This would permit that metropolis to continue its emergence as a regional economic hub and establish the city as a model of Progressive reform with well-watered public parks, adequate freshwater supplies, and a modern sewage system for all residents. Alfred Courchesne—an El Paso booster, who simultaneously was president of the El Paso Valley Water Users' Association, president of the El Paso Ice and

Refrigerator Company, a major real estate investor, and owner of a large rock quarry near the city—strongly supported the high-line canal as a civic enhancement to his city. Courchesne explained in 1912 to the Rio Grande Project's supervising engineer, Louis C. Hill, that the high-line canal would be "of the greatest value and importance to the development of the valley, this city [El Paso] and all sections of the country concerned."[15]

Frederick Newell was not as convinced of the high-line's advantages as were the inhabitants of southern New Mexico and western Texas, and as a result, he ordered that the Reclamation Service survey a low-line route. Newell's decision caused great consternation in the area. Fearing that his directive was a forerunner to actual low-line construction and the elimination of the high-line canal possibility, New Mexicans and Texans wired Congressman William Smith, urging him to convince Newell to rescind the order for the low-line study. Smith subsequently met with Newell, who assured him that the survey was merely intended to obtain enough information to compare the two canal options intelligently. In addition, Newell suggested that if local citizens felt so strongly about the need for the high-line canal, they should formally request that it be built through their representative organizations, the El Paso Valley Water Users' Association and the Elephant Butte Water Users' Association. Both groups dutifully passed resolutions to that effect on November 7, 1912; reacting to the growing public pressure, Newell began to secure options for the high-line canal's right-of-way.[16]

As a close adherent to Progressive-era ideology and one of the principal practitioners of that philosophy in the U.S. government, Newell also appointed a board of engineers to consider how a high-line canal might be constructed. Newell's action not only reflected his desire for detailed scientific analysis of the high-line idea but also was part of a broader U.S. government attempt to be more responsive to concerns voiced by settlers on many Reclamation Service projects throughout the West. By the end of the first decade of the twentieth century, the Reclamation Service had undertaken far more projects throughout the West than it could adequately carry out at one time, and a result was the growing view that the agency was arbitrary and high-handed. Moreover, complaints abounded on many projects that construction costs were soaring well beyond original estimates, and the passage of the Warren Act in 1911—which permitted the Reclamation Service to sell surplus project water to nonproject users—prompted criticism that the agency was drifting too far from its original goals of creating and serving new small family farms. All of these factors (and many others) caused Franklin K. Lane—who became secretary of the interior in early 1913—to initiate hearings for representatives of Reclamation Service projects from all over the West. The hearings and other discontent eventually led Congress to pass the Reclamation Extension Act of 1914, which instituted a multitude of reforms aimed at greater oversight of all Reclamation Service projects.[17]

In the meantime, however, Newell's authorization of a board of engineers to study a possible high-line canal for the Rio Grande Project was one manifestation of the irrigation concerns in the southern New Mexico and western Texas region. The board met in late March 1913. Theorizing that such a canal could head at a diversion dam to be built on the Rio Grande below Elephant Butte at Leasburg, New Mexico, the engineers hypothesized that the canal would then run down the east side of the Mesilla Valley to approximately ten miles southeast of Las Cruces, where there would be a significant drop in elevation and penstocks to generate hydroelectric power. Some of the water would be utilized in that area for crops, and the balance would be carried under the Rio Grande's channel by siphon for irrigation on the west side of the valley. Water not used there would continue in a canal to a generating plant near Montoya, Texas (about ten miles above El Paso), where more electricity would be generated. The water then would be released into the Rio Grande channel for use in the El Paso–Juárez area. The result of this system would be the creation of 15,000 horsepower on the high-line canal and another 5,000 to 10,000 horsepower at Elephant Butte Dam. Although electricity would be available only during the irrigation season, the Reclamation Service engineers conjectured that it could be used in El Paso, in Las Cruces, in nearby mining areas, and for groundwater pumping. The board of engineers cautioned, however, that the market for seasonal hydroelectric power was unknown, and they continued their studies in preparation for a final report.[18]

Amid growing public clamor for the high-line canal, the board of engineers reached its final conclusions in December 1913—findings that were decidedly unfavorable. The engineers' report observed that a high-line canal would seriously alter the Rio Grande's natural regimen and would cause the river to remain partly or completely dry for "probably periods of several years." This would allow phreatophytes (plants with deep roots that obtain their water supplies from the water table or the layer of soil just above it) to accumulate in the riverbed. Phreatophytes, the engineers realized, flourished in streambeds when periodic heavy floods did not wash them away, and sandbars were created as the plants trapped sediment in light flows. The engineers predicted that the outcome of building the high-line canal, therefore, would be a river channel with greatly diminished capacity. This situation, in turn, would cause severe flooding and damage to irrigation works on those occasions when Elephant Butte Dam could not control the river's entire flow. The board of engineers thus deemed "it essential to allow sufficient irrigation water to pass down the river channel to keep a definite course open and ready for the carriage of floods when they occur." To the board, the obvious way to do this was to use the river to carry Rio Grande Project waters instead of building a high-line canal. As to the issue of hydroelectric energy generation, the board concluded that the "necessity of using irrigation water for the above purpose [keeping the channel clear] renders development of power from irrigation canals in the Mesilla Valley impracticable."[19]

Despite the Reclamation Service's adverse findings, residents of the Mesilla and El Paso valleys remained unconvinced. Within three months, proposals to build a high-line canal again were raised by an organization called the Anthony High Line Association. Based in Anthony (a small town that straddled the Texas–New Mexico state line), the association advanced fresh reasons for building the high-line canal. Instead of stressing the multiple-use scientific efficiency of a system that would generate power and provide irrigation service and water supplies to El Paso city residents, the Anthony High Line Association appealed directly to New Mexico's desire to obtain the largest acreage possible within the Rio Grande Project and hence to New Mexico's drive to conquer the arid environment at the expense of its downstream neighbors.[20]

In mid-March 1914, the Anthony High Line Association asked Rio Grande Project manager L. M. Lawson to estimate both the cost and the increased acreage that would result from building a high-line canal. Lawson, however, referred the request to the Elephant Butte Water Users' Association, since any additional project lands in New Mexico would have to be represented by that organization. The Elephant Butte Water Users' Association already was predisposed to reopen the high-line canal discussion because the Anthony High Line Association played on the same concerns that had made the struggle over where to build a Rio Grande dam a stalemate prior to 1904—the fear that New Mexico water users would take a back seat to the El Paso Valley in any interstate apportionment of the Rio

Grande. Exploiting this deep-seated worry, the Anthony group cleverly had suggested that without a high-line canal, New Mexico irrigators would never obtain water for the full 110,000 acres allotted to them in the Reclamation Service's 1904 estimates. With this seed of doubt effectively planted, the Elephant Butte Water Users' Association passed resolutions in April and May 1914 insisting that the Rio Grande Project serve the full New Mexico acreage—if necessary, by means of a high-line canal.[21]

This stand by the New Mexico water users posed a particularly thorny question for the Reclamation Service: a dilemma that underscored the administrative difficulties that the Reclamation Act had created by establishing a federally sponsored irrigation program that operated under state water laws and required the cooperation of those whom it served in order to secure construction cost repayments. These problems were not unique to the Rio Grande Project and complicated Reclamation Service ventures throughout the West, but the Elephant Butte Water Users' Association resolutions brought to a head the critical question, Who was to have the final say in determining irrigable acreage for the Rio Grande Project?

The 1904 compromise had been based on the understanding by everyone at the national irrigation congress that the Reclamation Service would set the final interstate allocation based on the agency's scientific measurements and expert surveys. Congress's 1905 law authorizing a Rio Grande apportionment—based on the 1904 agreement—was predicated on the same expectation. The New Mexico position, however, challenged this basic premise, and it worried Reclamation Service officials. If the water users were to be allowed to compel the government to irrigate 110,000 acres in New Mexico—even if this proved to be impracticable—repayment obligations might become impossible because of both increased construction costs and continued land speculation. Yet if the Reclamation Service did not irrigate as many acres in one part of the project as originally proposed, the agency's credibility might suffer, or worse still, New Mexico water users might back out of the project altogether, since their agreement to support the Reclamation Service's plan had been based on estimates underlying the 1904 compromise. To find a solution, Lawson, assisted by the Reclamation Service's supervising engineer, Frank W. Hanna, studied the problem in depth.

Reporting to the Reclamation Service on July 25, 1914, Lawson and Hanna affirmed that the 110,000 acres demanded by the Elephant Butte Water Users' Association was indeed "originally assumed to be watered in the State of New Mexico from the Rio Grande Project as permitted to be contracted with by the Secretary of the Interior." Adding that a low-line canal would reach a substantially smaller acreage above the state line, Lawson and Hanna pointed out that the cost of serving the full 110,000 acres by a high-line canal would be prohibitively expensive.[22] Regardless of these observations, the question remained whether Hall's original estimate for irrigable acreage in New Mexico was fixed or whether it was subject to adjustments based on Reclamation Service judgments of what was practical as the Rio Grande Project was built.

Seeking further answers, Lawson and Hanna examined the articles of incorporation of the Elephant Butte Water Users' Association, amendments to those articles, and the original contract between the secretary of the interior and the water users' organization to determine what, if any, legal obligation the Reclamation Service had to fulfill the original 110,000-acre estimate. The articles of incorporation, Lawson and Hanna found, confirmed that "the determination of the irrigable area is left to the Reclamation Service through its surveys, so that the area of actually irrigated lands may be determined by the United States to be less than 110,000 acres." Lawson and Hanna also verified that the contract with the secretary of the interior stipulated that the government had the power "to limit the area of the project to the water supply." In addition, Lawson and Hanna reported that an amendment to the articles of incorporation of the Elephant Butte Water Users' Association required an adjustment in "the number of shares of stock in the association to the number of acres of land determined to be irrigable by the United States." Thus, Lawson and Hanna concluded that the U.S. government had reserved the right to determine the ultimate irrigable acreage within the Rio Grande Project "both from the viewpoint of the area feasible of reclamation by economical location of canals and by limiting the area to the available water supply." Because each acre of irrigated land would require a certain amount of water to be productive, Lawson and Hanna's conclusions meant that the government had retained the authority to apportion the Rio Grande between New Mexico and Texas based on its interpretation of the 1904 compromise, the 1905 legislation extending the Reclamation Act to the El Paso Valley, and subsequent contracts between the water users and the secretary of the interior.[23] These findings conformed with the ideology behind the Reclamation Act that projects would derive from centralized planning yet ultimately would be operated by local interests.

Lawson and Hanna's determinations settled the issue of who was to establish the irrigable area within the Rio Grande Project from the Reclamation Service's point of view, and they suggested that the Anthony High Line Association's idea was unacceptable owing to the large per-acre repayment costs that a high-line canal would bring. Even with these findings, however, the review by Lawson and Hanna underscored the need to define precisely which lands would be served by Rio Grande Project waters. Until this was done, other requests similar to that of the Anthony High Line Association could not be properly addressed, land speculation would continue unabated, and the problem of how the 1904 compromise would be implemented would remain unresolved. In mid-1914, with this in mind, Newell recommended to Secretary of the Interior Franklin Lane that a board be appointed to designate the actual lands to be served by the Rio Grande Project. The board was to survey Rio Grande valley lands pledged to both water users' associations and determine which parcels would eventually receive project water and have repayment duties. Newell believed that in addition to removing debate over the high-line canal, the board's review would also help diminish land speculation to some extent by identifying the precise parcels to be served—problems also confronting many other Reclamation Service projects elsewhere. Secretary Lane approved Newell's recommendation on August 3, 1914, less than two weeks before Congress passed the Reclamation Extension Act, implementing similar major reforms for all western Reclamation Service projects.[24]

Regardless of the new plan to define the Rio Grande Project's exact limits, pressure to expand the irrigable acreage continued to mount. This issue was compounded by difficulties in locating distribution canals, building drainage facilities, and legally changing the water users' associations to irrigation districts. This latter problem was a requirement then being imposed by the Reclamation Service on many federal projects for a multitude of reasons, not the least of which was to ensure construction cost repayments, because districts had the authority to levy local taxes whereas water users' associations did not.[25] All of these factors so complicated the board's task of defining the Rio Grande Project's irrigable area that immediate conclusions were impossible. The matter remained unresolved for several more years, and when Elephant Butte Reservoir began to store water regularly after 1916, the high-line canal proposal once again emerged. The new calls for a high-line canal's construction reopened the earlier debate over hydroelectric power and the role it could play in offsetting Rio Grande Project construction costs, which, as with many Reclamation Service undertakings elsewhere, were soaring way beyond initial expectations.

In 1902, when Congress passed the Reclamation Act, some backers of federal irrigation in the West believed that projects could be constructed for as little as five dollars an acre. Yet when the first five reclamation projects were authorized by the secretary of the interior in 1903, their costs were estimated to be about twelve or thirteen dollars an acre. In the following year, the Reclamation Service was predicting that the first million acres to be covered by Reclamation Act projects would cost twenty-seven dollars an acre, and estimates continued to increase.[26] As was occurring elsewhere, the growing expenses associated with building reclamation projects escalated on the Rio Grande, and this prompted calls for ways to offset them. One such means was the proposed high-line canal.

The revival of the high-line canal idea came in 1918 from an unlikely source—Nathan Boyd, the former president of the defunct Rio Grande Dam and Irrigation Company. Boyd, of course, had long been one of the most outspoken champions of protecting New Mexico's claims to Rio Grande waters, and having lost his final appeal in the U.S. Supreme Court in 1909, Boyd saw the possible construction of the high-line canal as a personal vindication of his firm's plans. Among his company's ideas had been the proposal to irrigate considerably larger areas in New Mexico's Mesilla Valley than the Reclamation Service was then contemplating without the high-line canal. Ironically, Boyd believed that among the advantages afforded by a high-line canal was the ability to provide major water supplies to the city of El Paso—a goal that had been advanced in the 1890s to support Boyd's rival project, the international dam at El Paso. Asserting that the high-line canal also would increase irrigable acreage in the Mesilla Valley and produce inexpensive hydroelectric power, Boyd actively promoted the proposition among civic and commercial groups throughout the area to redeem his name and the plans of the Rio Grande Dam and Irrigation Company (although the company was no longer in existence).[27]

Surprisingly, El Pasoans enthusiastically endorsed Boyd's proposal for a variety of reasons, even though the high-line canal might result in fewer acres in Texas receiving Rio Grande Project waters. Circumstances had changed considerably in the four years since the Anthony High Line Association's proposal had been eliminated by the 1914 Reclamation Service report. Elephant Butte Dam had been completed in 1916, and the Reclamation Service was continuing to refine its studies on the Rio Grande Project's final limits, even if there still was no official proclamation on this point. To El Pasoans, these factors made the new high-line proposal more likely to succeed, and with World War I then raging, the industrial demand for hydroelectric power in El Paso was greater than it had been previously. Most important, however, was that El Pasoans had begun to see a larger need for Rio Grande Project waters to serve their city; consequently, they took a far greater role in promoting the new high-line canal drive than they had previously.

To advance the high-line revival, a cooperative committee was organized with delegates representing several Rio Grande water interests, including the Elephant Butte Irrigation District and El Paso County Water Improvement District No. 1 (both of which had replaced the respective old water users' associations), as well as the city of El Paso and the El Paso Chamber of Commerce. As one of its first actions, the joint committee asked the engineering firm of Quinton, Code, and Hill to draft a preliminary report on the possibilities offered by the high-line canal.[28] This company had been chosen because one of its partners, Louis C. Hill, previously had been the Reclamation Service's supervising engineer who had overseen the construction of Elephant Butte Dam and the Salt River Project's Roosevelt Dam in Arizona; he was therefore presumed to understand the factors confronting the completion of the Rio Grande Project. In addition, Hill had been a member of the Reclamation Service's board of engineers that had recommended against the high-line canal in 1913. The cooperative committee hoped that with the functioning of the dam being less a matter of conjecture than it had been in 1913, Hill would change his opinion and support the high-line canal.

Quinton, Code, and Hill submitted their report to the cooperative committee on June 27, 1919, and the firm's findings undoubtedly pleased the committee's members. In his cover letter, Louis Hill stressed that, based on his company's studies, the building of a high-line canal and the development of hydroelectric power from both Elephant Butte Dam and the canal would be of great benefit to the two Rio Grande Project irrigation districts and to the city of El Paso. Moreover, the report affirmed that if the river was used to carry Rio Grande Project waters in the Mesilla Valley, the cost of drains to eliminate seepage problems would be greater than the expense of building the high-line canal.[29]

Aside from these conclusions, one of the main points of Quinton, Code, and Hill's report was that the high-line canal could greatly increase water supplies to El Paso. Noting that the city got most of its water from deep wells—circumstances that made the expense of water for urban consumption relatively high—the consultants observed that although the cost tended to enforce water conservation, the result was that El Paso was not aesthetically appealing, owing to a lack of trees, shrubs, flowers, and lawns. Quinton, Code, and Hill added that city officials had long recognized the need for another water supply because groundwater levels in El Paso's wells were declining, and the consultants believed that the only possible supplemental source for the city was Elephant Butte Reservoir and the Rio Grande Project. With a high-line canal in place, Quinton, Code, and Hill estimated that bringing the reservoir's waters to El Paso would be less expensive than existing groundwater pumping costs, and the consultants believed that the quality of water also would be better than water supplied by the city's wells. The engineers thought that a high-line canal could provide twenty to forty million gallons of water per day to El Paso, or roughly 22,400 to 44,800 acre-feet per year.[30]

Following the study by Quinton, Code, and Hill, Harold H. Brook, president of the Elephant Butte Irrigation District, wrote a more encompassing report, titled "Co-Operative Proposal for the Settlement, Completion, and Power Development of the Rio Grande Project and for Municipal Water Supply for [the] City of El Paso by a High Line Canal." Widely known as an expert on irrigation engineering, Brook was a strong advocate of the high-line canal, and he stressed many of the same points discussed by Quinton, Code, and Hill. Including more-sweeping arguments for the high-line canal, Brook colored the undertaking with a patriotic fervor. By the time Brook authored his report, World War I had ended. Brook therefore argued that the high-line canal would provide irrigated farmland for ex-military personnel under the then-proposed National Soldier Settlement Act—legislation aimed at helping veterans reestablish themselves as civilian farmers. Brook's views on this subject undoubtedly had been encouraged by considerable debate in the U.S. Congress over a flood of bills to assist veterans and by the January 1919 Soldier's, Sailor's, and Marine's Land Settlement Congress. This gathering had endorsed a proposal advanced by the Department of the Interior to reclaim millions of acres in the American West to provide farms for returning veterans, and the meeting also had helped spur advocates of developing the water resources of the Colorado River.[31]

In addition to supporting national policy, according to Brook, the high-line canal offered three other principal advantages. First, although the government previously had held that larger acreage within the Rio Grande Project would increase construction costs, Brook believed that the opposite was true. To Brook, more land within the project would allow a lower per-acre cost by dividing expenses over a greater area. This, in turn, would permit project water users to reaffirm their obligation to repay all project costs, because their expenses would be diminished. This was an important selling point, Brook believed, given dissatisfaction with the rate of the project's construction and increasing sentiments to "repudiate" the debt—circumstances that were occurring on reclamation projects throughout the West. Second, Brook thought the high-line canal could allow hydroelectric energy to be delivered to Rio Grande Project water users at cost. Third, El Paso could extend the high-line canal to its municipal users at its own expense, Brook pointed out, and in exchange the city would pay its proportionate share of costs for storage, operation, and maintenance. This would diminish these expenses for irrigators.[32]

With the study by Quinton, Code, and Hill supporting his report, Brook sent his conclusions to Washington, D.C., for Reclamation Service review. He also traveled there in late July 1919 to lobby personally for the high-line canal, a trip that turned out to be unnecessary. By the time Brook arrived in the nation's capital, Davis (who had succeeded Newell as director of the Reclamation Service in late 1914) already had ordered W. E. Weymouth, the Reclamation Service's chief of construction, to have a new board of engineers reexamine the high-line canal plan, although Davis remained skeptical about reviving the idea. Weymouth appointed David C. Henny, James Munn, and Charles T. Pease to draft the report, and they worked closely with the cooperative high-line canal committee, holding frequent hearings in El Paso and Las Cruces.[33]

The November 1919 report by Henny, Munn, and Pease found that "the plan of the High Line Canal Committee so far as it includes the construction of a High Line Canal and power plants thereon does not appear at the present time financially feasible unless far greater burdens be placed upon the city [of El Paso] than can be equitably justified." The Reclamation Service engineers thought that the consultants' estimated cost of the high-line canal was too low and that the creation of a dry riverbed through the use of a high-line canal would not bring about the large savings in drainage costs that the consultants had projected.[34]

In relation to providing El Paso with water, the Reclamation Service engineers estimated that the city's need might eventually balloon to as much as 45,000 acre-feet per year. This figure, they determined, represented 8.7 percent of the total irrigation supply of the entire Rio Grande Project, and the government engineers contended that to provide this much water to the city would require reducing the project's irrigable lands by the same percentage, thus eliminating about 13,500 acres. El Paso officials had argued in support of the findings by Quinton, Code, and Hill that the city's sewage effluent and seepage from lawn sprinkling would offset some of the need for project waters in the El Paso Valley. Yet Henny, Munn, and Pease concluded that these flows were not necessary, with the southernmost part of the Rio Grande Project receiving sufficient waters from existing upstream drainage. Furthermore, according to the Reclamation Service engineers, El Paso's return flow from lawn sprinkling already aggravated the Rio Grande Project's drainage problem in the Texas part of that system. Finally, Henny, Munn, and Pease pointed out that the annual draft of 720,000 acre-feet from Elephant Butte Reservoir was only enough water to serve about 155,000 acres in the United States—an acreage that when added to Mexico's irrigated lands under the 1906 treaty approximated the Reclamation Service's 1904 estimate of 180,000 acres for the entire reservoir service area. This obviously left no surplus supply for municipal and industrial uses.[35]

Henny, Munn, and Pease were persuasive, and their conclusions spelled the end of the high-line canal proposal. Nevertheless, the near-decade-long agitation for the high-line canal and the related issues of land speculation and hydroelectric power generation had raised important questions about the nature of the Rio Grande Project as it was being built. Foremost among these was whether the project's irrigable acreage would be considerably larger than that proposed by Benjamin Hall. By eliminating the high-line canal idea on several occasions, the Reclamation Service reaffirmed that Hall's original estimates of the possible acreage served by Elephant Butte Dam were fundamentally correct. The debate over the high-line proposal also established that the final interstate apportionment of waters among Rio Grande Project farmlands would be done by the Reclamation Service within the general outlines defined in 1904 by Hall and as authorized by Congress's 1905 extension of the Reclamation Act to the El Paso Valley.

Simultaneously, the struggle for the high-line canal had vividly illustrated that the construction of Elephant Butte Dam and the Rio Grande Project was a cooperative venture with power to control the final outcome flowing two ways. The Reclamation Service might have retained the final authority to determine irrigable lands within the project, but those who were to receive the water supplies maintained considerable ability to shape the Reclamation Service's views through their obligation to repay construction costs. In addition, the water users' capabilities to mobilize public opinion through representative organizations such as the Anthony High Line Association, the Elephant Butte Water Users' Association, and the El Paso County Water Users' Association (and the later irrigation districts with similar names) made the Reclamation Service reluctant to totally ignore the wishes of those being served by the Rio Grande Project. Finally, the Reclamation Act's limitation of providing water to parcels of 160 acres or fewer made the Reclamation Service more willing to consider the views of local interests to obtain compliance with the acreage restriction. All of these factors contributed to the federal construction of a reclamation project that was in large measure locally controlled and retained the essential features of the locally achieved 1904 National Irrigation Congress compromise on apportioning Rio Grande waters.

CHAPTER 9

The Rio Grande Compact, Part I

The Temporary 1929 Agreement

The 1919 Reclamation Service report by David C. Henny, James Munn, and Charles T. Pease concluded that the high-line canal was not feasible for the Rio Grande Project. This determination affirmed Benjamin Hall's 1904 estimate that Elephant Butte Reservoir and the Rio Grande Project could serve a maximum of 180,000 cumulative acres above and below El Paso. With the 1906 treaty providing water to about 25,000 acres in Mexico, supplies for the remaining 155,000 acres in the United States still had to be divided between water users in the Elephant Butte Irrigation District and those in El Paso County Water Improvement District No. 1. To carry out this apportionment, in the years after the elimination of the high-line canal proposal, the government began to examine factors such as soil quality, drainage problems, access to distributing canals, and the possibility of developing hydroelectric power just at Elephant Butte Dam. On the basis of these evaluations, by 1929 the Bureau of Reclamation (formerly the Reclamation Service) had established that the New Mexico part of the Rio Grande Project should consist of 88,000 acres and the Texas portion should be 67,000 acres. Water stored at Elephant Butte Reservoir was to be dispersed accordingly.[1]

Although New Mexico's acreage had been diminished from Hall's 1904 estimate and the Texas allotment had increased, officials in both districts

Elephant Butte Dam, partially completed, February 1915. Courtesy Bureau of Reclamation, National Archives II, College Park, Maryland.

were, for the most part, content with the division. Water stored at Elephant Butte Reservoir was then being delivered to farmlands each year under temporary contracts, thus reducing the unrest that had emerged concerning the practicality of the high-line canal. In addition, local water users in New Mexico and Texas had persuaded the government to lengthen the period for construction repayments, first from ten to twenty years, then to twenty-seven years, and finally to forty years. Demonstrating their satisfaction, the Elephant Butte Irrigation District and El Paso County Water Improvement District No. 1 eventually signed two interdistrict agreements—one in 1929 and the second in 1938—confirming their mutual acceptance of the apportionment within the Rio Grande Project. The districts also executed new contracts with the federal government providing for the distribution of final construction costs and operation and maintenance fees between New Mexico and Texas water users in a ratio of 88:67 based on the acreage allocations.[2]

The new contracts and the interdistrict agreements completed the last steps in dividing the Rio Grande's waters below Elephant Butte Dam among irrigators in New Mexico, Texas, and Mexico based on the 1904 National

Construction at Elephant Butte Dam site, December 1912. Courtesy Bureau of Reclamation, National Archives II, College Park, Maryland.

Irrigation Congress compromise, the 1905 congressional legislation extending the Reclamation Act to the El Paso Valley (which formally apportioned waters to be stored at Elephant Butte Reservoir as agreed in the 1904 accord), and the 1906 treaty with Mexico. Yet as the Rio Grande Project reached completion in the early 1920s, a larger geographic problem began to arise over the river's distribution between irrigators above Elephant Butte Reservoir (and not in the Rio Grande Project) and those below. The 1904 compromise as implemented by the Bureau of Reclamation had divided water among farmers below Elephant Butte Reservoir in the Mesilla and El Paso valleys, but this apportionment did not apply to Colorado's part of the Rio Grande basin—the San Luis Valley—nor did it address the increasing calls for water by irrigators in the middle Rio Grande valley around Albuquerque, New Mexico. As the Rio Grande Project was being completed, officials in the three states uneasily became aware that the activities of water users in the middle Rio Grande valley and in the San Luis Valley might have a profound impact on supplies destined for storage at Elephant Butte Reser-

Cableways carrying train engine across the Rio Grande at the Elephant Butte Dam construction site, April 1912. Courtesy Bureau of Reclamation, National Archives II, College Park, Maryland.

voir. This, in turn, might interfere with the agreement reached in 1904 and potentially could jeopardize the 1906 treaty with Mexico.

To avoid continued controversy, state leaders turned to drafting an interstate compact to settle this broader Rio Grande apportionment problem. The compact approach was a logical outgrowth of how the allocation of waters within the Rio Grande Project had been handled, simply on a larger scale. Much as the implementation of the 1904 National Irrigation Congress compromise had involved local cooperation as well as assistance by regional, state, and national organizations and governments, the compact process reflected a similar federalism. Like the talks that led to the 1922 Colorado River Compact (from which officials in Colorado, New Mexico, and Texas drew their inspiration for a similar agreement on the Rio Grande), the negotiations that led first to a temporary Rio Grande Compact in 1929 and then to a permanent interstate accord in 1938 were multilayered. Substantial input came from local concerns, notably the two Rio

Townsite for Elephant Butte Dam workers on the Rio Grande, looking south, September 1911. Courtesy Bureau of Reclamation, National Archives II, College Park, Maryland.

Grande Project irrigation districts and water users around Albuquerque and in Colorado's San Luis Valley. The local contributions to negotiations for the two Rio Grande compacts were strengthened by considerable state government direction, which was aimed in part at limiting federal influence over western water resources. U.S. government assistance for settling the Rio Grande's apportionment problems was also essential. Among the contributions by federal authorities were technical studies relied upon to help reach the 1938 agreement—surveys that collectively came to be known as the Rio Grande Joint Investigation. Consequently, although the settlement of the Rio Grande basinwide apportionment question took several decades to achieve after the 1904 National Irrigation Congress compromise, like that earlier accord, the final solution exhibited a multitude of interests, with authority emanating from many sources on different levels.

The direct need for compact negotiations on the Rio Grande had stemmed from the so-called embargo that Secretary of the Interior David R. Francis had ordered in 1896 to prevent new rights-of-way on that stream for reservoirs or irrigation canals. Various secretaries of the interior had

Construction workers preparing the foundation site for Elephant Butte Dam, May 1912. Courtesy Bureau of Reclamation, National Archives II, College Park, Maryland.

maintained the embargo over the following years with only minor modifications to ensure that while Elephant Butte Dam was being built, the terms of the 1906 treaty with Mexico would be carried out.[3] As time progressed, the embargo became extremely controversial; Colorado authorities had even threatened to sue over the matter in 1914.[4] The embargo had also split water users in New Mexico as to its continued usefulness. Northern New Mexicans above Elephant Butte tended to align with Colorado interests regarding the need to lift the restriction, while water users below Elephant Butte wanted the embargo to remain in place.[5]

The Rio Grande embargo was not unique, and similar restrictions on new private irrigation works had been implemented elsewhere to protect federal reclamation projects. Such limitations were part of a broader U.S. government policy to defend Reclamation Service projects in various ways, including withdrawing public domain lands from homestead entry until those ventures were in place. Not only did federal authorities deny requests for rights-of-way across the public domain for private canals and reservoirs in certain stream basins, but the government also locked up federally owned lands in areas where watersheds might provide irrigation supplies for reclamation works. So broad was this policy that shortly after Congress passed the Reclamation Act in 1902, the government withdrew from entry 40 million acres of the public domain, including many good reservoir sites and lands adjoining rivers and streams. This restricted access to federal lands guaranteed that water coming from that acreage would remain available for government projects for many years into the future.[6]

One such stream was the Salt River in Arizona, where the Reclamation Service had withdrawn from homestead entry a considerable portion of the upper Salt River basin's lands. The goal was to protect the water supplies for Roosevelt Dam, completed in 1911 to supply arid lands around Phoenix. With only a small amount of upstream settlement, the Salt River withdrawals had not produced much opposition.[7] Such was not the case, however, on the North Platte River, where the Reclamation Service had completed Pathfinder Dam in 1909. Located in southeastern Wyoming and with a capacity of over a hundred thousand acre-feet of water, that structure stored supplies for irrigation downstream in western Nebraska. As had been the case on the Rio Grande, the United States had implemented a moratorium on upstream North Platte developments in Wyoming to protect flows destined for Pathfinder Dam. Wyoming's North Platte water users, like those along the upper Rio Grande, had protested this restriction to no avail over the following years, even after Pathfinder had been completed. Wyoming's leaders had continued to complain about the North Platte limitations during some of the initial meetings in the early 1920s to discuss a possible interstate compact for the Colorado River. With major U.S. storage works then being considered for the Colorado River's lower reaches, Wyoming's officials were determined that a halt in upstream Colorado River developments—such as the one imposed on the Rio Grande's San Luis Valley—would not be created in the Colorado River's upstream areas—regions that included parts of Wyoming.[8]

Parallel to the circumstances on the North Platte River, the Rio Grande embargo had been allowed to remain in force over the years because Rio Grande Project farmers had insisted that the restriction on upriver development protected Elephant Butte Reservoir's water supply. Also contributing to the embargo's retention was the widespread news of the 1916 completion of Elephant Butte Dam—then the world's largest such struc-

Officials at the Elephant Butte construction site offices, March 1913. *Left to right:* L. Clapp, president of the Elephant Butte Water Users' Association; Homer Gault, engineer for the Reclamation Service; Frederick H. Newell, director of the Reclamation Service; and unidentified driver. Courtesy Bureau of Reclamation, National Archives II, College Park, Maryland.

ture. This major event was reported by multitudes of newspapers across the country, and the dedication ceremony was held in conjunction with the opening in El Paso of that year's irrigation congress (dubbed the international irrigation congress). Special trains carried participants 125 miles upriver to Elephant Butte, and President Woodrow Wilson was even scheduled to participate (he later decided not to attend). With the huge number of press stories about the success of this gargantuan engineering endeavor and its importance to the nation, government officials were reluctant to tamper with success by removing the embargo.[9]

Although Elephant Butte Dam was heralded by newspapers across the country, the simultaneous preservation of the Rio Grande embargo led to endless protests by upstream irrigators in the middle Rio Grande and San Luis valleys, who viewed the continuation of the embargo as an unjust restraint on their sections of the basin. By the early 1920s, complaints over the embargo had become extremely bitter, and to resolve the issue, several

Ceremonial setting of the last lamppost at the completed Elephant Butte Dam, July 1916. Courtesy Bureau of Reclamation, National Archives II, College Park, Maryland.

of those who were then attempting to negotiate a compact for the Colorado River concluded that a similar solution to the Rio Grande's problems might be possible. With a compact for the Rio Grande in place, the reasoning went, there would be no more need for the embargo.[10]

While the Rio Grande embargo was a direct factor leading to the Rio Grande Compact talks, on a broader level, the desire to solve the problems on both the Rio Grande and the Colorado via the compact process also derived from the fact that western water law as it pertained to interstate rivers was still poorly defined. Before the early 1920s, despite growing specifics about how prior appropriation applied within individual states, there were very few precedents in case (court-made) law or in legislation establishing how water supplies from a stream shared by two or more states were to be allocated. The Rio Grande below Elephant Butte Reservoir, of course, had been apportioned with the passage of the 1905 congressional measure extending the Reclamation Act to the El Paso Valley. Yet the 1905 law, while

Completed Elephant Butte Dam, July 1916. Courtesy Bureau of Reclamation, National Archives II, College Park, Maryland.

allotting water to New Mexico and Texas irrigators within the Rio Grande Project, largely had been forgotten as a model for interstate river allocation because, at the time it was passed, the legislation's more notable function had been to extend the Reclamation Act to a part of Texas. Two years later, in *Kansas v. Colorado*, the U.S. Supreme Court had established the principle of "equitable apportionment" in that interstate conflict over the Arkansas River—a decision that had appalled Coloradans because they believed that U.S. Attorney General Judson Harmon's 1895 statement that the United States, as a sovereign nation, had no obligation to deliver any Rio Grande water to Mexico applied equally well to their circumstances in relation to the struggle with Kansas over the Arkansas River.[11] Yet regardless of how one viewed Harmon's opinion, the establishment of the "equitable apportionment" doctrine did not provide specific details about just what "equitable" meant. *Wyoming v. Colorado*, which had been filed in the Supreme Court in 1911 to settle those two states' claims to the Laramie River, was not decided until mid-1922 (the same year that Colorado River Compact discussions began). In that case, Wyoming had contended that the principle of equitable apportionment as set forth in *Kansas v. Colorado* applied to Wyoming's claims to the Laramie River. Nevertheless, Wyoming had argued that its equitable rights ought to be defined based on establishing prior appropriation across the state line into Colorado because both states adhered to this legal tenet. (Not coincidentally, Wyoming also happened to have older priorities in general than those in Colorado.) Despite Wyoming's contention, the *Wyoming v. Colorado* ruling had held that where two adjacent states recognized priority in water law, that principle could be considered as a factor but not the sole determinant to help resolve claims to a river shared by both.[12] Thus, as of 1922, very little water law—case or statutory—dealt directly with interstate stream apportionment, and the principle of equitable apportionment, while establishing an important concept, remained frustratingly vague.

In theory, the *Wyoming v. Colorado* decision ought to have been at least partly useful in helping to settle interstate allocation problems on the Rio Grande relating to Colorado's San Luis Valley and the area around Albuquerque because New Mexico and Colorado both recognized the priority doctrine. Nevertheless, because of the U.S. government's history of aggressively intervening in litigation to assert federal domination over the non-navigable portions of western rivers, authorities in the Rio Grande region leaned toward compact making to preserve as much control over that stream as possible. For example, in the U.S. government's lawsuit against Boyd's Rio Grande Dam and Irrigation Company during the 1890s and early 1900s, the United States had maintained that flows from the non-navigable portion of the Rio Grande might contribute to navigability farther downstream. Therefore, the federal government had claimed that it should retain control over all parts of that river.[13] The United States had taken similar positions on other western streams—arguments that were well known to Rio Grande officials. Federal lawyers used the navigability theory in 1904 to try to block the ambitious plans for irrigation of California's Imperial Valley from the lower Colorado River by Rockwood's California Development Company.[14] In the same year that U.S. authorities were attempting to obstruct Rockwood's goals on the Colorado, the United States filed a petition to intervene in *Kansas v. Colorado* to stake a claim to control over the Arkansas River based on the stream's alleged navigability below Kansas.[15] Navigability was only one argument posited by federal lawyers to support U.S. claims to western rivers, however; in intervening in *Wyoming v. Colorado* in 1918, U.S. attorneys had contended that the federal government had sole authority over all unappropriated waters of the West's non-navigable rivers.[16]

Although none of these U.S. attempts to gain greater control over western rivers had been successful, the relentless federal attacks and the lack of precedent on how to accomplish an interstate apportionment led western authorities in the early 1920s to view compact deliberations as the best way to solve their problems with a minimum of federal interference. The Colorado River talks were the obvious model for Rio Grande interests, yet resorting to such an approach to divide the Rio Grande's waters was nevertheless a relatively novel idea.

The use of compacts to solve disputes between states—many of which had been boundary conflicts—had been sanctioned under Article I of the U.S. Constitution, and the process had been utilized since that charter had been ratified in 1789. (In fact, some observers have argued that a similar procedure was used to settle controversies among the states even before the Constitution took effect.)[17] Whatever the case may be about the origins of compact making, such interstate accords had a long history by the early twentieth century. Nonetheless, employing an interstate compact specifically with the intention of apportioning a river's supplies among several states remained untested until deliberations began in 1922 to divide the Colorado River's waters among Arizona, California, Colorado, Nevada, New Mexico, Utah, and Wyoming.[18] When the Colorado River discussions bore fruit in the form of a compact in 1922, the compact idea appeared so attractive that discussions quickly began on several other interstate streams. It was no coincidence that the state of Colorado was involved in several sets of these compact deliberations, because that state lay at the headwaters of several rivers. Two of these agreements—the La Plata River Compact and the South Platte River Compact—were approved barely two years after the Colorado River Compact had been signed (although neither the La Plata River Compact nor the South Platte River Compact was completely ratified for several more years).[19] Moreover, talks began on at least three other rivers arising in Colorado at about the same time: the Arkansas River (Colorado and Kansas),[20] the North Platte (Colorado, Nebraska, and Wyoming),[21] and the Rio Grande. Other proposals for interstate water allocation compacts that emerged in the 1920s that did not involve the state of Colorado included two other western rivers and one eastern stream.[22]

Compact talks concerning the Rio Grande were sanctioned in 1923 by both New Mexico and Colorado. New Mexico named to the deliberations Julian O. Seth, a former U.S. attorney with experience in the U.S. General Land Office and the Forest Service. Colorado designated Delph E.

Carpenter, a prominent water lawyer, as his state's negotiator for the Rio Grande.[23] Among his achievements, Carpenter had represented Colorado in the landmark case of *Wyoming v. Colorado* between 1910 and 1919 and in other actions involving the South Platte River (with Nebraska as an opponent) and the Republican River (against Kansas and Nebraska). By the time he was asked to deal with the Rio Grande matter, Carpenter had been given authority to negotiate all interstate river compacts relevant to his state (powers he held until 1933) because it had been his idea to use a compact for the Colorado River. Moreover, Carpenter had first suggested the same approach for the Arkansas River in 1921. To Carpenter, using a compact to settle an interstate stream dispute held the advantage that once any such accord was ratified by the affected state legislatures and the U.S. Congress, the agreement would bind the states as well as their citizens and corporations. Carpenter believed that a negotiated interstate water agreement was clearly preferable to litigation because once such an accord was ratified, it would become a permanent part of that stream's "law of the river"—a term, widely associated today with the Colorado River,[24] that meant the collective body of laws, court decisions, and administrative rulings that governed how a particular stream was regulated. Moreover, compacts would strengthen states' rights and would diminish competition among neighboring states by allowing each to grow at its own rate. In short, compacts would provide security and permanence and would encourage financial investments in participant states.[25]

With commissioners having been appointed, New Mexico governor James E. Hinkle and Colorado governor William E. Sweet asked Secretary of the Interior Hubert Work for a federal delegate to join the talks because of the U.S. government's many interests along the river. Federal concerns along the Rio Grande (as with the Colorado River in this respect) included irrigation (principally, the Rio Grande Project), Indian reservations, public lands, and the fulfillment of international obligations to Mexico under the 1906 treaty. Although Work replied that he believed that the United States should not take part until Texas was included on the Rio Grande Compact Commission, President Calvin Coolidge appointed Herbert Hoover to take part in the discussions on December 22, 1923. Not only was Hoover then secretary of commerce, but he also had demonstrated his ability to address difficult problems by his previous position as food administrator during World War I. More to the point, however, in relation to the Rio Grande dispute, Hoover had recently chaired the negotiations that had led to the successful agreement on the 1922 Colorado River Compact.[26]

The question of what was to be Texas's role on the Rio Grande Compact Commission became a major stumbling block to getting deliberations under way. Hovering ominously in the background was the fact that at the time the Texas issue was surfacing in the Rio Grande talks, Arizona was refusing to ratify the recently completed Colorado River Compact. This left the other six Colorado River states with the questions of whether they could proceed at all with ratification and, if so, how.[27] No one wanted a similar situation on the Rio Grande. Yet Coloradans and northern New Mexicans opposed allowing Texas to join the dialogue because they thought Texas's inclusion would give the Rio Grande Project's interests undue power in the negotiations. Residents of Colorado and northern New Mexico contended that Texas's only concern with the Rio Grande's flow lay in relation to its allocation under the Rio Grande Project. That allotment, Coloradans and northern New Mexicans believed, already had been decided with the 1905 extension of the Reclamation Act to the El Paso Valley (which also sanctioned the Rio Grande Project and the division of that venture's water supplies according to the 1904 National Irrigation Congress compromise).

To water users in the Mesilla and El Paso valleys, however, Texas's participation was essential to protect Elephant Butte Reservoir's water supplies and the apportionment within the Rio Grande Project. Texans especially saw a need to be represented on the Rio Grande Compact Commission. Voicing views typical of many El Paso Valley residents, Richard F. Burges— who had attended the El Paso National Irrigation Congress meeting where the 1904 compromise had been endorsed and who was the attorney for El Paso County Water Improvement District No. 1—wrote to Texas governor Pat M. Neff in mid-1924 asserting that the state ought to be included in any Rio Grande apportionment negotiations specifically because of Texas's interest in the Rio Grande Project.[28] Burges was persuasive, and acting on his advice, Governor Neff asked Herbert Hoover for Texas to be "accorded the same representation upon that Commission which is accorded the States of New Mexico and Colorado." Because the Texas legislature was not then in session, Neff requested that the Rio Grande Compact Commission postpone its deliberations until the new legislature could convene in January 1925 and pass a bill authorizing the appointment of a Texas commissioner.[29]

Regardless of Governor Neff's desires, Governor Hinkle of New Mexico believed that Texas's rights were adequately protected by the 1904 National Irrigation Congress compromise and the 1905 congressionally authorized apportionment within the Rio Grande Project. Hinkle was worried that supporting Texas's inclusion might be construed as an attempt to reinforce New

Mexico's interests below Elephant Butte Dam against Colorado's San Luis Valley water users. Also, to maintain Colorado's support for ratification of the Colorado River Compact, which was then pending, Hinkle was unwilling to include Texas in the Rio Grande proceedings. Nonetheless, he told Governor Neff that he did not want to interfere with any rights Texas might have, suggesting that if there were to be a possible adjustment of the Rio Grande Project's apportionment below Elephant Butte Dam, then Texas ought to be included in the negotiations.[30]

Although Hinkle was equivocal, Colorado interests strenuously objected to Texas's participation in Rio Grande Compact talks because, unlike in New Mexico (where water users' concerns were split between those above and below Elephant Butte Dam), the loyalties of water users in the El Paso Valley lay strictly with the Rio Grande Project. Colorado irrigators were willing to negotiate with New Mexico because the division of that state's Rio Grande interests made it a less formidable opponent than Texas. San Luis Valley residents also encouraged Colorado to oppose Texas's inclusion in Rio Grande Compact deliberations, because they feared that if Texas took part, that state's water users below the Rio Grande Project might demand more water for irrigation—worries that later events proved to be justified. These apprehensions made Colorado extremely wary about negotiating with Texas, even when Texas officials threatened to have that state's congressional delegation block federal ratification of any compact if Texas was excluded from the discussions.

The situation rapidly reached an impasse. To try to salvage the compact deliberations, the Elephant Butte Irrigation District's president, Joseph W. Taylor, went to Santa Fe to talk with New Mexico's leaders. Although Taylor knew that the federal government was responsible for protecting Rio Grande Project water rights at any compact debates, he was concerned that if negotiations went forward without Texas, the Bureau of Reclamation (to avoid becoming involved in the interstate dispute) would not champion the project's water rights strongly. Given this possibility, Taylor and other Mesilla and El Paso valley water users wanted Texas's participation so that the Texas commissioner could become an advocate for the entire Rio Grande Project.

Reaching Santa Fe in late September 1924, Taylor confronted Julian Seth, New Mexico's compact commissioner, over the state's apparent hesitancy to include Texas in the negotiations. Taylor pressed Texas's case hard, arguing that if that state were left out, El Paso–area water users could justifiably claim in times of drought that their share of Rio Grande Project water should not suffer simply because Texas had played no role in shaping the compact—an argument that echoed Anson Mills's earlier contention that the El Paso Valley held water rights that antedated those of New Mexico and Colorado. Taylor stressed that a Texas claim based on having been excluded from the compact deliberations could conceivably leave the Elephant Butte Irrigation District subject to Texas's demands. While still reluctant to include Texas, Seth accepted the logic of Taylor's reasoning, and the two met with Governor Hinkle, who likewise was converted. Hinkle then agreed to call for an early compact meeting so that the New Mexico and Colorado commissioners could decide formally whether Texas should participate. To be certain that no one would object to Hinkle's plan, Seth subsequently secured the approval of the middle Rio Grande valley's water users.[31]

The first meeting of the New Mexico and Colorado delegates to the Rio Grande Compact Commission was held at the exclusive Broadmoor Hotel in Colorado Springs, Colorado, on Sunday, October 26, 1924. With the central purpose being to discuss Texas's possible participation, Colorado's Delph Carpenter pointed out that the people of the San Luis Valley were worried that Texas would insist on Rio Grande water supplies to irrigate land as far down the river as Brownsville—hundreds of miles below the Rio Grande Project. Explaining that the burden of such a Texas demand would naturally fall upon the source of supply on the upper river in Colorado, Carpenter observed that the continued enforcement of the Rio Grande embargo had "caused a feeling that the whole lower end of the river is against the upper, and that what New Mexico and Texas want to do is to strangle any future developments in the upper country." This sentiment, Carpenter maintained, made San Luis Valley water users vehemently opposed to Texas's inclusion in the compact talks.[32] Carpenter was well aware of the impact such upriver beliefs might have on negotiations over an interstate stream. During the Colorado River Compact deliberations—which had taken place barely two years earlier and during which Carpenter had been Colorado's representative—fears by water users upstream that downstream uses might preclude later upriver developments had hampered those discussions for a considerable amount of time.[33] Having successfully defended his state's interests against such a downriver dominance on the Colorado River, Carpenter was equally loath to allow lower river interests to prevail on the Rio Grande. Moreover, the ever-present threat of federal intervention had been driven home by circumstances on the North Platte

River; Carpenter and representatives of Nebraska and Wyoming were meeting to negotiate a compact to prevent the Bureau of Reclamation from intervening in disputes over that stream's waters.[34]

Attempting to allay Carpenter's concerns on the Rio Grande, Richard Burges, who was attending the meeting as an unofficial Texas delegate, claimed that water users on that river near El Paso had as much reason as Colorado's irrigators to fear demands from downstream areas. Burges contended that because the lower Rio Grande was not dependent on the upper river for its irrigation supplies (since the lower stream's flows came largely from Mexican tributaries below the Rio Grande Project), water users along the lower Rio Grande would have no interest in the compact negotiations. New Mexico's state engineer, George M. Neel, who also was at the deliberations as an informal observer, agreed with Burges, pointing out that if lower Rio Grande interests became involved in the compact talks, it almost certainly would mean dealing with Mexico to discuss downstream Mexican tributary contributions in relation to Mexican diversions. Involving Mexico, Neel cautioned, would effectively kill any possibility of a compact.[35]

Neel was undoubtedly aware that the Colorado River Compact's negotiators assiduously had avoided including Mexico in those discussions for precisely the same reason. Following the creation of the Colorado River Compact Commission in 1921, Mexican authorities had asked the U.S. government for Mexico to be represented in the talks and for Mexican access to any studies or other information that might be used in achieving a Colorado River accord. The State Department, however, had denied Mexico's request, insisting that the Colorado talks were purely a domestic matter. Mexico had renewed its request the following year, and when the State Department referred the question to Herbert Hoover, he had issued a similar response for comparable reasons.[36]

Rio Grande negotiators were keenly aware of the Colorado Compact's history, and they likewise preferred not to complicate matters by making the Rio Grande's talks international as well as interstate in character. This was an ironic position to take, given that the original 1904 National Irrigation Congress compromise dividing the Rio Grande's flows had stemmed in large measure from the international conflict over the river in the southern New Mexico and El Paso–Juárez regions. Nevertheless, with the interstate issue now involving three states and a much larger geographic area, keeping Mexico out of the Rio Grande deliberations appeared to make sense — much as it had in relation to the Colorado River Compact talks.

Texas, however, was a different matter. After considerably more discussion, Seth, Carpenter, and Hoover concurred that Texas had to be included in the Rio Grande Compact negotiations to avoid future problems, and they decided to delay further discussions until early 1925, when the Texas legislature could authorize the appointment of a compact commissioner.[37] Shortly thereafter, however, the potential for compact negotiations—even with Texas's participation—became seriously clouded by a series of events that had begun to unfold three years earlier, when the idea for a Rio Grande Compact had first been broached. Within months, compact deliberations broke down completely.

Paradoxically, the seeds of the dispute that caused the collapse of the Rio Grande talks had germinated simultaneously with the original idea to try to achieve a Colorado River settlement through an interstate compact. The problem centered on the Rio Grande embargo. Deviating from the subject of the Colorado River's allocation at discussions on that stream's apportionment, the Colorado River Compact negotiators had roundly criticized the U.S. government for unnecessarily perpetuating the Rio Grande embargo to the detriment of upper Rio Grande basin water users. Secretary of the Interior Albert B. Fall—a New Mexican who had represented the Rio Grande Dam and Irrigation Company in its legal battles with the federal government more than two decades earlier—had responded to the charge, acknowledging that perhaps the U.S. had been dilatory in determining whether there was sufficient water in the river to satisfy the Rio Grande Project's needs yet still allow reservoirs to be built in Colorado's San Luis Valley. Fall then ordered Arthur Davis, director of the Reclamation Service, to study the situation and provide a report.[38]

Davis had completed his study in late 1922, about two weeks before the Colorado legislature authorized the appointment of a Rio Grande Compact Commissioner. In his report, Davis reviewed the history of the Rio Grande embargo, and he detailed the water needs and rights of the Rio Grande Project. On the basis of this survey, Davis then suggested a major modification of the Rio Grande embargo—one that would allow the government to approve or reject applications for rights-of-way for reservoirs and canals on a case-by-case basis.[39] Although there was no immediate action on Davis's recommendations, his report eventually found its way into the hands of Colorado's Rio Grande water users, and it inspired an application by the San Luis Valley's River Ranch Company for a right-of-way across public lands to build the Vega Sylvestre Reservoir near Del Norte, Colorado.[40] The application qualified for

Davis's recommended case-by-case review, but the Department of the Interior rejected it because of Secretary Fall's resignation in March 1923 and the government's desire to await his replacement before acting on the revised embargo policy.[41]

Although the River Ranch Company's request was temporarily turned down, water users in the Mesilla and El Paso valleys nonetheless worried that the Rio Grande embargo eventually might be altered to allow the Vega Sylvestre Dam to be built or, worse still, that the embargo order might be abolished. These anxieties became acute when rumors reached the southern New Mexico–El Paso area that the newly appointed secretary of the interior, Hubert Work (who was from Colorado), would issue a directive asking all interested parties to show cause why the embargo should not be abrogated. Despite assurances by Bureau of Reclamation Commissioner Elwood Mead (who had become head of that agency in 1924) and Acting Secretary of the Interior F. M. Goodwin that the embargo would not be altered during Rio Grande Compact negotiations, the uneasiness among Rio Grande Project irrigators persisted during and well after the October 26, 1924, meeting at which the Rio Grande Compact Commissioners discussed Texas's possible participation in the talks.[42] Mesilla Valley and El Paso Valley water users were especially upset by the persistence of the rumors, and this apprehension threatened to sabotage the compact deliberations just as they were getting under way.

With the embargo crisis reaching a flash point over the River Ranch Company's application for the Vega Sylvestre Reservoir, in January 1925 U.S. Senator Morris Sheppard of Texas and El Paso–area congressman Claude B. Hudspeth, accompanied by New Mexico and Texas water users, called on the Rio Grande Compact Commission's chairman, Herbert Hoover, to seek a solution. Explaining that Texas would not pass the necessary law to participate in the Rio Grande Compact negotiations unless the federal government pledged that the embargo would remain intact until the compact commission had finished its labors, the delegates asked Hoover to intervene on their behalf. In response, Hoover said that he would secure a commitment from Secretary Work that the embargo would stay in place, and Hoover later told Congressman Hudspeth that Work had given the necessary pledge. Rio Grande Project water users were pleased by Work's promise, but to reinforce their position, the president of the Elephant Butte Irrigation District, Joseph Taylor, recommended that a bill be introduced in the New Mexico legislature to appropriate $25,000 for use in litigation against Colorado should the embargo be altered.[43]

Secretary Work, regardless of the assurance he had given to Hoover, quietly responded on February 5, 1925, to a request from a fellow Coloradan, U.S. Senator Lawrence Phipps, that the Department of the Interior reconsider the River Ranch Company's request to build the Vega Sylvestre Dam. After a thorough review of the proposal and the Rio Grande embargo, Work found that the right-of-way had been denied solely because of the embargo. Ruling that "additional development through storage of water along the upper reaches of the Rio Grande and its tributaries will not be inimical to the interests of the Rio Grande reclamation project," Work concluded that the proposed Colorado reservoir would "in all probability tend to stabilize and regulate the flow of flood waters in the stream." With this determination, Work approved the River Ranch Company's application.[44]

The Department of the Interior's action did not become known to Rio Grande Project water users for over a month, and because of Work's guarantee to Hoover, New Mexico and Texas irrigators waited for the Texas legislature to authorize the appointment of a compact commissioner.[45] Also contributing to the delay were simultaneous compact negotiations between New Mexico and Texas over the Pecos River, for which a major dispute had erupted over possible future unused flows. The Pecos situation complicated events on the Rio Grande by creating an environment of distrust and ill will.[46] Finally, on March 21, 1925—six weeks after the Vega Sylvestre Reservoir had been approved—officials of the Elephant Butte Irrigation District and El Paso County Water Improvement District No. 1 were notified that the River Ranch Company's petition had been sanctioned by the Department of the Interior. The long delay between Secretary Work's approval and the districts' notification triggered strong suspicions among Rio Grande Project leaders that the right-of-way had been hushed up to avoid protests. As Richard Burges fumed to Senator Morris Sheppard, "while we do not charge that any effort was made to suppress the knowledge of the fact, it seems strange that it should have leaked out so slowly and in the way it did."[47]

There was great dismay when word of Work's decision reached water users in the Mesilla and El Paso valleys, and even New Mexico water users above Elephant Butte Reservoir were alarmed. Filing a formal protest with Secretary of State Frank Kellogg, the Middle Rio Grande Reclamation Association—which supported forming its own water district in the region near Albuquerque—asked Kellogg to intervene with Secretary Work on the grounds that the Vega Sylvestre Reservoir allegedly would interfere with water owed to Mexico under the 1906 treaty (not to mention flows that irrigators in the middle Rio Grande area hoped to put to use).[48] With so many

New Mexicans upset by Work's action, a convention was quickly scheduled for all concerned to meet with New Mexico's governor, Arthur T. Hannett (who had succeeded Governor Hinkle in January 1925), and Commissioner Julian Seth. Unanimously agreeing that under the circumstances further talks with Colorado would be useless, the New Mexico and Texas irrigators demanded that a lawsuit be filed in the U.S. Supreme Court to settle all water rights on the river. With Rio Grande Project and other New Mexico water users seething, Seth gloomily reported to Hoover that he was "convinced that sentiment in this state is practically unanimous against further continuance of the Compact proceeding." He added that unless Hoover had "something to suggest which will relieve the situation," New Mexico would have to withdraw from the compact negotiations.[49]

Following the meeting with Governor Hannett and Commissioner Seth, representatives of the Elephant Butte Irrigation District and El Paso County Water Improvement District No. 1 filed formal objections to the Vega Sylvestre Dam with President Coolidge, Secretary Work, and Secretary Kellogg. The complaints suggested that because the secretary of the interior legally could not reverse a right-of-way grant, perhaps the Justice Department could file a suit to block the permit—an idea that no doubt derived from the tactic used to stop the Rio Grande Dam and Irrigation Company's plans three decades earlier. The districts also sought to have the State Department intercede, on the theory that the Vega Sylvestre right-of-way might interfere with Mexico's rights under the 1906 treaty.[50]

The opposition by New Mexicans and Texans to the Vega Sylvestre Reservoir approval was considerable, but the protests were in vain. Within days, however, the situation went from bad to worse. Although the River Ranch Company's right-of-way had been accepted because of Arthur Davis's recommendation that each application be considered on its merits, the Rio Grande embargo technically was still in force, subject only to requests for exemption on a case-by-case basis. Yet on May 20, 1925, Secretary Work vacated the embargo order.[51] Terminating the restrictions imposed by the Rio Grande embargo had been under active federal consideration as early as 1921, when Secretary of the Interior Albert Fall had pledged to consider voiding the upper Rio Grande limitation as a means of garnering support for federal development of a dam on the lower Colorado River—a storage facility that later became Hoover Dam.[52] Nevertheless, the removal of the full Rio Grande embargo came as a shock to Rio Grande water users below Elephant Butte. An outraged editorial writer for the *El*

Paso Herald cynically speculated that Work had ended the embargo because he planned to resign from President Coolidge's cabinet to run for one of Colorado's U.S. Senate seats. Notwithstanding possible political ambitions, Work professed that his cancellation of the embargo stemmed from his conviction—endorsed by water officials in most western states—that if a threat to existing water rights arose on any given river, the proper arena to settle such a dispute was in court. According to Work, the federal government had no authority to interfere with the states' regulation of water rights (an assertion that directly countered the U.S. government's actions over the years), and the Rio Grande embargo had been a manifest violation of this basic principle.[53]

The lifting of the Rio Grande embargo ended any hope that New Mexico would stay in the compact negotiations. On June 1, 1925, Julian Seth withdrew from the proceedings and resigned as Rio Grande Compact commissioner, telling Hoover that the change in the embargo's status made a compact "impossible from the viewpoint of the people interested in this state."[54] Texas governor Miriam "Ma" Ferguson, who with the approval of the state legislature had recently appointed Houston lawyer W. G. Love as a commissioner from her state, favored continuing with the compact talks to demonstrate in any subsequent court action that all possible steps had been taken before litigation was commenced, yet she was unable to persuade Governor Hannett of New Mexico to follow this moderate course. Instead, Hannett called on Albuquerque attorneys Summers Burkhart and James A. Hall to prepare a U.S. Supreme Court suit against Colorado. Burkhart and Hall began to lay the groundwork for the interstate lawsuit by meeting with Rio Grande Project irrigation district officials and other interested New Mexico and Texas parties.[55] To provide technical data, the New Mexico State Engineer's Office simultaneously began to seek a qualified consultant to study Rio Grande water use in the entire basin above Fort Quitman, Texas.[56]

The search for a consultant and the time required to compile engineering data further postponed action against Colorado for about a year, and this additional delay allowed tempers to cool. The result was that the possibility of settling the Rio Grande dispute through an interstate compact was raised once again at conferences held in August and September 1927 on Colorado River water use.[57]

Various factors made talks on the Rio Grande look more promising (or at least more necessary) than when they had broken off two years earlier.

First, despite the successful negotiations that originally had led to the 1922 Colorado River Compact, that stream had remained controversial over the following years and in need of further discussions for several reasons. These included Arizona's refusal to ratify the Colorado River Compact, difficulties in persuading the remaining six Colorado River basin states to accept it fully, the Utah legislature's threatened repeal of its ratification, and differences over proposals to build storage works on the lower reaches of the Colorado River.[58] Thus, by mid-1927, there was considerable doubt over whether the Colorado River Compact ever would accomplish its goal, and these circumstances underscored to Rio Grande negotiators the need to reach a workable compact for their stream.

Moreover, not only was the Colorado River Compact proving to be unsettled, but another early interstate river accord—the La Plata River Compact—also faced challenges, especially when New Mexico's attorney general, Robert C. Dow, wired Colorado's Delph Carpenter insisting that the La Plata River Compact's terms be carried out immediately. The La Plata River Compact had been concluded at about the same time as the Colorado River Compact. Yet as with the Colorado River, circumstances on the La Plata had remained controversial over precisely how to apply that agreement even though the La Plata accord had been fully ratified. Nevertheless, Dow's demand intimated that further legal steps might be taken if the La Plata River Compact's terms were not implemented at once.[59]

The problems with both the Colorado River interstate allocations and those of the La Plata River underscored how vital it was to continue with compact negotiations on the Rio Grande and to reach an accord that would preclude similar future difficulties from arising on that stream. Moreover, disastrous flooding throughout the entire Mississippi River valley in 1927 had emphasized the need for concerted and unified responses to all of the nation's water resource problems.[60] Thus, it became clear that regardless of the shortcomings of other interstate allocation settlements, talks on the Rio Grande ought to move forward.

Following up on the revival of the Rio Grande settlement idea, Francis C. Wilson, New Mexico's interstate river commissioner, discussed the Rio Grande situation with Richard Burges and Elephant Butte Irrigation District lawyer Edwin Mechem. Both Burges and Mechem favored continuing the lawsuit against Colorado, primarily because they feared that without litigation, the River Ranch Company would build Vega Sylvestre Reservoir. They were willing to consider a compact solution once again, however, if it could be achieved in a short period of time. With this limited approval, Wilson told Carpenter that any accord would have to be arrived at quickly to avoid legal action. Wilson then suggested that Carpenter draft a compact providing for deliveries of water at the Colorado–New Mexico state line.[61] Because of Carpenter's prominent role in preparing the Colorado River Compact and in negotiations over several other interstate streams,[62] he appeared to be the logical choice for the Rio Grande situation.

With New Mexico, Colorado, and Texas interests willing to try once again to achieve a Rio Grande Compact, on December 19, 1928, Wilson, Carpenter, and T. H. McGregor met in Santa Fe as the respective delegates from the three states. Also attending the first Rio Grande Compact conference since the talks had been called off three years earlier were representatives from the San Luis Valley, the Middle Rio Grande Conservancy District (created in 1925 to coordinate reclamation efforts in the basin near Albuquerque), the Elephant Butte Irrigation District, El Paso County Water Improvement District No. 1, and the Indian Irrigation Service. Assistant U.S. Attorney General William J. "Wild Bill" Donovan was named the federal delegate to the Rio Grande Compact Commission by outgoing president Calvin Coolidge after Herbert Hoover resigned from that post to be sworn in as the new president of the United States.[63]

As discussions got under way, Commissioner Wilson defined New Mexico's position first. Arguing that neither New Mexico nor Texas asked for any new Rio Grande water supplies but that both sought to prevent further Colorado diversions, Wilson insisted on delivery of a specific amount of water at the Colorado–New Mexico state line. Wilson recognized Colorado's desire to increase development in the San Luis Valley, but he thought this could be done by draining the waterlogged part of the valley commonly known as the "dead" or "sump" area and more formally designated the Closed Basin.[64] Residents of the San Luis Valley had proposed utilizing this wasted water since as early as 1911,[65] and the recovered water, Wilson believed, could be used elsewhere in Colorado. Such a plan would allow Colorado to enlarge its irrigated acreage and expand its water supplies by as much as 200,000 acre-feet per year with no detrimental effects below the state line. Wilson pointed out, however, that without such drainage, Vega Sylvestre Dam would be a direct threat to Rio Grande Project water rights because it would impound existing flows coming out of the San Luis Valley—an amount of water estimated by Wilson to be about 600,000 acre-feet per year.[66]

Richard Burges spoke next on behalf of Texas, telling the meeting that his state relied on its rights as established by the U.S. government's appropriations for the Rio Grande Project in 1906 and 1908. This may not have been a particularly tactful approach, because according to two Colorado newspapers, those filings had not become known in Colorado until 1912—circumstances that led the papers to charge that the government had deprived "the people of the San Luis Valley of the right to reclaim their own lands with the waters of Colorado in order that the people of two other states and of a foreign nation may benefit thereby."[67] That issue notwithstanding, Burges asserted that Texas also held senior water rights for 20,000 acres under ditch above Fort Quitman, Texas, but below the end of the Rio Grande Project. Most of this land, Burges pointed out, was being served by project return flows. In addition, Burges said that he had been asked to "lay before the commission the claims of the City of El Paso to a municipal water supply from the waters of the Rio Grande," but he did not elaborate on this point.[68]

With the New Mexico and Texas positions established, Colorado's lieutenant governor, George M. Corlett (who spoke for San Luis Valley irrigators), outlined the history of the Rio Grande embargo and described how that restriction had been a grave injustice to Colorado water users. Corlett offered two reasons why additional storage of Rio Grande waters in Colorado would not hurt water supplies downriver. First, he contended that return flows from San Luis Valley irrigation would offset any supplemental Colorado diversions—an argument that Colorado was simultaneously advancing in the continuing interstate dispute with Kansas over the waters of the Arkansas River to justify increasing Colorado's depletions of that stream.[69] Second, Corlett contended that any Rio Grande water flowing into New Mexico was wasted by evaporation in the desert heat long before it could reach Elephant Butte Reservoir. For these reasons, Corlett asserted that the additional storage at the proposed Vega Sylvestre Reservoir would not adversely affect irrigators below the state line, and he suggested that the facility might even benefit farmers in northern New Mexico and in the middle Rio Grande valley by acting as storage for them as well as for Colorado interests. Corlett concluded that while he was reluctant to abandon the Vega Sylvestre Reservoir, he was willing to work with New Mexico and Texas representatives to secure federal aid for drainage of the Closed Basin area and to provide related storage works on the upper Rio Grande and on the Conejos River, a tributary of the Rio Grande.[70]

During several more negotiating sessions, the Rio Grande Compact commissioners and other delegates heard testimony by engineering consultants representing the three states, the New Mexico and Texas irrigation districts, and the San Luis Valley.[71] The commissioners also considered at least one compact proposal that would have established mandatory binding arbitration.[72] Yet regardless of the extensive engineering information, by February 11, 1929, the commissioners had come to realize that no final agreement could be reached. Because the three states' legislatures met only once every two years and were then in session, it became imperative that a temporary agreement be realized to avoid expensive litigation in the U.S. Supreme Court. Thus, on February 12, 1929, Wilson, McGregor, and Carpenter signed a compact that in essence established the status quo as a basis for apportioning the Rio Grande's waters.[73]

Colorado's legislature approved the temporary Rio Grande Compact in early April 1929, and New Mexico and Texas, which had waited for Colorado's ratification before taking any action of their own, followed suit shortly thereafter. Despite these relatively quick actions and hopes for a similar prompt response by Congress, federal ratification stalled for over a year because Secretary of the Interior Ray Lyman Wilbur expressed his official opposition to the accord. Wilbur stated that he could not support the agreement, partly because of its nature—a temporary pact that merely maintained the status quo—and partly because he believed that the compact could be construed to obligate the U.S. government to build the San Luis Valley drain.[74] Nevertheless, after considerable lobbying by the three states' congressional delegations (and a published endorsement of the compacting process in general to solve myriad interstate problems by the second U.S. delegate to the Rio Grande talks, William Donovan), federal lawmakers ratified the compact in late June 1930. Final approval came on June 17, 1930, when President Hoover signed the congressional bill approving the settlement.[75]

The temporary Rio Grande Compact recognized the right of the U.S. government to enter into treaties with foreign nations, but it asserted that the 1906 treaty with Mexico, which gave that country 60,000 acre-feet of water per year, had been made at the expense of citizens of Colorado, New Mexico, and Texas. To remedy this fault, the compact suggested (but, contrary to Secretary Wilbur's understanding, did not demand) that the United States construct a drain for the San Luis Valley's Closed Basin and a reservoir in Colorado near the state line to impound the increased Rio Grande flow from the drainage works. These new reclamation features were to benefit all three states. The compact provided that after the Closed Basin Drain and the reservoir were completed, the three states would meet again to work out a permanent agreement based on river flow measurements with these facilities in place. The accord noted, however, that if the drain and reservoir were not operating by June 1, 1935, or if no final settlement had been achieved by that date, then each state could do as it saw fit. Tied to the request that the federal government construct the Closed Basin Drain and the reservoir at the Colorado–New Mexico state line was the central point of the temporary compact. Until the drain and reservoir were built, Colorado agreed not to increase diversions, build more storage facilities, or impair the flow of the river as it then existed.[76] The idea, of course, was to assure federal authorities that U.S. aid for the proposed projects could go forward unimpeded by the interstate quarrel.

This concept of maintaining the status quo during deliberations over apportioning interstate streams was not unique to the Rio Grande watershed. Negotiators struggling over the allocations of other interstate rivers in the 1930s and 1940s also frequently turned to "freezing" existing uses temporarily—particularly on streams where immediate federal assistance was sought in one form or another during the Great Depression. For example, barely three years after the 1929 Rio Grande Compact was ratified, officials in Kansas and Colorado agreed to what became known as the Stipulation of 1933. This agreement to respect existing water uses on the Arkansas River was negotiated as part of the proceedings in *Colorado v. Kansas*, an interstate lawsuit that had grown out of the U.S. Supreme Court's failure to apportion that stream in the 1907 *Kansas v. Colorado* decision. The principal point behind the Stipulation of 1933 (much as the purpose behind the 1929 Rio Grande Compact was to secure federal funds for the Closed Basin Drain and the related reservoir) was to obtain U.S. assistance in building various flood control and irrigation works—including John Martin Dam—by assuring federal authorities that the interstate quarrel between Kansas and Colorado would not complicate government construction on the river.[77]

Protecting existing water uses on the Rio Grande, like elsewhere in the West, was not merely a ploy to garner U.S. dollars for reclamation projects. Recognizing that there were finite limits to growth in the arid part of the country, westerners everywhere strongly adhered to the sanctity of water appropriations as private property. Thus, the status quo concept was in part a protection of property rights. On the Rio Grande, Colorado's willingness to accept the situation the way it then existed meant by implication that the Bureau of Reclamation's division of water between users above and below El Paso within the Rio Grande Project remained firmly in place and vested property rights there would be protected while a permanent interstate compact was negotiated.

CHAPTER 10

The Rio Grande Compact, Part II
The Permanent 1938 Accord

Delph Carpenter, Francis Wilson, and T. H. McGregor had intended for the 1929 Rio Grande Compact to buy enough time to allow the construction of the San Luis Valley drain (then becoming known formally as the Closed Basin Drain) and a reservoir just inside Colorado (dubbed the State Line Reservoir). The three negotiators believed that with these structures completed, an accurate measurement could be made of how much water the drain would return to the Rio Grande and a permanent compact could then be consummated fixing each state's share of the river. Yet the negotiators of the 1929 Rio Grande Compact could not have anticipated that less than nine months after they had signed the accord, the stock market crash would trigger the worst economic crisis the United States had experienced to that date. With the Great Depression making Congress and President Herbert Hoover reluctant to approve major expenditure bills, projects such as the Closed Basin Drain and the State Line Reservoir were temporarily shelved.

Franklin D. Roosevelt's inauguration as president in 1933, however, and his New Deal programs brought renewed faith to Rio Grande water users, who hoped that federal legislation funding the two projects in Colorado might finally allow a lasting compact to be realized. Such a permanent accord, all parties understood, would finally accomplish a fixed interstate division of the river's flows—one that from the perspective of Rio Grande Project water users would incorporate the provisions of the 1904 local compromise and the 1905 congressional allocation of water below Elephant Butte Reservoir.

The involvement of the New Deal in Rio Grande apportionment issues began with the passage of the 1933 National Industrial Recovery Act, a part of which was aimed at improving the economy through a massive government jobs program administered by the Public Works Administration (PWA).[1] Seeing an opportunity to have the Closed Basin Drain and State Line Reservoir built as PWA programs, the governors of Colorado, New Mexico, and Texas and other interested parties applied for federal funds. On June 20, 1934, the PWA recommended that $900,000 be allotted to the Department of the Interior to build the drain and to survey the reservoir site.[2]

Despite the good news, the PWA's recommendation came too late to be implemented before the June 1935 deadline for a permanent compact. As a result, in late 1934 Colorado governor Edwin "Big Ed" Johnson called for new talks to take place without the information about how much return flow the Closed Basin Drain would provide. Colorado State Engineer Michael C. (usually known as "M.C.") Hinderlider, who had taken over Delph Carpenter's duties as interstate river commissioner the previous year because of Carpenter's advancing Parkinson's disease, became Colorado's delegate to the new compact sessions.[3] Eventually becoming the longest-serving state engineer in Colorado's history, Hinderlider was a graduate of Purdue University. Before he had gone to work for the state, he had been an engineer for the City of Denver, the U.S. Geological Survey, and the Reclamation Service. Ultimately, Hinderlider played important roles in the negotiation of several interstate compacts involving rivers that Colorado shared with its neighbors.

The governors of New Mexico and Texas, Andrew W. Hockenhull and James V. Allred, respectively, concurred that new deliberations should be held. Governor Hockenhull appointed as commissioner New Mexico State Engineer Thomas M. McClure. (The previous governor of New Mexico, Richard C. Dillon, had fired Francis Wilson as his state's Rio Grande commissioner in July 1929, apparently in a political dispute over his state's position with regard to a potential interstate oil compact.)[4] Governor Allred named T. H. McGregor, who had negotiated the 1929 Rio Grande

Compact for Texas, to the new Rio Grande discussions. President Franklin Roosevelt directed the Bureau of Reclamation's assistant chief engineer, Sinclair O. Harper, to take part for the federal government.[5]

The Rio Grande was not the only western river for which compact proposals, both new and revived, were again being suggested. The specific reasons varied from basin to basin, but in many cases the severe drought circumstances of the 1930s emphasized the need for mutual cooperation within watersheds to avoid lengthy and expensive litigation — something states could ill afford during the Great Depression. Moreover, the gradual completion of Bureau of Reclamation projects in the 1920s on some interstate streams altered historical river regimens and prompted new controversies to emerge. And Roosevelt's 1932 election prompted hopes of securing federal funds from New Deal programs to pay for new developments. All of these factors spurred new rounds of compact discussions (some successful and others not) starting in the early 1930s on a variety of streams.

For example, beginning in 1931, Colorado, Nebraska, and Wyoming tried to continue compact discussions originally commenced a half decade earlier for the North Platte River.[6] On the Columbia River, where compact talks also had started in the mid-1920s, Idaho, Montana, Oregon, and Washington again hoped to reach a settlement. In addition, at about the same time, Colorado, Kansas, and Nebraska discussed compact possibilities for the Republican River and its tributaries (both as separate streams and together). Other compact discussions took place between Idaho and Wyoming for the Snake River and among Montana, Wyoming, and (later) North Dakota for the Yellowstone River and its tributaries. Colorado and Kansas continued to struggle over the Arkansas River, including renewed compact deliberations. And on the Colorado River, the situation with regard to Arizona's failure to ratify that accord not only remained unresolved but also had been complicated by that state's lawsuit against California and discussions about possible separate lower and upper Colorado River basin compacts.[7]

On the Rio Grande, the first meeting of that stream's revived compact commission took place on December 10, 1934, in Santa Fe, New Mexico. In addition to those officially representing the three states, other delegates came on behalf of water users in the San Luis Valley, the middle Rio Grande valley, and the Rio Grande Project.[8] Among the first to speak was George M. Corlett, who, as in 1929, once again represented San Luis Valley interests. Corlett reiterated the reasons for a new compact, and he pointed out that the commissioners needed to discuss how to handle the

Farmer and son in rye field, Rio Grande Project, 1918. Courtesy Bureau of Reclamation, National Archives II, College Park, Maryland.

PWA's recommendations regarding the Closed Basin Drain and the State Line Reservoir. Noting that the government's action provided $900,000 to build the drain but merely funded a survey for the reservoir and not its actual construction, Corlett concluded that the assumption underlying the 1929 Rio Grande Compact that the two features could form the basis for a new agreement was no longer valid. Corlett then demanded that Colorado be "placed upon a parity with New Mexico and Texas insofar as our present requirements are concerned," an equality that to Corlett and San Luis Valley water users meant having the right to build new storage reservoirs in Colorado regardless of whether the Closed Basin Drain and the State Line Reservoir were constructed. Such Colorado irrigation facilities, of course, would benefit San Luis Valley water users at the expense of downstream farmers in New Mexico and Texas.[9]

In response, Richard Burges, who had come to the meeting as a legal adviser to McGregor, insisted that Texas was unwilling to allow Colorado to have more storage until the extent of return flows from the Closed Basin Drain was known. Favoring the construction of the drain and a determination of its augmentation to the river before allowing new reservoirs in Colorado, Burges saw clear limits to the Rio Grande's water supply. He was willing to permit additional dams above the New Mexico–Colorado state line only after measurements of the Closed Basin Drain had been made and then only to the extent that the drain conserved water that had previously been lost through evaporation or seepage in the Closed Basin. Burges suggested that the most important question before the commissioners was whether Colorado intended to accept the $900,000 grant from the PWA. He explained that Colorado's decision would influence whether the 1929 Rio Grande Compact should be extended while the drain was built or whether the negotiators should instead try to reach a new pact without the drain data. New Mexico's representatives supported Burges's position, recognizing that without the Closed Basin Drain information, Colorado's upstream position could allow San Luis Valley water users to take ever-larger amounts of the Rio Grande's flow.[10]

Colorado delegates opposed keeping the 1929 Rio Grande Compact in effect beyond June 1935 because such an extension of the status quo would only postpone further San Luis Valley development while the Closed Basin Drain was built and return flow measurements were being made. Future Colorado governor Ralph L. Carr, who, like Corlett, had joined the gathering as a spokesman for San Luis Valley residents, insisted that although Colorado intended to construct the drain eventually, the real purpose of the existing discussions was to establish an equitable apportionment of the Rio Grande, not to deliberate over the Closed Basin Drain. Carr maintained that the 1929 Rio Grande Compact had specified that any subsequent negotiations were to create a permanent division of the river's waters regardless of whether Closed Basin Drain statistics were available or not. With more debate amply demonstrating that Colorado's negotiators would not retreat from their position, the commissioners realized that no quick agreement was likely, and the session adjourned for the time being.[11]

Even after another meeting in late January 1935, the Rio Grande Compact negotiators still could reach no conclusion on how to proceed, essentially because of Colorado's insistence on continuing with compact talks without the Closed Basin Drain study.[12] The delegates then turned to their respective legislatures for a two-year extension of the 1929 Rio Grande Compact, during which time the commissioners hoped to sort out their differences and conclude a permanent accord.[13] Although an extension to June 1, 1937, was readily approved by all three states, tensions were not relieved, and events involving the Middle Rio Grande Conservancy District quickly clouded the interstate apportionment situation.

The Middle Rio Grande Conservancy District had been formed in 1925 to reclaim farmland near Albuquerque through a combination of drainage systems, flood control facilities, and irrigation works. To avoid depleting flows that normally went down the river to Elephant Butte Reservoir for the Rio Grande Project and for Mexico, organizers of the Middle Rio Grande Conservancy District had planned that water from drainage works would offset increased irrigation and storage in their area. Because studies had estimated that the Rio Grande Project's water supply would not be affected so long as the conservancy district reclaimed just the immediate Rio Grande valley and not higher mesa lands, officials of the Elephant Butte Irrigation District and El Paso County Water Improvement District No. 1 had not objected strenuously to the conservancy district's organization.[14]

With most of the Middle Rio Grande Conservancy District's features taking shape within a decade of its formation, however, Rio Grande Project water users had changed their minds and had come to view the conservancy district as a direct threat to Elephant Butte Reservoir's water supplies. Charging that the conservancy district was extending beyond its original river-valley limits, Rio Grande Project farmers believed that the district was likely to consume large quantities of water destined for Elephant Butte Reservoir. Worse still to water users in the Mesilla and El Paso valleys was that conservancy district officials had started to promote the proposed State Line Reservoir as a flood control project, although Rio Grande Project backers feared that the facility would be used more for storage than flood abatement. The conservancy district, moreover, in a move that alarmed downstream water users, was constructing the El Vado Reservoir on the Rio Chama, a tributary of the Rio Grande, which irrigators below Elephant Butte Dam thought might be operated to hold back waters that they considered to rightfully belong to the Rio Grande Project. All of these concerns were exacerbated by memories of a season of unusually low runoff in 1934, which had left water levels at Elephant Butte Reservoir well below normal.[15]

With Rio Grande Project water users believing that their supplies were being severely threatened, Texas filed a lawsuit in October 1935 in the U.S. Supreme Court to halt the Middle Rio Grande Conservancy District's activities until a compact could be reached.[16] Texas's complaint named the State of New Mexico and the conservancy district as defendants, and *Texas v. New Mexico and the Middle Rio Grande Conservancy District* thus became leverage to ensure that deliberations on a new compact moved forward as rapidly as possible. The significance of the Texas suit was not missed by the regional press. The *Albuquerque Journal* reported that the conflict had been characterized as "one of the most important legal battles ever engaged in with relation to water rights," while the *El Paso Herald-Post* observed that "attorneys on both sides are calling . . . [the lawsuit] 'a life and death struggle.'"[17]

Understandably, the pace of the lawsuit was directly tied to progress in the compact negotiations, much as the timing of the U.S. government's legal action against the Rio Grande Dam and Irrigation Company several decades earlier had been linked to debates about how best to allocate the Rio Grande's flows in the region that later came to encompass the Rio Grande Project. In both situations, litigation was a potentially explosive weapon wielded for economic and political power.[18] In both circumstances, however, a multilayered approach to negotiated settlement ultimately defused the ticking bomb.

The heated Rio Grande situation soon caught the attention of federal officials. The United States was involved in Rio Grande matters in a variety of ways, which included carrying out the terms of the 1906 treaty with Mexico, operating the Rio Grande Project, collecting payments on the Middle Rio Grande Conservancy District's construction costs (which had been subsidized by government-backed bonds), providing the $900,000 to build the Closed Basin Drain, acting as trustee for all Indian tribes with reservations in the area, and finally, managing public lands in New Mexico and Colorado along the river. Because of the multitude of federal interests in the Rio Grande valley, on September 23, 1935, President Franklin Roosevelt directed the National Resources Committee to act as a clearinghouse for any federal agency with Rio Grande basin plans and to help resolve the apportionment problem.[19]

Originally created in 1933 as the National Planning Board, the ideology behind the operations of the National Resources Committee was firmly rooted in the earlier Progressive era's support for comprehensive development of natural resources of the United States. The National Planning Board (subsequently reorganized as the National Resources Board in 1934, the National Resources Committee in 1935, and the National Resources Planning Board in 1939) had been established by Franklin Roosevelt's New Deal under the provisions of the National Industrial Recovery Act. To ensure that the agency's activities would have significant impact, the National Resources Committee worked closely with Administrator of Public Works (and Secretary of the Interior) Harold Ickes. The National Resources Committee performed four major functions: developing and scheduling public works, encouraging local and state planning, coordinating federal agencies in relation to natural resource programs, and conducting research to further its other three purposes. Having considerable sway in shaping federal policies, the National Resources Committee was highly influential in determining resource development, especially in the American West.[20] Thus, that Roosevelt ordered the agency to oversee federal activities in the Rio Grande basin is not surprising.

Following up on Roosevelt's directive, Charles W. Eliot II, the executive officer of the National Resources Committee, suggested that the Rio Grande Compact Commission work with the U.S. government to secure sufficient data to permit an equitable apportionment of the river's waters among the three concerned states.[21] The compact negotiators readily agreed to this proposal, and with the two-year extension to the 1929 Rio Grande Compact's deadline already obtained, work by state and federal officials began on what came to be called the Rio Grande Joint Investigation. Limited in authority to the collection and preservation of data, the fruit of the joint investigation's labors was not to include recommendations for a new compact unless specifically requested by the Rio Grande Compact commissioners—a restriction aimed at retaining the three states' autonomy in the face of rapidly escalating federal influence in the West under various New Deal programs. In the meantime, *Texas v. New Mexico and the Middle Rio Grande Conservancy District*—which had begun in late 1936 with testimony on the impact of Elephant Butte Reservoir on waters flowing to Texas—was postponed by Charles Warren, who had been appointed as special master by the Supreme Court to hear the case. Warren hoped the results of the joint investigation would facilitate the conclusion of a compact and make further prosecution of the case unnecessary.[22]

By late September 1937—aided by another brief extension of the 1929 Rio Grande Compact's deadline—the Rio Grande Joint Investigation had finished its work, and the compact commission met again to discuss the investigation's findings.[23] Even with the massive amounts of new information, however, the negotiators reluctantly concurred that no permanent accord could be reached without additional analysis of proposed water delivery schedules to the three principal regions of the Rio Grande in Colorado, New Mexico, and Texas: Colorado's San Luis Valley, the Rio Grande basin in New Mexico above Elephant Butte Reservoir, and the Rio Grande Project's lands below Elephant Butte in New Mexico and Texas. Disregarding the October 1, 1937, expiration of the second 1929 Rio Grande Compact extension, the compact commissioners then adjourned to study recommendations by the National Resources Committee.[24] To discuss possible deliveries and the conclusions made by the National Resources Committee, the Rio Grande Compact Commission's engineering advisers met with the Bureau of Reclamation; after considerable effort, a breakdown of contemplated deliveries to each section of the river was forwarded to the commissioners in December 1937 for use in continued negotiations.[25]

Although the engineers' conclusions represented their combined positions, not everyone was happy with the proposed schedule of deliveries. Demonstrating the differing Rio Grande interests within New Mexico, H. C. Neuffer, the chief engineer for the Middle Rio Grande Conservancy District, told New Mexico's commissioner, Thomas McClure, not to "accept this report as a basis for further compact negotiations" because it "would result in permanent damage to the Middle Rio Grande Conservancy District and other water users in New Mexico above Elephant Butte Dam." Neuffer alleged that the proposed deliveries provided too much water to Elephant Butte Reservoir, and he suggested that the engineers give the matter more thought before their findings were used for compact deliberations.[26]

McClure agreed with Neuffer and criticized the engineers' report as being "too vague and indefinite in some respects." Ignoring the fact that Elephant Butte Reservoir served water users in the Rio Grande Project in both New Mexico and Texas, McClure asserted that "the report fixes a basis for water supply to the State of Texas which, in my judgment and in the judgment of others in authority in New Mexico, is so far out of reason that it could not be considered as a basis for negotiations." McClure concluded that the engineers had exceeded their authority by the scope of their recommendations, but he also added that they ought to study the subject further.[27]

McClure's objections to the engineers' analysis angered Raymond A. Hill, Texas's engineering adviser. Because the engineers' report had called for one dividing point for Rio Grande waters to be at the head of Elephant Butte Reservoir—which, as everyone knew, was well above the New Mexico–Texas state line—Hill considered that McClure's position necessitated a decision on where the measurement for Texas's allotment ought to be located. Fully aware that in some cases in the past, Texas had acted to protect all Rio Grande Project interests to safeguard water supplies flowing across the state line to the El Paso Valley, Hill asserted that "the time has come when the State of Texas should cease being the direct representative" of the Elephant Butte Irrigation District. Hill observed that as long as Texas had to act as an advocate for the water rights of all lands under the Rio

Grande Project, New Mexico's official position on Rio Grande matters would always be identical to that of the Middle Rio Grande Conservancy District. He added that if New Mexico's McClure was forced to represent the Elephant Butte Irrigation District more effectively, then that district could insist on a schedule of deliveries into Elephant Butte Reservoir for its own water users. Texas, Hill concluded, could then protect just the interests of El Paso County Water Improvement District No. 1.[28]

To compel McClure to represent both the Elephant Butte Irrigation District and the Middle Rio Grande Conservancy District, Hill suggested that "demand be made for a schedule of deliveries at Courchesne [near El Paso]." This schedule, Hill proposed, would cover all water allotted to Mexico under the 1906 treaty, supplies for consumptive use below El Paso in Texas, flows needed to balance salt levels, operating waste of the Rio Grande Project, and water that was not divertible in winter and in excess of irrigation needs in summer (mostly storm runoff). Hill estimated that these combined amounts totaled about 500,000 acre-feet per year. With a schedule of deliveries near El Paso written into a compact, Hill argued, "the interests of the Elephant Butte Irrigation District will be better served thereby than will be the case if the full burden of providing for deliveries into Elephant Butte Reservoir is placed upon Texas."[29]

By the time the Rio Grande Compact Commission met again in early March 1938, despite some initial heated discussions,[30] the need for a specific schedule of deliveries at the New Mexico–Texas state line had been rendered irrelevant by the interdistrict agreement reached in February 1938. This accord had verified the Bureau of Reclamation's determination that the maximum irrigable acreage of the Elephant Butte Irrigation District was 88,000 acres and that of El Paso County Water Improvement District No. 1 was 67,000 acres. This finding had been made in line with the 1905 congressional legislation extending the Reclamation Act of 1902 to the El Paso Valley and authorizing the U.S. government to fix the final allotments of water within the Rio Grande Project on the basis of studies by the Bureau of Reclamation. With the 1938 interdistrict contract between the two Rio Grande Project sections making a schedule of deliveries at El Paso unnecessary (because irrigated acreage was roughly equivalent to a volume of water), the compact commission slightly scaled back the amount of water the engineers had allocated to Elephant Butte Reservoir—primarily to placate McClure—and they then unanimously adopted the engineers' report as the technical basis for a new compact.[31]

To prepare the actual wording of the compact agreement, the commissioners created a committee composed of two legal advisers from each state, and although no formal compact hearings took place while the draft was being written, the legal committee held spontaneous talks with the commissioners to resolve controversial issues. By mid-March 1938, the legal committee's members had finished their work, and they presented a completed draft of an accord to the full Rio Grande Compact Commission. After considering it overnight, the negotiators met one final time on March 18, 1938, to sign the agreement. Shortly thereafter, *Texas v. New Mexico and the Middle Rio Grande Conservancy District* was postponed yet again to await the compact's ratification by the three states' legislatures and Congress.[32]

The new Rio Grande Compact established a permanent commission to carry out the agreement's apportionment—the first such regulatory body created by any interstate river compact.[33] This was a feature that the Rio Grande Compact's negotiators hoped would avoid problems that had confronted signatory states of other early western river settlements such the accords over the Colorado and La Plata rivers. On the Colorado, although Congress's passage of the 1928 Boulder Canyon Act had approved the Colorado River Compact with six of the seven basin states in agreement, several years later Arizona had filed suit against California over the lower basin's allocation. This litigation dragged on for decades (and eventually culminated in the 1963 landmark U.S. Supreme Court ruling in *Arizona v. California*).[34] The lengthy—and costly—struggle over the water supplies of the Colorado River was vivid evidence to the negotiators of the Rio Grande Compact that a means had to be provided in their accord to mediate comparable difficulties.

With regard to the La Plata River, representatives of Colorado and New Mexico had approved that compact in 1922, barely three days after the Colorado River Compact had offered the original model for using such agreements to allocate stream flows.[35] Nevertheless, in 1928, the La Plata and Cherry Creek Ditch Company, a Colorado water user, had sued the state, claiming that it had been denied flows that were being utilized to satisfy Colorado's settlement with New Mexico. By early 1938—with no interstate mechanism for compact enforcement to help settle the La Plata conflict—the case had reached the U.S. Supreme Court to answer the fundamental question of whether interstate river compacts could be enforced to the detriment of existing vested water rights.[36] The negotiators of the Rio Grande

Compact hoped that their agreement's establishment of a permanent commission would help prevent a similar situation on the Rio Grande.

As if problems with other interstate compacts were not proof enough that a new approach had to be tried on the Rio Grande, pending interstate river litigation in the U.S. Supreme Court that did not stem directly from existing compacts pointed to the need for a long-lasting deliberative body to discuss possible future problems. For instance, on the Arkansas River, two lawsuits in lower federal court by Kansas water users against upstream Colorado appropriators had prompted Colorado to return to the U.S. Supreme Court in 1928 to block the Kansas actions. Colorado contended in *Colorado v. Kansas* that it sought the "equitable apportionment" the high court had ruled in 1907 in *Kansas v. Colorado* that either state might be entitled to if an unfair water-use situation developed. *Colorado v. Kansas*—which remained unresolved as the Rio Grande Compact was being ratified— offered yet another example of expensive interstate litigation that had to be avoided if at all possible.[37]

While the Arkansas River was a reminder that Supreme Court lawsuits over interstate streams could be long and costly, so too were events on the North Platte, for which, although proposals for compacts had taken place repeatedly since as early as 1924, no agreement had ever been achieved. As a result, in frustration, Nebraska had filed an action before the Supreme Court in 1934 (even though proposals for a compact on that stream continued to be advanced).[38] The North Platte lawsuit had not been pending as long as that on the Arkansas River, but it nonetheless was a salient reminder that if discussions failed, expensive litigation would be the outcome on interstate streams.

The various legal actions on interstate streams also illustrated yet another threat to be avoided at all cost—intervention by the U.S. government. The permanent Rio Grande Compact Commission was a means to maintain state sovereignty over water by establishing a body to settle disputes before they went to venues in which federal courts or U.S. agencies might be able to impose their own solutions. This was a decades-old worry that had grown in proportion to the federal government's size and power during the New Deal years, and U.S. intervention in the North Platte Supreme Court case had driven this point home to the Rio Grande negotiators. The La Plata case also had demonstrated a similar concern when eastern states had intervened to argue that the U.S. Supreme Court did not have jurisdiction over interstate compacts.[39]

Thus, the permanent Rio Grande Compact Commission was aimed at solving myriad problems. Comprising one representative each from Colorado, New Mexico, and Texas and one from the U.S. government, the permanent Rio Grande Compact Commission was to collect data and carry out the apportionment provided in the three-state accord. The commission was to oversee twelve fixed gauging stations on the river to help determine water deliveries by Colorado at the Colorado–New Mexico state line and by New Mexico at San Marcial, the head of Elephant Butte Reservoir. A system of debits and credits was to accommodate annual variations from agreed-upon schedules, and the downstream states could demand water releases up to the limit of the upstream states' accrued debits. In essence, this method of apportioning the Rio Grande treated water as a commodity to be spent or banked, depending on the needs of a particular locale and on precipitation changes from year to year. New Mexico and Texas agreed that the compact settled their pending Supreme Court case, but all three states concurred that the compact did not preclude future legal action if the quantity or quality of Rio Grande water changed. Finally, the compact provided that it would become effective when ratified by all three states and Congress.[40]

With the signing of the Rio Grande Compact, the commissioners returned to their home states to lobby for quick ratification by their respective legislatures when the state lawmakers reconvened in early 1939. Having overcome such formidable disagreements to reach a final pact, however, little could the commissioners have imagined the dangers facing the new accord's formal acceptance. First, the Supreme Court lawsuit over the La Plata River Compact continued to overshadow the Rio Grande Compact's ultimate viability. With no resolution yet of the La Plata case's key question of whether compacts could compromise vested state water rights, the legitimacy of the Rio Grande Compact hung partially in the La Plata outcome.[41]

Not only did the possible outcome of the La Plata case cloud the possible usefulness of an interstate compact for the Rio Grande, but so too did events that took place within the three signatory states to the Rio Grande Compact as it went out to the legislatures for ratification. When the Rio Grande Compact commissioners signed off on that accord in March 1938, they could not have anticipated that ratification would become an almost insurmountable obstacle in Texas because of a major dispute about how the compact's terms affected that state. Like the earlier New Mexico struggles between water users in the Middle Rio Grande Conservancy District and the Elephant

Butte Irrigation District, the Texas fight demonstrated that intrastate water conflicts could flare in any of the three states and that local interests could severely disrupt the settlement of an interstate apportionment.

The Rio Grande, of course, was not unique in this regard. Conflicts among intrastate interests had severely complicated ratification of the 1922 Colorado River Compact when that accord was considered in the seven states sharing that stream's flows.[42] Similarly, ten years after the Rio Grande Compact had been signed by its negotiators, intrastate issues in Colorado and Kansas would threaten ratification of the 1948 Arkansas River Compact.[43] Unlike these other two interstate compacts, however, the Rio Grande Compact's intrastate ratification difficulties centered on a lack of understanding of the history of that stream's existing apportionment along one reach of the river—the region that lay within the Bureau of Reclamation's Rio Grande Project. Congress had already made an interstate allocation in this section of the Rio Grande when it passed the 1905 law extending the Reclamation Act to the El Paso Valley in Texas—a statute that was intended to implement the national irrigation congress compromise reached the preceding year. Yet this history was not widely known.

The Rio Grande Compact's complete lack of mention of specific deliveries at the New Mexico–Texas state line triggered the ratification problem in Texas, and the dispute centered on the same issue that had compelled Raymond Hill to recommend a schedule for water deliveries at El Paso during the compact negotiations. Although an idea similar to Hill's proposal had been discussed by the Rio Grande Compact commissioners in late September and early October 1937, it later had been rejected because of the existing apportionment within the Rio Grande Project. That allocation, of course, had been established by the Bureau of Reclamation under the terms of the 1904 National Irrigation Congress compromise, the 1905 congressional legislation extending the Reclamation Act to the El Paso Valley in Texas, and the 1929 and 1938 interdistrict agreements. The compact commission's reasons for rejecting a schedule of deliveries at the New Mexico–Texas state line, however, had never been made clear to Texans on the lower Rio Grande between Fort Quitman and the Gulf of Mexico—although some lower Rio Grande parties had been scheduled to attend Rio Grande Compact negotiations. As a result, many of these water users thought that because the compact provided for water deliveries only at Elephant Butte Reservoir and not at the New Mexico–Texas state line, Texas had no solid guarantee to any Rio Grande water.[44]

Studies done at the turn of the century by William W. Follett in relation to the Rio Grande Dam and Irrigation Company litigation had demonstrated that relatively little of the upper river's flow contributed to the lower stream. Nonetheless, to residents on the lower Rio Grande, the supposed lack of an apportionment at the New Mexico–Texas state line appeared to be a sellout of the majority of Texas's interests in favor of a handful of Rio Grande Project farmers in the El Paso Valley—irrigators who already enjoyed the benefits of Elephant Butte Dam and federally constructed canals. Even more galling to lower Rio Grande water users was that the assumed abandonment of their needs had taken place during the severe drought of the 1930s. Furthermore, the lack of rules governing Mexican diversions below Fort Quitman (which was not remedied until a 1944 treaty) made downstream Texans all the more suspicious that their requirements had been completely ignored by the Rio Grande Compact Commission.[45]

Dismay over the compact among lower Rio Grande water users had arisen even before the interstate accord had been signed. Seeking provisions guaranteeing that Rio Grande water would be delivered to their part of Texas, representatives from below Fort Quitman had attended the January 1938 compact session to discuss the commission engineers' report.[46] At that meeting, Texas's commissioner, Frank Clayton, responded to the lower Rio Grande water users' concerns by advising them that it would be misguided to ask for water for areas below Fort Quitman in the compact negotiations because of how such a demand would be perceived by New Mexico and Colorado. Nonetheless, Clayton had assured the water users from along the lower river that once the compact was signed, neither New Mexico nor Colorado could control what Texas did with its share of Rio Grande waters—a position endorsed by Charles S. Clark, chairman of the Texas Board of Water Engineers. Stressing the need for a united Texas front in the Rio Grande Compact deliberations, Clayton then invited the lower Rio Grande representatives to appear at subsequent hearings.[47]

This did not end the matter, however. Two months later, Clayton sent a copy of the compact draft for review to Charles Clark and to Frank Robertson, who represented the Water Conservation Association of the Lower Rio Grande Valley (an organization of irrigation districts, water companies, cities, counties, and other water users' groups near Brownsville). Immediately wiring back, Robertson and his constituents called for an assurance from Rio Grande Project water users that a minimum of 200,000 acre-feet per year would pass Fort Quitman—a figure based on the average flow at that point during the previous ten years. The lower Rio Grande water users insisted on this commitment even though 200,000 acre-feet was only a tiny fraction of water usage below Fort Quitman and notwithstanding the fact that much of that amount was lost to evaporation and seepage before it ever reached the lower basin.[48] Regardless of the demands submitted by the lower valley's conservation association, Clayton executed the Rio Grande Compact for Texas three days after receiving the telegrams, mistakenly believing that the water users of the lower valley understood that the 1905 congressional allocation below Elephant Butte Dam was intended to be included in the compact's provisions.

Nevertheless, water users on the lower river continued to press Clayton to secure a pledge from the Rio Grande Project's irrigation districts for a fixed quantity of water to pass Fort Quitman each year. Realizing belatedly that the Water Conservation Association of the Lower Rio Grande Valley might oppose the compact's ratification by the Texas legislature if that organization's demands were not addressed, Clayton reluctantly broached the matter with Roland Harwell, manager of El Paso County Water Improvement District No. 1. Harwell, however, pointed out that even if Rio Grande Project water users had wanted to enter into such an agreement, they could not do so, because the Bureau of Reclamation had made the original water appropriations for the entire Rio Grande Project and the bureau controlled all releases of water from Elephant Butte Dam. Clayton then forwarded Harwell's response to the lower Rio Grande interests, hoping it would persuade them not to obstruct the compact's ratification. Attempting to defuse the situation further, Clayton also suggested the unlikelihood that existing flows passing Fort Quitman could ever be diminished, because water going beyond that point derived from supplies necessary to maintain an acceptable salt level farther upstream. Clayton counseled lower Rio Grande water users that if they wished to pursue the topic further, they should deal directly with the two Rio Grande Project irrigation districts and the Bureau of Reclamation.[49]

By mid-April 1938, concern along the lower Rio Grande had grown to the point where a large group of irrigation district managers, attorneys, and water engineers from the region adopted a resolution asking the Water Conservation Association of the Lower Rio Grande Valley to seek assurances that the Rio Grande Compact would provide ample water for areas below Fort Quitman. The group also encouraged the lower Rio Grande association to meet with representatives of the Rio Grande Project and the Bureau of Reclamation.[50]

Acting on this request and Clayton's similar advice, the Water Conservation Association of the Lower Rio Grande Valley sent a delegation to El Paso in late May 1938 to consult with officials of the Rio Grande Project's irrigation districts and the bureau. At the meeting, the lower Rio Grande water users again tried to obtain a guaranteed minimum flow past Fort Quitman of at least 200,000 acre-feet per year, but officials of the Elephant Butte and El Paso districts reiterated that they had no authority over Elephant Butte Dam. Moreover, they added, regardless of who controlled releases from the reservoir, the districts could not make the type of promise sought by the lower basin, because there were too many Mexican diversions beyond the end of the Rio Grande Project that might interfere with flows farther downriver.[51]

This response did not satisfy lower Rio Grande water users, and they became further alarmed by a recommendation aimed at mollifying their worries made at the El Paso gathering by Harlan H. Barrows of the National Resources Committee. Suggesting a survey of the lower river similar to the one done for the Rio Grande Joint Investigation, Barrows proposed that the results of the lower Rio Grande study could then be used to negotiate a treaty with Mexico to settle the long-standing international conflict over irrigation supplies on the river below Fort Quitman. Barrows assumed that the treaty would help alleviate lower Rio Grande water users' problems on the U.S. side of the river, since much of the lower river's water came from Mexican tributaries. Despite Barrow's good intentions, however, lower river interests took his offer to be a veiled threat that if they blocked the Rio Grande Compact's ratification by the Texas legislature, Barrows would use his considerable influence in the federal government (he had served on a variety of President Roosevelt's natural resource management committees since the early 1930s) to obstruct a future treaty with Mexico. Lower Rio Grande water users wanted an international accord covering their part of the river regardless of their request for guaranteed supplies from the Rio Grande Project. The outcome of the El Paso meeting, therefore, was a resolute unification of all water users below Fort Quitman and the initiation of lobbying against the compact's approval in the Texas legislature.[52]

Simultaneously with the upheaval over the compact in Texas, other issues arose in Colorado and New Mexico in July 1938 threatening ratification by any of the three states. In Colorado, George Corlett vowed to fight approval by his state's legislature if the National Resources Committee did not recommend that the Public Works Administration sanction two new proposed reclamation works in the San Luis Valley: the Wagon Wheel Gap Reservoir and Conejos Reservoir. Complicating Corlett's warning was a U.S. government plan to build the Jemez Reservoir near Albuquerque. Although New Mexico was willing to endorse federal approval for Colorado's projects to secure construction of the Jemez Reservoir, Texas— which had the most to lose if any of these works were built—opposed all three propositions.[53]

With only a few months to pass before the states' legislatures convened to consider the Rio Grande Compact, Frank Clayton conceived an unorthodox method to salvage the interstate agreement before the widening controversies in all three states permanently doomed the accord. In desperation, Clayton suggested to Richard Burges in August 1938 that perhaps a solution lay in the final disposition of *Texas v. New Mexico and the Middle Rio Grande Conservancy District*, which had remained pending to allow time for the compact's ratification. Proposing that Texas would not object to the Colorado or New Mexico projects if Colorado would become a party to the U.S. Supreme Court suit, Clayton submitted that all three states could then adopt a consent decree to embody the terms of the compact and end the litigation. The advantage of such a procedure, Clayton observed, was that when the Supreme Court accepted the consent decree, the court's order would make the Rio Grande Compact's terms binding without ratification by the states' governments (although Clayton contended that for public relations reasons, he also still favored legislative approval). Clayton believed that in addition to solving the Colorado and New Mexico issues, the consent decree plan would circumvent the widening opposition to the compact's approval by Texas's lower Rio Grande water users.[54]

Clayton fully understood that his idea might prompt charges in southern Texas that it was an attempt to impose the Rio Grande Compact's terms on the state without formal ratification—which, of course, it was. Nonetheless, he rationalized that the proposal was not really an end run around the Texas legislature, because the consent decree would be signed by the state's attorney general. To Clayton, that official represented Texas as much as the state's legislators did. Yet Clayton knew that this reasoning might not satisfy everyone, and to convince other Texans that he was not trying to have the compact adopted surreptitiously, on September 6, 1938, he met with Richard Burges; Texas Assistant Attorney General H. Grady Chandler; the chairman of the Texas Board of Water Engineers, Charles Clark; and the attorney for the Texas Board of Water Engineers, J. E. Sturrock. Also invited to the meeting were Sawnie B. Smith, A. L. Cramer, and Albert Tamm, all of whom represented the Water Conservation Association of the Lower Rio Grande Valley.[55]

At the gathering, Clayton tried to explain the necessity for the consent decree, but the lower Rio Grande water users were unconvinced. Complaining that they would not receive enough water under the Rio Grande Compact's terms, they asserted that the only place the accord should be considered for approval was in the state legislature—where lower Rio Grande interests believed they could have it defeated. Clayton, however, refused to drop the consent decree plan, and he persuaded the Texas attorney general's office to try the maneuver.[56]

Lower Rio Grande water users were furious, and their regional newspapers reflected that anger. For example, the page-wide headline of the *Valley Star-Monitor-Herald* (Brownsville) declared, "Attorney General Aide Ignores Valley Plea on Rio Grande Suit," and the subtitle charged, "Pact Action without Ratification." The article then described how Albert Tamm had insisted to Texas Assistant Attorney General Chandler that the consent decree plan was unjust because "no consideration for the rights of water users along the lower Rio Grande, except those in the Rio Grande project, was given in the Compact, and that there was nowhere stated how much water from the upper Rio Grande Texas would get."[57] Nevertheless, Chandler went ahead and suggested to New Mexico Attorney General Frank H. Patton and Colorado Attorney General Byron G. Rogers that all three states agree to the consent decree to speed a resolution of the Rio Grande's problems and to allow their states' respective storage projects to go forward.[58] Indeed, Texas's officials were so certain that the consent decree solution was the only workable way to protect their state's interests and resolve the Rio Grande conflict among the three states that they subsequently declared that Texas would only agree to water projects then being considered for New Mexico and Colorado if those two states acceded to the consent decree.[59]

While Chandler awaited replies from Colorado and New Mexico, members of the Water Conservation Association of the Lower Rio Grande Valley discussed the consent decree proposal and the issue of the compact's ratification by the Texas legislature. Turning to the question of how much water Texas would receive under the compact's terms, one association member charged that there was nothing in the interstate agreement guaranteeing that Texas would get any water at all. Sturrock, who had been at the September 6 gathering with Clayton, Burges, and Chandler, agreed. Proposing that the lower Rio Grande water users might need to intervene in *Texas v. New Mexico and the Middle Rio Grande Conservancy District* if the consent decree idea went forward, Sturrock suggested that such a legal action could be based on an allegation of bad faith on the part of the Texas assistant attorney general and on "the indefiniteness of the compact as to how much water Texas was going to get." Obviously unaware that the Rio Grande Compact commissioners had intended to include the 1905 congressionally authorized apportionment within the Rio Grande Project in the compact's terms, Sturrock asserted that intervention in the court case would be intended to secure an injunction preventing the attorney general from signing the proposed consent decree, because, as Sturrock explained, "nobody can tell just how much water Texas is entitled to under that compact." As legal counsel for the Texas Board of Water Engineers, however, Sturrock was unable to offer his services to fight the consent decree plan, so the Water Conservation Association of the Lower Rio Grande Valley retained Smith & Hall, a law firm from the lower Rio Grande town of Edinburg, Texas, which offered to do the work without charge. Like Sturrock, the law firm's senior partner, Sawnie B. Smith, had been at the September 6th meeting with Clayton, Burges, and Chandler.[60]

Before developing a legal strategy, Smith realized that he needed to know whether the Rio Grande Compact commissioners deliberately had not provided for a specific amount of water to go to Texas, and if so, why. Writing to Frank Clayton, Smith noted that there had been considerable comment on the fact that the new Rio Grande Compact "makes no provision for the division of waters below Elephant Butte between the States of New Mexico and Texas and makes no provision concerning the amount of water to which Texas is entitled." This apparent omission, to Smith, was puzzling, and he told Clayton that it was "too obvious to have been inadvertent, and, therefore, unquestionably, the commissioners had what they considered valid reasons for it." Smith wanted an explanation, therefore, of "why the respective rights of Texas and New Mexico to those waters were not defined and provided for in the compact in express terms."[61]

In reply, Clayton wrote that the negotiators for the new Rio Grande Compact had recognized an existing apportionment of the river's waters between New Mexico and Texas below Elephant Butte Dam through the allocation made by the Bureau of Reclamation and the operation of the Rio Grande Project—a division of the Rio Grande's waters authorized by the 1905 congressional law extending the Reclamation Act to the El Paso

Valley. Clayton explained that "the question of the division of the water released from Elephant Butte reservoir is taken care of by contracts between the districts under the Rio Grande Project and the Bureau of Reclamation." Observing that these contracts provided that the lands within the project would all have the same rights, Clayton confirmed that the water was allocated according to the respective areas involved in the two states—areas defined by the Bureau of Reclamation under the terms of the 1905 legislation sanctioning the 1904 apportionment compromise. "By virtue of the contract recently executed [the 1938 interdistrict agreement]," Clayton continued, "the total area is 'frozen' at the figure representing the acreage now actually in cultivation: approximately 88,000 acres for the Elephant Butte Irrigation District, and 67,000 for the El Paso County Water Improvement District No. 1, with a 'cushion' of three per cent for each figure." Adding optimistically his belief that "there will never be any difficulty about the allocation of this water," Clayton told Smith that he hoped his answer would satisfy lower Rio Grande water users.[62]

Because of the evident misunderstanding about the Rio Grande Compact commissioners' intentions, Clayton sent explanatory letters similar to his reply to Smith to all the incoming Texas state legislators, and he went in person to the lower Rio Grande valley in early October 1938—armed with copies of the compact and histories of the Rio Grande controversy—to explain the commission's aim.[63] The campaign to clarify the compact quickly paid off, and Clayton won the support of lower Rio Grande water users for the compact's ratification or, if necessary, for the consent decree approach to implement the compact's terms.[64]

This change of heart with respect to the consent decree plan in the lower Rio Grande valley no doubt was gratifying to Clayton, but his efforts turned out to be superfluous on this point. In late October 1938, Colorado's attorney general, Byron Rogers, notified New Mexico and Texas that his state could not accept the consent decree idea because there was no way to guarantee that the U.S. Supreme Court would enter a decree worded exactly like the compact. Also making the consent decree proposal less appealing, the Public Works Administration had rejected Colorado's applications to fund the Wagon Wheel Gap and Conejos reservoirs, and New Mexico had withdrawn its application for the Jemez Reservoir. Thus, these structures no longer posed an immediate threat to Texas water users.[65]

With most sources of controversy resolved, the legislatures of Colorado, New Mexico, and Texas soon ratified the Rio Grande Compact. On Feb-

ruary 21, 1939, Colorado's governor, Ralph L. Carr, signed his state's ratification bill. Texas's governor, W. Lee "Pappy" O'Daniel, executed his state's
approval measure on March 1, 1939. New Mexico's governor, John E.
Miles, followed suit the next day. When President Franklin Roosevelt
signed Congress's consent on May 31, 1939, the Rio Grande Compact took
effect.[66]

Not surprisingly, multiple accounts of the compact's final ratification
process appeared in Colorado, New Mexico, and Texas newspapers,
although most of these were relatively brief notices (the bigger story had
been the compact's approval by its negotiators nearly a year earlier).[67] Other
stories of the Rio Grande Compact's approval appeared in the press in more-
distant parts of the country, and these news stories emphasized the significance of the achievement to the American West and to the United States as
a whole. For instance, the *Hammond (IN) Times*, the *Cedar Rapids (IA)
Tribune*, and the *Portsmouth (NH) Herald* all carried the nearly identical
story that "conquest of America's great southwestern desert—started 400
years ago by Spanish explorers—is underway again, this time for a prize
more valuable than the fabulous gold sought by the helmeted Conquista-
dores." The accounts continued that "guns and lances have no part in the
modern conquest of the modern southwest—rather the weapons will be
dams, reservoirs and irrigation canals. The result will produce a fortune in
tillable land far surpassing in value the wildest dreams of the conquering
Spaniards when they marched northward from Mexico centuries ago." All
that remained for this remarkable scenario to transpire, the *Times*, *Tribune*,
and *Herald* added before filling in details, was the final approval by Congress of the Rio Grande Compact.[68]

With such laudatory accounts appearing in the press, the subsequent dis-
missal of *Texas v. New Mexico and the Middle Rio Grande Conservancy District* by the Supreme Court the following October was an anticlimax, but it
brought to a close almost sixty years of controversy over the use and apportionment of the waters of the Rio Grande in Colorado, New Mexico, and
Texas.[69] Moreover, the ratification of the 1938 Rio Grande Compact that
had permitted the interstate litigation to be dropped was a milestone in western water law, and the agreement set a valuable example for how future
compacts could be negotiated with federal help in the form of studies and
surveys. In fact, even before the Rio Grande accord had been completely
ratified, negotiators for New Mexico and Texas hoped it would provide guidance for similar talks aimed at allocating flows between the two states on the

Pecos River.[70] Not only did the Rio Grande Compact provide a model for utilizing U.S. assistance, but it also created a regulatory oversight body—known, like the original negotiating organization as the Rio Grande Compact Commission—which served as a prototype for other interstate river compacts. Perhaps most important to Rio Grande water users, however, was that the 1938 Rio Grande Compact renewed Congress's original 1905 interstate apportionment within the Rio Grande Project by including that division in a broader agreement covering the entire basin in Colorado, New Mexico, and Texas above Fort Quitman. Thus, for the time being at least, peace was restored to the region in regard to the water supplies of the Rio Grande.

Conclusion

As the history of the Rio Grande water struggles amply demonstrates, irrigators in southern New Mexico's Mesilla Valley and those in the El Paso Valley grappled with multitudes of problems in relation to achieving interstate and international apportionments of that river. In this sense, the conflict over the Rio Grande was similar to other water confrontations that crossed political lines in the western United States. Yet unlike other transboundary western water battles, the Rio Grande's allocation problems arose and were dealt with far earlier than elsewhere and thus shed significant light on the evolution of water law and natural resource management and control in the late nineteenth- and early twentieth-century American West.

The difficulties on the Rio Grande typified but generally preceded many similar water contests in the arid part of the United States for several reasons. Foremost among these was the fact that settlement came to the Mesilla and El Paso valleys when western water law was in its infancy. When the Rio Grande controversy first erupted, the legal doctrine of prior appropriation was young and just beginning to be refined in the western states and territories. Nonetheless, even in those jurisdictions where prior appropriation had developed some guise of legal acceptance either by court decisions or statutes, there was still considerable room for dispute over the details of the priority principle and whether it had completely replaced the East's water law doctrine of riparian rights.

Whatever limited certitude there might have been about the rules of prior appropriation as they applied within each state or territory when the Rio Grande's water difficulties began, those sureties ended at state and national boundaries. Further complicating these questions for water users on the Rio Grande were doubts about what authority the U.S. government might have over western rivers. Most nineteenth-century westerners assumed that through federal acts passed in 1866, 1870, and 1877, the U.S. government had relinquished its power over water allocation. Federal officials, however, did not all agree with this conclusion, as the lawsuit against the Rio Grande Dam and Irrigation Company manifestly illustrated. Embodying fundamental issues of what right the United States had to restrict access to water supplies for irrigation, the suit against the firm also posed a broader question about the federal government's ability to apportion western rivers. So too did simultaneous congressional debates over the degree to which the United States should be involved in reclaiming all parts of the arid West—a dialectic that revealed a decline in the belief that national resource development was the domain of private enterprise and the simultaneous advent of the Progressive-era faith in government-directed, scientific natural resource management.

The emerging federal involvement in the control and use of western water was not a manifestation of a centralized autocracy using a scarce natural resource to dominate a weak region of the United States, however. On the Rio Grande, the multiform nature of American law in the late nineteenth century complicated the lack of precision in defining prior appropriation and the uncertainty about federal authority over western rivers. Thus, when conflict began to arise over water use and control in the Mesilla and El Paso valleys, irrigators were unsure about what level or branch of government might help resolve the problem—a lack of certainty that was compounded by the relatively sparse western population and the obstacles involved in communicating with different governmental entities. The result initially was a patchwork approach to resolving the Rio Grande apportionment difficulty that involved the New Mexico territorial government, the El Paso City Council, the Texas state government, Congress, the federal courts, the International (Water) Boundary Commission, the Corps of Engineers, and the Departments of State, Interior, and Justice, as well as the Mexican government.

With the unrefined nature of western water law forcing the question of the allocation of the Rio Grande into a multiplicity of legal venues, the

answer to the river's apportionment understandably became extremely perplexing. It is not surprising, therefore, that water users in southern New
Mexico and western Texas sought their own resolution to the issue through
a compromise at the 1904 National Irrigation Congress. These were circumstances that added an unofficial governmental body to the multiform
mix of possible sites of resolution of the water crisis—yet one that also
encouraged local compromise as a starting point to a settlement.

The agreement in part grew out of the legal system's unclear rules for
water control in the West, but the need to find a consensus on the Rio
Grande also was due to the reality of settlement patterns in the region at the
turn of the century. Isolated by miles of remote and arid terrain and with little convenient contact to other areas of the country, the communities in the
Mesilla and El Paso valleys understandably wanted to remain on good terms
with each other, especially because the regional economy was inextricably
bound together regardless of state or international borders.

Compromise on the Rio Grande was especially vital at the end of the
nineteenth century because interstate and international water conflicts
were essentially local problems. Isolation attributable to the arid environment and distance from national, state, and territorial powers created a
sense of community and mutual confidence among the Rio Grande groups.
As the battle between the proponents of the international dam at El Paso
and the backers of the Elephant Butte site amply illustrates, that mutual
confidence did not come easily; in fact, it emerged only with the proposal
of the Reclamation Service at the 1904 National Irrigation Congress to sup-
plant the Rio Grande Dam and Irrigation Company's Elephant Butte project with a federal version at roughly the same locale. While this revealed the
emerging Progressive ideology of natural resource management, nevertheless, the Reclamation Service's plans were made possible only by a local
understanding on just how waters to be stored by the federal dam would be
divided among New Mexico, Texas, and Mexico.

It is perhaps ironic that the participants in the 1904 localized compromise on the Rio Grande called for something that no self-respecting present-
day westerner would endorse as a legal canon to guide the allocation of water
in the arid part of the United States. Once the decision had been reached at
the 1904 National Irrigation Congress on how the Rio Grande's waters
would be divided, representatives of New Mexico and Texas (supported by
Mexico) heavily lobbied the U.S. Congress to do exactly what as a general
principle their successors would abhor—pass federal laws carrying out the

apportionment. The 1905 congressional allocation of the Rio Grande grew from complex reasons and found its way through myriad levels and forms of official and unofficial governmental action involving a vast array of individuals. Yet that division of the Rio Grande's flows applied only to waters stored behind Elephant Butte Dam, and it only covered lands below that facility and above Fort Quitman, Texas. Nonetheless, the same multiform and multilevel approach to resolving the allocation of supplies from Elephant Butte Reservoir continued to drive the larger allocation of the stream that was accomplished by the 1929 and 1938 Rio Grande Compacts. Just as carrying out the 1904 National Irrigation Congress compromise had necessitated cooperation among local, regional, state, and national organizations and governments, so too did the compact process reflect a similar type of federalism. Substantial aid in reaching the two compacts came from the local Rio Grande Project irrigation districts (and their forerunner water users' associations) as well as the Middle Rio Grande Conservancy District and irrigators in Colorado's San Luis Valley. The local input in achieving the 1929 and 1938 compacts was supplemented by considerable state government assistance, which partly was intended to restrict U.S. governmental control over western water resources. Federal aid to the two compact processes—particularly through the efforts of the Rio Grande Joint Investigation—was vital in ultimately reaching the 1938 accord.

Thus, the 1938 Rio Grande Compact was the result of efforts by many diverse parties—disparate in terms of geographic location, level of government, and partisan interests as well as dissimilar in time. The Rio Grande Compact of 1938 was not only the creation of its negotiators and those they represented but also embodied the desires and compromises that had been made more than three decades earlier by incorporating into the compact the division of the river's waters below Elephant Dam that had been the fruit of a local 1904 compromise and federal legislation the following year implementing that agreement.

The Rio Grande, therefore, demonstrates a fusing process in western resource management and control that has involved fragments from countless conflicts and compromises.

Notes

Introduction

1. "Dam Is Assured," *Houston Post*, Nov. 18, 1904.

2. *Rio Grande Republican*, Nov. 18, 1904.

3. "Unanimity," *El Paso Herald*, Nov. 17, 1904; "Our Path Clearly Marked Out for Us," ibid.

4. "Elephant Butte Dam Approved," *El Paso Daily Times*, Nov. 18, 1904.

5. For detailed discussions of water rights in general, see R. Clark, *Water and Water Rights*; Hutchins, *Water Rights*.

6. See, for example, Angell, *Treatise*; Bannister, "Question of Federal Disposition"; Chandler, *Elements of Western Water Law*; Clayberg, "Genesis and Development"; Durst, "Riparian Rights"; Farnham, *Law of Waters*; Haight, "Riparian Rights"; Hess, "Illustration of Legal Development"; Kinney, *Treatise*; Long, "Early History"; Long, *Treatise*; Pomeroy, *Treatise*; Shaw, "Development of the Law of Waters"; Shaw, "Development of Water Law"; Wiel, "Origin and Comparative Development"; Wiel, "Political Water Rights"; Wiel, "'Priority' in Western Water Law"; Wiel, "Public Policy"; Wiel, "Theories of Water Law"; Wiel, "Water Law of the Public Domain"; Wiel, *Water Rights*; Wiel, "Waters."

7. On the early evolution of the appropriation doctrine, see Littlefield, "Water Rights."

8. Radosevich et al., *Evolution and Administration*, 23–24.

9. On the evolution of prior appropriation in New Mexico, see I. Clark, *Water in New Mexico*, 42.

10. Dunbar, *Forging New Rights*, 84–85, 128.

11. *Wyoming v. Colorado*, 259 U.S. 419 (1922). This decision did not say that prior appropriation *must* be recognized across state borders where both states accept priority, merely that priority *could* be considered in making an equitable apportionment between those states. See Sherow, "Latent Influence of Equity."

12. The 1907 decision in *Kansas v. Colorado* was the first interstate river ruling by the Supreme Court, but there had been one other such case heard in a lower federal court before the *Kansas* action. That case, *Howell v. Johnson*, 89 Fed. 556 (1898), was heard by the U.S. District Court for the District of Montana; it involved the States of Wyoming and Montana in a suit over the waters of Sage Creek. Although Kansas lost in *Kansas v. Colorado*, Kansas did not adopt a comprehensive water code making all waters within the state subject to a prior appropriation permit process until 1945. On the history of water use on the Arkansas River, see Sherow, *Watering the Valley*. See also *Kansas v. Colorado*, 206 U.S. 46 (1907).

13. *Arizona v. California*, 373 U.S. 546 (1963); Hundley, *Dividing the Waters*.

14. U.S. Senate, *Report of the Special Committee*, vol. 4, *Statements by Director Powell and Other Officers of the U.S. Geological Survey, Consular Reports, General Report on Irrigation in the United States, Miscellaneous Papers.*

15. "Report of the Commissioner of the General Land Office," Oct. 1, 1896, contained in U.S. Department of the Interior, *Report of the Secretary of the Interior . . . Second Session of the Fifty-fourth Congress*, 1:60; "Our Rapidly Growing Irrigation Areas," *Scientific American.*

16. Pisani, *To Reclaim a Divided West*, 64–68.

17. U.S. House, *Preliminary Examination*, 58.

18. Animas–La Plata Project Compact, 82 Stat. 898 (1968); Arkansas River Compact, 63 Stat. 145 (1949); Bear River Compact, 94 Stat. 4 (1980); Belle Fourche River Compact, 58 Stat. 94 (1944); Big Blue River Compact, 86 Stat. 193 (1972); Canadian River Compact, 66 Stat. 74 (1952); Colorado River Compact, 45 Stat. 1057 (1928); Costilla Creek Compact, 77 Stat. 350 (1963); Klamath River Basin Compact, 71 Stat. 497 (1957); Lake Tahoe (California-Nevada) Interstate Compact (approved by both states but not yet ratified by Congress); La Plata River Compact, 43 Stat. 796 (1925); Pecos River Compact, 63 Stat. 159 (1949); Red River Compact, 94 Stat. 3305 (1980); Red River of the North Compact, 52 Stat. 150 (1938); Republican River Compact, 57 Stat. 86 (1943); Rio Grande Compact, 53 Stat. 785 (1939); Sabine River Compact, 68 Stat. 690 (1954); Snake River Compact, 64 Stat. 29 (1950); South Platte River Compact, 44 Stat. 195 (1926); Upper Colorado River Compact, 63 Stat. 31 (1949); Upper Niobrara River Compact, 83 Stat. 86 (1969); and Yellowstone River Compact, 65 Stat. 663 (1951). Two of these interstate stream struggles have been the subject of book-length published historical studies. On the Colorado River, see Hundley, *Water and the West*. For a general history of water use on the Arkansas River, see Sherow, *Watering the Valley*. For details on the Arkansas River Compact's history with specific reference to the interstate allocation issues, see Littlefield, "History of the Arkansas River Compact"; Littlefield, *Transcripts of Testimony*; and the exhibits Littlefield introduced in that case. For a legal analysis of the compacting process as it applies to interstate rivers (as well as litigation over such rivers), see Sherk, *Dividing the Waters*, which reprints most interstate river compacts and major court decisions affecting interstate streams.

19. See Pisani, *To Reclaim a Divided West*.

20. On the struggle to control water and mineral rights for profit, see Limerick, *Legacy of Conquest*.

21. Worster, *Rivers of Empire*.

22. Maass and Anderson, *And the Desert Shall Rejoice*, 371.

23. Albert B. Fall to Charles L. McNary, Jan. 19, 1923, file 149.67, Entry 7, Records of the Bureau of Reclamation.

24. See Hays, *Conservation*; Pisani, "Reclamation"; Pisani, *To Reclaim a Divided West*; Pisani, *Water and American Government*.

25. See Horwitz, *Transformation of American Law*.

26. Hurst, *Law and the Conditions*; An Act to Authorize the Formation of Companies for the Purpose of Constructing Irrigating and Other Canals and the Colonization and Improvement of Lands Contained in Acts of the Legislative Assembly of the Territory of New Mexico, Twenty-seventh Session (1887, printed by J. A. Carruth of Las Vegas, N.Mex.); An Act Granting the Right of Way to Ditch and Canal Owners over the Public Lands, and for Other Purposes, 14 Stat. 251 (1866).

27. On law's multiform levels, see Hall, *Magic Mirror*.

28. *Kansas v. Colorado*, 206 U.S. 46 (1907). See also Hundley, *Water and the West*. On Roosevelt's policies as they affected the West, see Lowitt, *New Deal*.

Chapter 1. A Dry River at El Paso and Juárez

1. U.S. House, *El Paso Troubles, Texas—Letter from the Secretary of War Transmitting a Report from Colonel Hatch on the Subject of El Paso Troubles*, 3 (hereafter cited as U.S. House, *Hatch Report*).

2. For details on Luis Cardis and Charles Howard, see Timmons, *El Paso*, 189–96.

3. U.S. House, *Hatch Report*, 3.

4. U.S. House, *Hatch Report*, 1–5; U.S. House, *El Paso Troubles in Texas—Letter from the Secretary of War in Response to a Resolution of the House of Representatives Transmitting Reports of the Commission Appointed to Investigate the El Paso Troubles in Texas*, 3–5, 13–18 (hereafter referred to as U.S. House, *El Paso Commission Report*). For more details on the salt-pond conflicts, see Sonnichsen, *El Paso Salt War*. For the history of the El Paso–Juárez area, see Sonnichsen, *Pass of the North*; Timmons, *El Paso*; Luckingham, *Urban Southwest*; Martinez, *Border Boom Town*.

5. The quotations are in U.S. House, *El Paso Commission Report*, 2–3, 18. See also U.S. House, *Hatch Report*, 3, 5–6. For a complete analysis of U.S.-Mexico problems involving the use of waters from international rivers, see Hundley, *Dividing the Waters*. On Mexico's water policies at the turn of the century, see Kroeber, *Man, Land, and Water*.

6. The discussion of the Rio Grande's characteristics is taken primarily from U.S. National Resources Committee, *Rio Grande Joint Investigations*, 1:7; Hundley, *Dividing the Waters*, 4–9.

7. Letter to the editor, *Thirty-four*, March 24, 1880.

8. Petition to the Honorable County Commissioners' Court of El Paso County, April 6, 1880, in U.S. Department of State, *Papers Relating to the Foreign Relations, . . . 1880*, 754–55 (hereafter cited as State Department, *Foreign Relations, 1880*).

9. The quotation is in O. M. Roberts to William M. Evarts, May 10, 1880, in State Department, *Foreign Relations, 1880*, 752–53. See also Henry C. Cook to Roberts, April 6, 1880, in ibid., 753–54; Evarts to P. H. Morgan, June 12, 1880, in ibid., 752. Evarts also protested to the Mexican foreign minister in Washington, D.C. See "Statement in re the International Dam Project," in a letter from Nathan Boyd to Secretary of State John Hay, May 26, 1902, reproduced in U.S. Senate, *Message from the President of the United States . . . in Regard to the Equitable Distribution of the Waters of the Rio Grande*, 61 (hereafter cited as U.S. Senate, *Equitable Distribution*, S. Doc. 154). For a brief synopsis of Roberts's life, see www.tsha.utexas.edu/handbook/online/articles/RR/fro18.html.

10. The quotation is in U.S. Senate, *Message from the President of the United States . . . of Certain Dams in the Rio Grande*, 2 (hereafter cited as U.S. Senate, *Dams in the Rio Grande*). See also ibid., 1–9, 22–23; Oswald H. Ernst to Thomas F. Bayard with enclosures, Dec. 12, 1888, in U.S. Department of State, *Papers Relating to the Foreign Relations, . . . 1889*, 621–36 (hereafter cited as State Department, *Foreign Relations, 1889*); U.S. Department of State, *Papers Relating to the Foreign Relations, . . . 1888*, 1110–11, 1200–1201, 1241–46 (hereafter cited as State Department, *Foreign Relations, 1888*); U.S. House, *International Commission with Mexico*, 1–3.

11. A. Mills, *My Story*, 25, 47, 53–54; U.S. House, *International Dam*, 3; White, *Out of the Desert*, 333–38. For a contemporary and highly favorable review of Mills's autobiography (carried by the Associated Press news service), see "West Point Failure Who Came Back," *Ada Evening News*, May 31, 1918. For more details on Mills, see www.tsha.utexas.eduhandbookonlinearticlesMMfmi36.html and www.arlingtoncemetery.net/a-mills.htm.

12. Anson Mills and William W. Follett, "Reports on the Investigations and Survey for an International Dam and Reservoir on the Rio Grande del Norte to Preserve the Boundary between the United States and Mexico by Controlling the Flood Waters of Said River, with Appendices A, B, and C," Oct. 10, 1889, in International Boundary Commission, *Proceedings*, 2:392; "A Damming Proposition," *Reno Evening Gazette*, Nov. 13, 1888.

13. On Powell's background, see Worster, *River Running West*; Stegner, *Beyond the Hundredth Meridian*; Darrah, *Powell of the Colorado*.

14. "Report of the Commissioner of the General Land Office," in U.S. Department of the Interior, *Report of the Secretary of the Interior, 1885*, 231.

15. For details on the Powell Irrigation Survey and Powell, see Pisani, *To Reclaim a Divided West*, 140–53; Alexander, "Powell Irrigation Survey"; Sterling, "Powell Irrigation Survey."

16. On Mills's meeting with Powell, see Mills and Follett, "Reports on the Investigations," in International Boundary Commission, *Proceedings*, 2:392; U.S. House, *Ceding the Arid Lands to the States and Territories*, 14.

17. U.S. House, *International Dam*, 3–6. The quotation is on 3.

18. Ibid., 3–6. Mills's scheme as he outlined it to Secretary Bayard was reproduced in 1896 in this same work.

19. Frazer, *Forts of the West*, 143–44.

20. Mills and Follett, "Reports on the Investigations," in International Boundary Commission, *Proceedings*, 2:392. On Powell's views and how westerners perceived his ideas for watershed development, see Pisani, *To Reclaim a Divided West*, 143–68.

21. On the struggle to control water and mineral rights for profit, see Limerick, *Legacy of Conquest*.

22. Mills and Follett, "Reports on the Investigations," in International Boundary Commission, *Proceedings*, 2:392.

23. *Who Was Who in America* (1943), 1:410.

24. Mills and Follett, "Reports on the Investigations," in International Boundary Commission, *Proceedings*, 2:392–93. For Nettleton's role and his positive assessment of the El Paso dam site, see "An Irrigation Plan," *Los Angeles Times*, June 30, 1889; A. Mills, *My Story*, 273.

25. For current detailed legal analyses of water rights, see R. Clark, *Water and Water Rights*; Hutchins, *Water Rights*. For late-nineteenth- and early-twentieth-century discussions of water rights, see Chandler, *Elements of Western Water Law*; Farnham, *Law of Waters*; Kinney, *Treatise*; Long, *Treatise*; Pomeroy, *Treatise*; Wiel, *Water Rights*.

26. On the interstate struggle over the Arkansas River, see Littlefield, "History of the Arkansas River Compact"; Littlefield, *Transcripts of Testimony*; and the exhibits Littlefield introduced in *Kansas v. Colorado*. See also Sherow, *Watering the Valley*.

27. *Wyoming v. Colorado*, 259 U.S. 419 (1922). See also Sherk, *Dividing the Waters*, 5; Gibbard, "*Wyoming v. Colorado*," 37.

28. Mills and Follett, "Reports on the Investigations," in International Boundary Commission, *Proceedings*, 2:393.

29. Ibid., 393–94.

30. Ibid., 285, 299, 392–93, 395–99. The quotation is on 393. Follett also had examined a dam site about one and three-quarters miles above El Paso. He ultimately favored the location slightly upriver because, from a cursory inspection, the canyon was narrower with strong cliffs on either side. Later, more thorough examinations showed that this site had a much greater depth to bedrock—a fact that substantially increased projected costs and might have made the lower location a better choice.

31. Pisani, *To Reclaim a Divided West*, 151. For varying contemporary views of irrigation in the West and what role government might play in aiding reclamation, see Newell, *Irrigation in the United States*; Smythe, *Conquest of Arid America*; Teele, *Irrigation in the United States*; Mead, *Irrigation Institutions*. For a useful summary of the growing demand for reclamation in the West, see Lilley and Gould, "Western Irrigation Movement."

32. U.S. Senate, *Report of the Special Committee*, vol. 3, *Rocky Mountain Region and Great Plains*, 13–16, 19–20.

33. U.S. Senate, *Report of the Special Committee*, vol. 4, *Statements by Director Powell and Other Officers of the U.S. Geological Survey, Consular Reports, General Report on Irrigation in the United States, Miscellaneous Papers*, 22–27, 31, 63, 68, 101.

34. Ibid., 101.

35. Ibid., 27. Powell had given similar testimony on February 6, 1890, to the House Select Committee on Irrigation of Arid Lands. See U.S. House, *Ceding the Arid Lands to the States and Territories*, 13.

36. U.S. Senate, *Report of the Special Committee*, vol. 4, *Statements by Director Powell and Other Officers of the U.S. Geological Survey, Consular Reports, General Report on Irrigation in the United States, Miscellaneous Papers*, 27.

37. S. 1644, 51st Cong., 1st sess., Jan. 6, 1890, *Congressional Record* 21:1, 385.

38. "The Rio Grande Dam," *Galveston Daily News*, July 24, 1889.

39. H.R. 3924, 51st Cong., 1st sess., Jan. 6, 1890, *Congressional Record* 21:1, 406.

40. U.S. House, *Ceding the Arid Lands to the States and Territories*, 13–20.

41. H.R. 3924, 51st Cong., 1st sess., Feb. 27, 1890, *Congressional Record* 21:2, 1789; U.S. House, *Irrigation of Arid Lands*, 1, 9. The quotations are on 1.

42. "The International Dam," *San Antonio Daily Express*, Feb. 22, 1890; "The International Dam," *Chillicothe Morning Constitution*, Feb. 23, 1890.

43. S. 1644, 51st Cong., 1st sess., Feb. 21, March 6 and 18, 1890, *Congressional Record* 21:2, 1576, 1958; 21:3, 2340–42.

44. S. 1644, 51st Cong., 1st sess., April 5 and 23, 1890, *Congressional Record* 21:4, 3064–66, 3703; U.S. House, *International Dam*, 6.

45. H.R. 3924, 51st Cong., 1st sess., April 29, 1890, *Congressional Record* 21:4, 3977–78.

Chapter 2. A Dry River in New Mexico and Texas

1. Sherow, *Watering the Valley*, 106; Tyler, *Silver Fox*, 89; Gibbard, "*Wyoming v. Colorado*"; Hundley, *Water and the West*, 53–54.

2. *Kansas v. Colorado*, 206 U.S. 46 (1907); *Wyoming v. Colorado*, 259 U.S. 419 (1922); *Arizona v. California*, 283 U.S. 423 (1931); *Arizona v. California*, 292 U.S. 341 (1934); *Arizona v. California*, 298 U.S. 558 (1936); *Arizona v. California*, 373 U.S. 546 (1963); *Arizona v. California*, 376 U.S. 340 (1964). For synopses of these cases and brief descriptions of other interstate water conflicts, see Sherk, *Dividing the Waters*. For a detailed discussion of the *Wyoming v. Colorado* case, see Sherow, "Latent Influence of Equity."

3. Sherow, *Watering the Valley*, 108. See also *Kansas v. Colorado*, 185 U.S. 125 (1902); *Wyoming v. Colorado*, 259 U.S. 419 (1922).

4. *United States v. Rio Grande Dam and Irrigation Company*, 174 U.S. 690 (1899); *United States v. Rio Grande Dam and Irrigation Company*, 184 U.S. 416 (1902); *Rio Grande Dam and Irrigation Company v. United States*, 215 U.S. 266 (1909).

5. An Act Granting the Right of Way to Ditch and Canal Owners over the Public Lands, and for Other Purposes, 14 Stat. 251 (1866); An Act to Amend "An Act Granting the Right of Way to Ditch and Canal Owners over the Public Lands, and for Other Purposes," 16 Stat. 217 (1870); An Act to Provide for the Sale of Desert Lands in Certain States and Territories, 19 Stat. 377 (1877).

6. Kinney, *Treatise*, 1:1025.

7. For a perceptive analysis on whether the states or the federal government had control over western waters in the late nineteenth and early twentieth centuries, see Pisani, "State vs. Nation."

8. William W. Follett, "A Study of the Use of Water for Irrigation in the Rio Grande del Norte," in International Boundary Commission, *Proceedings*, 2:286; U.S. Senate, *Report of the Special Committee*, vol. 3, *Rocky Mountain Region and Great Plains*, 325–26. On the settlement of the San Luis Valley, see Simmons, *San Luis Valley*; Abbott et al., *Colorado*, 35–51; Steinel, *History of Agriculture*, 28–30. For the history of settlement in the El Paso and Mesilla valleys, see Sonnichsen, *Pass of the North*; Martinez, *Border Boom Town*; Luckingham, *Urban Southwest*; Timmons, *El Paso*; Baldwin, "Short History."

9. Price, *Pioneers of the Mesilla Valley*, 1–58; Harris, *Las Cruces*, 11–59. For descriptions of the Mesilla Valley and its commercial center, Las Cruces, see "The Mesilla Valley," *Thirty-four*, Jan. 1, 1879; "The Mesilla Valley, Its Resources and Attractions," ibid., March 10, 1880.

10. "The Drought," *Thirty-four*, Sept. 3, 1879. For the comparison to Egypt and the Nile, see "Dona Ana County," *Rio Grande Republican*, Dec. 17, 1896.

11. U.S. Senate, *Report of the Special Committee*, vol. 3, *Rocky Mountain Region and Great Plains*, 5–6; U.S. Department of the Interior, *Report of the Secretary of the Interior, . . . Second Session of the Fifty-first Congress*, 3:457–58.

12. "Artificial Lakes," *Thirty-four*, July 30, 1879; "Our Water Supply," ibid., Sept. 24, 1879; *Rio Grande Republican*, Oct. 22, 1887.

13. *Deming Headlight*, April 27, 1893.

14. U.S. Department of the Interior, *Report of the Secretary of the Interior. . . Second Session of the Fifty-first Congress*, 3:608–609.

15. Hurst, *Law and the Conditions*; An Act to Authorize the Formation of Companies for the Purpose of Constructing Irrigating and Other Canals and the Colonization and Improvement of Lands contained in Acts of the Legislative Assembly of the Territory of New Mexico, Twenty-seventh Session (1887, printed by J. A. Carruth of Las Vegas, N.Mex.), 29–37; An Act Granting the Right of Way to Ditch and Canal Owners over the Public Lands, and for Other Purposes, 14 Stat. 251 (1866); An Act to Provide for the Sale of Desert Lands in Certain States and Territories, 19 Stat. 377 (1877); An Act to Repeal Timber-culture Laws, and for Other Purposes, 26 Stat. 1095 (1891); I. Clark, *Water in New Mexico*, 62, 64; "Prospectus for Rio Grande Irrigation and Land Co., Ltd.," in U.S. Senate, *Equitable Distribution of the Waters of the Rio Grande*, S. Doc. 229, 5.

16. Pisani, *To Reclaim a Divided West*, 71–74.

17. For more details on Rockwood's scheme, see Hundley, *Water and the West*, 21–27.

18. "An Irrigation Project," *Los Angeles Times*, Aug. 30, 1892; "To Dam the Rio Grande," *Washington Post*, Aug. 30, 1892; "An Immense Dam," *Hamilton Daily Republican*, Aug. 30, 1892; "An International Dam," *Titusville Morning Herald*, Aug. 30, 1892; "A Gigantic Dam," *Richwood Gazette*, Sept. 1, 1892.

19. J. Boyd, "Entrepreneur." James Boyd is Nathan E. Boyd's great-grandson. On Nathan Boyd's early involvement in New Mexico irrigation, see Nathan E. Boyd to Charles S. Teller, April 14, 1914, McDonald Papers; Boyd to John W. Griggs, Aug. 29, 1900, in International Boundary Commission, *Proceedings*, 2:374–75.

20. Anson Mills to chairman of subcommittee of the House Foreign Affairs Committee, Feb. 18, 1901, in International Boundary Commission, *Proceedings*, 2:373–74; "Memorandum Presented to the Congressional Subcommittee on Foreign Affairs, in re H.R. 9710, by Max Weber, of Ciudad Juarez, Mexico, Feb. 11, 1901," in ibid., 376–77. For Mills's opinion that Campbell had relied on Mills's information, see "Testimony Submitted to the Committee on Foreign Affairs on Bill (H.R. 9710) to Provide for the Equitable Distribution of the Waters of the Rio Grande between the United States of America and the United States of Mexico, and for the Purpose of Building an International Dam and Reservoir on Said River at El Paso, Texas," in ibid., 371.

21. "Prospectus for Rio Grande Irrigation and Land Co., Ltd.," in U.S. Senate, *Equitable Distribution of the Waters of the Rio Grande*, S. Doc. 229, 5.

22. "Petition to President and Directors of the Elephant Butte Water Users' Association," undated, Prince Papers; "Prospectus for Rio Grande Irrigation and Land Co., Ltd.," in U.S. Senate, *Equitable Distribution of the Waters of the Rio Grande*, S. Doc. 229, 6; "Map of the Rio Grande Valley from Engle, New Mexico, to Fort Quitman, Texas, Showing Dams, Reservoirs, Canals, and Irrigable Lands of the Rio Grande Dam and Irrigation Company," in International Boundary Commission, *Proceedings*, 2:356; Nathan E. Boyd to secretary of state, May 26, 1902, in U.S. Senate, *Equitable Distribution*, S. Doc. 154, 62.

23. On the need for scientific study of irrigation during the nineteenth century, see Pisani, *To Reclaim a Divided West*, 153–68. For details on another nineteenth-century irrigation company whose plans were equally unrealistic in relation to the area to be served, see Sherow, "Watering the Plains."

24. Nathan E. Boyd to secretary of state, May 26, 1902, in U.S. Senate, *Equitable Distribution*, S. Doc. 154, 61; "Prospectus for Rio Grande Irrigation and Land Co., Ltd.," in U.S. Senate, *Equitable Distribution of the Waters of the Rio Grande*, S. Doc. 229, 6. On the community ditch system in New Mexico, see Hutchins, "Community Acequia."

25. Pisani, *Water and American Government*, xiii.

26. Rio Grande Dam and Irrigation Company, power of attorney to Nathan E. Boyd, Dec. 11, 1893 (copy enclosed with Price, Waterhouse and Co. to Sir Cecil Hurst, Oct. 12, 1923), FO5/2624, Records of the Foreign Office; *History of New Mexico*, 2:1001.

27. Memorandum and articles of association of the Rio Grande Irrigation and Land Company, Oct. 10, 1895, BT31/34376–45577, Records of the Board of Trade.

28. The conversion to values in U.S. dollars was accomplished by changing the value of pounds in 1900 to pounds as of 2008, then changing pounds to dollars: www.nationalarchives.gov.uk/currency; www.translatum.gr/converter/currency.htm.

29. Memorandum of agreement between the Rio Grande Dam and Irrigation Company and the Rio Grande Irrigation and Land Company, May 30, 1896, BT31/34376–45577, Records of the Board of Trade. See also "Rio Grande Claim (Claim No. 83)." By

early 1900, Boyd had sold about a third of his stock in the English company. On the stock transfers by Boyd and Chetham-Strode, see the summaries of capital and shares of the Rio Grande Irrigation and Land Company, filed in compliance with British law in late 1897, early 1899, and early 1900, copies in ibid. The Rio Grande Irrigation and Land Company went into liquidation in April 1900, and there were no further stock filings with the English government. See record of extraordinary general meeting of the Rio Grande Irrigation and Land Company, April 20, 1900, ibid.; John A. Simmers to the registrar, Register of Companies, April 25, 1900, ibid.

30. On Boyd's stake in the Rio Grande Irrigation and Land Company's bonds, see list of debenture holders, Feb. 25, 1901 (copy enclosed with Price, Waterhouse and Co. to Sir Cecil Hurst, Oct. 12, 1923), FO897/24, Records of the Foreign Office.

31. On English investments in the nineteenth-century American West, see Clements, "British-Controlled Enterprise."

32. Summaries of capital and shares of the Rio Grande Irrigation and Land Co., filed in compliance with British law in late 1897, early 1899, and early 1900, copies in BT31/34376–45577, Records of the Board of Trade; list of debenture holders, Feb. 25, 1901 (copy enclosed with Price, Waterhouse and Co. to Sir Cecil Hurst, Oct. 12, 1923), FO897/24, Records of the Foreign Office; *History of New Mexico*, 2:1001.

33. U.S. Senate, *History of the Rio Grande Dam*, 3. See also "Prospectus for Rio Grande Irrigation and Land Co., Ltd.," in U.S. Senate, *Equitable Distribution of the Waters of the Rio Grande*, S. Doc. 229, 5. See also "*Ex Parte* J.L. Campbell, et al., and Rio Grande Dam and Irrigation Company, Petition for Reimbursement" (date-stamped Jan. 27, 1914), file 253–1, Rio Grande Project files, Records of the Bureau of Reclamation.

34. "Prospectus for Rio Grande Irrigation and Land Co., Ltd.," in U.S. Senate, *Equitable Distribution of the Waters of the Rio Grande*, S. Doc. 229, 6.

35. Ibid.

36. Ibid., 6–7.

37. N. E. Baker to S. B. Newcomb, July 12, 1895, in ibid., 4; S. W. Lamoreux to Hoke Smith, Aug. 15, 1896, in ibid., 14–17; Hoke Smith to commissioner of the General Land Office, Feb. 1, 1895, in U.S. Senate, *Equitable Distribution*, S. Doc. 154, 147–48.

38. The quotation is in "Petition to President and Directors of the Elephant Butte Water Users' Association," undated, Prince Papers. See also "Testimony Submitted to the Committee on Foreign Affairs on Bill (H.R. 9710) to Provide for the Equitable Distribution of the Waters of the Rio Grande between the United States of America and the United States of Mexico, and for the Purpose of Building an International Dam and Reservoir on Said River at El Paso, Texas," in International Boundary Commission, *Proceedings*, 2:371.

39. Matias Romero to Richard Olney, Oct. 21, 1895, in U.S. Senate, *Equitable Distribution*, S. Doc. 154, 7–9. The quotation is on 9. See also Richardson, *Compilation*, 9:527; U.S. Department of State, *Papers Relating to the Foreign Relations, . . . 1894* (hereafter cited as State Department, *Foreign Relations, 1894*), 395–97.

40. McCaffrey, "Water, Water Everywhere," 326. McCaffrey notes that Congress established the State Department's own legal office when it passed An Act for the

Grading and Classification of Clerks in the Foreign Service of the United States of America, and Providing for Compensation Therefor, 46 Stat. 1214 (1931).

41. Richard Olney to attorney general, Nov. 5, 1895, in U.S. Senate, *Equitable Distribution*, S. Doc. 154, 9–10.

42. Judson Harmon to Richard Olney, Dec. 12, 1895, in ibid., 10–16.

43. On the interstate struggle for the Arkansas River and Harmon's reply, see Sherow, *Watering the Valley*, 108. For the U.S. Supreme Court's decision in *Kansas v. Colorado*, see 206 U.S. 46 (1907). For Harmon's reply in relation to the Colorado River, see Hundley, *Water and the West*, 23, 81, 205.

44. On the history of the International Boundary Commission, see International Boundary Commission, *Proceedings*, 2:iii, 4–8; U.S. Department of State, *Papers Relating to the Foreign Relations . . . 1897*, 402–405 (hereafter cited as State Department, *Foreign Relations, 1897*); U.S. Department of State, *Papers Relating to the Foreign Relations . . . 1900* (hereafter cited as State Department, *Foreign Relations, 1900*), 788–89.

45. International Boundary Commission, *Proceedings*, 2:iii, 4–8, 278.

46. The quotation is in "Proceedings of the International Commission on the Equitable Distribution of the Waters of the Rio Grande," journal entry, Aug. 17, 1896, in U.S. Senate, *Equitable Distribution of the Waters of the Rio Grande*, S. Doc. 229, 34. See also Richard Olney to Anson Mills, May 13, 1896, in ibid., 31.

47. Andres Horcasitas to M. Romero, June 22, 1896, in ibid., 2; W. W. Rockhill to Anson Mills, Aug. 8, 1896, in ibid., 3; Mills to Rockhill, Nov. 17, 1896, in ibid., 11. See also Richard Olney to secretary of the interior, Nov. 30, 1896, in U.S. Senate, *Equitable Distribution*, S. Doc. 154, 144–45.

48. "Cause for Rejoicing," *Galveston Daily News*, April 2, 1896. Diaz repeated his support for the international dam to the Mexican Congress on September 16, 1897. See "Mexican Congress Opened," *Los Angeles Times*, Sept. 17, 1897.

49. International Boundary Commission, *Proceedings*, 2:279.

50. Ibid.

51. Hays, *Conservation*, 22–26; Dodds, "Stream-Flow Controversy," 59–69; Pisani, *To Reclaim a Divided West*, 161–62. A brief New Mexico newspaper article that appeared more than a decade before Follett's report, however, suggests that even then, at least some westerners suspected that there were links between water storage and forests. See *Rio Grande Republican*, Sept. 22, 1888.

52. W. W. Follett, "A Study of the Uses of Water for Irrigation in the Rio Grande del Norte," in International Boundary Commission, *Proceedings*, 2:290–91, 296–300. The quotations are on 298.

53. "Proceedings of the International Commission on the Equitable Distribution of the Waters of the Rio Grande," journal entry, Nov. 25, 1896, in U.S. Senate, *Equitable Distribution of the Waters of the Rio Grande*, S. Doc. 229, 38–39.

54. Richard Olney to secretary of the interior, Nov. 30, 1896, in U.S. Senate, *Equitable Distribution*, S. Doc. 154, 144–45.

55. On the question of state or federal reclamation, see Pisani, *To Reclaim a Divided West*, 225–326. On the Progressive reclamation movement, see Hays, *Conservation*; Pisani, "Reclamation."

56. D. R. Francis to S. W. Lamoreux, Dec. 5, 1896, in U.S. House, *Letter from the Secretary of the Interior . . . Touching Use, Appropriation, or Disposition for Irrigation of the Waters of the Rio Grande . . .* , H. Doc. 39, 2; Francis to secretary of state, Dec. 19, 1896, in U.S. Senate, *Equitable Distribution of the Waters of the Rio Grande*, S. Doc. 229, 17–19; Richard Olney to Anson Mills, Jan. 4, 1897, in ibid. See also "In the Matter of the Rio Grande Dam and Irrigation Company—Memorandum for the Secretary of the Interior," in U.S. Senate, *Equitable Distribution*, S. Doc. 154, 20–25.

57. Matias Romero to Richard Olney, Dec. 19, 1896, in U.S. Senate, *Equitable Distribution of the Waters of the Rio Grande*, S. Doc. 229, 178; Romero to Olney, Jan. 5, 1897, in ibid.

58. Richard Olney to Matias Romero, Jan. 4, 1897, in ibid., 179.

59. An Act Making Appropriations for the Construction, Repair and Preservation of Certain Public Works on Rivers and Harbors, and for Other Purposes, 26 Stat. 426 (1890); An Act Making Appropriations for the Construction, Repair and Preservation of Certain Public Works on Rivers and Harbors, and for Other Purposes, 27 Stat. 88 (1892).

60. Richard Olney to Anson Mills, Jan. 4, 1897, in U.S. Senate, *Equitable Distribution of the Waters of the Rio Grande*, S. Doc. 229, 18–19.

61. Anson Mills to Richard Olney, Jan. 7, 1897, in ibid., 19–23. The quotation is on 23. On the Rio Grande and navigability, see Kelley, *River of Lost Dreams*.

62. Richard Olney to the secretary of war, Jan. 13, 1897, in U.S. Senate, *Equitable Distribution of the Waters of the Rio Grande*, S. Doc. 229, 24–26.

63. Hays, *Conservation*, 199–218.

64. A. MacKenzie to A. M. Miller, Jan. 25, 1897, in U.S. Senate, *Equitable Distribution of the Waters of the Rio Grande*, S. Doc. 229, 184–85; George McDerby to W. P. Craighill, Feb. 1, 1897, in ibid., 185–86.

65. *Steamer Daniel Ball v. United States*, 77 U.S. 557 (1870).

66. A. MacKenzie to A. M. Miller, Jan. 25, 1897, in U.S. Senate, *Equitable Distribution of the Waters of the Rio Grande*, S. Doc. 229, 184–85; George McDerby to W. P. Craighill, Feb. 1, 1897, in ibid., 185–86.

67. Russell A. Alger to attorney general, May 4, 1897, in ibid., 192; Holmes Conrad to secretary of war, May 7, 1897, in ibid.

Chapter 3. The United States versus the Rio Grande Dam and Irrigation Company

1. Horwitz, *Transformation of American Law*, 266.

2. *Kansas v. Colorado*, 206 U.S. 46 (1907); *Winters v. United States*, 207 U.S. 564 (1908); *Wyoming v. Colorado*, 259 U.S. 419 (1922); *United States v. Appalachian Electric Power Company*, 310 U.S. 377 (1940); *Nebraska v. Wyoming*, 325 U.S. 589 (1945); *Arizona v. California*, 373 U.S. 546 (1963). For early federal claims to western rivers, see Pisani, "State vs. Nation."

3. On Anson Mills's prominence in El Paso and Washington, D.C., see his autobiography, *My Story*. The names of Mills and his wife appeared frequently in the society pages of the eastern press. For several examples (among many), see "Washington Society Notes," *New York Times*, Dec. 21, 1900; "Society in Washington," ibid., Feb. 24,

27. Ibid., 695–710. The quotation is on 696.

28. W. T. Johns to H. D. Bowman, May 30, 1899, Bowman Bank Records.

29. Max Weber interview in the *El Paso Times*, quoted in "The Dam Decision," *Rio Grande Republican*, May 26, 1899.

30. Unidentified Denver newspaper, quoted in "Rio Grande Dam Case," *Rio Grande Republican*, May 26, 1899.

31. "Dispute with Mexico," *Fort Collins Weekly Courier*, Dec. 7, 1899. For a similar sentiment voiced by another Colorado newspaper, see "Colorado Items," *New Castle Nonpareil*, Dec. 21, 1899. The same story appeared virtually verbatim under the headline "Colorado Items" in the following Colorado newspapers: *Elbert County Banner*, Dec. 22, 1899; *Fairplay Flume*, Dec. 22, 1899; *Summit County Journal*, Dec. 23, 1899.

32. "The Rio Grande Dispute," *Los Angeles Times*, Nov. 27, 1899; "Elephant Butte Dam," ibid., Dec. 1, 1899.

33. *United States v. Rio Grande Dam and Irrigation Company*, 184 U.S. 416 (1902), 420–21.

34. For details on the testimony, see *Rio Grande Republican*, Dec. 15, 1899; "The Dam Case," ibid., Dec. 22, 1899; "The Dam Case," ibid., Dec. 29, 1899; "Elephant Butte Dam Case," *Los Angeles Times*, Dec. 24, 1899.

35. *United States v. Rio Grande Dam and Irrigation Co. et al.*, 10 N.M. 617 (1900), 621–34. The quotations are on 633 and 634. For the lower court's decision as summarized in the regional press, see "The Dam Case," *Rio Grande Republican*, Jan. 5, 1900; "Against the Government," *Akron Pioneer Press*, Jan. 5, 1900; "Against the Government," *Castle Rock Journal*, Jan. 5, 1900. The outcome of the case also was carried in newspapers throughout the rest of the United States. See, for example, "Decided against the Government," *Chester Times*, Jan. 2, 1900.

36. Editorial, *Aspen Tribune*, Jan. 14, 1900.

37. *United States v. Rio Grande Dam and Irrigation Company*, 184 U.S. 416 (1902), 421–22.

38. John W. Griggs to secretary of state, Jan. 24, 1900, in International Boundary Commission, *Proceedings*, 2:401; John Hay to Anson Mills, Jan. 30, 1900, in ibid. The quotation is in the former letter.

39. John W. Griggs to secretary of state, Jan. 24, 1900, in International Boundary Commission, *Proceedings*, 2:401; John Hay to Anson Mills, Jan. 30, 1900, in ibid., 402; Mills to secretary of state, Feb. 7, 1900, in ibid.; Mills and Jacobo Blanco to consulting engineers, International (Water) Boundary Commission, Feb. 10, 1900, in ibid.; Mills to secretary of state, Feb. 13, 1900, in ibid., 2:403; "Joint Journal of the International (Water) Boundary Commission," Feb. 6 and 13, 1900, in ibid., 2:403–404.

40. *United States v. Rio Grande Dam and Irrigation Co. et al.*, 10 N.M. 617 (1900), 619–21.

41. Ibid., 634.

42. Ibid., 636.

43. Ibid., 637.

44. Nathan Boyd to H. D. Bowman, Aug. 24, 1900, Bowman Bank Records; Boyd to Bowman, Jan. 16, 1901, ibid.; Boyd to John W. Griggs, Aug. 29, 1900, in International

Boundary Commission, *Proceedings*, 2:374–75; "Memorial of Nathan Boyd to the U.S. Senate, Jan. 10, 1901," in U.S. Senate, *History of the Rio Grande Dam*, 8; A. Mills, *My Story*, 278.

45. National Safe Deposit Company Limited to N. E. Boyd, May 3, 1900, FO897/24, Records of the Foreign Office.

46. Rio Grande Irrigation and Land Company to debenture holders, April 21, 1900 (copy enclosed with Charles B. Woodward to Cecil J. B. Hurst, Oct. 29, 1923), FO897/24, Records of the Foreign Office.

47. List of debenture holders, Feb. 25, 1901 (copy enclosed with Price, Waterhouse and Co. to Sir Cecil Hurst, Oct. 12, 1923), FO897/24, Records of the Foreign Office; summary of capital and shares of the Rio Grande Irrigation and Land Co., Jan. 1900, BT31/34376–45577, Records of the Board of Trade; record of extraordinary general meeting of the Rio Grande Irrigation and Land Company, April 20, 1900, ibid.; John A. Simmers to the registrar, Register of Companies, April 25, 1900, ibid. On the conversion to modern values in U.S. dollars, see chapter 2, note 28. Boyd also owned about 200,000 shares of stock in the Rio Grande Irrigation and Land Company, valued at the firm's formation in 1896 at £1 each, although they held little value as of 1900.

48. Nathan Boyd to H. D. Bowman, Aug. 24, 1900, Bowman Bank Records; Boyd to Bowman, Jan. 16, 1901, ibid.; Boyd to John W. Griggs, Aug. 29, 1900, in International Boundary Commission, *Proceedings*, 2:374–75; "Memorial of Nathan Boyd to the U.S. Senate, Jan. 10, 1901," in U.S. Senate, *History of the Rio Grande Dam*, 8.

49. "Joint Engineers' Report," Feb. 12, 1901, in International Boundary Commission, *Proceedings*, 2:403–404; "Joint Journal of the International (Water) Boundary Commission," Dec. 13, 1901, in ibid., 403–404.

50. M. C. Burch to John H. Stephens, Feb. 13, 1901, in ibid., 2:376.

51. Ibid.; "Petition to the President and Directors of the Elephant Butte Water Users' Association," undated, Prince Papers.

52. "Petition to the President and Directors of the Elephant Butte Water Users' Association," undated, Prince Papers.

53. E. Roberts to H. D. Bowman, Dec. 27, 1900, Bowman Bank Records.

54. *United States v. Rio Grande Dam and Irrigation Company*, 184 U.S. 416 (1902), 416, 422, 425. The quotation is on 422.

55. *United States v. Rio Grande Dam and Irrigation Co. et al.*, 10 N.M. 617 (1900), 636; *United States v. Rio Grande Dam and Irrigation Company*, 184 U.S. 416 (1902), 424–25.

56. E. V. Berrien to Miguel A. Otero, March 12, 1902, frames 261–62, roll 132, Territorial Archives of New Mexico.

57. John D. Bryan to Henry D. Bowman, March 2, 1902, Bowman Bank Records; New Mexico, Secretary, *Report*, 212.

58. *The United States v. Rio Grande Dam and Irrigation Co. et al.*, 13 N.M. 386 (1906), 393–97.

59. Ibid., 393–407.

60. "Big Suit to Save River," *Janesville Daily Gazette*, Dec. 18, 1906; "Big Suit to Save River," *Oelwein Daily Register*, Dec. 18, 1906. In another story about *Kansas v. Col-*

orado published at about the same time, the *New Castle News* of Pennsylvania referred to the lawsuit as "the now famous case." See "Briefs Filed in the Kansas vs. Colorado Case," *New Castle News*, Dec. 28, 1906.

61. *Kansas v. Colorado*, 206 U.S. 46 (1907), 54–57, 64–76.

62. "Hague Tribunal May Decide Elephant Butte Claims," unidentified newspaper clipping, Dec. 24, 1904, file 253–1, Rio Grande Project files, Records of the Bureau of Reclamation.

63. Sir H. M. Durand to the British Foreign Office, April 18, 1905, FO5/2624, Records of the Foreign Office.

64. Confidential draft of letter to Rio Grande Irrigation and Land Company, June 15, 1905, FO5/2624, Records of the Foreign Office; memoranda to R. Chetham-Strode, Oct. 28 and Dec. 4, 1905, ibid.

65. Nathan Boyd to Felix Martinez, Jan. 11, 1905, quoted in "Petition to the President and Directors of the Elephant Butte Water Users' Association," undated, Prince Papers. For similar sentiments, see Boyd to H. B. Holt, Nov. 23, 1905, folder 7, box 14, Elephant Butte Irrigation District Records.

66. The following Colorado newspapers carried the same story under the headline "Restrains Irrigation": *Colorado Transcript*, March 8, 1906; *Fairplay Flume*, March 9, 1906; *Breckenridge Bulletin*, March 10, 1906; *Creede Candle*, March 10, 1906.

67. Nathan Boyd to Thomas Ryan, Jan. 8, 1907, file 253–1, Rio Grande Project files, Records of the Bureau of Reclamation. For a sample of Boyd's views and opinions, see Boyd, *Statement*; Boyd, *Commentary*; Boyd, *Shall the Elephant Butte Project*; Boyd, *Perjury and Other Charges*; Boyd, *In the Dept. of the Interior*; Boyd, *Memorial to the Senate*. On Boyd's being declared a "dangerous man" by the Secret Service, see A. Mills, *My Story*, 278.

68. Nathan Boyd to Thomas Ryan, Jan. 8, 1907, file 253–1, Rio Grande Project files, Records of the Bureau of Reclamation. For more-temperate views of Davis, see Gressley, "Arthur Powell Davis"; Gressley, "Reclamation and the West."

69. Morris Bien to secretary of the interior, May 20, 1907, file 253–1, Rio Grande Project files, Records of the Bureau of Reclamation.

70. B. M. Hall to director, May 28, 1907, ibid.

71. *Rio Grande Dam and Irrigation Company v. United States*, 215 U.S. 266 (1909), 266–78.

72. Abstract statement of receipts and payments, Rio Grande Irrigation and Land Company, June 28, 1911, BT31/34376–45577, Records of the Board of Trade.

73. On Boyd's battles in the international arbitration, see "Rio Grande," *American and British Claims Arbitration under the Special Agreement Concluded between the United States and Great Britain, August 18, 1910*, 332–46 (the quotations are on 332); Boyd, *In the Dept. of the Interior*.

74. Liquidator's statement of account, May 26, 1926, BT31/34376–45577, Records of the Board of Trade; notice of dissolution, Rio Grande Irrigation and Land Company, Feb. 11, 1949, ibid.

Chapter 4. Congress Seeks a Solution

1. For the Carey Act, see An Act Making Appropriations for Sundry Civil Expenses of the Government for the Fiscal Year Ending June Thirtieth, Eighteen Hundred and Ninety-five, and for Other Purposes, 28 Stat. 372 (1895). For the Reclamation Act, see An Act Appropriating from the Sale and Disposal of Public Lands in Certain States and Territories to the Construction of Irrigation Works for the Reclamation of Arid Lands, 32 Stat. 388 (1902).

2. On the history of the Reclamation Act, see Pisani, *To Reclaim a Divided West*; Pisani, *Water and American Government*; Dunbar, *Forging New Rights*, 1–58; Ganoe, "Origin"; Gates and Swenson, *History*, 439–56; Holmes, *History*; Robbins, *Our Landed Heritage*, 330–33; Worster, *Rivers of Empire*, 156–69. On the history of the Bureau of Reclamation and its projects, see Golze, *Reclamation in the United States*; Institute for Government Research, *United States Reclamation Service*; James, *Reclaiming the Arid West*; Reisner, *Cadillac Desert*; Robinson, *Water for the West*; U.S. Bureau of Reclamation, *Bureau of Reclamation Organizational Structure*; Warne, *Bureau of Reclamation*.

3. Hundley, "Clio Nods."

4. Arthur P. Davis, "The Rio Grande Project," undated, unpublished report, 6, box 17, Davis Papers.

5. Harvey B. Fergusson to John Sherman, June 1, 1897, in U.S. Senate, *Equitable Distribution*, S. Doc. 154, 16–18.

6. On the drive for New Mexico statehood, see Larson, *New Mexico's Quest*. For a view of the statehood battle shortly before it bore fruit, see Prince, *New Mexico's Struggle*.

7. H.R. 161, 55th Cong., 2d sess., Jan. 14, 1898, *Congressional Record* 31:1, 643; H.R. 161, 55th Cong., 2d sess., March 2, 1898, ibid., 31:3, 2230–31; S. Res. of Inquiry, 55th Cong., 2d sess., Feb. 26, 1898, ibid., 31:3, 2372; S. Res. of Inquiry, 55th Cong., 2d sess., April 7, 1898, ibid., 31:4, 3651; H.R. 161, 55th Cong., 2d sess., April 7, 1898, ibid., 31:4, 3693. See also U.S. Senate, *Equitable Distribution of the Waters of the Rio Grande*, S. Doc. 229, 1.

8. Boyd explained his role in defeating these measures in his "Statement in re the International El Paso Dam Project," a copy of which is contained in Nathan Boyd to secretary of state, May 26, 1902, reprinted in U.S. Senate, *Equitable Distribution*, S. Doc. 154, 55–57. On competition among local groups in the West to dominate natural resources, see Limerick, *Legacy of Conquest*. On the Progressive-era interest in scientific management of natural resources, see Hays, *Conservation*.

9. John H. Stephens to Anson Mills, Dec. 29, 1899, U.S.-Mexican Border files, Records Relating to International Boundaries; John W. Griggs to secretary of state, March 15, 1900, in International Boundary Commission, *Proceedings*, 2:357; "Testimony Submitted to the Committee on Foreign Affairs on Bill (H.R. 9710) to Provide for the Equitable Distribution of the Waters of the Rio Grande between the United States of America and the United States of Mexico, and for the Purpose of Building an International Dam and Reservoir on Said River at El Paso, Texas," ibid., 2:364–66, 368 (here-

after cited as "Testimony Submitted on H.R. 9710); "Statement of the Losses of the Citizens of El Paso County, Tex., Because of Lack of Water for Irrigation, Caused by the Unlawful Appropriations of the Waters of the Rio Grande River in New Mexico and Colorado during the Four Years Next Past," ibid., 2:372; H.R. 9710, 56th Cong., 1st sess., March 19, 1900, *Congressional Record* 33:4, 3063; S. 3794, 56th Cong., 1st sess., March 26, 1900, ibid., 33:4, 3297.

10. "Testimony Submitted on H.R. 9710," in International Boundary Commission, *Proceedings*, 2:357.

11. "Proposed Dam Legislation," *Rio Grande Republican*, April 20, 1900.

12. Proclamation by Governor Miguel A. Otero calling convention, May 3, 1900, frame 682, roll 147, Territorial Archives of New Mexico; Miguel A. Otero to chairman, Board of County Commissioners, Doña Ana County, May 7, 1900, frame 547, roll 141, ibid.; "Testimony Submitted on H.R. 9710," in International Boundary Commission, *Proceedings*, 2:358. For background on Otero, see Otero, *My Life on the Frontier*; Otero, *My Nine Years as Governor*.

13. "Testimony Submitted on H.R. 9710," in International Boundary Commission, *Proceedings*, 2:358–61.

14. Ibid., 2:360–64. The quotations are on 360. On William W. Mills, see his *Forty Years at El Paso*.

15. "Testimony Submitted on H.R. 9710," in International Boundary Commission, *Proceedings*, 2:363.

16. Miguel A. Otero to Nathan E. Boyd, Jan. 3, 1901, in vol. 1, box 2, 21P, Otero Papers; Otero to William B. Childers, Jan. 3, 1901, ibid.; Otero to B. S. Rodey, Jan. 5, 1901, ibid.; Otero to secretary of the interior, Jan. 8, 1901, ibid.

17. S. 3794, 56th Cong., 1st sess., Dec. 19, 1900, *Congressional Record* 34:1, 418.

18. U.S. Senate, *Equitable Distribution of the Waters*, S. Rpt. 1755, 7–8.

19. Miguel A. Otero to E. P. Kenna, Dec. 26, 1900, vol. 1, box 2, 21P, Otero Papers.

20. B. S. Rodey to H. D. Money, Jan. 5, 1901, in International Boundary Commission, *Proceedings*, 2:386; H. D. Money to Governor Otero, Jan. 15, 1901, ibid. The quotation is in the second letter.

21. S. 3794, 56th Cong., 1st sess., Jan. 22, 1901, *Congressional Record* 34:2, 1284; S. 3794, 56th Cong., 1st sess., Feb. 18, 1901, ibid., 34:3, 2560.

22. "Memorial of Nathan Boyd to the U.S. Senate, Jan. 10, 1901," reprinted in U.S. Senate, *History of the Rio Grande Dam*, 10; *Kansas v. Colorado*, 206 U.S. 46 (1907). For a brief synopsis of *Kansas v. Colorado* and its history, see Sherk, *Dividing the Waters*, 4–5. For other details on New Mexicans' efforts to defeat this version of the Culberson-Stephens bill, see "Mill's [sic] Scheme," *Rio Grande Republican*, Jan. 18, 1901.

23. "Memorial of Nathan Boyd to the U.S. Senate, Jan. 10, 1901," reprinted in U.S. Senate, *History of the Rio Grande Dam*, 8.

24. Ibid., 11–13.

25. An Act Granting the Right of Way to Ditch and Canal Owners over the Public Lands, and for Other Purposes, 14 Stat. 251 (1866); An Act to Amend "An Act Granting the Right of Way to Ditch and Canal Owners over the Public Lands, and for Other

Purposes," 16 Stat. 217 (1870); An Act to Provide for the Sale of Desert Lands in Certain States and Territories, 19 Stat. 377 (1877).

26. Nathan E. Boyd to M. A. Otero, Feb. 21, 1901, frames 234–38, roll 130, Territorial Archives of New Mexico; Boyd to Otero, Aug. 31, 1901, frames 386–90, roll 131, ibid.; Otero to Boyd, Aug. 5, 1901, vol. 2, box 2, 21P, Otero Papers; N. Boyd, *New Mexico and Statehood*. Despite his opposition to calling a state constitutional convention without a congressional enabling act, in September 1901 Otero issued a gubernatorial proclamation calling for a gathering to consider the issue and to pass appropriate resolutions. See "Call for a Statehood Convention," *Rio Grande Republican*, Oct. 11, 1901.

27. "To Preserve Water Rights," *Akron Pioneer Press*, March 7, 1902. Demonstrating the importance of the New Mexico Rio Grande situation to Coloradans, the same article with the identical headline was printed in the following Colorado newspapers: *Range Ledger*, March 6, 1902; *Basalt Journal*, March 8, 1902; *Breckenridge Bulletin*, March 8, 1902; *Glenwood Post*, March 8, 1902.

28. H.R. 115, 57th Cong., 1st sess., Dec. 2, 1901, *Congressional Record* 35:1, 53; S. 453, 57th Cong., 1st sess., Dec. 4, 1901, ibid., 35:1, 127; H.R. 13361, 57th Cong., 1st sess., April 4, 1902, ibid., 35:4, 3704; S. 4974, 57th Cong., 1st sess., April 5, 1902, ibid., 35:4, 3707; H.R. 13963, 57th Cong., 1st sess., April 23, 1902, ibid., 35:5, 4604; Nathan Boyd, "Statement in re the International El Paso Dam Project," included in Boyd to secretary of state, May 26, 1902, reprinted in U.S. Senate, *Equitable Distribution*, S. Doc. 154, 46.

29. Miguel A. Otero to Nathan E. Boyd, Feb. 15, 1902, vol. 3, box 2, 21P, Otero Papers; Otero to Boyd, March 6, 1902, vol. 4, box 2, 21P, ibid.; Otero to Bernard S. Rodey, March 6, 1902, ibid.; Otero to Rodey, March 29, 1902, ibid.; Otero to Boyd, March 29, 1902, ibid.; Larson, *New Mexico's Quest*, 303.

30. Nathan Boyd, "Statement in re the International El Paso Dam Project," included in Boyd to secretary of state, May 26, 1902, reprinted in U.S. Senate, *Equitable Distribution*, S. Doc. 154, 46.

31. Ibid., 47–51, 55–56, 59–62. The quotation is on 60.

32. S. Res. of Inquiry, 57th Cong., 1st sess., June 6, 1902, *Congressional Record* 35:7, 6368.

33. S. Res. of Inquiry, 57th Cong., 1st sess., Feb. 14, 1903, *Congressional Record* 36:3, 2188–89; H.R. 12, 58th Cong., 1st sess., Nov. 9, 1903, ibid., 37:1, 151; S. 2130, 58th Cong., 1st sess., Dec. 7, 1903, ibid., 37:1, 544.

34. "Eternal Vigilance Is Necessary," *Albuquerque Morning Journal*, Oct. 23, 1903.

35. Coloradans, in particular, clearly saw the relevance of the Arkansas River litigation to the conflict over the Rio Grande inasmuch as Colorado had an interest in both streams. See the following Colorado newspaper articles, all published under the headline "To Preserve Water Rights": *Range Ledger*, March 6, 1902; *Akron Pioneer Press*, March 7, 1902; *Basalt Journal*, March 8, 1902; *Breckenridge Bulletin*, March 8, 1902; *Glenwood Post*, March 8, 1902.

36. "Late Washington News and Congressional Proceedings," *Colorado Transcript*, June 11, 1902.

37. Horwitz, *Transformation of American Law*.

Chapter 5. The Compromise of 1904

1. Pisani, *Water and American Government*, xiii.

2. Ibid., xiii–xv. For a detailed discussion of the events that contributed to the passage of the 1902 Reclamation Act, see Pisani, *To Reclaim a Divided West*. For the Carey Act, see An Act Making Appropriations for Sundry Civil Expenses of the Government for the Fiscal Year Ending June Thirtieth, Eighteen Hundred and Ninety-five, and for Other Purposes, 28 Stat. 372 (1894).

3. An Act Appropriating from the Sale and Disposal of Public Lands in Certain States and Territories to the Construction of Irrigation Works for the Reclamation of Arid Lands, 32 Stat. 388 (1902). On the history of the Reclamation Act, see Pisani, *To Reclaim a Divided West*; Dunbar, *Forging New Rights*, 1–58; Ganoe, "Origin"; Gates and Swenson, *History*, 439–56; Holmes, *History*; Robbins, *Our Landed Heritage*, 330–33; Worster, *Rivers of Empire*, 156–69. On the history of the Bureau of Reclamation and its projects, see Golze, *Reclamation in the United States*; Institute for Government Research, *United States Reclamation Service*; James, *Reclaiming the Arid West*; Pisani, *Water and American Government*; Reisner, *Cadillac Desert*; Robinson, *Water for the West*; Warne, *Bureau of Reclamation*.

4. Pisani, "Reclamation," 46–63; the quotation is on p. 53. See also Pisani, *Water and American Government*, 24–26; Hays, *Conservation*.

5. On Davis's background, see Gressley, "Reclamation," 78–101.

6. On Newell's role in drafting the Reclamation Act, see Pisani, *To Reclaim a Divided West*, 301–303. See also Arthur P. Davis, "The Rio Grande Project," undated, unpublished report, 6–10, box 17, Davis Papers; U.S. Reclamation Service, *Third Annual Report*, 93; F. H. Newell to G. A. Richardson, Oct. 28, 1902, frames 518–25, roll 15, Territorial Archives of New Mexico; Charles D. Walcott to Richardson, Jan. 24, 1903, ibid.; Newell to Richardson, Jan. 28, 1903, ibid.; Newell to W. W. Follett, Jan. 28, 1903, file 253–4, Rio Grande Project files, Records of the Bureau of Reclamation; Follett to Newell, Feb. 6, 1903, ibid.; Newell to J. A. French, Feb. 5, 1903, file 46, ibid.

7. *Who Was Who in America*, 1943 ed., 1:504; "Georgian Solve[s] Problem of Reclaiming Arid Lands," *Atlanta Constitution*, Dec. 11, 1904; "Atlanta Engineer Named to Irrigate Porto [sic] Rico," ibid., Feb. 26, 1908; "Hall to Address Engineer Bodies on 'Water Power,'" ibid., Jan. 25, 1921; "Benjamin M. Hall, Noted Atlantan, Dies," ibid., Nov. 20, 1929.

8. *Kansas v. Colorado*, 185 U.S. 125 (1902), 126.

9. Ibid., 126–37.

10. Sherow, *Watering the Valley*, 108.

11. The final decision in this round of the Arkansas River litigation was rendered in *Kansas v. Colorado*, 206 U.S. 46 (1907), although Kansas continued to struggle with Colorado over the stream's diversions for decades to come.

12. See Edward Bartlett to Miguel Otero, June 6, 1904, roll 135, Territorial Archives of New Mexico. See also *Kansas v. Colorado*, 185 U.S. 125 (1902); *Kansas v. Colorado*, 206 U.S. 46 (1907).

13. On the international Colorado River dispute, see Hundley, *Dividing the Waters*, 31–38.

14. M. de Aspiroz to John Hay, June 3, 1904, roll 135, Territorial Archives of New Mexico.

15. John Hay to Ethan A. Hitchcock, June 27, 1904 (two letters of same date), ibid.

16. Hundley, *Dividing the Waters*, 31–38.

17. U.S. Bureau of Reclamation, *Bureau of Reclamation Organizational Structure*, 14.

18. F. H. Newell to Charles D. Walcott (with draft of letter to Secretary Hay), July 16, 1904, roll 135, Territorial Archives of New Mexico.

19. Ibid.

20. Hall, "Discussion of Past and Present Plans."

21. Ibid., 7, 43–53, 56–57, 71.

22. Ibid., 53–54.

23. Ibid.

24. See B. M. Hall to A. P. Davis, Nov. 21, 1904, file 46, Rio Grande Project files, Records of the Bureau of Reclamation; Davis to Hall, Nov. 25, 1904, ibid.

25. Hall, "Discussion of Past and Present Plans," 61–65.

26. "The Proposed Dam," *El Paso Morning Times*, Oct. 16, 1904; B. M. Hall to F. H. Newell, Oct. 25, 1904, file 253–2, Rio Grande Project files, Records of the Bureau of Reclamation.

27. "Mesilla Valley Dam Will Be Recommended," *El Paso Herald*, Oct. 21, 1904; "El Paso Approves the Reclamation Plan," ibid., Oct. 21, 1904; "Reclamation Engineers at Vegas," ibid., Oct. 22, 1904; Hall, "Discussion of Past and Present Plans," 72; resolution adopted at Las Cruces irrigation meeting, Oct. 20, 1904, file 253–2, Rio Grande Project files, Records of the Bureau of Reclamation; "Transcript of Stenographic Memo of Remarks Made by Mr. A. P. Davis . . . October, 1904 . . .," folder 1, box 17, Elephant Butte Irrigation District Records. The Reclamation Extension Act of 1914 transferred the power to authorize federal irrigation projects from the secretary of the interior directly to Congress. See An Act Extending the Period of Payment under Reclamation Projects, and for Other Purposes, 38 Stat. 686 (1914). See also Hays, *Conservation*, 248.

28. Hall, *Magic Mirror*, 5.

29. Pisani, *To Reclaim a Divided West*, 238–40.

30. See Articles II, III, and VI, Constitution of the National Irrigation Congress, July 1, 1903, copy in file 562–12, General Administrative files, Records of the Bureau of Reclamation.

31. For a brief synopsis of Lippincott's life, see Volk and Rowe, "Memoir [of Joseph Barlow Lippincott]."

32. Kluger, *Turning On Water*.

33. General directive to U.S. Reclamation Service engineers, March 1, 1904, file 562–12, General Administrative files, Records of the Bureau of Reclamation; C. B. Booth to F. H. Newell, March 24, 1904, ibid.; Newell to B. M. Hall, Sept. 26, 1904, ibid.; Newell to commissioners of the District of Columbia, Oct. 12, 1904, ibid.; William Tin-

dall to Newell, Oct. 14, 1904, ibid.; Tindall to H. C. Rizer, Oct. 18, 1904, ibid.; flier listing officers of the national irrigation congress, ibid.; list of engineers invited to attend the national irrigation congress, ibid.

34. Flier listing officers of the national irrigation congress, ibid.; Mitchell, *Official Proceedings*, 82–88.

35. C. R. Morehead to Richard Burges, Nov. 1, 1904, box 2B79, Burges Papers; Mitchell, *Official Proceedings*, 82–88; "Proceedings of the Second Conference of Engineers of [the] Reclamation Service at El Paso, Texas, November 14 to 18, 1904, and at Washington, D.C., January 9 to 14, 1905," in file 562–12, General Administrative files, Records of the Bureau of Reclamation; White, *Out of the Desert*, 365–67, 407–409; Coan, *History of New Mexico*, 271–73.

36. "Proceedings of the Second Conference of Engineers of [the] Reclamation Service at El Paso, Texas, November 14 to 18, 1904, and at Washington, D.C., January 9 to 14, 1905," in file 562–12, General Administrative files, Records of the Bureau of Reclamation; W. R. Smith to Richard Burges, Feb. 21, 1908, box 2B80, Burges Papers.

37. The quotation is in Mitchell, *Official Proceedings*, 211. See also "Proceedings of the Second Conference of Engineers of [the] Reclamation Service at El Paso, Texas, November 14 to 18, 1904, and at Washington, D.C., January 9 to 14, 1905," in file 562–12, General Administrative files, Records of the Bureau of Reclamation.

38. B. M. Hall, "Rio Grande Project," in U.S. Geological Survey, *Proceedings of the Second Conference*, 77–78.

39. Mitchell, *Official Proceedings*, 218. Slichter's report was later published as *Observations on the Ground Waters of [the] Rio Grande Valley*. On Hall's request that Slichter study Rio Grande groundwaters, see B. M. Hall to Charles S. Slichter, July 9, 1904, file 432, Rio Grande Project files, Records of the Bureau of Reclamation.

40. B. M. Hall, "Rio Grande Project," in U.S. Geological Survey, *Proceedings of the Second Conference*, 76–77.

41. The quotation is in "The Elephant Butte Project," *El Paso Herald*, Nov. 17, 1904. See also "Unanimity," ibid.

42. "Unanimity," *El Paso Herald*, Nov. 17, 1904.

43. The quotation is in Mitchell, *Official Proceedings*, 108. See also "Unanimity," *El Paso Herald*, Nov. 17, 1904; "The Elephant Butte Project," ibid.; stenographic report of 1904 Irrigation Congress Proceedings, 135–41, enclosed with B. M. Hall to F. H. Newell, Feb. 7, 1905, file 562–12, General Administrative files, Records of the Bureau of Reclamation.

44. "Unanimity," *El Paso Herald*, Nov. 17, 1904; Mitchell, *Official Proceedings*, 82, 108; stenographic report of 1904 Irrigation Congress Proceedings, 135–41, enclosed with B. M. Hall to F. H. Newell, Feb. 7, 1905, file 562–12, General Administrative files, Records of the Bureau of Reclamation.

45. "Original Agreement between [sic] Mexico, New Mexico and Texas Delegates, Preparatory to the Starting of the Rio Grande Irrigation System, Signed at Irrigation Congress, El Paso, Texas, Nov. 18th, 1904," file 78–25, Rio Grande Historical Collections;

"Mexican Representatives Join with the Americans," *El Paso Herald*, Nov. 18, 1904; "Unanimity," ibid., Nov. 17, 1904; Mitchell, *Official Proceedings*, 107–109.

46. B. M. Hall to A. P. Davis, Nov. 19, 1904, file 46, Rio Grande Project files, Records of the Bureau of Reclamation.

47. Ibid.

48. "Georgian Solve[s] Problem of Reclaiming Arid Lands," *Atlanta Constitution*, Dec. 11, 1904.

49. "Praised by Newlands," *Washington Post*, Nov. 26, 1904.

50. "Dam Is Assured," *Houston Post*, Nov. 18, 1904; *Rio Grande Republican*, Nov. 18, 1904; "Elephant Butte Dam Approved," *El Paso Daily Times*, Nov. 18, 1904.

51. See the following Colorado newspaper articles, all published under the same headline of "Portland Next": *Eagle County Times*, Nov. 19, 1904; *Colorado Transcript*, Nov. 24, 1904; *Eagle County Blade*, Nov. 24, 1904; *Longmont Ledger*, Nov. 25, 1904; *Yampa Leader*, Nov. 26, 1904.

52. "Probe Water Rights," *Washington Post*, April 15, 1905.

53. "Mexican Representatives Join with the Americans," *El Paso Herald*, Nov. 18, 1904.

54. For Hall's presentation as it was printed in one regional newspaper, see "Government's Plan," *Rio Grande Republican*, Nov. 25, 1904.

Chapter 6. The 1905 Congressional Apportionment of the Rio Grande

1. On the Supreme Court's interpretation of the historical record behind the Boulder Canyon Act and how the court may have misunderstood that record, see Hundley, "Clio Nods." See also Hundley, *Water and the West*. Consult the same work for details on the Colorado River Compact. For the Boulder Canyon Act, see An Act to Provide for the Construction of Works for the Protection and Development of the Colorado River Basin, for the Approval of the Colorado River Compact, and for Other Purposes, 45 Stat. 1057 (1928). For details on *Wyoming v. Colorado*, 259 U.S. 419 (1922), see Sherk, *Dividing the Waters*, 5; Tyler, *Silver Fox*, 88–122; Radosevich et al., *Evolution and Administration*, 224–25; Dunbar, *Forging New Rights*, 136–37, 197; Sherow, "Latent Influence of Equity." See also Sherk's *Dividing the Waters* for brief descriptions of most other interstate stream disputes in the United States.

2. See Pisani, "Reclamation." See also Hays, *Conservation*.

3. "Elephant Butte Reservoir Convention," *Rio Grande Republican*, Dec. 9, 1904; "Another Mass Meeting Called for December 27," *El Paso Herald*, Dec. 19, 1904.

4. "Mesilla Valley Water Users Are in Session," *El Paso Herald*, Dec. 22, 1904; "Texas Water Users Must Prepare to Act," ibid., Dec. 23, 1904; "To Reclaim This Valley," ibid., Dec. 13, 1904; "Water Users' Convention a Crowning Success," *Rio Grande Republican*, Dec. 23, 1904; "Petition [to] the President and Directors, The Elephant Butte Water Users' Association," undated flier, file 253–1, Rio Grande Project files, Records of the Bureau of Reclamation; "Transcript of Stenographic Memo of Remarks . . . by Mr. A. P. Davis . . . ," folder 1, box 17, Elephant Butte Irrigation District Records; "To the

Chairman and Members of the Elephant Butte Reservoir Convention," resolution to form the Elephant Butte Water Users' Association, folder 5, box 14, ibid. For the articles of incorporation of both water users' associations, see file 655, Rio Grande Project files, Records of the Bureau of Reclamation. See also folder 1, box 15, Elephant Butte Irrigation District Records.

5. Gates and Swenson, *History*, 670–72.

6. H.R. 15579, 58th Cong., 3d sess., Dec. 5, 1904, *Congressional Record* 39:1, 5.

7. "A Bill Extending the Operation of the Irrigation Reclamation Act of Congress to the State of Texas in Certain Cases," copy in file 286–2, General Administrative files, Records of the Bureau of Reclamation; director of U.S. Geological Survey to secretary of the interior, Jan. 25, 1905, file 286–3, ibid.

8. On Newell's role in drafting the original Reclamation Act, see Pisani, *To Reclaim a Divided West*, 302–303. On other aspects of Newell's background, see Pisani, *Water and American Government*, 23–24; Smith, *Magnificent Experiment*, 12–13.

9. "Memorandum Regarding Rio Grande Legislation," Jan. 18, 1905, in file 690, Rio Grande Project files, Records of the Bureau of Reclamation; draft entitled "A Bill Relating to the Construction of a Dam and Reservoir on the Rio Grande for the Impounding of the Flood Waters of Said River for Purposes of Irrigation and Providing for the Distribution of Said Stored Waters among the Irrigable Lands in New Mexico, Texas, and the Republic of Mexico," H.R. 17939, 58th Cong., 3d sess., Jan. 18, 1905, *Congressional Record* 39:2, 1059; "A Bill (H.R. 17939) Relating to the Construction of a Dam and Reservoir on the Rio Grande, in New Mexico, for the Impounding of the Floodwaters of Said River for the Purposes of Irrigation, and Providing for the Distribution of Said Stored Waters among the Irrigable Lands in New Mexico, Texas, and the Republic of Mexico, and to Provide for a Treaty for the Settlement of Certain Alleged Claims of the Citizens of the Republic of Mexico against the United States of America," 58th Cong., 3d sess., copy in ibid. See also "Dam on the Rio Grande," *Galveston Daily News*, Jan. 25, 1905.

10. See memorandum and bills listed in preceding note.

11. H.R. 17939, 58th Cong., 3d sess., Jan. 26, 1905, *Congressional Record* 39:2, 1437, 1901. The quotation is on 1903.

12. Ibid.

13. Ibid.

14. Ibid., 39:2, 1904 (emphasis added).

15. The Frenger and Boyd telegrams to Hall (both dated Feb. 1, 1905) are quoted in B. M. Hall to A. P. Davis, Feb. 2, 1905, file 430, Rio Grande Project files, Records of the Bureau of Reclamation.

16. B. M. Hall to A. P. Davis, Feb. 2, 1905, ibid. On the Reclamation Service's attitude toward water users in general, see Worster, *Rivers of Empire*, 156–88.

17. B. M. Hall to N. C. Frenger, Feb. 2, 1905, file 430, Rio Grande Project files, Records of the Bureau of Reclamation.

18. S. 7018, 58th Cong., 3d sess., Feb. 1, 1905, *Congressional Record* 39:2, 1669; H.R. 17939, 58th Cong., 3d sess., Feb. 4, 1905, ibid., 39:2, 1905.

19. H. B. Holt to Charles E. Miller, Feb. 8, 1905, frames 309–12, roll 136, Territorial Archives of New Mexico.

20. Ibid.

21. El Paso Valley Water Users' Association telegram to F. H. Newell, Feb. 8, 1905, file 655, Rio Grande Project files, Records of the Bureau of Reclamation.

22. Acting chief engineer to El Paso Valley Water Users' Association, Feb. 10, 1905, ibid.

23. H.R. 17939, 58th Cong., 3d sess., Feb. 6 and 15, 1905, *Congressional Record* 39:2, 1914, 2603; H.R. 17939, 58th Cong., 3d sess., Feb. 17 and 20, 1905, ibid., 39:3, 2894–95; Joint Memorial 3, 36th Legislative Assembly of the Territory of New Mexico, passed Feb. 10, 1905, copy in file 690, Rio Grande Project files, Records of the Bureau of Reclamation.

24. H.R. 17939, 58th Cong., 3d sess., Feb. 20 and 21, 1905, *Congressional Record* 39:3, 2886–87, 2993; H.R. 17939, 58th Cong., 3d sess., Feb. 25, 1905, ibid., 39:4, 3584; An Act Relating to the Construction of a Dam and Reservoir on the Rio Grande, in New Mexico, for the Improvement of the Flood Waters of Said River for Purposes of Irrigation, 33 U.S. Stat. 814 (1905); "Condensed Telegrams," *Creede Candle*, March 25, 1905.

25. An Act to Extend the Irrigation Act to the State of Texas, 34 Stat. 259 (1906).

26. An Act Relating to the Construction of a Dam and Reservoir on the Rio Grande, in New Mexico, for the Improvement of the Flood Waters of Said River for Purposes of Irrigation, 33 U.S. Stat. 814 (1905).

27. For the treatment of interstate apportionment by writers around the time of the 1905 congressional division of the Rio Grande, see Chandler, *Elements of Western Water Law*; Farnham, *Law of Waters*; Kinney, *Treatise*; Long, *Treatise*; Pomeroy, *Treatise*; Wiel, *Water Rights*.

28. *Howell v. Johnson*, 89 Fed. 556 (1898), was a dispute between Montana and Wyoming over the waters of Sage Creek and was settled by the U.S. Circuit Court for Montana. The first U.S. Supreme Court case actually to apportion an interstate river was *Wyoming v. Colorado*, 259 U.S. 419 (1922), a case that is also important for establishing that prior appropriation could be enforced across state lines if two adjoining states each recognized the priority principle within their boundaries. That decision, however, did not say that prior appropriation had to be used across state lines, merely that it could be considered in determining an equitable apportionment between the states involved.

29. Kinney, *Treatise*, 3:2210.

30. Indeed, Jerome C. Muys asserted in a 1995 article published by the American Bar Association as part of a review of the status of water law that "Congress has [legislated the apportionment of an interstate river] only once since 1963 when it learned that it had such power. That was in 1990, when it legislated an equitable apportionment of the Truckee and Carson Rivers and Lake Tahoe between California and Nevada" ("Approaches and Considerations," 312). See also Clark, *Water and Water Rights*; Hutchins, *Water Rights*; Sherk, *Dividing the Waters*; Frankfurter and Landis, "Compact

Clause"; Muys, "Interstate Compacts"; Thursby, *Interstate Cooperation*; Zimmermann and Wendell, *The Law and Use of Interstate Compacts*.

31. On this point, see *Bean v. Morris*, 221 U.S. 485 (1911).

32. A. P. Davis to B. M. Hall, Feb. 28, 1905, file 46, Rio Grande Project files, Records of the Bureau of Reclamation.

33. H. B. Holt to F. H. Newell, Nov. 7, 1905, ibid.; B. M. Hall to the chief engineer, Nov. 20, 1905, ibid.; Holt to Hall, Nov. 20, 1905, ibid.; Felix Martinez to Hall, Nov. 20, 1905, ibid.

34. B. M. Hall to David L. White, Jan. 23, 1906, file 41-D, General Administrative files, Records of the Bureau of Reclamation; supervising engineer to Vernon L. Sullivan, April 14, 1908, ibid.

35. "Articles of Agreement between the Elephant Butte Water Users' Association and the El Paso Valley Waters Users' Association and the United States of America," June 27, 1906, reprinted in U.S. House, *Letter from the Secretary of the Interior . . . Touching Use, Appropriation, or Disposition for Irrigation of the Waters of the Rio Grande . . .* , 10–12.

Chapter 7. An International Apportionment

1. See Hays, *Conservation*.

2. F. H. Newell to E. A. Hitchcock, March 25, 1905, file 690, Rio Grande Project files, Records of the Bureau of Reclamation.

3. E. A. Hitchcock to director of the U.S. Geological Survey, March 30, 1905, ibid.; F. H. Newell to secretary of the interior, April 3, 1905, ibid.

4. Pisani, *Water and American Government*, 14–15.

5. "Probe Water Rights," *Washington Post*, April 15, 1905.

6. "Canada Watching Niagara," *Galveston Daily News*, April 20, 1905.

7. "Want the Whole Stream," *Manitoba Free Press*, May 1, 1905.

8. "International Water Rights," ibid., May 11, 1905.

9. "The Milk River Irrigation Project," ibid., May 25, 1925 (quoting the *Great Falls [MT] Tribune*, n.d.).

10. "Canadian Waterways," *Ogden Standard*, May 27, 1905; "Awaiting Taft's Decision," *Washington Post*, May 27, 1905.

11. E. A. Hitchcock to director of the U.S. Geological Survey, March 30, 1905, file 690, Rio Grande Project files, Records of the Bureau of Reclamation; F. H. Newell to secretary of the interior, April 3, 1905, ibid.

12. E. A. Hitchcock to director of the U.S. Geological Survey, March 30, 1905, ibid.; F. H. Newell to secretary of the interior, April 3, 1905, ibid.

13. *Who Was Who in America*, 1943 ed., 93.

14. For details on Bien's proposed water code, see Pisani, *Water and American Government*, 38–40.

15. Draft of letter from director of the U.S. Geological Survey to secretary of the interior, April 26, 1905, file 690, Rio Grande Project files, Records of the Bureau of Reclamation.

16. For details on Slater's life and contributions to the El Paso area, see www.tsha.utexas.edu/handbook/online/articles/SS/fsl13.html.

17. H. D. Slater to F. H. Newell, April 17, 1905, file 253, Rio Grande Project files, Records of the Bureau of Reclamation; Newell to Slater, April 22, 1905, ibid.

18. H. D. Slater's draft of a letter to the secretary of the interior, undated but preceding May 13, 1905, file 690, Rio Grande Project files, Records of the Bureau of Reclamation; Slater's draft of a proposed treaty with Mexico, ibid.

19. On the negotiations for the 1944 treaty, see files 032 and 032.5 (both of which deal with water rights and treaty matters), Entry 7, General Administrative and Project Records, 1919–1929, and 1930–1945, Records of the Bureau of Reclamation. See also Hundley, *Dividing the Waters*.

20. See chapter 7, note 18.

21. See chapter 7, note 18.

22. H. D. Slater to F. H. Newell, May 29, 1905, ibid.

23. Ibid.

24. B. M. Hall to F. H. Newell, June 3, 1905, file 690, Rio Grande Project files, Records of the Bureau of Reclamation.

25. "Suggestions for a Treaty between the United States and Mexico," as amended Oct. 23, 1905, initialed by M.B. [Morris Bien], ibid.

26. F. H. Newell to secretary of the interior, Oct. 31, 1905, ibid.; Joaquin D. Casasus to Elihu Root, March 28, 1906, ibid.; Elihu Root to secretary of the interior, April 2, 1906, ibid.

27. Morris Bien to secretary of the interior, April 18, 1906, ibid.

28. W. R. Smith to Richard Burges, Jan. 5, 1906, box 2B79, Burges Papers.

29. A. S. Burleson to Richard Burges, April 23, 1906, ibid.; Burges to Burleson, May 1, 1906, ibid.

30. A. S. Burleson to Richard Burges, May 11, 1906, ibid.

31. "Waters of the Rio Grande—Message from the President of the United States Transmitting a Convention between the United States and Mexico, Signed at Washington on May 21, 1906, Providing for the Equitable Distribution of the Waters of the Rio Grande for Irrigation Purposes," copy in file 690, Rio Grande Project files, Records of the Bureau of Reclamation.

32. The quotation is in Richard F. Burges to A. S. Burleson, May 23, 1906, box 2B79, Burges Papers. See also Burleson to Burges, June 24, 1906, ibid.; Charles A. Culberson telegram to Burges, June 26, 1906, ibid.; Burleson to Burges, June 30, 1906, with enclosed copy of a letter of the same date from Burleson to Max Weber, ibid.; "Water Supply of [the] Rio Grande—From Official Records, 1912," unpublished report, file 46, Rio Grande Project files, Records of the Bureau of Reclamation; Convention Providing for the Equitable Distribution of the Waters of the Rio Grande for Irrigation Purposes, 34 Stat. 2953 (1906).

33. For a brief synopsis of the history of the Hondo Project, see I. Clark, *Water in New Mexico*, 87. For more details, see Bogener, *Ditches across the Desert*.

34. Acting chief engineer to B. M. Hall, Nov. 25, 1904, file 46, Rio Grande Project files, Records of the Bureau of Reclamation.

35. A. P. Davis to B. M. Hall, Feb. 28, 1905, ibid.

36. B. M. Hall to chief engineer, Jan. 29, 1907, file 690, Rio Grande Project files, Records of the Bureau of Reclamation.

37. F. H. Newell to B. M. Hall, Feb. 4, 1907, ibid.

38. F. H. Newell to A. S. Burleson, Feb. 13, 1907, with enclosed portion of an appropriation bill, ibid.

39. Arthur P. Davis to Charles Denby, Feb. 8, 1907, ibid.; Davis, "The Rio Grande Project," undated, unpublished report, 13, box 17, Davis Papers.

40. Nathan E. Boyd to Henry Moody, Oct. 27, 1906, file 253–1, Rio Grande Project files, Records of the Bureau of Reclamation.

41. An Act Making Appropriations for Sundry Civil Expenses of the Government for the Fiscal Year Ending June Thirtieth, Nineteen Hundred and Eight, and for Other Purposes, 34 Stat. 1295 (1907).

42. "Water Supply of [the] Rio Grande — From Official Records, 1912," unpublished report in file 46, Rio Grande Project files, Records of the Bureau of Reclamation; B. M. Hall to chief engineer, Feb. 13, 1907, file 46, ibid.; Hall to chief engineer, Feb. 27, 1907, ibid.; W. R. Smith to Richard Burges, Feb. 26, 1907, box 2B79, Burges Papers.

Chapter 8. The Reclamation Service Begins Work

1. See Horwitz, *Transformation of American Law.*

2. For the history of the Colorado River's apportionment, see Hundley, *Water and the West.*

3. Hall, *Magic Mirror,* 5.

4. See Hays, *Conservation.*

5. See Limerick, *Legacy of Conquest.*

6. On the politics behind the Reclamation Act's enactment, see Pisani, *To Reclaim a Divided West.* On the 160-acre limit to federal reclamation projects, see McDonald, *One Hundred and Sixty Acres.*

7. Pisani, *Water and American Government,* 56–60. The quotation from the secretary of the interior appears on 57.

8. Ibid., 203.

9. Ibid., 203–20.

10. Elephant Butte Realty Company letterhead, ca. 1908, file 46, Rio Grande Project files, Records of the Bureau of Reclamation.

11. "Leasburg Dam Causes Land Values to Soar," *Rio Grande Republican,* July 15, 1910.

12. F. H. Newell to supervising engineer, July 20, 1914, file 46, Rio Grande Project files, Records of the Bureau of Reclamation.

13. Charles H. Stoll to Richard F. Burges, Sept. 6, 1910, box 2B80, Burges Papers; "Statement of Final Settlement of Accounts of the Mesilla Valley and El Paso Interurban

Railway Company," undated, ibid.; G. R. Scrugham to R. F. Burges, Nov. 21, 1910, ibid.; Burges to J. W. Bailey, Jan. 25, 1911, ibid.; Wade H. Ellis to Burges, Feb. 1, 1911, ibid.; Ellis to Burges, Feb. 3, 1911, ibid.; Scrugham to Burges, Feb. 7, 1911, ibid.; Scrugham telegram to Burges, Feb. 18, 1911, ibid.; W. R. Smith telegram to Burges, Feb. 20, 1911, ibid.; Scrugham to Burges, Feb. 24, 1911, ibid.; Scrugham to Burges, Feb. 25, 1911, ibid.; Smith to Burges, Feb. 28, 1911, ibid.

14. www.usbr.gov/dataweb/html/riograndeh.html\#32a.

15. A. Courchesne to Louis C. Hill, dated 1912, file 46, Rio Grande Project files, Records of the Bureau of Reclamation. On Courchesne's background, see Paddock, *Twentieth Century History*, 1:626–27.

16. W. R. Smith to R. F. Burges, Oct. 17, 1912, with a copy of Frederick Newell memorandum to L. C. Hill, Oct. 9, 1912, box 2B81, Burges Papers; Burges to Smith, Nov. 12, 1912, ibid.; A. P. Davis to supervising engineer, Nov. 14, 1912, file 46, Rio Grande Project files, Records of the Bureau of Reclamation; Louis C. Hill to chief engineer, Nov. 23, 1912, ibid.; Hill to chief engineer, Nov. 23, 1912, ibid.; "High Line Canal," chronology of events, folder 1, box 17, Elephant Butte Irrigation District Records.

17. Pisani, Water and American Government, 103–17. For the Warren Act, see An Act to Authorize the Government to Contract for Impounding, Storing, and Carriage of Water, and to Cooperate in the Construction and Use of Reservoirs and Canals under Reclamation Projects, and for Other Purposes, 36 Stat. 925 (1911). For the Reclamation Extension Act, see An Act Extending the Period of Payment under Reclamation Projects, and for Other Purposes, 38 Stat. 686 (1914).

18. A. P. Davis, Louis C. Hill, D. C. Henny, L. M. Lawson, and Homer J. Gault to director, March 27, 1913, file 46, Rio Grande Project files, Records of the Bureau of Reclamation; Davis to supervising engineer, April 17, 1913, ibid.; "To the Members of the Council of the Elephant Butte Water Users' Association of New Mexico," annual report, May 5, 1913, folder 5, box 16, Elephant Butte Irrigation District Records.

19. William L. Marshall, D. C. Henny, W. W. Follett, Louis C. Hill, and L. M. Lawson to the director, Dec. 4, 1913, file 46, Rio Grande Project files, Records of the Bureau of Reclamation; Hill to chief engineer, Dec. 8, 1913, ibid. The board's conclusions are also quoted in L. M. Lawson to director, July 3, 1919, file 301.5, Rio Grande Project files, Records of the Bureau of Reclamation.

20. A. P. Davis to W. A. Ryan, March 5, 1914, file 46, Rio Grande Project files, Records of the Bureau of Reclamation; F. W. Hanna and L. M. Lawson to the Reclamation Commission, July 25, 1914, file 458, Rio Grande Project files, Records of the Bureau of Reclamation; "To the Members of the Council of the Elephant Butte Water Users' Association of New Mexico," annual report for 1914, folder 5, box 16, Elephant Butte Irrigation District Records.

21. F. W. Hanna and L. M. Lawson to Reclamation Commission, July 25, 1914, file 458, Rio Grande Project files, Records of the Bureau of Reclamation; "To the Members of the Council of the Elephant Butte Water Users' Association of New Mexico," annual

report for 1914, folder 5, box 16, Elephant Butte Irrigation District Records; "High Line Canal," chronology of events, folder 1, box 17, ibid.

22. F. W. Hanna and L. M. Lawson to Reclamation Commission, July 25, 1914, file 458, Rio Grande Project files, Records of the Bureau of Reclamation.

23. Ibid. The documents are quoted in the letter.

24. F. H. Newell to supervising engineer and project manager, Aug. 20, 1914, file 458, Rio Grande Project files, Records of the Bureau of Reclamation; Newell to Secretary Lane, July 15, 1914, ibid.

25. For details on the change from water users' associations to districts, see Pisani, *Water and American Government*, 133–34.

26. Ibid., 52–53.

27. Project manager to chief of construction, Feb. 8, 1918, file 46, Rio Grande Project files, Records of the Bureau of Reclamation; "Develop Hydro-Electric Power; Irrigate Bench Lands," *Rio Grande Republican*, Jan. 4, 1918. For an idea of the scale of the Rio Grande Dam and Irrigation Company's plans, see "Map of the Rio Grande Valley from Engle, New Mexico, to Fort Quitman, Texas, Showing Dams, Reservoirs, Canals, and Irrigable Lands of the Rio Grande Dam and Irrigation Company," in International Boundary Commission, *Proceedings*, 2:356.

28. H. H. Brook, "Co-operative Proposal for the Completion of the Rio Grande Project, Texas–New Mexico," 7–8, unpublished report, July 7, 1919, copy in file 301.5, Rio Grande Project files, Records of the Bureau of Reclamation.

29. Quinton, Code, and Hill, "Proposed High Line Canals and Power Plants of the Rio Grande Project and the Future Water Supply of the City of El Paso, Texas," unpublished report, June 1919, copy in ibid.

30. Ibid.

31. H. H. Brook, "Co-operative Proposal for the Completion of the Rio Grande Project, Texas–New Mexico," 1, 12–15, unpublished report, July 7, 1919, copy in ibid.; Pisani, *Water and American Government*, 126–29; Hundley, *Water and the West*, 44, 84–85. On Brook's background, see Coan, *History of New Mexico*, 39–41.

32. H. H. Brook, "Co-operative Proposal for the Completion of the Rio Grande Project, Texas–New Mexico," 1, 12–15, unpublished report, July 7, 1919, copy in file 301.5, Rio Grande Project files, Records of the Bureau of Reclamation.

33. A. P. Davis to chief of construction, July 12, 1919, file 301.5, Rio Grande Project files, Records of the Bureau of Reclamation; Davis to chief of construction, July 26, 1919, ibid.; Davis to H. H. Brook, July 26, 1919, ibid.; D. C. Henny, James Munn, and C. T. Pease, "Report on Water Supply and Project Area, High Line Canal Construction, Power Development, and City Water Supply from Storage, Rio Grande Project," unpublished report, Nov. 1919, 1, copy in ibid. Another copy of this report is in the library of the New Mexico State Engineer, Santa Fe.

34. Henny, Munn, and Pease report cited in preceding note, pp. 1–6, 35–70.

35. Ibid., 1–6, 37–42.

Chapter 9. The Rio Grande Compact, Part I

1. B. P. Fleming telegram to R. F. Walter, Feb. 16, 1929, file 301, Rio Grande Project files, Records of the Bureau of Reclamation; Roland Harwell to R. F. Walter, Feb. 16, 1929, ibid.; "Memorandum Relating to Additional Work for El Paso County Water Improvement District Number One," Feb. 16, 1929, ibid.

2. B. P. Fleming to L. R. Fiock, April 4, 1931, file 222, Rio Grande Project files, Records of the Bureau of Reclamation; R. F. Walter to the commissioner, Nov. 2, 1937, ibid.; L. R. Fiock to Roland Harwell, Nov. 9, 1937, ibid.; "Contract between the Elephant Butte Irrigation District and the El Paso County Water Improvement District No. 1," Feb. 16, 1938, file 222, box 918, ibid.

3. One change in the embargo had taken place in 1906 when the U.S. government permitted construction of some Rio Grande basin reservoir projects to proceed, provided that those ventures had filed applications prior to 1903. See "Rio Grande Case," *Colorado Transcript*, July 31, 1906. The same story under the identical headline appeared in other Colorado newspapers, including the *Akron Pioneer Press*, June 1, 1906; *Castle Rock Journal*, June 1, 1906; *Elbert County Banner*, June 1, 1906; *Yampa Leader*, June 2, 1906.

4. "Will Urge Lane to Throw Open San Luis Valley," *Alamosa Independent Journal*, April 17, 1914.

5. For northern New Mexico's views, see, for example, a 1910 editorial in the *Santa Fe New Mexican* favoring removal of the embargo. The editorial is reprinted in "As the New Mexican Views It," *Rio Grande Republican*, Sept. 30, 1910.

6. Pisani, *Water and American Government*, 53–54.

7. On the Salt River withdrawals, see file labeled "Reclamation Bureau, Salt River Project, Withdrawals & Restorations, March 4, 1908, to March 18, 1913," box 1648, Central Classified Files, 1907–1936, Record Group 48, Records of the Office of the Secretary of the Interior. On the Salt River Project generally, see Smith, *Magnificent Experiment*.

8. Hundley, *Water and the West*, 96–101, 104–105.

9. For a partial list of news reports about the completion of Elephant Butte Dam, see "Uncle Sam Opens Great Irrigation Project on Rio Grande," *Evening Observer*, May 12, 1916; "Work Completed on Huge Dam," *Portsmouth Daily Times*, May 13, 1916; "Greatest Reservoir in World in Service," *Syracuse Herald*, May 13, 1916; "Great Dam Finished," *Oelwein Daily Register*, May 15, 1916; "Immense Dam Finished," *Washington Post*, May 15, 1916; "Elephant Butte Dam Builders Praised," *Oakland Tribune*, May 17, 1916; "U.S. Finishes Huge Dam," *Akron Weekly Pioneer Press*, May 19, 1916; "Huge New Dam Finished by U.S.," *Fairplay Flume*, May 19, 1916; "Huge New Dam Finished by U.S.," *Plateau Voice*, May 19, 1916; "Elephant Butte Dam on Mexican Border Complete," *Newcastle News*, June 14, 1916; "Reclaiming an Empire," *Van Nuys News*, July 21, 1916; "Elephant Butte Dam Is to Be Set to Work Oct. 14," *Logansport Daily Tribune*, Sept. 15, 1916; "International Irrigation and Farm Congress Problems," *Fort Collins Weekly Courier*, Sept. 15, 1916; "New U.S. Dam Largest Mass of Masonry in the World,"

Wisconsin State Journal, Sept. 17, 1916; "Twelve Years Construction [of] the Butte Dam," *Daily Kennebec Journal*, Sept. 23, 1916; "Largest Dam in the World," *San Juan Prospector*, Oct. 7, 1916; "To Dedicate Big Irrigation Dam," *Lincoln Daily Star*, Oct. 8, 1916; "World's Greatest Water Reservoir Opened Today," *Edwardsville Intelligencer*, Oct. 14, 1916; "Nation Builds Huge Reservoir," *Star and Sentinel*, Nov. 7, 1916; "Nation Builds Huge Reservoir," *Tyrone Herald*, Nov. 20, 1916; "Elephant Butte Dam Will Curb the Rio Grande Floods," *Grand Rapids Tribune*, May 3, 1917.

10. On the history of the Rio Grande embargo and water use in northern New Mexico and in Colorado's San Luis Valley, see the following unpublished reports in the New Mexico State Engineer Office, Santa Fe: French, "Irrigation on the Rio Grande"; Hamele, "Embargo"; Stannard, "Report of Operations"; Yeo, "General Description"; Yeo, "Report on Hydrographic and Irrigation Conditions"; Yeo, "Tabulation of Ditches." See also files 41-D, 64-A, and 64-A2, General Administrative files, Records of the Bureau of Reclamation; file 032.02, Rio Grande Basin files, Records of the Bureau of Reclamation; file 8–3, boxes 1638 and 1639, Central Classified files, 1907–1936, Records of the Office of the Secretary of the Interior; boxes 2B80, 2B81, and 2B82, Burges Papers.

11. *Kansas v. Colorado*, 206 U.S. 46 (1907). On Coloradans' views of *Kansas v. Colorado*, see Tyler, *Silver Fox*, 75.

12. *Wyoming v. Colorado*, 259 U.S. 419 (1922); Tyler, *Silver Fox*, 77–78. Contrary to popular perception, the decision in *Wyoming v. Colorado* did not extend priorities across state lines; the ruling considered priorities in making a bulk allocation to each state. See Sherk, *Dividing the Waters*, 5.

13. *United States v. Rio Grande Dam and Irrigation Company*, 174 U.S. 690 (1899), 690–92.

14. Hundley, *Water and the West*, 24–26.

15. *Kansas v. Colorado*, 206 U.S. 46 (1907), 54–57, 64–76.

16. *Wyoming v. Colorado*, 259 U.S. 419 (1922), 443.

17. For example, a recent interstate disagreement involved the 1785 "Mount Vernon" compact (named for negotiations that took place at George Washington's home) between Maryland and Virginia and the latter state's proposed diversions of water from the Potomac River, which lies along the border between the two states. In that case, Virginia's authorities argued before the U.S. Supreme Court that the 1785 accord was in effect a compact that granted their state the right to use Potomac waters even though Maryland's 1632 colonial charter extended Maryland's territory under the Potomac River to the Virginia shoreline. In 2003, the Supreme Court sustained Virginia's point of view. The high court ruled that the 1785 agreement—which took place four years before the U.S. Constitution was ratified—gave Virginia the modern-day "privilege of making and carrying out wharfs and other improvements" in the river. Although this provision in the 1785 compact most likely was intended to govern waterborne commerce on the Potomac, the Supreme Court nonetheless held that the wording also applied to activities involving present water diversions. See *Virginia v. Maryland*, 540 U.S. 56 (2003).

18. On the Colorado River Compact, see Hundley, *Water and the West*. On interstate river compacts, see Muys, "Interstate Compacts"; Sherk, *Dividing the Waters*; Stinson, "Western Interstate Water Compact." On compacts in general, see Thursby, *Interstate Cooperation*; Zimmermann and Wendell, *Interstate Compact since 1925*; Leach and Sugg, *Administration of Interstate Compacts*; Leach, "Interstate Compact."

19. The La Plata River Compact was signed by delegates of Colorado and New Mexico in 1922 and took effect after final ratification in 1925. The South Platte River Compact was approved in 1923 but not fully ratified until 1926. For details on the negotiation of these two compacts, see Tyler, *Silver Fox*. For specifics about the La Plata River Compact, see Sherk, *Dividing the Waters*, 54–55, 737–39. For the South Platte River Compact, see ibid., 49–50, 857–64. For news reports of the South Platte River Compact's ratification, see "River Approval Given," *Havre Daily News Promoter*, March 9, 1926; "Platte Bill," *Helena Independent*, March 10, 1926.

20. Discussions began on a compact for the Arkansas River in the early 1920s, but the parties' failure to reach a conclusion at that time resulted in more interstate litigation between Colorado and Kansas over the next two decades. Although those two states finally approved the Arkansas River Compact in 1948, that agreement went back to the U.S. Supreme Court in the mid-1980s. For details on the Arkansas River Compact's history, with specific reference to the interstate allocation issues of the case that was brought in the 1980s, see Littlefield, "History of the Arkansas River Compact"; Littlefield, *Transcripts of Testimony*; and the exhibits Littlefield introduced in that case. For the compact itself, see Sherk, *Dividing the Waters*, 51, 517–26. On the history of water use on the Arkansas River more generally, see Sherow, *Watering the Valley*.

21. "Name Board to Cut North Platte Water among Three States," *Billings Gazette*, July 8, 1924.

22. Other proposals for interstate river allocation compacts that appeared by the mid-1920s included agreements for the Columbia, Delaware, and Pecos rivers. For news reports of the suggested compact for the Columbia, see "Columbia Compact Boosted in House," *Anaconda Standard*, March 30, 1926; "Columbia Basin Bill Finds Favor in House," *Helena Independent*, March 30, 1926. For press accounts about the Delaware River Compact among New Jersey, New York, and Pennsylvania, see "Delaware River Compact Ratified," *Middleton Daily Herald*, Feb. 11, 1925. For the Pecos, see "Pecos Pact Is Vital to State Says Engineer," *Albuquerque Morning Journal*, Feb. 25, 1925; "Ratification of Pecos River Compact Is Urged by Engineer Neel before Senate Committee," ibid., March 6, 1925; "Pecos Compact Amended to Put Up Safeguards," ibid., March 11, 1925; "Texas Will Accept Reservations to the Pecos River Compact," ibid., March 12, 1925.

23. Delph E. Carpenter telegram to attorney general of Kansas, June 7, 1921, file 11, Kansas Attorney General Records; Richard J. Hopkins to Delph E. Carpenter, June 7, 1921, ibid.; J. F. Hinkle telegram to W. E. Sweet, March 11, 1923, Hinkle Papers; Hale Smith telegram to Hinkle, March 14, 1923, ibid.; Hubert Work to Hinkle, Dec. 10, 1923, ibid.; C. B. Slemp to Hinkle, Dec. 22, 1923, ibid.; A. B. McMillan and W. C. Reid to governor of New Mexico, Feb. 25, 1925, Hannett Papers; Calvin Coolidge to Herbert

Hoover, Dec. 23, 1923, Commerce Papers; Hoover to Coolidge, December 27, 1923, ibid.; "Report of the Rio Grande Valley Survey Commission," undated and unpublished report, copy in folder 21, box 15, Dillon Papers.

24. See, for example, Arizona Department of Water Resources, *Law of the River*.

25. On Carpenter's background and his views on compact making, see Tyler, *Silver Fox*, esp. 88–122. See also Hundley, *Water and the West*, 105–106; *Who Was Who in America*, 1960 ed., 3:319; Sherow, *Watering the Valley*, 127.

26. J. F. Hinkle telegram to W. E. Sweet, March 11, 1923, Hinkle Papers; Hale Smith telegram to Hinkle, March 14, 1923, ibid.; Hubert Work to Hinkle, Dec. 10, 1923, ibid.; C. B. Slemp to Hinkle, Dec. 22, 1923, ibid.; A. B. McMillen and W. C. Reid to governor of New Mexico, Feb. 25, 1925, Hannett Papers; Calvin Coolidge to Herbert Hoover, Dec. 23, 1923, Commerce Papers; Hoover to Coolidge, Dec. 27, 1923, ibid.

27. Hundley, *Water and the West*, 215–81.

28. Pat Neff to Richard F. Burges, Sept. 6, 1924, box 2B86, Burges Papers.

29. Pat Neff to Herbert Hoover, Sept. 20, 1924, Commerce Papers.

30. Governor [James F. Hinkle] to Pat M. Neff, Sept. 24, 1924, Hinkle Papers. See also generally folder 8, box 39, Elephant Butte Irrigation District Records.

31. Elephant Butte Irrigation District president and manager [J. W. Taylor] to D. C. Henny, Sept. 30, 1924, box 2F468, Burges Papers; J. O. Seth to R. F. Burges, Oct. 8, 1924, ibid.; J. W. Taylor and T. D. Porcher to Charles E. Hughes, Sept. 3–4, 1924, Commerce Papers; Delph E. Carpenter to Herbert Hoover, Oct. 9, 1924, ibid.

32. "First Meeting, Rio Grande River Compact Commission," 1, 24–25, copy in Commerce Papers.

33. On Colorado's concerns about how downstream water uses might hinder later upriver Colorado River developments, see Hundley, *Water and the West*.

34. On the initial proposal for a compact on the North Platte, see "Name Board to Cut North Platte Water among Three States," *Billings Gazette*, July 8, 1924.

35. "First Meeting, Rio Grande River Compact Commission," 2–6, 25–37, copy in Commerce Papers.

36. On the desire to avoid dealing with Mexico during the Colorado River Compact talks, see Hundley, *Water and the West*, 175–77, 204–205.

37. "First Meeting, Rio Grande River Compact Commission," 35–37, copy in Commerce Papers; "Rio Grande Action Delayed by Texas," *San Antonio Express*, Oct. 27, 1924.

38. A. P. Davis to secretary of the interior, March 2, 1923, file 032, Rio Grande Project files, Records of the Bureau of Reclamation.

39. Ibid.

40. A. P. Davis to V. E. Keyes, Dec. 12, 1922, file 032.02, Rio Grande Basin files, Records of the Bureau of Reclamation; Davis to Delph Carpenter, Feb. 7, 1923, ibid.

41. Corlett, "Statement to the Secretary," copy in Hamele, "Embargo."

42. F. M. Goodwin to J. W. Taylor, Sept. 16, 1924, folder 1, box 40, Elephant Butte Irrigation District Records; Goodwin to H. O. Bursum, Sept. 17, 1924, file 8–3, box 1638, Central Classified files, 1907–1936, Records of the Office of the Secretary of the

Interior; Elwood Mead memorandum for the secretary [of the interior], Sept. 6, 1924, box 2F468, Burges Papers; Richard F. Burges to James E. Ferguson, April 8, 1925, ibid.; undated report, Hannett Papers; Taylor to Burges, Nov. 3, 1924, folder 4, box 39, Elephant Butte Irrigation District Records; Taylor to J. O. Seth, Nov. 3, 1924, folder 7, box 39, ibid.; D. C. Henny to Seth, Nov. 7, 1924, ibid.; Taylor to Seth, Nov. 8, 1924, ibid.

43. Undated report, Hannett Papers; J. W. Taylor to J. O. Seth, Jan. 21, 1925, folder 6, box 39, Elephant Butte Irrigation District Records; Taylor to Seth, Feb. 26, 1925, ibid.

44. "Motion for Rehearing," Feb. 5, 1925, copy in Hamele, "Embargo," 137–38. Work's conclusions regarding the paramount need for river control were remarkably similar to contemporaneous findings by a state commission created by New Mexico to study Rio Grande problems. See "River Control Most Important Need in Valley," *Albuquerque Morning Journal*, March 6, 1925.

45. Richard F. Burges to D. C. Henny, March 12, 1925, box 2F468, Burges Papers; Burges to James E. Ferguson, April 8, 1925, ibid.

46. "Pecos Pact Is Vital to State Says Engineer," *Albuquerque Morning Journal*, Feb. 25, 1925; "Ratification of Pecos Compact Is Urged by Engineer Neel before Senate Committee," ibid., March 6, 1925. After a long and sometimes bitter fight (and one that sometimes influenced events on the Rio Grande and sometimes vice versa), New Mexico and Texas ultimately ratified the Pecos River Compact in 1949. Congress approved the pact in 1950. Eventually, however, that accord became the focus of U.S. Supreme Court litigation. See "Pecos Compact Amended to Put Up Safeguards," *Albuquerque Morning Journal*, March 11, 1925; "Texas Will Accept Reservations to the Pecos River Compact," ibid., March 12, 1925; "How about These Matters Gov. Tingley?" *Santa Rosa News*, Oct. 2, 1936; "The Truth about Pecos Water Agreement," *Albuquerque Journal*, Oct. 30, 1936; "Why Hatch, Chavez and Tingley Are Trying to Slip from under the Dirty Deal They Tried to Hand New Mexico in the Pecos River Compact," ibid., Nov. 1, 1936; "Texas Approves Pecos Compact," ibid., March 23, 1939; "Pecos Valley Survey, Las Vegas to Carlsbad, Precedes River Compact," ibid., Aug. 2, 1939. See also *Texas v. New Mexico*, 482 U.S. 124 (1987); *Texas v. New Mexico*, 485 U.S. 388 (1988); *Texas v. New Mexico*, 494 U.S. 111 (1990). See also I. Clark, *Water in New Mexico*, esp. 537–38; Bogener, *Ditches across the Desert*; Sherk, *Dividing the Waters*, 52–53, 781–88.

47. Richard F. Burges to Morris Sheppard, April 18, 1925, box 2F468, Burges Papers.

48. "Formal Protest Filed with Kellogg against Work Granting Permit to Build Storage Dam," *Albuquerque Morning Journal*, April 30, 1925.

49. J. O. Seth to Herbert Hoover, May 15, 1925, Commerce Papers.

50. Protest to secretary of the interior, May 9, 1925, ibid.; Richard F. Burges to Morris Bien, April 30, 1925, Burges Papers; Bien to Burges, May 6, 1925, ibid.; Bien to secretary of state, May 28, 1925, folder 5, box 21, Elephant Butte Irrigation District Records. For correspondence on the protests over the approval of the River Ranch Company's application, see folder 12, box 39, ibid. Most of this correspondence is between district officials and Morris Bien, a former U.S. Bureau of Reclamation legal counsel hired by the districts to coordinate the complaints in Washington, D.C.

51. "Secretary Work Raises Embargo Imposed in 1896," *Albuquerque Morning Journal*, May 21, 1925.

52. Hundley, *Water and the West*, 133–35.

53. "Department of the Interior Memorandum for the Press," May 20, 1925, Commerce Papers; undated editorial in *El Paso Herald*, reprinted in "Broken Faith?" *Santa Fe New Mexican*, May 23, 1925; Hubert Work to commissioner of the General Land Office, May 20, 1925, file 8–3, box 1639, Central Classified files, 1907–1936, Records of the Office of the Secretary of the Interior.

54. J. O. Seth to Herbert Hoover, June 1, 1925, Wilson Papers. See also Seth to A. T. Hannett, June 1, 1925, Commerce Papers.

55. Miriam A. Ferguson telegram to Arthur T. Hannett, June 4, 1925, Hannett Papers; J. W. Taylor telegram to Hannett, June 4, 1925, ibid.; Hannett telegram to Ferguson, June 6, 1925, ibid.; Hannett to Summers Burkhart and James A. Hall, June 8, 1925, ibid.; Burkhart to J. W. Taylor, June 16, 1925, folder 11, box 40, Elephant Butte Irrigation District Records.

56. New Mexico and Texas jointly hired E. P. Osgood in April 1927 to do their engineering study. J. W. Taylor to Morris Bien, Sept. 26, 1925, box 2F468, Burges Papers; George M. Neel to Richard F. Burges, Oct. 23, 1926, ibid.; D. C. Henny to Burges, Nov. 3, 1926, ibid.; Taylor to Henny, Feb. 7, 1927, ibid.; Burges to T. H. McGregor, June 29, 1926, box 2F469, Burges Papers; "The Water Fund Ruling," *Albuquerque Evening Herald*, Dec. 21, 1925; "New Mexico to Bring Suit," *Grand Junction Daily Sentinel*, Aug. 18, 1926; A. T. Hannett to Summers Burkhart, Sept. 9, 1926, Hannett Papers; J. W. Taylor to Morris Bien, Sept. 26, 1925, folder 5, box 21, Elephant Butte Irrigation District Records.

57. Francis C. Wilson to T. H. McGregor, Oct. 7, 1927, Wilson Papers.

58. Hundley, *Water and the West*, 215–81.

59. "Suit Looms in Two-State Row on River Rights," *Los Angeles Times*, Jan. 16, 1927.

60. See Barry, *Rising Tide*. See also Hundley, *Water and the West*, 272.

61. Francis C. Wilson to Delph E. Carpenter, Nov. 17, 1927, folder 5, box 21, Elephant Butte Irrigation District Records; Wilson to Carpenter, Dec. 2, 1927, ibid.; Edwin Mechem to Wilson, Nov. 22, 1927, box 2F469, Burges Papers; Richard F. Burges to Wilson, Nov. 25, 1927, ibid.; Burges to Wilson, Feb. 1, 1928, ibid.

62. See Tyler, *Silver Fox*.

63. "Proceedings of the Rio Grande Compact Conference Held December 19–20–21, 1928, at Santa Fe, New Mexico," 1, archived at New Mexico Interstate Stream Commission, Santa Fe (hereafter cited as Rio Grande Compact Commission, "Proceedings," with relevant dates specified in title). On the history of the Middle Rio Grande Conservancy District, see I. Clark, *Water in New Mexico*, 209–12.

64. Rio Grande Compact Commission, "Proceedings . . . December 19–20–21, 1928," 6–11.

65. See, for example, "To Solicit Government Co-operation in Utilizing Waste Water of San Luis Valley," *Alamosa Independent Journal*, Sept. 22, 1911.

66. Rio Grande Compact Commission, "Proceedings . . . December 19–20–21, 1928," 6–11.

67. "U.S. Grabs Colorado Water," *Colorado Transcript*, July 18, 1912. The same article was also published in the *Brandon Bell*, July 19, 1912.

68. Rio Grande Compact Commission, "Proceedings . . . December 19–20–21, 1928," 13.

69. For Kansas's perception of Colorado's return flow argument in the Arkansas River case, see W. E. Stanley to John G. Egan, Aug. 20, 1930, box 2, *Kansas v. Colorado* files, Kansas Attorney General Records. For Colorado views on this matter as they were presented later in *Kansas v. Colorado*, see "Patterson Plan," as reproduced in "Record of Proceedings of Kansas-Colorado Meeting (March 27 and 28, 1944, Denver, Colorado) Concerning Temporary Plan of Administration of Water of Arkansas River," file 9, box 18, Schoeppel Papers. See also Littlefield, "History of the Arkansas River Compact"; and Littlefield, *Transcripts of Testimony*.

70. Rio Grande Compact Commission, "Proceedings . . . December 19–20–21, 1928," 15–22.

71. Reports were summarized and testimony given by D. C. Henny, who represented the Elephant Butte Irrigation District and El Paso County Water Improvement District No. 1; R. G. Hosea, who worked for the States of New Mexico and Texas; and Ralph I. Meeker, who spoke on behalf of Colorado. See ibid., 22–78. See also "States Close Water Parley," *Galveston Daily News*, Dec. 22, 1928.

72. "Rio Grande Pact Commission in Second Session," *Reno Evening Gazette*, Jan. 21, 1929; "Three State Water Conference Resumed," *San Antonio Express*, Jan. 21, 1929; "New Rio Grande Compact Offered by New Mexico," ibid., Jan. 23, 1929; "Rio Grande Compact Commission Recesses," ibid., Jan. 26, 1929.

73. "Rio Grande Compact—Report of the Commissioner for New Mexico and Memorandum of Law on Interstate Compacts on Interstate Streams," copy in Wilson Papers.

74. Francis C. Wilson telegram to Richard F. Burgess [*sic*], April 5, [1929], box 2F469, Burges Papers; Herbert W. Yeo to Burges, May 29, 1929, ibid.; unidentified and undated news clipping in Wilson Papers. On Secretary Wilbur's opposition to the 1929 Rio Grande Compact, see "Interior Department Opposes Rio Grande Compact Plan," *Greeley Daily Tribune*, Oct. 30, 1929; "River Compact Is Disapproved by Department," *Galveston Daily News*, Oct. 31, 1929; "Ratification of River Compact Will Be Urged," ibid., Oct. 31, 1929; "Winbourn Pleased at Modification of Public Land Closing," *Greeley Tribune-Republican*, Nov. 4, 1929; "Secretary Wilbur's Rio Grande Water Stand Assailed," *San Antonio Express*, Nov. 6, 1929.

75. "Ratification of River Compact Will Be Urged," *Galveston Daily News*, Oct. 31, 1929; "President Approves Rio Grande Compact," *Amarillo Globe*, June 19, 1930; "Water Rights Bill Is Effective Today," *Brownsville Herald*, June 19, 1930; "Rio Grande Compact," *Galveston Daily News*, June 19, 1930. For Donovan's arguments supporting the compact process, see William J. Donovan, "Law and the Crook," *Abilene Morning*

News, June 16, 1929. This article was published as part of a Sunday supplement that appeared in at least seven newspapers.

76. "Rio Grande Compact—Report of the Commissioner for New Mexico and Memorandum of Law on Interstate Compacts on Interstate Streams," copy in Wilson Papers.

77. "Stipulation between Colorado and Kansas," Dec. 18, 1933, box 4, *Kansas v. Colorado* files, Kansas Attorney General Records. See the *Kansas v. Colorado* files generally for the history of the struggle to apportion the Arkansas River. Although these files are labeled *Kansas v. Colorado* at the Kansas State Historical Society, in reality they cover all aspects of the interstate litigation leading up to the 1943 Supreme Court's decision in *Colorado v. Kansas,* 320 U.S. 383 (1943). The complete record of that case can be found in *Colorado v. Kansas,* Original No. 14, Oct. Term 1928, U.S. Supreme Court Records, Record Group 267, National Archives, Washington, D.C. See also Littlefield, "History of the Arkansas River Compact"; Littlefield, *Transcripts of Testimony.*

Chapter 10. The Rio Grande Compact, Part II

1. On the New Deal in the West, see Lowitt, *New Deal;* Patterson, "New Deal"; Swain, "Bureau of Reclamation." See also An Act to Encourage National Industrial Recovery, to Foster Fair Competition, and to Provide for the Construction of Certain Useful Public Works, and for Other Purposes, 48 Stat. 195 (1933).

2. Richard F. Burges to Pearce Rodey, July 8, 1933, box 2F471, Rio Grande Compact Commission Records; Burges to Rodey, July 14, 1933, ibid.; M. C. Hinderlider to Burges, July 18, 1933, ibid.; Burges to Hinderlider, Aug. 2, 1933, ibid.; Miriam A. Ferguson to Burgess [*sic*], Aug. 5, 1933, ibid.; George M. Neel to Burges, Aug. 8, 1933, ibid.; "Resolution for Special Board," June 20, 1934, ibid.

3. "Lineups Are Changed for Water Fight," *Greeley Daily Tribune,* Jan. 27, 1933; "D.E. Carpenter, Father of River Pacts between States, Dies Here Tuesday after 20 Years of Illness," ibid., Feb. 27, 1951. On Carpenter's life, see Tyler, *Silver Fox.*

4. "Commissioner Wilson Fired by Governor Dillon," *Las Vegas Daily Optic,* July 31, 1929.

5. Thomas M. McClure to Clyde Tingley, Feb. 1, 1935, Tingley Papers; governor [Clyde Tingley] to James V. Allred, March 21, 1935, ibid.; Allred telegram to governor of New Mexico, April 27, 1935, ibid.; Harold Ickes telegram to A. W. Hockenhull, Dec. 8, 1934, Hockenhull Papers.

6. "Wyoming, Colorado Hold River Confab," *Billings Gazette,* Feb. 5, 1931; "Record Drouth Is Reported in State," *Greeley Daily Tribune,* Oct. 7, 1931. Ultimately, the North Platte Compact talks failed to stop Nebraska from filing a U.S. Supreme Court case in 1934 against Wyoming (Colorado became an impleaded defendant). Attempts to settle that dispute with an interstate compact were unsuccessful, and the case was decided by the high court in *Nebraska v. Wyoming,* 325 U.S. 589 (1945). This ruling contains a detailed synopsis of the history of the case. For the attempt to settle the lawsuit through compact discussions, see "Miller Asks North Platte Pact," *Greeley Daily Tribune,* Jan. 25,

1936; "Governor Names Trio on North Platte Deal," ibid., Jan. 22, 1936; "Tri-State Water Compact Sought," *Billings Gazette,* May 8, 1936; "Delegates Make River Proposals," ibid., May 15, 1936. Nebraska went back to the Supreme Court again in 1986, but this revival of the litigation eventually was resolved before trial. For the settlement details, see www.dnr.ne.gov/legal/nebraska.html.

7. Many of the compact debates are detailed in records held by the respective states' archives. Because the federal government was involved in most of these discussions, see also the Records of the Bureau of Reclamation and Records of the Secretary of the Interior. For details on the Arkansas River Compact's history, see Littlefield, "History of the Arkansas River Compact"; Littlefield, *Transcripts of Testimony;* and the exhibits Littlefield introduced in that case. For the compact itself, see Sherk, *Dividing the Waters,* 51, 517–26. For the full story of the Colorado River Compact, see Hundley, *Water and the West.*

8. Rio Grande Compact Commission, "Proceedings . . . December 10, 11, 1934," 1–2.

9. Ibid., 3–13. The quotation is on 10.

10. Ibid., 13–21.

11. Ibid., 22–38.

12. For details in the press on Colorado's arguments, see "Colorado Rio Grande Idea Shown," *Albuquerque Journal,* Jan. 29, 1935.

13. Rio Grande Compact Commission, "Proceedings . . . January 28th to January 30th, 1935," 2–45; "Extension of River Compact Requested," *Brownsville Herald,* Feb. 26, 1935.

14. On the development of the Middle Rio Grande Conservancy District, see the New Mexico governors' papers beginning in 1917. Most of these are in the New Mexico State Records Center and Archives in Santa Fe, although Governor Richard Dillon's papers are at the University of New Mexico in Albuquerque. For reports on the purpose and nature of the Middle Rio Grande Conservancy District, see Debler and Elder, "Preliminary Report"; Burkholder, *Report of the Chief Engineer.* See also I. Clark, *Water in New Mexico,* 209–12.

15. E. B. Debler to Elwood Mead, Feb. 27, 1935, file 301, Rio Grande Project files, Records of the Bureau of Reclamation; R. E. Thomason to Mead, April 16, 1935, ibid.; Roland Harwell and N. B. Phillips to L. R. Fiock, July 30, 1934, file 031, Rio Grande Project files, Records of the Bureau of Reclamation; Harwell to Morris Sheppard, May 6, 1935, folder 4, box 82, Elephant Butte Irrigation District Records.

16. Frank B. Clayton to N. B. Phillips and Roland Harwell, May 14, 1935, box 2F467, Rio Grande Compact Commission Records; Clayton to William McCraw, Oct. 19, 1935, ibid.; Raymond A. Hill to Clayton, Sept. 20, 1936, ibid.; H. Grady Chandler to R. M. Clark, Sept. 9, 1938, box 2F466, ibid.

17. "Historical Phases of Water Dispute Set Out in Hearings," *Albuquerque Journal,* Nov. 10, 1936; "Ancient Water Rights Issue in River Clash," *El Paso Herald-Post,* Nov. 30, 1936.

18. See Horwitz, *Transformation of American Law.*

19. Franklin D. Roosevelt to federal agencies concerned with projects or allotments for water use in the upper Rio Grande valley above El Paso, Sept. 23, 1935, file 032, Rio Grande Project files, Records of the Bureau of Reclamation; S. O. Harper to the National Resources Committee, Nov. 8, 1935, box 2F464, Rio Grande Compact Commission Records; Harper to secretary of the interior, Dec. 14, 1935, file 8–3, box 1638, Central Classified files, 1907–1936, Records of the Office of the Secretary of the Interior.

20. On the National Planning Board and its successors, see Lowitt, *New Deal*, 79–80.

21. See chapter 10, note 19; see also "Survey of Rio Grande Suggested," *Albuquerque Journal*, Dec. 3, 1935; "Water Dispute Compromised," *Abilene Daily Reporter*, Dec. 4, 1935; "States Agree on Probe Plan," *Amarillo Globe*, Dec. 4, 1935.

22. Rio Grande Compact Commission, "Proceedings . . . December 2–3, 1935," 1–7; Rio Grande Compact Commission, "Proceedings . . . March 3 and 4, 1937," 1–2, 6, 24–25; Charles Elmore Croply to William McCraw, April 6, 1937, box 2F467, Rio Grande Compact Commission Records; Raymond A. Hill to L. R. Fiock, May 18, 1937, ibid.; Hill to Fiock, July 8, 1937, ibid.; Hill to F. B. Clayton, Sept. 3, 1937, ibid. For a press account of the initial testimony in *Texas v. New Mexico and the Middle Rio Grande Conservancy District*, see "Flow of Salt into Valleys Hit at Hearing," *El Paso Herald-Post*, Dec. 11, 1936.

23. For the details of the Rio Grande Joint Investigation's findings, see U.S. National Resources Committee, *Rio Grande Joint Investigations*; Sloan, "Report." See also "Will Examine Water Report," *El Paso Herald-Post*, March 6, 1937.

24. Rio Grande Compact Commission, "Proceedings . . . September 27 to October 1, 1937," 6–8. The delay in the compact talks and litigation coincided well with negotiations between the two Rio Grande Project irrigation districts and the U.S. government on an exchange of hydroelectric power rights for a credit toward construction charges and on an interdistrict agreement to fix maximum irrigable acreage in either district. The latter agreement was to contractually confirm the 1904 apportionment of Rio Grande waters below Elephant Butte Reservoir, and this would facilitate any compact settlement, particularly because the districts' representatives were taking part in the compact hearings. See telegram to Raymond Hill, Dec. 26, 1937 (sender not identified), box 2F466, Rio Grande Compact Commission Records; L. R. Fiock to commissioner, file 222, Rio Grande Project files, Records of the Bureau of Reclamation; Fiock to John C. Page, Nov. 9, 1937, ibid. See also "Experts Meet for Division of Rio Grande," *Las Vegas Daily Optic*, Sept. 27, 1937; "River Allotment Is Discussed in Secret Sessions," ibid., Sept. 29, 1937; "Three States Meet to Discuss Division of Rio Grande Water," *Abilene Reporter-News*, Sept. 28, 1937; "River Pact Group Split," *San Antonio Light*, Sept. 29, 1937; "Water Compact Is Still Effective," *Amarillo News-Globe*, Oct. 3, 1937.

25. E. B. Debler, Royce J. Tipton, John H. Bliss, and R. A. Hill to Rio Grande Compact Commission, Dec. 27, 1937, copy in appendix 1 of Rio Grande Compact Commission, "Proceedings . . . March 3rd to March 18th inc. 1938," 40–47.

26. H. C. Neuffer to Thomas M. McClure, Jan. 12, 1938, copy in Rio Grande Compact Commission, "Proceedings . . . March 3rd to March 18th inc. 1938," 47.

27. Thomas M. McClure to S. O. Harper, Jan. 25, 1938, folder 4, box 82, Elephant Butte Irrigation District Records.

28. Raymond A. Hill to Frank B. Clayton, Feb. 8, 1938, box 2F466, Rio Grande Compact Commission Records. For Hill's recollections of the compact deliberations three decades after they had ended, see Hill, *Development of the Rio Grande Compact*; Hill, "Development."

29. Raymond A. Hill to Frank B. Clayton, Feb. 8, 1938, box 2F466, Rio Grande Compact Commission Records.

30. "Clash Opens Water Meeting," *Albuquerque Journal*, March 4, 1938; "New Compact Hope Is Seen," ibid., March 5, 1938.

31. Rio Grande Compact Commission, "Proceedings . . . March 3rd to March 18th inc. 1938," 3–37; E. B. Debler, Royce J. Tipton, John H. Bliss, and R. A. Hill to Rio Grande Compact Commission, March 9, 1938, copy in appendix 7 of ibid., 58–65; Frank B. Clayton to Charles Warren, March 28, 1938, box 2F466, Rio Grande Compact Commission Records.

32. See previous note.

33. Article XII, Rio Grande Compact, 53 Stat. 785 (1939). The Red River of the North Compact among Minnesota, North Dakota, and South Dakota (approved on June 23, 1937, and ratified in 1938) also created a permanent interstate river commission. That compact, however, did not create an apportionment among the three states but simply asked that the three states "undertake to cooperate with the other two states for the most advantageous utilization of the waters of the Red River of the North, for the control of the flood waters of this river and for the prevention of the pollution of such waters." See Article II, Red River of the North Compact, 52 Stat. 150 (1938).

34. The formal title for the Boulder Canyon Act is An Act to Provide for the Construction of Works for the Protection and Development of the Colorado River Basin, for the Approval of the Colorado River Compact, and for Other Purposes, 45 Stat. 1057 (1928). For the ratification battle over the Colorado River Compact, see Hundley, *Water and the West*, 215–81. For the Arizona litigation against California, see ibid., 282–306; *Arizona v. California*, 283 U.S. 423 (1931); *Arizona v. California*, 292 U.S. 341 (1934); *Arizona v. California*, 298 U.S. 558 (1936); *Arizona v. California*, 373 U.S. 546 (1963); *Arizona v. California*, 376 U.S. 340 (1964).

35. The La Plata River Compact was approved by its negotiators on November 27, 1922, although it was not finally ratified until 1925. See La Plata River Compact, 43 Stat. 796 (1925); Sherk, *Dividing the Waters*, 54–55, 737–39.

36. *Hinderlider v. La Plata River and Cherry Creek Ditch Co.*, 304 U.S. 92 (1938); "Water Compact Threat," *Albuquerque Journal*, Jan. 27, 1938.

37. Littlefield, "History of the Arkansas River Compact," 17–30. See also *Colorado v. Kansas*, 320 U.S. 383 (1943).

38. "Name Board to Cut North Platte Water among Three States," *Billings Gazette*, July 8, 1924; "Wyoming, Colorado Hold River Confab," ibid., Feb. 5, 1931; "Edward T.

Taylor Comes to Attend Water Conference," *Greeley Daily Tribune*, Oct. 7, 1931; "Governor Names Trio on North Platte Deal," ibid., Jan. 22, 1936. See also *Nebraska v. Wyoming*, 325 U.S. 589 (1945).

39. "Appeals for Preservation of New England Sovereignty," *Lowell Sun*, Sept. 18, 1937; "Water Compact Threat," *Albuquerque Journal*, Jan. 27, 1938; "Nevada's Position Is Defined by Attorney General in Water Control Controversy with United States," *Reno Evening Gazette*, April 30, 1938; "Tri-State Compact Status Improved," *El Paso Herald-Post*, Oct. 11, 1938.

40. Rio Grande Compact Commission, "Proceedings . . . March 3rd to March 18th inc. 1938," 72–82; Articles II–XVII, Rio Grande Compact, 53 Stat. 785 (1939).

41. The Supreme Court eventually ruled that interstate compacts were superior to state-held water rights. See "Federal Supreme Court Upsets Colorado's High Tribunal on La Plata River Compact," *Albuquerque Journal*, April 26, 1938; "Tri-State Compact Status Improved," *El Paso Herald-Post*, Oct. 11, 1938; *Hinderlider v. La Plata River and Cherry Creek Ditch Co.*, 304 U.S. 92 (1938).

42. For a comprehensive discussion of ratification battles over the Colorado River Compact, see Hundley, *Water and the West*, 215–81. See also Tyler, *Silver Fox*, 167.

43. Littlefield, "History of the Arkansas River Compact"; Littlefield, *Transcripts of Testimony*; and exhibits used in Littlefield's testimony. For the compact itself, see Sherk, *Dividing the Waters*, 51, 517–26. See also Sherow, *Watering the Valley*.

44. Oscar C. Dancy to Tom Connally, Dec. 8, 1936, box 2F466, Rio Grande Compact Commission Records. For the possible attendance of lower Rio Grande interests at compact negotiating sessions, see "Delegates Named to Water Meet," *Brownsville Herald*, Jan. 21, 1938; "Robertson Will Attend Interstate Water Meet," ibid., March 1, 1938.

45. See note 44, above.

46. "Delegates Named to Water Meet," *Brownsville Herald*, Jan. 21, 1938.

47. Frank B. Clayton to C. S. Clark, Jan. 26, 1938, box 2F466, Rio Grande Compact Commission Records; Clark to Clayton, Feb. 2, 1938, ibid.

48. C. S. Clark telegram to Frank B. Clayton, March 15, 1938, ibid.; Frank S. Robertson telegram to Clayton, March 15, 1938, ibid.; Robertson to Clayton, March 16, 1938, ibid. See also "Valley Requires Binding Pact on Volume of Water," *Brownsville Herald*, March 16, 1938; "Valley's Minimum Water Need Placed at 200,000 Acre Feet," *San Antonio Express*, March 20, 1938.

49. Frank B. Clayton to F. S. Robertson, March 26, 1938, folder 4, box 82, Elephant Butte Irrigation District Records.

50. "Valley Seeks Assurance of Adequate Water Supply," *Brownsville Herald*, April 13, 1938.

51. "Proceedings of the Executive Board of the Water Conservation Association of the Lower Rio Grande Valley, June 1, 1938," copy in box 2F466, Rio Grande Compact Commission Records.

52. Ibid.

53. Frank Clayton to Harlan H. Barrows, July 5, 1938, box 2F466, Rio Grande Compact Commission Records; Barrows to Clayton, June 30, 1938, ibid.; N. B. Phillips to

Clayton, July 8, 1938, ibid.; Clayton to Richard F. Burges, Aug. 30, 1938, ibid.; H. Grady Chandler to R. M. Clark, Sept. 7, 1938, ibid.; Alfred Tamm to Lower Rio Grande Water Conservation Association, Sept. 12, 1938, ibid. See also "Another Dam on Upper Rio Is Opposed," *El Paso Herald-Post*, July 9, 1938.

54. Frank B. Clayton to Richard F. Burges, Aug. 30, 1938, box 2F466, Rio Grande Compact Commission Records.

55. Alfred Tamm to Lower Rio Grande Valley Water Conservation Association, Sept. 12, 1938, ibid.

56. H. Grady Chandler to Frank W. Patton and Byron G. Rogers, Sept. 8, 1938, ibid.

57. "Attorney General Aide Ignores Valley Plea on Rio Grande Suit," *Valley Star-Monitor-Herald*, Sept. 18, 1938.

58. H. Grady Chandler to Frank W. Patton and Byron G. Rogers, Sept. 8, 1938, box 2F466, Rio Grande Compact Commission Records.

59. "Texas Demands Supreme Court Water Decree," *Albuquerque Journal*, Sept. 23, 1938.

60. "Proceedings of the Executive Committee of Water Conservation Association of the Lower Rio Grande Valley," Sept. 16, 1938, copy in box 2F466, Rio Grande Compact Commission Records.

61. Sawnie B. Smith to Frank B. Clayton, Sept. 29, 1938, box 2F466, Rio Grande Compact Commission Records.

62. Frank B. Clayton to Sawnie B. Smith, Oct. 4, 1938, ibid. Clayton made a similar statements to C. S. Clark, chairman of the Texas Board of Water Engineers, and to state legislator Augustine Celaya. See Clayton to Clark, Oct. 16, 1938, ibid.; Clayton to Celaya, Sept. 21, 1938, ibid.

63. Frank B. Clayton to Harlan H. Barrows, Sept. 24, 1938, ibid.

64. Oscar D. Dancy to L. M. Lawson, Oct. 13, 1938, ibid.

65. Harlan H. Barrows to Frank B. Clayton, Sept. 29, 1938, ibid.; Clayton to Barrows, Oct. 1, 1938, ibid.; Barrows to Clayton, undated, ibid.; Byron G. Rogers to William McCraw, Oct. 28, 1938, ibid.

66. Thomas M. McClure to M. C. Hinderlider and Frank B. Clayton, Feb. 23, 1939, ibid.; Harlan H. Barrows to Clayton, March 7, 1939, ibid.; Ralph L. Carr to John E. Miles, Feb. 21, 1939, Miles Papers; governor of New Mexico [John E. Miles] to W. Lee O'Daniel, March 2, 1939, ibid.; O'Daniel to Miles, March 9, 1939, ibid.; Cordell Hull to Miles, June 28, 1939, ibid.

67. See, for example, "Early Action on Rio Grande Water Compact Seen," *Galveston Daily News*, Jan. 16, 1939; "Texas, Colorado, New Mexico Renew River Pact," ibid., March 19, 1938; "Governor Signs 3-State Treaty on Rio Grande," *Greeley Daily Tribune*, Feb. 21, 1939; "Rio Grande Pact before Senate," *Las Cruces Sun-News*, March 16, 1939; "Approve Compact," ibid., June 8, 1939; "Texas Senate Paves Way to Ratify Rio Grande Compact," *Albuquerque Journal*, March 1, 1939; "Colorado Legislature Affirms Texas Pact," *San Antonio Express*, Feb. 11, 1939; "Rio Grande Compact Ratified by Senate," ibid., May 20, 1939; "Rio Grande Pact Is Signed by O'Daniel," *San Antonio Light*,

March 2, 1939; "Commissioners of Compact to Hold Meeting," *El Paso Herald-Post*, June 1, 1939.

68. "Water Riches Soon to Flow into 3 States," *Hammond Times*, April 27, 1939; "Will Conquer Great Desert," *Cedar Rapids Tribune*, June 2, 1939; "Will Conquer Great Desert," *Portsmouth Herald*, June 2, 1930. The *Tribune* and *Herald* apparently did not know that Congress already had ratified the Rio Grande Compact and President Roosevelt had signed the ratification bill two days before the articles in those papers appeared.

69. *State of Texas v. State of New Mexico and the Middle Rio Grande Conservancy District*, decree, Oct. 16, 1939, copy in Miles Papers.

70. "$100,000 Allocated to PWA for Survey of Pecos River Basin," *Albuquerque Journal*, Feb. 21, 1939; "Pecos River Problems Will Be Discussed at El Paso, Hatch Says," ibid., March 10, 1939; "Pecos River Survey Believed Probable," *El Paso Herald-Post*, Feb. 21, 1939.

Bibliography

Document Collections

Bowman Bank Records. New Mexico State Records Center and Archives, Santa Fe.

Burges, Richard F. Papers. Eugene C. Barker Texas History Collection, University of Texas, Austin.

Colorado River Compact Commission Papers. Herbert Hoover Presidential Library, West Branch, Iowa.

Commerce Papers. Herbert Hoover Presidential Library, West Branch, Iowa.

Davis, Arthur P. Papers. Archives–American Heritage Center, University of Wyoming, Laramie.

Dillon, Richard C. Papers. Special Collections, University of New Mexico, Albuquerque.

Elephant Butte Irrigation District Records. Rio Grande Historical Collections, New Mexico State University, Las Cruces.

Hannett, Arthur T. Papers. New Mexico State Records Center and Archives, Santa Fe.

Hinkle, James F. Papers. New Mexico State Records Center and Archives, Santa Fe.

Hockenhull, Andrew W. Papers. New Mexico State Records Center and Archives, Santa Fe.

Kansas Attorney General Records. Kansas State Historical Society, Topeka.

McDonald, William C. Papers. New Mexico State Records Center and Archives, Santa Fe.

Miles, John E. Papers. New Mexico State Records Center and Archives, Santa Fe.

Otero, Miguel A. Papers. Special Collections, University of New Mexico, Albuquerque.

Prince, L. Bradford. Papers. New Mexico State Records Center and Archives, Santa Fe.

Records of the Board of Trade. Public Record Office, U.K. National Archives, London.

Records of the Bureau of Reclamation. Record Group 115. National Archives Branch, Rocky Mountain Region, Denver.

Records of the Foreign Office. Public Record Office, U.K. National Archives, London.

Records of the Office of the Secretary of the Interior. Record Group 48. National Archives II, College Park, Maryland.

Records Relating to International Boundaries. Record Group 76. National Archives II, College Park, Maryland.

Rio Grande Compact Commission Records. Eugene C. Barker Texas History Collection, University of Texas, Austin.

Schoeppel, Andrew F. (Governor). Papers. Kansas State Historical Society, Topeka.

Territorial Archives of New Mexico (microfilm). New Mexico State Records Center and Archives, Santa Fe.

Tingley, Clyde. Papers. New Mexico State Records Center and Archives, Santa Fe.

U.S. Supreme Court Records. Record Group 267. National Archives, Washington, D.C.

Wilson, Francis C. Papers. New Mexico State Records Center and Archives, Santa Fe.

Wilson, Fred C. Papers. Archives–American Heritage Center, University of Wyoming, Laramie.

Court Cases

Arizona v. California, 283 U.S. 423 (1931)

Arizona v. California, 292 U.S. 341 (1934)

Arizona v. California, 298 U.S. 558 (1936)

Arizona v. California, 373 U.S. 546 (1963)

Arizona v. California, 376 U.S. 340 (1964)

Bean v. Morris, 221 U.S. 485 (1911)

Colorado v. Kansas, 320 U.S. 383 (1943)

El Paso v. S. E. Reynolds, 563 F. Supp. 379 (1983)

Hinderlider v. La Plata River and Cherry Creek Ditch Co., 304 U.S. 92 (1938)

Howell v. Johnson, 89 Fed. 556 (1898)

Kansas v. Colorado, 185 U.S. 125 (1902)

Kansas v. Colorado, 206 U.S. 46 (1907)

Nebraska v. Wyoming, 325 U.S. 589 (1945)

Rio Grande Dam and Irrigation Company v. United States, 215 U.S. 266 (1909)

Steamer Daniel Ball v. United States, 77 U.S. 557 (1870)

Texas v. New Mexico, 482 U.S. 124 (1987)

Texas v. New Mexico, 485 U.S. 388 (1988)

Texas v. New Mexico, 494 U.S. 111 (1990)

Texas v. New Mexico and the Middle Rio Grande Conservancy District, 296 U.S. 547 (1935)

United States v. Appalachian Electric Power Company, 310 U.S. 377 (1940)

United States v. Rio Grande Dam and Irrigation Company et al., 9 N.M. 292 (1898)

United States v. Rio Grande Dam and Irrigation Company et al., 10 N.M. 617 (1900)

United States v. Rio Grande Dam and Irrigation Company et al., 13 N.M. 386 (1906)

United States v. Rio Grande Dam and Irrigation Company, 174 U.S. 690 (1899)

United States v. Rio Grande Dam and Irrigation Company, 184 U.S. 416 (1902)

Virginia v. Maryland, 540 U.S. 56 (2003)
Winters v. United States, 207 U.S. 564 (1908)
Wyoming v. Colorado, 259 U.S. 419 (1922)

Interstate River Compacts (Cited as U.S. Statutes)

Animas–La Plata Project Compact, 82 Stat. 898 (1968)
Arkansas River Compact, 63 Stat. 145 (1949)
Bear River Compact, 94 Stat. 4 (1980)
Belle Fourche River Compact, 58 Stat. 94 (1944)
Big Blue River Compact, 86 Stat. 193 (1972)
Canadian River Compact, 66 Stat. 74 (1952)
Colorado River Compact, 45 Stat. 1057 (1928)
Costilla Creek Compact, 77 Stat. 350 (1963)
Klamath River Basin Compact, 71 Stat. 497 (1957)
Lake Tahoe (California-Nevada) Interstate Compact (ratified by California and Nevada
    but not yet by Congress)
La Plata River Compact, 43 Stat. 796 (1925)
Pecos River Compact, 63 Stat. 159 (1949)
Red River Compact, 94 Stat. 3305 (1980)
Red River of the North Compact, 52 Stat. 150 (1938)
Republican River Compact, 57 Stat. 86 (1943)
Rio Grande Compact, 46 Stat. 767 (1930)
Rio Grande Compact, 53 Stat. 785 (1939)
Sabine River Compact, 68 Stat. 690 (1954)
Snake River Compact, 64 Stat. 29 (1950)
South Platte River Compact, 44 Stat. 195 (1926)
Upper Colorado River Compact, 63 Stat. 31 (1949)
Upper Niobrara River Compact, 83 Stat. 86 (1969)
Yellowstone River Compact, 65 Stat. 663 (1951)

U.S. Statutes (Not Including Compacts)

An Act Appropriating from the Sale and Disposal of Public Lands in Certain States and
    Territories to the Construction of Irrigation Works for the Reclamation of Arid Lands,
    32 Stat. 388 (1902).
An Act Extending the Period of Payment under Reclamation Projects, and for Other Pur-
    poses, 38 Stat. 685 (1914).
An Act for the Grading and Classification of Clerks in the Foreign Service of the United
    States of America, and Providing for Compensation Therefor, 46 Stat. 1214 (1931).
An Act Granting the Right of Way to Ditch and Canal Owners over the Public Lands,
    and for Other Purposes, 14 Stat. 251 (1866).

An Act Making Appropriations for Sundry Civil Expenses for the Government for the Fiscal Year Ending June Thirtieth, Eighteen Hundred and Ninety-five, and for Other Purposes, 28 Stat. 372 (1894).

An Act Making Appropriations for Sundry Civil Expenses of the Government for the Fiscal Year Ending June Thirtieth, Eighteen Hundred and Ninety-six, and for Other Purposes, 28 Stat. 372 (1895).

An Act Making Appropriations for Sundry Civil Expenses of the Government for the Fiscal Year Ending June Thirtieth, Nineteen Hundred and Eight, and for Other Purposes, 34 Stat. 1295 (1907).

An Act Making Appropriations for the Construction, Repair and Preservation of Certain Public Works on Rivers and Harbors, and for Other Purposes, 26 Stat. 426 (1890).

An Act Making Appropriations for the Construction, Repair and Preservation of Certain Public Works on Rivers and Harbors, and for Other Purposes, 27 Stat. 88 (1892).

An Act Relating to the Construction of a Dam and Reservoir on the Rio Grande, in New Mexico, for the Improvement of the Flood Waters of Said River for Purposes of Irrigation, 33 U.S. Stat. 814 (1905).

An Act to Amend "An Act Granting the Right of Way to Ditch and Canal Owners over the Public Lands, and for Other Purposes," 16 Stat. 217 (1870).

An Act to Authorize the Government to Contract for Impounding, Storing, and Carriage of Water, and to Cooperate in the Construction and Use of Reservoirs and Canals under Reclamation Projects, and for Other Purposes, 36 Stat. 925 (1911).

An Act to Encourage National Industrial Recovery, to Foster Fair Competition, and to Provide for the Construction of Certain Useful Public Works, and for Other Purposes, 48 Stat. 195 (1933).

An Act to Extend the Irrigation Act to the State of Texas, 34 Stat. 259 (1906).

An Act to Provide for the Construction of Works for the Protection and Development of the Colorado River Basin, for the Approval of the Colorado River Compact, and for Other Purposes, 45 Stat. 1057 (1928).

An Act to Provide for the Sale of Desert Lands in Certain States and Territories, 19 Stat. 377 (1877).

An Act to Repeal Timber-Culture Laws, and for Other Purposes, 26 Stat. 1095 (1891).

Convention Providing for the Equitable Distribution of the Waters of the Rio Grande for Irrigation Purposes, 34 Stat. 2953 (1906).

New Mexico Territorial Statutes

An Act to Authorize the Formation of Companies for the Purpose of Constructing Irrigating and Other Canals and the Colonization and Improvement of Lands Contained in Acts of the Legislative Assembly of the Territory of New Mexico, Twenty-seventh Session. Las Vegas, N.Mex.: J. A. Carruth, 1887.

Newspapers

Abilene Daily Reporter (Texas)
Abilene Morning News (Texas)
Abilene Reporter-News (Texas)
Ada Evening News (Oklahoma)
Akron Pioneer Press (Colorado)
Akron Weekly Pioneer Press (Colorado)
Alamosa Independent Journal (Colorado)
Albuquerque Evening Herald (New Mexico)
Albuquerque Journal (New Mexico)
Albuquerque Morning Journal (New Mexico)
Amarillo Globe (Texas)
Amarillo News-Globe (Texas)
Anaconda Standard (Montana)
Aspen Tribune (Colorado)
Atlanta Constitution (Georgia)
Basalt Journal (Colorado)
Billings Gazette (Montana)
Brandon Bell (Colorado)
Breckenridge Bulletin (Colorado)
Brownsville Herald (Texas)
Castle Rock Journal (Colorado)
Cedar Rapids Tribune (Iowa)
Chester Times (Pennsylvania)
Chillicothe Morning Constitution (Missouri)
Colorado Transcript (Golden, Colorado)
Creede Candle (Colorado)
Daily Kennebec Journal (Maine)
Deming Headlight (New Mexico)
Eagle County Blade (Red Cliff, Colorado)
Eagle County Times (Red Cliff, Colorado)
Edwardsville Intelligencer (Illinois)
Elbert County Banner (Elizabeth, Colorado)
El Paso Daily Times (Texas)
El Paso Herald (Texas)
El Paso Herald-Post (Texas)
El Paso Morning Times (Texas)
Evening Observer (Dunkirk, New York)
Fairplay Flume (Colorado)
Fort Collins Weekly Courier (Colorado)
Fort Wayne News (Indiana)
Fresno Bee (California)

Galveston Daily News (Texas)
Glenwood Post (Colorado)
Grand Junction Daily Sentinel (Colorado)
Grand Rapids Tribune (Wisconsin)
Greeley Daily Tribune (Colorado)
Hamilton Daily Republican (Ohio)
Hammond Times (Indiana)
Havre Daily News Promoter (Montana)
Helena Independent (Montana)
Houston Post (Texas)
Janesville Daily Gazette (Wisconsin)
Las Cruces Sun-News (New Mexico)
Las Vegas Daily Optic (New Mexico)
Lincoln Daily Star (Nebraska)
Logansport Daily Tribune (Indiana)
Longmont Ledger (Colorado)
Los Angeles Times (California)
Lowell Sun (Massachusetts)
Manitoba Free Press (Winnipeg, Canada)
Middleton Daily Herald (New York)
New Castle News (Pennsylvania)
Newcastle News (Wyoming)
New Castle Nonpareil (Colorado)
New York Times (New York)
Oakland Tribune (California)
Oelwein Daily Register (Iowa)
Ogden Standard (Utah)
Ogden Standard-Examiner (Utah)
Plateau Voice (Collbran, Colorado)
Portsmouth Daily Times (Ohio)
Portsmouth Herald (New Hampshire)
Range Ledger (Hugo, Colorado)
Reno Evening Gazette (Nevada)
Richwood Gazette (Ohio)
Rio Grande Farmer (Las Cruces, New Mexico)
Rio Grande Republican (Las Cruces, New Mexico)
San Antonio Daily Express (Texas)
San Antonio Express (Texas)
San Antonio Light (Texas)
San Juan Prospector (Colorado)
Santa Fe New Mexican (New Mexico)
Santa Rosa News (New Mexico)
Star and Sentinel (Gettysburg, Pennsylvania)

Summit County Journal (Breckenridge, Colorado)
Syracuse Herald (New York)
Thirty-four (Las Cruces, New Mexico)
Titusville Morning Herald (Pennsylvania)
Tribune-Republican (Greeley, Colorado)
Tyrone Herald (Pennsylvania)
Valley Star-Monitor-Herald (Brownsville, Texas)
Van Nuys News (California)
Washington Post (Washington, D.C.)
Wisconsin State Journal (Madison)
Yampa Leader (Colorado)

Other Works

Abbott, Carl., Stephen J. Leonard, and Thomas J. Noel. *Colorado: A History of the Centennial State*. Boulder: University of Colorado Press, 1982.

Alexander, Thomas G. "The Powell Irrigation Survey and the People of the Mountain West." *Journal of the West* 7 (1968): 48–54.

American and British Claims Arbitration under the Special Agreement Concluded between the United States and Great Britain, August 18, 1910. Washington, D.C.: U.S. Government Printing Office, 1926.

Angell, Joseph K. *A Treatise on the Law of Watercourses: With an Appendix, Containing Statutes of Flowing, and Forms of Declarations*. Boston: Little Brown, 1877.

Arizona Department of Water Resources. *The Law of the River*. Phoenix: Colorado River Management Section, Arizona Department of Water Resources, 2000.

Baldwin, P. M. "A Short History of the Mesilla Valley." *New Mexico Historical Review* 13 (1938): 314–24.

Bannister, L. W. "The Question of Federal Disposition of State Waters in the Priority States." *Harvard Law Review* 28 (1915): 270–93.

Barrows, E. L. "Report of Seepage Study on Rio Grande between Elephant Butte Dam and Leasburg Dam" (typescript of unpublished report). November 26–28, 1928. Archived at New Mexico State Engineer Office, Santa Fe.

Barry, John M. *Rising Tide: The Great Mississippi Flood of 1927 and How It Changed America*. New York: Simon and Schuster, 1998.

Black, R. F. "Improvement of the Rio Grande in Socorro County, N. Mex., during 1929–1930" (typescript of unpublished report). May 1, 1930. Archived at New Mexico State Engineer Office, Santa Fe.

Bliss, John H. "Memorandum to Mr. McClure—Analysis of Stream-Flow Depletions, Otowi to San Marcial, during Months of July, August, and September" (typewritten). March 1938. Archived at New Mexico State Engineer Office, Santa Fe.

———. "Report on Investigation of Invisible Gains and Losses in the Channel of the Rio Grande from Elephant Butte to El Paso, Texas, February 1936" (typescript of unpublished report). February 1936. Archived at New Mexico State Engineer Office, Santa Fe.

——, and E. P. Osgood. "Report on Seepage Investigations of the Rio Grande and Data of Previous Investigations, 1913–1927" (typescript of unpublished report). July 20, 1928. Archived at New Mexico State Engineer Office, Santa Fe.

Bogener, Stephen. *Ditches across the Desert: Irrigation in the Lower Pecos Valley*. Lubbock: Texas Tech University Press, 2003.

Bowman, Arthur C. "The History and Present Status of Water Utilization on the Rio Grande." Ph.D. diss., University of Texas, 1955.

Boyd, James S. "An Entrepreneur and His Untold Contribution to the Reclamation of the Southwest." Unpublished manuscript, Dec. 9, 1983, copy in possession of author.

Boyd, Nathan E. *Commentary on Secretary Root's Memorandum in re the Elephant Butte Dam Project*. N.p., 1906.

——. *In the Dept. of the Interior in re the Rio Grande Claim, Statement of Case for Claimant*. Las Cruces, N.Mex.: Rio Grande Irrigation and Land Co., 1915.

——. *Memorial to the Senate of the United States in re Bill 3794*. N.p., n.d.

——. *New Mexico and Statehood—Admission into the Union Essential to Territory's Material Progress—An Analysis of Culberson-Stephens Bill*. Washington, D.C.: n.p., 1902.

——. *Perjury and Other Charges against Brigadier General Anson Mills, Comm. for the U.S., of U.S. and Mexico Boundary Comm., Preferred in Petition Signed by Citizens of N. Mex.; in the Dept. of State in re the Elephant Butte Dam Affair*. Las Cruces, N.Mex.: Rio Grande Irrigation and Land Co., 1914.

——. *Shall the Elephant Butte Project (Alias the Engle Project) Be Made a Blessing or a Curse?* El Paso, Texas: J. D. Hughes Printing Co., [1908?].

——. *Statement by Dr. Nathan Boyd in re Elephant Butte [New Mexico] Dam Enterprise and General Anson Mills' International [El Paso] Dam Scheme; Proposed Treaty with the Republic of Mexico; Injunction Suit, United States vs. Rio Grande Dam and Irrigation Co.; Abstracts from Official Documents, Court Decisions, Etc*. Washington, D.C.: Judd and Detweiler, 1902.

Brook, Harold H. *The International Aspects of the Rio Grande Project, Texas and New Mexico*. Las Cruces, N.Mex.: n.p., 1923.

Burkholder, Joseph L. "Report of the Chief Engineer, Submitting a Plan for Flood Control, Drainage, and Irrigation of the Middle Rio Grande Conservancy Project." 3 vols. N.p., August 15, 1928. Archived in New Mexico State Interstream Commission Records, New Mexico State Records Center and Archives, Santa Fe.

Carroll, S. S. "Report on Rio Grande Improvements" (typescript of unpublished report). December 1, 1912. Archived at New Mexico State Engineer Office, Santa Fe.

Chandler, Albert E. *Elements of Western Water Law*. San Francisco: Technical Publishing Co., 1913; rev. ed., 1918.

Clark, Ira G. "The Elephant Butte Controversy: A Chapter in the Emergence of Federal Water Law." *Journal of American History* 61 (1975): 1006–33.

———. *Water in New Mexico: A History of Its Management and Use*. Albuquerque: University of New Mexico Press, 1987.

Clark, J. W. "The Upper Rio Grande." *Natural Resources Journal* 18 (1978): 69–75.

Clark, Robert E., ed. *Water and Water Rights: A Treatise on the Law of Waters and Allied Problems, Eastern, Western, Federal*. 7 vols. Indianapolis: Allen Smith Co., 1967; rev. ed., 1984.

Clayberg, John B. "The Genesis and Development of the Law of Waters in the Far West." *Michigan Law Review* 1 (1902): 91–101.

Clements, Roger V. "British-Controlled Enterprise in the West between 1870 and 1900, and Some Agrarian Reactions." *Agricultural History* 27 (1953): 132–40.

Coan, Charles F. *A History of New Mexico*. Chicago: American Historical Society, 1925.

Cone, William S. "Report on Possible Power Development at Elephant Butte Dam" (typescript of unpublished report). August 1936. Archived at New Mexico State Engineer Office, Santa Fe.

Conkling, Harold, and Erdman Debler. "Report on Water Supply for Possible Development of Irrigation and Drainage Projects on the Rio Grande River above El Paso, Texas" (typescript of unpublished report). 1919. Archived at New Mexico State Engineer Office, Santa Fe.

Corlett, George M. "Statement to the Secretary of the Interior on Appeal from Action of the Commissioner of the General Land Office on the Application of the River Ranch Company for the Approval of a Right of Way for the Vega Sylvestre Reservoir." Copy in Hamele, "Embargo on the Upper Rio Grande."

Darrah, William Culp. *Powell of the Colorado*. Princeton, N.J.: Princeton University Press, 1951.

Davis, Arthur Powell. *Irrigation Works Constructed by the United States Government*. New York: J. Wiley and Sons, 1917.

Debler, Erdman B. "Final Report on Middle Rio Grande Investigations" (typescript of unpublished report). May 1932. New Mexico State Engineer and Interstate Stream Commission Records, New Mexico State Records Center and Archives, Santa Fe.

———. *Final Report on the Middle Rio Grande Investigation*. Washington, D.C.: U.S. Bureau of Reclamation, 1932.

———. "Rio Grande Project—Project Water Supply Requirements" (typescript of unpublished report). September 27, 1924. Archived at New Mexico State Engineer Office, Santa Fe.

———, and C. C. Elder. "Preliminary Report on Middle Rio Grande Valley Investigations" (typescript of unpublished report). December 15, 1927. New Mexico State Engineer and Interstate Stream Commission Records, New Mexico State Records Center and Archives, Santa Fe.

———, and B. F. Walker. "Rio Grande" (typescript of unpublished report). August 1924. New Mexico State Engineer and Interstate Stream Commission Records, New Mexico State Records Center and Archives, Santa Fe.

Dictionary of American Biography, Supplement Three, 1941–1945. New York: Charles Scribner's Sons, 1973.

Dodds, Gordon B. "The Stream-Flow Controversy: A Conservation Turning Point." *Journal of American History* 56 (June 1969): 59–69.

Dunbar, Robert G. *Forging New Rights in Western Waters*. Lincoln: University of Nebraska Press, 1983.

Durst, John H. "Riparian Rights from Another Standpoint." *Overland Monthly* 6 (1885): 10–14.

Eisenhart, Henry A. "The History of Elephant Butte Dam, Lake, and State Park." Ph.D. diss., University of New Mexico, 1980.

Farnham, Henry P. *Law of Waters and Water Rights: International, National, State, Municipal, and Individual, Including Irrigation, Drainage, and Municipal Water Use*. 3 vols. Rochester, N.Y.: Lawyers' Cooperative Publishing, 1904.

Fergusson, Harvey. *Rio Grande*. New York: Alfred K. Knopf, 1933.

Follett, W. W. "A Study of the Use of Water for Irrigation in the Rio Grande del Norte above Fort Quitman, Texas, November 1896" (typescript of unpublished report). 1896. Archived at New Mexico State Engineer Office, Santa Fe.

Frankfurter, Felix, and James M. Landis. "The Compact Clause of the Constitution— A Study in Interstate Adjustments." *Yale Law Journal* 34 (1925): 685–758.

Frazer, Robert W. *Forts of the West: Military Forts and Presidios and Posts Commonly Called Forts West of the Mississippi River to 1898*. Norman: University of Oklahoma Press, 1965.

French, James A. "Irrigation on the Rio Grande, Colorado Area; Also List of Ditches" (typescript of unpublished report). 1910. Archived at New Mexico State Engineer Office, Santa Fe.

———. "A Report of [the] State Engineer for [the] Fifth and Sixth Fiscal Years" (typescript of unpublished report). 1918. New Mexico State Engineer and Interstate Stream Commission Records, New Mexico State Records Center and Archives, Santa Fe.

Ganoe, John T. "The Beginnings of Irrigation in the United States." *Mississippi Valley Historical Review* 25 (1938): 59–78.

———. "The Origin of a National Reclamation Policy." *Mississippi Valley Historical Review* 18 (1931): 34–52.

Gates, Paul W., and Robert W. Swenson. *History of Public Land Law Development*. Washington, D.C.: U.S. Government Printing Office, 1968.

Gault, Homer J. "Middle Rio Grande Reclamation Project" (typescript of unpublished report). December 1922. Archived at New Mexico State Engineer Office, Santa Fe.

———. "Report on the Middle Rio Grande Reclamation Project" (typescript of unpublished report). 1923. New Mexico State Engineer and Interstate Stream Commission Records, New Mexico State Records Center and Archives, Santa Fe.

Gibbard, Frank. "*Wyoming v. Colorado*: A 'Watershed' Decision." *Colorado Lawyer* 34 (2005): 37.

Golze, Alfred. *Reclamation in the United States*. New York: McGraw-Hill, 1952.

Gressley, Gene M. "Arthur Powell Davis, Reclamation, and the West." *Agricultural History* 42 (1968): 241–57.

———. "Reclamation and the West via Arthur Powell Davis." In *The Twentieth-Century American West: A Potpourri*, ed. Gene M. Gressley. Columbia: University of Missouri Press, 1977.

Haight, George W. "Riparian Rights." *Overland Monthly* 5 (1885): 561–69.

Hall, B. M. "A Discussion of Past and Present Plans for Irrigation of the Rio Grande Valley." Unpublished report. Archived as file 46, Rio Grande Project files, Records of the Bureau of Reclamation.

Hall, Kermit L. *The Magic Mirror: Law in American History*. New York: Oxford University Press, 1989.

Hamele, Ottomar. "The Embargo on the Upper Rio Grande" (typescript of unpublished report). November 11, 1924. Archived at New Mexico State Engineer Office, Santa Fe.

Harris, Linda G. *Las Cruces: An Illustrated History*. Las Cruces, N.Mex.: Arroyo Press, 1993.

Hays, Samuel P. *Conservation and the Gospel of Efficiency: The Progressive Conservation Movement, 1890–1920*. Cambridge, Mass.: Harvard University Press, 1959.

Hedke, Charles R. "Consumptive Use of Water by Crops, Rio Grande Valley" (typescript of unpublished report). July 1924. New Mexico State Engineer and Interstate Stream Commission Records, New Mexico State Records Center and Archives, Santa Fe.

———. "A Report on the Irrigation Development and Water Supply of the Middle Rio Grande Valley, N. Mex., as It Relates to the Rio Grande Compact" (typescript of unpublished report). January 1925. Archived at New Mexico State Engineer Office, Santa Fe.

Henny, D. C. "Comments of D.C. Henny on Meeker's Report on Embargo Dated August 1924" (unpublished typescript). January 3, 1925. Archived at New Mexico State Engineer Office, Santa Fe.

———. "Exhibit VIII, Part of a Statement of Elephant Butte Irrigation District to Colorado—New Mexico Compact Commission" (unpublished typescript). June 1925. Archived at New Mexico State Engineer Office, Santa Fe.

———, James Munn, and Charles Pease. "Rio Grande Project: Report on Water Supply and Project Area; High Line Canal Construction; Power Development and City Water Supply from Storage" (typescript of unpublished report). November 1919. Archived at New Mexico State Engineer Office, Santa Fe.

Hess, Ralph H. "An Illustration of Legal Development—The Passing of the Doctrine of Riparian Rights." *American Political Science Review* 2 (1907): 15–31.

Hetrick, Nancy E. "Recent Developments in the El Paso/New Mexico Interstate Groundwater Controversy—The Constitutionality of New Mexico's New Municipality Water Planning Statute." *Natural Resources Journal* 29 (1989): 223–49.

Hill, Raymond A. "Development of the Rio Grande Compact of 1938." *Natural Resources Journal* 14 (1974): 163–200.

———. *Development of the Rio Grande Compact of 1938*. San Francisco: Leeds, Hill and Jewett, 1968.

Hinderlider, M. C., T. M. McClure, and F. B. Clayton. "Rio Grande Compact, Rio Grande above Fort Quitman, Colorado, New Mexico, Texas" (typescript of unpublished report). March 18, 1938. Archived at New Mexico State Engineer Office, Santa Fe.

History of New Mexico, Its Resources and People, Illustrated. 2 vols. Los Angeles: Pacific States Publishing, 1907.

Holmes, Beatrice H. *A History of Federal Water Resources Programs, 1800–1960.* Washington, D.C.: U.S. Department of Agriculture, 1972.

Horwitz, Morton J. *The Transformation of American Law, 1780–1860.* Cambridge, Mass.: Harvard University Press, 1977.

Hosea, R. G. "Report on Irrigation in the Rio Grande Valley" (typescript of unpublished report). 1928. Archived at New Mexico State Engineer Office, Santa Fe.

Hundley, Norris, Jr. "Clio Nods: *Arizona v. California* and the Boulder Canyon Act—A Reassessment." *Western Historical Quarterly* 3 (1972): 455–82.

———. *Dividing the Waters: A Century of Controversy between the United States and Mexico.* Berkeley: University of California Press, 1966.

———. *Water and the West: The Colorado River Compact and the Politics of Water in the American West.* Berkeley: University of California Press, 1975.

———. "The West against Itself: The Colorado River—An Institutional History." In *New Courses for the Colorado River: Major Issues for the Next Century,* edited by Gary D. Weatherford and F. Lee Brown, 9–50. Albuquerque: University of New Mexico Press, 1986.

Hurst, James Willard. *Law and the Conditions of Freedom in the Nineteenth-Century United States.* Madison: University of Wisconsin Press, 1964.

Hutchins, Wells A. "The Community Acequia: Its Origins and Development." *Southwest Historical Review* 31 (1928): 261–84.

———. *Water Rights in the Nineteen Western States.* 3 vols. Washington, D.C.: U.S. Department of Agriculture, 1972–77.

"Index of Data in the Office of the State Engineer Relating to Irrigation, Water Supply, Hydrology and Geology of the Rio Grande Basin above Fort Hancock, Texas" (unpublished typescript). 1927. Archived at New Mexico State Engineer Office, Santa Fe.

Institute for Government Research. *The United States Reclamation Service: Its History, Activities, and Organization.* New York: D. Appleton and Co., 1919.

International Boundary Commission. *Proceedings of the International (Water) Boundary Commission, United States and Mexico, Treaties of 1884 and 1889: Equitable Distribution of the Waters of the Rio Grande.* 2 vols. Washington, D.C.: U.S. Government Printing Office, 1903.

Irby, Frank E. "The Ground-Water Situation in the Rio Grande Underground Water Basin, New Mexico," paper delivered before the Albuquerque chapter, Society of American Military Engineers, August 14, 1957. Archived at New Mexico State Engineer Office, Santa Fe.

James, George Wharton. *Reclaiming the Arid West: The Story of the United States Reclamation Service.* New York: Dodd, Mead, and Co., 1917.

Jenkins, Myra Ellen. "The Rio Grande Compact of 1938" (typescript of unpublished paper). 1982. Archived at New Mexico State Engineer Office, Santa Fe.

Kelley, Pat. *River of Lost Dreams: Navigation on the Rio Grande.* Lincoln: University of Nebraska Press.

Kinney, Clesson S. *A Treatise on the Law of Irrigation Including the Law of Water Rights and the Doctrine of Appropriation of Waters as the Same Are Construed and Applied in the States and Territories of the Arid and Semi-Humid Regions of the United States, and Also Including the Statutes of the Respective States and Territories, and Decisions of the Courts Relating to Those Subjects.* 4 vols. Washington, D.C.: W. H. Lowdermilk and Co., 1893; rev. ed., San Francisco: Bender-Moss, 1912.

Kluger, James R. *Turning On Water with a Shovel: The Career of Elwood Mead.* Albuquerque: University of New Mexico Press, 1992.

Kroeber, Clifton B. *Man, Land, and Water: Mexico's Farmlands Irrigation Policies, 1885–1911.* Berkeley: University of California Press, 1983.

Larson, Robert W. *New Mexico's Quest for Statehood, 1846–1912.* Albuquerque: University of New Mexico Press, 1968.

Leach, Richard H. "The Interstate Compact, Water and the Southwest: A Case Study in Compact Utility." *Southwestern Social Science Quarterly* 38 (1957): 236–47.

——, and Redding S. Sugg, Jr. *The Administration of Interstate Compacts.* Baton Rouge: Louisiana State University Press, 1959.

Lee, Lawrence B. *Reclaiming the Arid West: An Historiography and Guide.* Santa Barbara, Calif.: ABC-Clio Press, 1980.

——. "William Ellsworth Smythe and the Irrigation Movement: A Reconsideration." *Pacific Historical Review* 41 (1972): 289–311.

Lee, Willis Thomas. *Water Resources of the Rio Grande Valley in New Mexico and Their Development.* U.S. Geological Water Supply Paper 188. Washington, D.C.: U.S. Government Printing Office, 1907.

Lilley, William, III, and Lewis L. Gould. "The Western Irrigation Movement, 1878–1902." In *The American West: A Reorientation*, edited by Gene M. Gressley, 57–74. Laramie: University of Wyoming Press, 1966.

Limerick, Patricia Nelson. *The Legacy of Conquest: The Unbroken Past of the American West.* New York: W. W. Norton, 1987.

Linford, P. D. "Background Information—Rio Grande Compact" (undated typescript of unpublished report). Archived at New Mexico State Engineer Office, Santa Fe.

Littlefield, Douglas R. "The History of the Arkansas River Compact." Exhibit 129, 2 vols., *Kansas v. Colorado*, Original No. 105, Oct. Term 1985.

——. "Interstate Water Conflicts, Compromises, and Compacts: The Rio Grande, 1880–1938." Ph.D. dissertation, University of California, Los Angeles, 1987.

——. "The Rio Grande Compact of 1929: A Truce in an Interstate River Apportionment War." *Pacific Historical Review* 60 (1991): 497–515.

——. *Transcripts of Testimony in "Kansas v. Colorado."* 13 vols. Original No. 105, Oct. Term 1985.

——. "Water Rights during the California Gold Rush: Conflicts over Economic Points of View." *Western Historical Quarterly* 14 (1983): 415–34.

Long, Joseph R. "Early History of the Doctrine of Appropriation." *Case and Comment* 19 (1913): 675–77.

———. *A Treatise on the Law of Irrigation Covering the States and Territories.* St. Paul, Minn.: Keefe-Davidson Law Book Co., 1901; rev. ed., Denver: W. H. Courtright Publishing, 1916.

Lowitt, Richard. *The New Deal and the West.* Bloomington: Indiana University Press, 1984.

Luckingham, Bradford. *The Urban Southwest: A Profile History.* El Paso: Texas Western Press, 1982.

Maass, Arthur, and Raymond L. Anderson. *And the Desert Shall Rejoice: Conflict, Growth, and Justice in Arid Environments.* Cambridge, Mass.: MIT Press, 1978.

———, and Hiller Zobel. "Anglo-American Water Law: Who Appropriated the Riparian Doctrine?" *Public Policy* 10 (1960): 109–56.

Martinez, Oscar. *Border Boom Town: Ciudad Juarez since 1848.* Austin: University of Texas Press, 1978.

McCaffrey, Stephen C. "Water, Water Everywhere, but Too Few Drops to Drink: The Coming Fresh Water Crisis and International Environmental Law." *Denver Journal of International Law and Policy* 28, no. 3 (2003): 326.

McDonald, Angus. *One Hundred and Sixty Acres of Water: The Story of the Antimonopoly Law.* Washington, D.C.: Public Affairs Institute, 1958.

Mead, Elwood. *Irrigation Institutions: A Discussion of the Economic and Legal Questions Created by the Growth of Irrigated Agriculture in the West.* New York: McMillan, 1903.

Meeker, R. I. "Preliminary Report—Water Supply, Irrigation and Drainage, Present and Future Conditions, San Luis Valley, Colorado" (typescript of unpublished report). May 1924. Archived at New Mexico State Engineer Office, Santa Fe.

———. "Review of Water Supply, Drainage, Irrigated Areas, and Consumptive Use of Water in the Rio Grande Basin above Fort Quitman, Texas" (typescript of unpublished report). 1924. Archived at New Mexico State Engineer Office, Santa Fe.

Mills, Anson. *My Story.* Washington, D.C.: privately published, 1918.

Mills, William W. *Forty Years at El Paso, 1858–1898.* El Paso, Texas: Hertzog, 1962.

Mitchell, Guy Elliot, comp. and ed. *The Official Proceedings of the Twelfth National Irrigation Congress Held at El Paso, Texas, November 15–16-17–18, 1904.* Galveston, Texas: Clarke and Courts, 1905.

Muys, Jerome C. "Approaches and Considerations for Allocation of Interstate Waters." In *Water Law: Trends, Policies, and Practice,* edited by Kathleen Marion Carr and James D. Crammond, 311–19. Chicago: American Bar Association, 1995.

———. "Interstate Compacts and Regional Water Resources Planning Management." *Natural Resources Lawyer* 6 (1973): 153–88.

Neuffer, H. C. "Memorandum-Subject: Rio Grande Joint Investigation, Volume 1, Part 1" (unpublished typescript). 1937. New Mexico State Engineer and Interstate Stream Commission Records, New Mexico State Records Center and Archives, Santa Fe.

Newcomer, A. W. "Depletion of Flow of the Rio Grande at the Colorado–New Mexico Interstate Line" (typescript of unpublished report). May 6, 1930. Archived at New Mexico State Engineer Office, Santa Fe.

Newell, Frederick. *Irrigation in the United States*. New York: Thomas Y. Crowell and Co., 1902.

New Mexico, Secretary of the Territory of. *Report of the Secretary of the Territory, 1903–1904, and Legislative Manual, 1905*. Santa Fe: New Mexican Printing Company, 1905.

Osgood, E. P. "Irrigation, San Luis Valley, Colorado, Critical Years" (typescript of unpublished report). September 1928. Archived at New Mexico State Engineer Office, Santa Fe.

——— . "Preliminary Report upon the Use, Control, and Disposition of the Waters of the Rio Grande and Its Tributaries above Fort Quitman, Texas" (typescript of unpublished report). March 31, 1928. Archived at New Mexico State Engineer Office, Santa Fe.

——— . "Report on Irrigation in the Rio Grande Basin in Texas above Fort Quitman and in New Mexico" (typescript of unpublished report). 1928. Archived at New Mexico State Engineer Office, Santa Fe.

——— . "Report on Water Supply, Irrigation, and Drainage in the San Luis Valley, Colorado" (typescript of unpublished report). 1928. Archived at New Mexico State Engineer Office, Santa Fe.

——— . "Rio Grande Project, 1919–1927: Effects of Rains on Consumptive Use of Irrigation Water" (typescript of unpublished report). August 1928. Archived at New Mexico State Engineer Office, Santa Fe.

Otero, Miguel A. *My Life on the Frontier*. New York: Press of the Pioneers, 1935.

——— . *My Nine Years as Governor of the Territory of New Mexico, 1897–1906*. Albuquerque: University of New Mexico Press, 1940.

"Our Rapidly Growing Irrigation Areas." *Scientific American* 82 (1900): 131.

Paddock, B. B. *A Twentieth Century History and Biographical Record of North and West Texas*. 2 vols. Chicago: Lewis Publishing, 1906.

Patterson, James T. "The New Deal in the West." *Pacific Historical Review* 38 (1969): 317–27.

Pease, Charles T. "Report on Floods and Drainage at San Marcial, New Mexico—Elephant Butte Reservoir" (typescript of unpublished report). October 1925. New Mexico State Engineer and Interstate Stream Commission Records, New Mexico State Records Center and Archives, Santa Fe.

Perkins, W. A. "Rio Grande Project, New Mexico–Texas Community Ditches in the Rio Grande Valley" (typescript of unpublished report). December 1914. Archived at New Mexico State Engineer Office, Santa Fe.

Pisani, Donald J. "Reclamation and Social Engineering in the Progressive Era." *Agricultural History* 57 (1983): 46–63.

——— . "State vs. Nation: Federal Reclamation and Water Rights in the Progressive Era." *Pacific Historical Review* 51 (1982): 265–82.

——— . *To Reclaim a Divided West: Water, Law, and Public Policy, 1848–1902*. Albuquerque: University of New Mexico Press, 1992.

———. *Water and American Government: The Reclamation Bureau, National Water Policy, and the American West, 1902–1935*. Berkeley: University of California Press, 2002.

Pomeroy, John Norton. *A Treatise on the Law of Riparian Rights as the Same Is Formulated and Applied in the Pacific States, Including the Doctrine of Appropriation*. St. Paul, Minn.: West Publishing, 1887; rev. ed., 1893.

Price, Paxton L. *Pioneers of the Mesilla Valley*. Las Cruces, N.Mex.: Yuca Tree Press, 1995.

Prince, L. Bradford. *New Mexico's Struggle for Statehood: Sixty Years of Effort to Obtain Self Government*. Santa Fe: New Mexican Printing Company, 1910.

Radosevich, G. E., K. C. Nobe, D. Allardice, and C. Kirkwood. *Evolution and Administration of Colorado Water Law, 1876–1976*. Fort Collins, Colo.: Water Resources Publications, 1978.

Reisner, Marc. *Cadillac Desert: The American West and Its Disappearing Water*. New York: Pantheon Books, 1985.

Resch, W. F. "Report on Mexican Canal Diversion—Rio Grande Project" (typescript of unpublished report). March 29, 1935. Archived at New Mexico State Engineer Office, Santa Fe.

Reynolds, S. E. "The Rio Grande Compact." In *International Water Law along the Mexican-American Border*, edited by Clark S. Knowlton, 48–62. Contribution no.11 of the Committee on Desert and Arid Zones Research, Southwestern and Rocky Mountain Division, American Association for the Advancement of Science. El Paso: University of Texas, 1968.

Richardson, James, ed. *A Compilation of the Messages and Papers of the Presidents*. 10 vols. Washington, D.C.: U.S. Government Printing Office, 1898.

"Rio Grande Claim (Claim No. 83)." *American Journal of International Law* 19 (1925): 206–14.

Rio Grande Compact Commission. "Proceedings of the Rio Grande Compact Commission." 1928–1938. Archived at New Mexico Interstate Stream Commission, Santa Fe.

Robbins, Roy. *Our Landed Heritage: The Public Domain, 1776–1936*. Princeton, N.J.: Princeton University Press, 1942.

Robinson, Michael C. *Water for the West: The Bureau of Reclamation, 1902–1977*. Chicago: Public Works Historical Society, 1979.

Roder, Wolf. "Distribution and Use of the Waters of an International River: The Rio Grande." Ph.D. diss., University of Chicago, 1956.

Rodey, Pearce C., and Joseph L. Burkholder. "The Middle Rio Grande Valley Project— Status and Information Relative to Development of Official Plan for Flood Control, Drainage, and Irrigation" (typescript of unpublished report). January 1, 1927. Archived at New Mexico State Engineer Office, Santa Fe.

Shaw, Lucien. "Development of the Law of Waters in the West." *American Bar Association Journal* 8 (1922): 562–68.

———. "The Development of Water Law in California." *California Bar Association Proceedings* 13 (1922): 154–73.

Sherk, George William. *Dividing the Waters: The Resolution of Interstate Water Conflicts in the United States.* London: Kluwer Law International, 2000.

Sherow, James Earl. "The Latent Influence of Equity in *Wyoming v. Colorado* (1922)." *Great Plains Research* 2 (1992): 7–26.

———. "Watering the Plains: An Early History of Denver's Highland Canal." *Colorado Heritage* 4 (1988): 2–13.

———. *Watering the Valley: Development along the High Plains Arkansas River, 1870–1950.* Lawrence: University of Kansas Press, 1990.

Simmons, Virginia McConnell. *The San Luis Valley: Land of the Six Armed Cross.* Boulder, Colo.: Pruett Publishing, 1979.

Slichter, Charles S. *Observations on the Ground Waters of [the] Rio Grande Valley.* U.S. Geological Survey Water Supply Paper 141. Washington, D.C.: U.S. Government Printing Office, 1905.

Sloan, W. G. "Report on Rio Grande Joint Investigations" (typescript of unpublished report). August 1937. New Mexico State Engineer and Interstate Stream Commission Records, New Mexico State Records Center and Archives, Santa Fe.

Smith, Karen L. *The Magnificent Experiment: Building the Salt River Reclamation Project, 1890–1917.* Tucson: University of Arizona Press, 1986.

Smythe, William E. *The Conquest of Arid America.* New York: Harper, 1900.

Sonnichsen, C. L. *The El Paso Salt War, 1877.* El Paso: Texas Western Press, 1961.

———. *Pass of the North: Four Centuries on the Rio Grande.* 2 vols. El Paso: Texas Western Press, 1968.

Stannard, Jay D. "Report of Operations in San Luis Valley, Colorado, 1912 and 1913" (typescript of unpublished report). 1912–1913. Archived at New Mexico State Engineer Office, Santa Fe.

Stegner, Wallace. *Beyond the Hundredth Meridian: John Wesley Powell and the Second Opening of the West.* Boston: Houghton Mifflin, 1954.

Steinel, Alvin T. *History of Agriculture in Colorado.* Fort Collins, Colo.: State Agricultural College, 1926.

Sterling, Everett. "The Powell Irrigation Survey, 1888–1893." *Mississippi Valley Historical Review* 27 (1940): 421–34.

Stinson, Howard R. "Western Interstate Water Compact." *California Law Review* 45 (1957): 655–64.

Stout, O.V.P., F. H. Fowler, and Erdman B. Debler. "Report of San Luis Valley Drain Committee to Administrator Harold L. Ickes, Federal Emergency Administration of Public Works, Denver, Colorado" (typescript of unpublished report). February 26, 1935. Archived at New Mexico State Engineer Office, Santa Fe.

Sullivan, Vernon L. "Report and Recommendation for the Reclamation of the Middle Rio Grande Valley of New Mexico" (typescript of unpublished report). December 1924. Archived at New Mexico State Engineer Office, Santa Fe.

Swain, Donald C. "The Bureau of Reclamation and the New Deal, 1933–1940." *Pacific Northwest Quarterly* 61 (1970): 137–46.

Tarlock, A. Dan. "The Law of Equitable Apportionment Revisited, Updated, and Restated." *University of Colorado Law Review* 56 (1985): 381–411.

Taylor, Joseph S. "Statement of Elephant Butte Irrigation District to Colorado–New Mexico Compact Commission" (typewritten). 1924. Archived at New Mexico State Engineer Office, Santa Fe.

Teele, Ray P. *Irrigation in the United States: A Discussion of Its Legal, Economic, and Financial Aspects.* New York: D. Appleton and Co., 1915.

Thursby, Vincent V. *Interstate Cooperation: A Study of the Interstate Compact.* Washington, D.C.: Public Affairs Press, 1953.

Timmons, W. H. *El Paso: A Borderlands History.* El Paso: Texas Western Press, 2004.

Tipton, Royce J. "Deduction of Acreage Irrigated in San Luis Valley" (typescript of unpublished report). March 24, 1924. Archived at New Mexico State Engineer Office, Santa Fe.

——. "Resume of the Problem Concerning the Rio Grande above Fort Quitman, Texas" (typescript of unpublished report). 1935. Archived at New Mexico State Engineer Office, Santa Fe.

——. "Soil Conditions and Drainage in San Luis Valley, Colorado" (typescript of unpublished report). September 1924. Archived at New Mexico State Engineer Office, Santa Fe.

——. "Storage for Irrigation, Colorado Area Rio Grande Basin" (typescript of unpublished report). May 1924. Archived at New Mexico State Engineer Office, Santa Fe.

Tyler, Daniel. *Silver Fox of the Rockies: Delphus E. Carpenter and Western Water Compacts.* Norman: University of Oklahoma Press, 2003.

U.S. Bureau of Reclamation. *Bureau of Reclamation Organizational Structure.* Denver: U.S. Bureau of Reclamation History Program, 1997.

U.S. Congress. *Congressional Record.* 1890–1905. Washington, D.C.

U.S. Department of State. *Papers Relating to the Foreign Relations of the United States, Transmitted to Congress with the Annual Message of the President, December 6, 1880.* Washington, D.C.: U.S. Government Printing Office, 1881.

——. *Papers Relating to the Foreign Relations of the United States, Transmitted to Congress with the Annual Message of the President, December 3, 1888.* Washington, D.C.: U.S. Government Printing Office, 1889.

——. *Papers Relating to the Foreign Relations of the United States, Transmitted to Congress with the Annual Message of the President, December 3, 1889.* Washington, D.C.: U.S. Government Printing Office, 1890.

——. *Papers Relating to the Foreign Relations of the United States, Transmitted to Congress with the Annual Message of the President, December 3, 1894.* Washington, D.C.: U.S. Government Printing Office, 1895.

——. *Papers Relating to the Foreign Relations of the United States, Transmitted to Congress with the Annual Message of the President, December 6, 1897.* Washington, D.C.: U.S. Government Printing Office, 1898.

——. *Papers Relating to the Foreign Relations of the United States, Transmitted to Congress with the Annual Message of the President, December 3, 1900.* Washington, D.C.: U.S. Government Printing Office, 1902.

U.S. Department of the Interior. *Annual Report of the Department of the Interior for the Fiscal Year Ending June 30, 1897.* Washington, D.C.: U.S. Government Printing Office, 1897.

——. *Annual Report of the Department of the Interior for the Fiscal Year Ending June 30, 1898.* Washington, D.C.: U.S. Government Printing Office, 1898.

——. *Annual Report of the Secretary of the Interior for the Fiscal Year Ending June 30, 1885.* 5 vols. Washington, D.C.: U.S. Government Printing Office, 1886.

——. *Annual Report of the Secretary of the Interior for the Fiscal Year Ending June 30, 1888.* 6 vols. Washington, D.C.: U.S. Government Printing Office, 1888.

——. *Annual Report of the Secretary of the Interior for the Fiscal Year Ending June 30, 1891.* 5 vols. Washington, D.C.: U.S. Government Printing Office, 1892.

——. *Report of the Secretary of the Interior, Being Part of the Message and Documents Communicated to the Two Houses of Congress at the Beginning of the First Session of the Fifty-first Congress.* 5 vols. Washington, D.C.: U.S. Government Printing Office, 1890.

——. *Report of the Secretary of the Interior, Being Part of the Message and Documents Communicated to the Two Houses of Congress at the Beginning of the Second Session of the Fifty-first Congress.* 5 vols. Washington, D.C.: U.S. Government Printing Office, 1890.

——. *Report of the Secretary of the Interior, Being Part of the Message and Documents Communicated to the Two Houses of Congress at the Beginning of the Second Session of the Fifty-second Congress.* 5 vols. Washington, D.C.: U.S. Government Printing Office, 1892.

——. *Report of the Secretary of the Interior, Being Part of the Message and Documents Communicated to the Two Houses of Congress at the Beginning of the First Session of the Fifty-fourth Congress.* 5 vols. Washington, D.C.: U.S. Government Printing Office, 1896.

U.S. Geological Survey. *Proceedings of the Second Conference of Engineers of the Reclamation Service with Accompanying Papers.* U.S. Geological Survey Water Supply Paper 146. Washington, D.C.: U.S. Government Printing Office, 1905.

U.S. House of Representatives. *Ceding the Arid Lands to the States and Territories.* H. Rpt. 3767 (serial 2888), 51st Cong., 2d sess., 1891.

——. *Dam and Reservoir on the Rio Grande in New Mexico.* H. Rpt. 3990 (serial 4767), 58th Cong., 3d sess., 1905.

——. *El Paso Troubles, Texas—Letter from the Secretary of War in Response to a Resolution of the House of Representatives Transmitting Reports of the Commission Appointed to Investigate the El Paso Troubles in Texas.* H. Ex. Doc. 93 (serial 1809), 45th Cong., 2d sess., 1878. Cited in the notes as *El Paso Commission Report.*

———. *El Paso Troubles, Texas—Letter from the Secretary of War Transmitting a Report from Colonel Hatch on the Subject of El Paso Troubles.* H. Ex. Doc. 84 (serial 1809), 45th Cong., 2d sess., 1878. Cited in the notes as *Hatch Report.*

———. *Equitable Distribution of the Waters of the Rio Grande.* H. Rpt. 598 (serial 3719), 55th Cong., 2d sess., 1898.

———. *International Commission with Mexico.* H. Rpt. 1008 (serial 1809), 45th Cong., 2d sess., 1878.

———. *International Dam in Rio Grande River near El Paso, Tex.* H. Doc. 125 (serial 3414), 54th Cong., 1st sess., 1896.

———. *Irrigation of Arid Lands—International Boundary—Mexican Relations.* H. Rpt. 490 (serial 2808), 51st Cong., 1st sess., 1890.

———. *Letter from the Secretary of State Transmitting a Copy of a Communication from the Acting Secretary of State Submitting an Estimate of Appropriation for Carrying Out Convention with Mexico as to Distribution of the Waters of the Rio Grande.* H. Doc. 548 (serial 5155), 59th Cong., 2d sess., 1907.

———. *Letter from the Secretary of the Interior, Transmitting, by Direction of the President, Orders and Regulations of the Interior Department Touching Use, Appropriation, or Disposition for Irrigation of the Waters of the Rio Grande and Its Tributaries in Colorado and New Mexico,* H. Doc. 39 (serial 6117), 62d Cong., 1st sess., 1911.

———. *Negotiations with Mexico.* H. Rpt. 1967 (serial 2812), 51st Cong., 1st sess., 1890.

———. *Preliminary Examination of Reservoir Sites in Wyoming and Colorado.* H. Doc. 141 (serial 3666), 55th Cong., 2d sess., 1897.

———. *Report on the Lands of the Arid Region of the United States.* H. Ex. Doc. 73, 45th Cong., 2d sess, 1878.

U.S. National Resources Committee. *The Rio Grande Joint Investigations in the Upper Rio Grande Basin in Colorado, New Mexico, and Texas, 1936–1937.* 5 vols, undated. Regional Planning, Part 6. [Washington, D.C.: 1938.]

U.S. President's Water Resources Policy Commission. *Ten Rivers in America's Future.* 3 vols. Washington, D.C.: U.S. Government Printing Office, 1950.

U.S. Reclamation Service. *First Annual Report of the Reclamation Service from June 17 to December 1, 1902.* Washington, D.C.: U.S. Government Printing Office, 1903.

———. *Second Annual Report of the Reclamation Service, 1902–1903.* Washington, D.C.: U.S. Government Printing Office, 1904.

———. *Third Annual Report of the Reclamation Service, 1903–1904.* 2 vols. Washington, D.C.: U.S. Government Printing Office, 1905.

———. *Fifth Annual Report of the Reclamation Service, 1906.* Washington, D.C.: U.S. Government Printing Office, 1907.

———. *Seventh Annual Report of the Reclamation Service, 1907–1908.* Washington, D.C.: U.S. Government Printing Office, 1908.

———. *Ninth Annual Report of the Reclamation Service, 1909–1910.* Washington, D.C.: U.S. Government Printing Office, 1911.

———. *Tenth Annual Report of the Reclamation Service, 1910–1911.* Washington, D.C.: U.S. Government Printing Office, 1912.

——. *Eleventh Annual Report of the Reclamation Service, 1911–1912.* Washington, D.C.: U.S. Government Printing Office, 1913.

——. *Twelfth Annual Report of the Reclamation Service, 1912–1913.* Washington, D.C.: U.S. Government Printing Office, 1914.

U.S. Senate. *Dam and Reservoir on the Rio Grande in New Mexico.* S. Rpt. 3915 (serial 4756), 58th Cong., 3d sess., 1905.

——. *Equitable Distribution of the Waters of the Rio Grande—Message from the President of the United States Transmitting in Response to Resolution of the Senate of February 26, 1898, Reports . . . Relative to the Equitable Distribution of the Waters of the Rio Grande River.* S. Doc. 229 (serial 3610), 55th Cong., 2d sess., 1898.

——. *Equitable Distribution of the Waters of the Rio Grande, etc.* S. Rpt. 1755 (serial 4064), 56th Cong., 2d sess., 1900.

——. *History of the Rio Grande Dam and Irrigation Company and the Elephant Dam Case.* S. Doc. 104 (serial 4033), 56th Cong., 2d sess., 1900.

——. *Investigation of the Department of the Interior and the Bureau of Forestry.* S. Doc. 719 (serials 5892–5903), 61st Cong., 3d sess., 1911.

——. *Message from the President of the United States Transmitting a Report from the Secretary of State with Accompanying Papers, in Regard to the Equitable Distribution of the Waters of the Rio Grande.* S. Doc. 154 (serial 4428), 57th Cong., 2d sess., 1903.

——. *Message from the President of the United States Transmitting a Report Relative to the Construction of Certain Dams in the Rio Grande.* S. Ex. Doc. 144 (serial 2613), 50th Cong., 2d sess., 1889. Cited in the notes as *Dams in the Rio Grande.*

——. *Report of the Special Committee of the United States Senate on the Irrigation and Reclamation of Arid Lands.* S. Rpt. 928 (serial 2708), 51st Cong., 1st sess., 1890.

Vlasich, Anthony. "Pueblo Indian Agriculture, Irrigation, and Water Rights." Ph.D. diss., University of Utah, 1980.

Volk, Kenneth Q., and Edgar Alan Rowe. "Memoir [of Joseph Barlow Lippincott]." *Transactions of the American Society of Civil Engineers* 108 (1943): 1543–50.

Walker, B. F., and Erdman B. Debler. "Development of the Middle Rio Grande: Rio Grande Project Water Supply—Irrigable Area of Project" (typescript of unpublished report). August 1924. Archived at New Mexico State Engineer Office, Santa Fe.

Warne, William E. *The Bureau of Reclamation.* New York: Praeger, 1973.

White, Owen. *Out of the Desert: The Historical Romance of El Paso.* El Paso, Texas: McMath Company, 1923.

Who Was Who in America. Chicago: A. N. Marquis, 1943; rev. ed., 1960.

Wiel, Samuel C. "Origin and Comparative Development of the Law of Watercourses in the Common Law and in the Civil Law." *California Law Review* 6 (1918): 245–67, 342–71.

——. "Political Water Rights." *California Law Review* 10 (1922): 111–19.

——. "'Priority' in Western Water Law." *Yale Law Journal* 18 (1908–1909): 189–98.

——. "Public Policy in Western Water Decisions." *California Law Review* 1 (1912–13): 11–31.

——. "Theories of Water Law." *Harvard Law Review* 27 (1913–14): 530–44.

———. "The Water Law of the Public Domain." *American Law Review* 43 (1909): 481–515.

———. *Water Rights in the Western States: The Law of Prior Appropriation of Water as Applied Alone in Some Jurisdictions and as in Others Confined to the Public Domain, with the Common Law of Riparian Rights for Water upon Private Lands.* San Francisco: Bancroft-Whitney, 1905; 2d ed., 1908; 3d ed., 2 vols., 1911.

———. "Waters: American Law and French Authority." *Harvard Law Review* 33 (1919): 133–67.

Wilson, Francis C. "Rio Grande Compact" (typescript of unpublished report). 1929. Archived at New Mexico State Engineer Office, Santa Fe.

Worster, Donald. *A River Running West: The Life of John Wesley Powell.* New York: Oxford University Press, 2001.

———. *Rivers of Empire: Water, Aridity, and the Growth of the American West.* New York: Pantheon Books, 1985.

Yeo, Herbert W. "General Description of the Rio Grande Valley from White Rock Canyon of the Rio Grande to Old Fort Craig, N. Mex.," unpublished report, 1910. Archived in the New Mexico State Engineer Office, Santa Fe.

———. "Report on Hydrographic and Irrigation Conditions in the Rio Grande Valley, New Mexico," unpublished report, 1910. Archived in the New Mexico State Engineer Office, Santa Fe.

———. "Report on Irrigation in the Rio Grande Basin in Texas above Fort Quitman and in New Mexico during 1907, 1920, and 1928" (undated typescript of unpublished report, 1928?). Archived at New Mexico State Engineer Office, Santa Fe.

———. "Report on Water Supply, Irrigation, and Drainage in the San Luis Valley and Adjacent Mountain Areas in the State of Colorado" (typescript of unpublished report). 1931. Archived at New Mexico State Engineer Office, Santa Fe.

———. "Tabulation of Ditches, Rio Grande, New Mexico Area," unpublished report, 1910. Archived in the New Mexico State Engineer Office, Santa Fe.

Zimmermann, Frederick L., and Mitchell Wendell. *The Interstate Compact since 1925.* Chicago: Council of State Governments, 1951.

———, and ———. *The Law and Use of Interstate Compacts.* Lexington, Ky.: Council of State Governments, 1976.

Index

www.ingramcontent.com/pod-product-compliance
Lightning Source LLC
Chambersburg PA
CBHW020537100426
42813CB00038B/3471/J